WATERLOO.

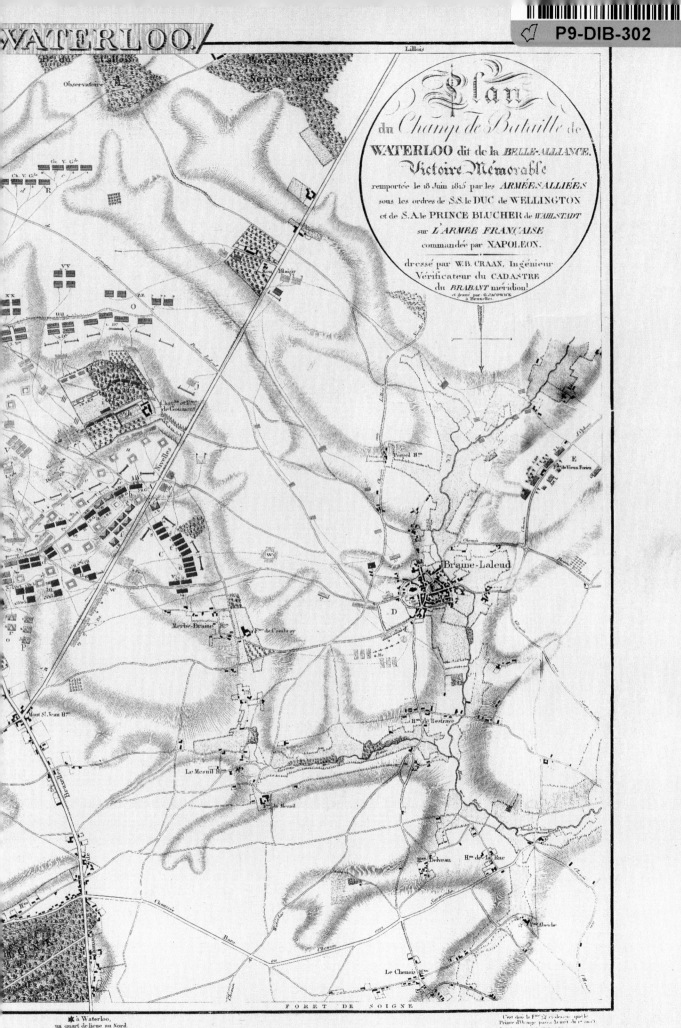

Plan du Champ de Bataille de WATERLOO dit de la BELLE-ALLIANCE. Victoire Mémorable remportée le 18 Juin 1815 par les ARMÉES ALLIÉES sous les ordres de S.S. le DUC de WELLINGTON et de S.A. le PRINCE BLÜCHER de WAHLSTADT sur L'ARMÉE FRANÇAISE commandée par NAPOLÉON.

dressé par W.B. CRAAN, Ingénieur Vérificateur du CADASTRE du BRABANT méridiol. et gravé par G. JACOWICK à Bruxelles.

FORET DE SOIGNE.

à Waterloo, un quart de lieue au Nord.

A
DESPERATE
BUSINESS

Wellington, the British Army
and the Waterloo Campaign

A DESPERATE BUSINESS

Wellington, the British Army and the Waterloo Campaign

It was the most desperate business I was ever in. I never took so much trouble about any battle, and never was so near being beat. Our loss is immense particularly in that best of all instruments, British infantry. I never saw the infantry behave so well.

Wellington to his brother, William, the day after Waterloo

The hour has come when an old soldier feels it is his duty to remind your Majesty, that while the Duke of Wellington's position is one which he cannot contemplate for permanent occupation, you are now in front of an infantry which, during the whole of the Spanish war, I never saw give way.

General Maximilien Foy, a veteran of the Peninsula, to Napoleon, on the morning of Waterloo

Ian Fletcher

SPELLMOUNT
Staplehurst

Acknowledgements

Thanks to Alix Baker, Chris Collingwood, Matt Deadman, Tim Edwards,
David Grant, Ian Hughes, Derek Stone, John Strecker and to my publisher, Jamie Wilson.
Special thanks to Martin Windrow for casting his expert eye over the MSS. Thanks.

British Library Cataloguing in Publication Data:
A catalogue record is available from the British Library

ISBN 1-86227-118-6

First published in the UK in 2001 by
Spellmount Limited
The Old Rectory
Staplehurst
Kent TN12 0AZ

Tel: 01580 893730
Fax: 01580 893731

E-mail: enquiries@spellmount.com
Website: www.spellmount.com

1 3 5 7 9 8 6 4 2

All illustrations from the author's collection

Designed by Louise Millar

Printed in China

CONTENTS

INTRODUCTION

On 14 June 1814 the Duke of Wellington issued his General Order of Thanks to his victorious Peninsular army before setting off to Paris and the waiting appointment as British Ambassador to the Court of King Louis XVIII. Six years earlier Wellington, then Lieutenant General Sir Arthur Wellesley, watched as his army struggled through the surf to land at Mondego Bay in Portugal to begin its long campaign that would eventually end at Bordeaux. With the war at an end he embarked upon his journey to Paris, leaving his army to sail home from Pauillac, whilst the British cavalry marched through France to embark from the ports of Calais and Boulogne for Dover. Little did he know that in less than a year, his army would make the return journey, albeit to Ostend, to help put the final nail in Napoleon Bonaparte's coffin following the Waterloo Campaign of June 1815.

The British Army had waged war on the French in the Peninsula since 1808 and, along with its Portuguese allies, had marched back and forth across Spain and Portugal, engaging in countless skirmishes in addition to the twenty-odd major battles and sieges, before it invaded France in October 1813. On 27 February 1814 Wellington defeated Marshal Soult at the Battle of Orthes, the last major action in open country, before he brought the war to a successful conclusion following the Battle of Toulouse on 10 April. Bonaparte had already abdicated on 6 April, following which he was exiled to the tiny Mediterranean island of Elba. Peace had apparently descended upon Europe after years of constant war.

During the six years of war in the Peninsula, Wellington, who had himself grown immensely in stature, saw his army develop from a small, relatively untried one, with a less than spectacu-lar record behind it, into what he called 'the most complete machine' existing in Europe at the time. This was no exaggeration. The army that stormed the French positions at the Battle of the Nivelle on 10 November 1813 was as good a fighting army as Britain has ever sent into battle. Indeed, the reputations and traditions of many British regiments were won in the Peninsula. Sadly, the end of the war saw the break up of this fine army, for the politicians considered the Napoleonic Wars to be at an end and the tri-umphant army was disbanded with almost obscene haste. Several regiments had parted company with Wellington even before the year of 1813 was at an end, in order to join Sir Thomas Graham for his campaign at Bergen-op-Zoom. The rest remained until the final depar-tures from France in July, August and September 1814, whereupon regiments sailed for America, Canada, Sicily, Gibraltar, Ireland and England. Hence, Wellington's great army was all but dis-banded forever.

With his army dispersed and the Napoleonic Wars seemingly at an end, Wellington set off for Paris, arriving there in August to take up his appointment as British Ambassador. He trav-elled to Paris by way of the Low Countries and during his journey took the opportunity of mak-ing a reconnaissance of the defences along the border with France. He was accompanied by Colonels Smyth, Chapman and Pasley of the Royal Engineers and his observations were writ-ten down in a memorandum which he sent to Lord Bathurst. Given the events that were to take place in June the following year Wellington's memorandum makes interesting reading.[1] We know that he possessed a great 'eye for the ground', whilst his ability to foresee the proba-ble course of events is equally well known. For example, in October 1809, following a detailed study of the ground which he made in August and September 1808 and in 1809, he issued to Colonel Richard Fletcher, of the Royal Engineers, his memorandum for the construction of the famous Lines of Torres Vedras. He appears to have known that the situation would arise when he would have to retreat from the Spanish-Portuguese border to the Lisbon peninsula and so it proved. His prediction was eerily correct, for his retreating army entered the Lines almost a year to the day after he issued Fletcher with his instructions. Now, in August 1814, he was examining a position to the south of Brussels where the main road from the south enters the forest of Soignies. The low ridge there, situated just south of the main road to Nivelles, was nothing like those which he had used to great effect at Busaco or Sorauren, for example, but it did, nevertheless, provide him with the sort of characteristics which he required to fight one of his classic defensive battles. He did not know it at the time but he was looking at the battlefield with which he would forever be synonymous; it was the field of Waterloo.

Wellington's memorandum singled out the importance of Antwerp as a naval base and the dangers of it falling into the hands of a single hostile power. However, he did not think that the British government should suffer from any great anxiety, as there was little likelihood at the time of such a power rising to the fore. Nevertheless, he was under no illusions about the importance of Antwerp both as a naval base and as a centre for communications with Britain. And so it proved, for during the campaign of June 1815 Wellington would forever be wary of any move against his right flank and his communications with Antwerp. It was a wariness that has attracted much criticism ever since. As we shall see later, his preoccupation with an imagined French threat to his right flank caused him to leave thousands of troops there who might otherwise have been used during the battle on 18 June. Furthermore, it caused him to keep his army dangerously scattered over a wide area, the consequence being that it would not be possible to concentrate it at any great speed.

The following month the Congress of Vienna opened with the various victorious powers, including Britain, Austria, Prussia and Russia, picking over the bones of Bonaparte's former empire and setting about redrawing the boundaries of European states. It was a thankless task for those involved, with the participants harbouring ambitions far different from those that had been originally set down at the outset of the Congress. Indeed, far from proceeding as a Congress between friendly allied powers, it quickly degenerated into an atmosphere of hostility and distrust, prompting Wellington, who had arrived in February 1815 to replace Castlereagh, to describe it as being 'totally stagnant'.

Castlereagh himself returned home to find England in the grip of a frenzied optimism of a long-standing peace. The major topics of discussion were the reduction of the armed forces and the lowering of taxes. And yet, all of the time, whilst politicians in London and Vienna engaged in their verbal sparring, the dethroned Emperor of the French lay just a few miles off the coast of France, whilst in nearby Naples Joachim Murat, one of Bonaparte's great lieutenants, still sat upon the throne. It was all a little too threatening for Castlereagh who urged Lord Liverpool not to be lulled into any false sense of security. Indeed, he went so far as to advocate a campaign against Murat to prise him from his throne.

The air of despondency in Vienna continued until 7 March when the members of the Congress were brought to their senses by the shattering news that Bonaparte had escaped from Elba. It had taken nine days for the news of Bonaparte's escape to reach Vienna by which time events were beginning to overtake the Allied leaders. Gradually news began to filter through of what was unfolding in France, including the duplicity of Marshal Ney who, after being sent to confront Bonaparte on his march towards Paris, went over to his old master instead, despite having promised Louis XVIII that he would bring Bonaparte back to the French capital in an iron cage. On 13 March Bonaparte was declared an outlaw by the Congress of Vienna – not that this judgement would have bothered him much. Indeed, with all of France in the grip of the old fever, Bonaparte was swept into Paris on 20 March, with the King leaving rather ignominiously the night before.

With Bonaparte back in Paris the Allied powers at Vienna, galvanised into action by this latest outrage, agreed to implement the Treaty of Chaumont, which had been signed on 10 March 1814. Under the terms of the treaty Britain, Prussia, Austria and Russia should each put into the field 150,000 men to rid Europe once and for all of Bonaparte, who it was estimated would not be able to field more than 150,000 men himself.

The actual strengths of the coalition powers make frightening reading, for the grand total came to over 700,000 men. The Army of the Upper Rhine, consisting of 255,000 Austrians and Bavarians under Schweidnitz, was to concentrate around Koblenz, from where it would be able to advance west through the Ardennes and into France. Farther north, the Army of the Upper Rhine, under Marshal Blücher, consisted of 155,000 Prussians and Saxons, who would march to link up with Wellington in the Low Countries. The Anglo-Dutch Army or Army of Flanders, under Wellington himself, numbered 155,000 and was to assemble in the Low Countries on France's northern border. Finally, 170,000 Russians, under Barclay de Tolly, were to march and gather as a reserve.

On paper, the Allies' task appeared to be relatively straightforward, advancing into France with overwhelming numerical superiority in their favour. The reality was far different, however, for it would take a great deal of time for them to organise themselves and implement a joint, synchronised plan for the invasion. Furthermore, such a plan had yet to be conceived. This lapse would allow Bonaparte to snatch the initiative and make the first moves himself, moves that would come mightily close to achieving victory.

For Wellington the considerations were not purely military. Not only was he given command of the Anglo-Dutch Army gathering to the south of Brussels but he was also responsible for the safety of the exiled Louis XVIII, residing at Ghent, as well as the King of the Netherlands in Brussels. Furthermore, he was only too aware of the importance of Antwerp as a military base, mentioned earlier, and his instructions from London related largely to the need to maintain this vital port. Hence his preoccupation with his right flank. From a military standpoint the retention of Antwerp was of major importance, whilst on the political front any move against Brussels by the French would, in Wellington's own words, 'have a terrible effect on public opinion in France and here [the Low Countries]'. It was a situation that might have troubled lesser men than Wellington, but he had been performing a military and political juggling act for the last six years and demonstrated that he was no ordinary soldier. After all, it was no coincidence that he had been appointed British Ambassador to Paris, nor that he had been sent to Vienna where he made a vital contribution to the Congress. He was, quite simply, the best man for the job.

Wellington's task was made easier in many respects by the presence of Marshal Blücher's Prussian Army, which would muster on his left flank. The two men had become great friends during the Congress of Vienna and although the Prussian commander was almost thirty years Wellington's senior, their friendship was to pay dividends during the coming campaign. This was not to say that many Prussian officers did not view Wellington and Britain with a good deal of suspicion. Gneisenau, Blücher's chief of staff, was particularly distrustful of Wellington but, again, when the vital hour arrived he was persuaded to do the right thing and act in accordance with the wishes of his commander in chief. To smooth the flow of communications between the two armies, Colonel Henry Hardinge, a veteran of the Peninsular War, and General Baron von Müffling, a similarly experienced officer, were appointed as liaison officers.

The Allied plans having being formed, the various commanders took themselves off to join their armies. For some it would be a long journey. Wellington's involved a six-day trip by carriage across the Danube, through Bavaria and on to Brussels. During his long journey, accompanied by Lord William Lennox and Colonel Fremantle of the Coldstream Guards, he must have wondered what awaited him in the Belgian capital for he knew full well the extent to which his old Peninsular army had been broken up. No sooner had news of Bonaparte's escape reached him than he began to make requests for various regiments to be recalled from foreign stations. He would even request a brigade of Portuguese troops, his trusty 'fighting cocks'. Sadly, his request could not be granted and, whereas in the Peninsula in 1813 he was able to call his army 'the most complete military machine', he would fight the Waterloo campaign with what he called, 'an infamous army'.

Historians have been picking over the bones of the Waterloo campaign for years. In fact, the blood had barely finished seeping into the Belgian soil before pens were drawn and accounts of the campaign written. From the outset, Wellington set himself against writing an account of the battle and assured those who wrote to him, asking for advice, that they would never write a satisfactory account. 'The history of a battle is much like the history of a ball,' he said, each participant seeing things in their own different light. He was also irritated by the number of accounts that were published both in England and throughout Europe, and by the number of inaccurate versions in particular. Writing to the British Ambassador to the Netherlands, two years after the battle, he said,

> The truth regarding the battle of Waterloo is this: there exists in England an insatiable curiosity

upon every subject which has occasioned a mania for travelling and writing. The battle of Waterloo having been fought within reach, every creature who could afford it, travelled to the field; and almost every one who came who could write, wrote an account. It is inconceivable the number of lies that were published and circulated in this manner by English travellers; and other nations, seeing how successfully this could be done, thought it as well to adopt the same means of circulating their own stories. This has been done with such industry, that it is now quite certain that I was not present and did not command in the battle of Quatre Bras, and it is very doubtful whether I was present in the battle of Waterloo. It is not easy to dispose of the British army as it is of an individual: but although it is admitted they were present, the brave Belgians, or the brave Prussians, won the battle; and neither in histories, pamphlets, plays, nor pictures, are the British troops ever noticed. But I must say that our travellers began this warfare of lying; and we must make up our minds to the consequences. [2]

Visitors to the battlefield today will probably feel the same as Wellington; that he was never there, particularly as the place is awash with Bonaparte souvenirs. Indeed, with Europe seemingly intent on displaying a united front – which was, after all, Bonaparte's dream – and with Brussels at the very heart of the 'community', it is little wonder that it is so difficult for the uninformed visitor to discover who actually won the battle.

Historians, notably Jac Weller, in his excellent *Wellington at Waterloo*, have often tried to write the battle from Wellington's point of view, but they have invariably brought in Bonaparte, the Prussians and the French Army. However, *A Desperate Business* is an attempt to tell the story entirely from the British point of view using only the information that Wellington had, and drawing upon eye-witness accounts of the men who fought under him. Hence, there are hardly any references to specific French soldiers or regiments. After all, would the ordinary private soldier at Waterloo really have known the regiments opposed to him? I doubt it. To the men from the shires of England, from Scotland, Wales and from Ireland, the French were simply that; they were the French. And that was all they needed to know. They recognised different types of French troops, particularly the cavalry, but beyond that the French were all the same. Thus, our story concentrates on the British and King's German Legion troops, whilst the French simply appear as the enemy. Napoleon, meanwhile, is referred to throughout as Bonaparte, which was Wellington's favoured term for his great adversary.

Twenty-three years have passed since I first visited the battlefield of Waterloo and still the place is as fascinating as ever. Situated virtually in the suburbs of Brussels it marks the one great meeting between Wellington and Bonaparte. It also marks the site of the last great battle fought by Wellington's army. By the very high standards set by his old Peninsular army, the army of 1815 was a poor one indeed, but when called upon to hammer the final nail in Bonaparte's coffin it rose to the occasion and responded with the same sort of determination that had been displayed at Talavera, Badajoz, Salamanca, Vittoria and other Peninsular battlefields. An infamous army it may well have been, but it was also a victorious army, and one that would provide Wellington with his most famous but 'close run' victory.

But the Battle of Waterloo was not a British victory, and it certainly wasn't a German one. It was an Allied victory. It is true that there were more Germans present – eventually – on the battlefield than any other nation, but many thousands of them, serving in the King's German Legion, were part of the British Army and had been ever since 1803. They were trained in the British system, wore the same uniforms, were armed and equipped by the British government, and contained many British officers. For this reason, the KGL features in this book, which is an unashamed tribute to the Duke of Wellington and the British Army. There were men of several other nationalities, most of whom served with great distinction during the Waterloo campaign, including Nassauers, Hanoverians and Belgians, but this is not their story. It is the story of the British Army, how it arrived in Belgium, its part in the campaign, its march to Paris and its final return from there from 1815 to 1818.

IAN FLETCHER,
Rochester, 2001.

---

1 Wellington to Bathurst, 22 September 1814. *The Despatches of Field Marshal the Duke of Wellington* (London, 1832).
2 Wellington to the Earl of Clancarty, 3 December 1817, *Supplementary Despatches* (London, 1857).

Chapter I
WELLINGTON'S INFAMOUS ARMY

*I have got an infamous army, very weak and ill-equipped,
and a very inexperienced staff.*

Wellington to Charles Stewart, 8 May 1815

The Duke of Wellington left Vienna on 29 March, bound for Brussels where he arrived on 4 April. Here, he was to assume command of the Anglo-Dutch Army that would form the northern tip of the great Allied scythe threatening France from the north and east. But when he arrived in the Belgian capital he found little cause for optimism. His oft-quoted opinion of his army, as being 'infamous...very weak and ill-equipped' is a little harsh given the number of Peninsular veterans he would count among his staff and at the head of his divisions when hostilities began in June 1815. But in May it certainly was a weak army, for the British government could place under his command no more than twenty-five battalions of infantry and six regiments of cavalry. The troops immediately at his disposal were fifteen battalions of infantry that had been present with Sir Thomas Graham during the ill-fated attack on Bergen-op-Zoom in 1814, the strongest of which were the three battalions of Foot Guards, the 2/1st Foot Guards, the 2/Coldstream Guards and the 2/3rd Foot Guards. None of these battalions had been present in the Peninsula, although the latter two contained many men and officers who left their first battalions in the Peninsula to join Graham's force. Eventually, ten of Graham's fifteen battalions would join Wellington's army for the Waterloo campaign, of which only the 3/1st Foot Guards and the 2/30th could claim active service in the Peninsula. The others, the 2/1st Foot Guards, 2/Coldstream, 2/3rd Foot Guards, 33rd, 2/69th, 2/73rd, 2/35th and 1/54th could not. There were also four companies from all three battalions of the 95th Rifles, all four of which had served in the Peninsula.

The 30-year-old William Wheeler, of the 51st Light Infantry, was a veteran of the Peninsular War. He had joined the army in 1809 and had served at Walcheren and in the Peninsula, during which time he rose from private to sergeant. He had been severely wounded at the Battle of the Nivelle on 10 November 1813. So bad was his wound, in fact, that he did not rejoin his regiment until September 1814. When he did so, he was alarmed to see so few of his old comrades. It was a view shared by many a Peninsular veteran and is one that sums up the quality of many of the regiments now on their way to join Wellington in the Low Countries:

> It was a joyful meeting, [wrote Wheeler] but when I look around me and see so many strange faces, I am a wonder to myself, scarcely four years has rolled over, ere, at this place I embarked with about 900 of my comrades. Where are they now? I could not muster one company out of the whole number. The battle field, fatigue, privations and sickness has made sad havoc in the ranks of as fine a set of young fellows as ever belonged to the service. The blanks are filled up and the Regiment is fit for any service the country should require of them.[1]

Years after Waterloo, Wellington declared that he would have attacked Bonaparte at Waterloo had the old Peninsular army been present on the slopes of Mont St Jean on 18 June 1815, adding, somewhat fancifully, that it would have taken him about three hours to have won the battle. Needless to say, this claim has to be taken with a huge pinch of salt. But it is, nevertheless, tempting to consider what might have happened had the men who had stormed Badajoz, who had shed gallons of blood at Albuera, thrashed the French at Salamanca and Vittoria and who had driven deep into French soil in 1814, been present at Waterloo. What might Bonaparte's Imperial legions have made of the Connaught Rangers, for example? And what of the Fusilier brigade that 'reeled and staggered' at Albuera? Who could have withstood their might at Waterloo? The list of glorious absentees is long indeed and includes the Buffs, the Die-Hards, Fusiliers, Northamptons, Worcesters and the Connaught Rangers, to name just a few.

Despite the absence of many fine veteran British regiments there was still a large number of very experienced troops available to Wellington, many of whom were diverted from other destinations to join him. The suddenness of Bonaparte's escape caught many British regiments by surprise and whilst many, such as the 43rd Light Infantry, failed to arrive in time to play a part in the campaign, others were turned back even as they sailed for North America. Charles Cadell, of the 28th, had sailed with his regiment for Bermuda in late January 1815, but ill-winds kept him in port at Cove in Ireland until 17 March, when his convoy sailed once more. That same afternoon, however, a frigate caught up with them bringing the news that Bonaparte had escaped from Elba. The convoy immediately returned to port to await further orders. Sailing for Bermuda in the same convoy were the 71st, 79th, 91st and 92nd Regiments, all Peninsular veterans. One shudders to think what might have happened at Waterloo had these fine regiments not been able to return in time. One of the 71st's men later wrote,

> We lay on board for six weeks before setting sail. When on our way, a schooner fired a gun and brought us to and gave us orders for Deal…After the ship was put about for England, a load was taken from my mind and I became more happy. We landed all our heavy baggage at Deal, then sailed round to Gravesend and disembarked. We lay there only one afternoon, then were put on board the smacks and were landed at Antwerp.[2]

Whilst some regiments were stopped in mid-Atlantic, others already based in England prepared for the coming campaign. Many of Wellington's veteran heavy cavalry regiments were simply not prepared after enduring such a hard campaign in the Peninsula. Indeed, of the experienced heavy cavalry regiments that had served in Spain, only the 1st (Royal) Dragoons were to take part in the Waterloo campaign. True, the Life Guards and Horse Guards had been in the Peninsula, but they had arrived only in late 1812 and had seen very little action between then and the close of the war, particularly as much of the time Wellington's army was fighting in the Pyrenees and in southern France, where the terrain precluded any real effective use of heavy cavalry. Added to the Royals and the Household Cavalry were the 2nd (Royal North British) Dragoons, known more famously as the Scots Greys, the 6th (Inniskilling) Dragoons, and the 1st (King's) Dragoon Guards, regiments that had seen very little service during the previous twenty-odd years. The light cavalry regiments, on the other hand, did prepare for war, despite having got through an amazing amount of work in the Peninsula. The post-Peninsula months were spent in refitting and recruiting, and by the time of Bonaparte's escape from Elba they were once again in a fit state for war.

Of the light dragoon regiments that had served in the Peninsula, the 11th, 12th, 13th, 16th and 23rd were to join Wellington in the Low Countries, with the 14th Light Dragoons being the only notable absentees. Of the hussar regiments the 7th, 10th, 15th and 18th, all of which had seen service in the Peninsula, served in the Waterloo campaign. While Bonaparte was making his escape from Elba, the 16th Light Dragoons were making their way to Westminster Bridge in readiness for the riots that were expected following the passing of the Corn Laws. In the event, Bonaparte's escape brought all disturbances to an end and the regiment was ordered to prepare for embarkation for the Low Countries. The strength of the regiment at embarkation was six troops, each consisting of fifty-five men and horses each. Captain William Tomkinson, one of the great diarists of the period, was one of the regiment's officers. Born in 1790, Tomkinson was gazetted to the 16th Light Dragoons in December 1807 and joined his regiment in April the following year. In 1809 he sailed for the Peninsula and was severely wounded in his very first fight. He returned to England and recovered and sailed again for Portugal in 1810. He subsequently served for the remainder of the war in numerous battles and skirmishes without so much as a scratch. In his journal for the Waterloo campaign, he wrote:

> The vessels we embarked in were small colliers, holding from ten to thirty-five horses each. The horses were put loose in the hold, and it being fine weather we did not lose any from there being no bails. Larger vessels could not have passed the bar at Ostend, and to have fitted them up regularly for cavalry would have required so many, and caused so much delay, that the passage of any considerable body of cavalry would have been much retarded.[3]

The 16th Light Dragoons arrived at Ostend on 12 April, landing the horses on the sand, and by the end of the day the regiment had marched inland about six miles to a village called Ghristiles. Like their comrades of the 16th, the 12th Light Dragoons were also being held in readiness to march to London in anticipation of riots brought on by the Corn Laws. The regiment marched from its barracks at Dorchester, but upon arrival in London was greeted with the news that Bonaparte had escaped. A 23-year-old Scot, Captain William Hay, had served in the Peninsula with the famous 52nd Light Infantry, one of the British Army's finest regiments. He was later gazetted to the 12th Light Dragoons. Hay was amongst a group of officers of the 12th who were dining at an inn when a mail-coach drew up:

> The guard, a good-humoured fellow and a great favourite with all our officers, who had travelled to town by this coach, exclaimed, 'Well, gentlemen, I have brought you news today.' All exclaimed: 'What! The route?' 'Yes,' was the reply, 'the route in earnest, old Boney has broken out again and got to Paris.' We were astonished, and indeed could not believe our ears; but on the delivery of newspapers and letters the news we heard was not only confirmed, but an immediate order for us to march by Canterbury, en route to Dover, there to embark for Ostend, and, I must confess, the news gave me the greatest satisfaction, as I had no liking for the life of a soldier in idleness.[4]

The regiment's heavy baggage was put into stores and campaign equipment loaded. Then, after an inspection at Canterbury, the 12th Light Dragoons marched to Dover before sailing for Ostend, which they reached after an uneventful voyage. Meanwhile, other cavalry regiments followed. The 1st Life Guards also sailed for Ostend, although their passage across the English Channel was not as smooth. Assistant Surgeon Haddy James had already endured an uncomfortable journey from London to Ramsgate in the company of Colonel George O'Malley, of the 44th Regiment. They found Ramsgate virtually deserted by the military apart from a few companies of infantry, waiting to get across the Channel. After getting their horses on board, the Life Guards set out in their transports, bound for Ostend. James later wrote:

> I had not been on board more than three hours when that vile sensation, sea-sickness, came upon me. Wrapped in my cloak I lay upon deck, until the spray obliged me to go below. By keeping myself in a perfectly horizontal position I escaped much suffering, but I am well aware that in a storm I should experience

it in a severe degree. After a sail of about thirteen hours we made the coast of Flanders, which is not inviting in its aspect. Besides the steeples of Nieuport, nothing is to be seen but a low range of sandbanks. The mouth of the harbour of Ostend is narrow and guarded by a wooden fort, opposite which is a handsome lighthouse, which, with the steeple of the principal church, form the conspicuous features. Disembarking our baggage and horses consumed a great part of the morning, and these strenuous hours, after the depletion I had undergone at sea, rendered me exceedingly hungry. Several times I endeavoured to get a moment to find breakfast, but the morning was far advanced before I managed to obtain a hurried meal at an indifferent hotel.[5]

One of the most experienced cavalry regiments in the British Army, the 1st (Royal) Dragoons, were mortified to learn that they were not amongst those selected for service.

> So the Ruler's [Colonel Clifton] heart began to ache. He saw that every cavalry regiment that could be spared had already been disposed of, and yet no notice had been taken of the Royals, and it was little comfort to his wishes and vanity that the regiment should remain dispersed over the Kingdom. Part of it was in the fishing coves of Cornwall, part in Dorset, part in Devon, part in Somerset. In short, the Ruler only nominally commanded his regiment, his headquarters merely a depot in Exeter consisting of the riding master, young officers, and raw

Arthur Wellesley, 1st Duke of Wellington 1769-1852. Wellington had fought a successful campaign in the Iberian Peninsula between 1808 and 1814, but had yet to face an army commanded by Napoleon Bonaparte himself. At Waterloo he was required to do so with what he called, 'an infamous army'. Fortunately for him his army proved a worthy successor to his triumphant Peninsular army.

Major General Sir Denis Pack. A veteran of many a campaign including Buenos Aires in 1806-7, where he was taken prisoner, Pack commanded the 9th British brigade of Picton's 5th Division.

Elba reached them, some artillery units were still undergoing reductions in strength in order to bring them into line with peace-time establishments. The 32-year-old Captain Cavalié Mercer had not been present in the Peninsula, but he had, nevertheless, seen action in South America during the ill-fated campaign against Buenos Aires in 1807. Mercer, author of the classic *Journal of the Waterloo Campaign*, was at Colchester when he heard of Bonaparte's escape. His troop had already begun the necessary reductions when he received orders to equip once more for foreign service. Many of his horses had already departed and in order to get new ones another troop of artillery which found itself in the same barracks, was broken up and the horses given over to Mercer. Three days later the troop was ready to move and on 9 April it marched for Harwich where the transports *Adventure*, *Philarea* and *Salus* were waiting to ferry them across the Channel. 'As might be expected,' wrote Mercer,

> the little town of Harwich presented a most animated spectacle. Its narrow streets of modest houses, with brick trottoirs, were crowded with soldiers – some, all over dust, just arrived; some, who had already been a day or two in the place, comparatively at home, lounging about in undress; others, about to embark, hurrying along to the beach with baggage and stores; sailors marketing, or rolling about half-seas-over; country people bringing in vegetables and the like, and townspeople idling at their windows, or in groups at corners of the streets – in short, the usual picture incident on such occasions.[7]

recruits. So before long he could contain his patience no longer, and wrote to the Adjutant-General entreating his Royal Highness that the Royals might have the honour of forming part of the army in Belgium.[6]

The reply from Horse Guards was disappointing. Coastal duties were considered too important and the Royals were told they simply could not be spared. And so, while other regiments, experienced and raw alike, were despatched across the English Channel, the Royals, the regiment that had charged on many a dusty Spanish battlefield, were left to contemplate the bleak prospect of acting as a police force in the West Country. And then, to the complete surprise of everyone, the regiment received orders to prepare for embarkation at Dover and on 13 May the first two squadrons of the regiment embarked, followed by two more squadrons during the next few days.

Like the cavalry, the artillery required a great amount of preparation before embarking for the Continent. Matters were not helped by the fact that, when news of Bonaparte's escape from

It was some days before the flotilla carrying Mercer's troop finally got underway. The morning of 10 April was too foggy, whilst a nice breeze that got up the following day died down before sunset, forcing the transports to anchor at the harbour's mouth. The same occurred on 12 April, but on the morning of the 13th the wind had got up considerably and soon Mercer found himself sailing out across the English Channel, bound for Ostend which soon hove into sight. The scene on the beaches at Ostend and, indeed, right across the Channel, must have been a wonderful sight with ships of all sizes – transports, supply ships, frigates acting as escorts and innumerable other craft, the landing ships vying with each other to get in close to the shore. The majority of the landing vessels simply bumped themselves up on to the shore before their cargoes came tumbling out, whether it be cavalry, infantry or artillery. Mercer again:

Those immediately above us had just arrived, and from them a regiment of light dragoons was in the act of disembarking by throwing the horses overboard, and then hauling them ashore by a long rope attached to their head-collars. What a scene! What hallooing, shouting, vociferating, and plunging! The poor horses did not appear much gratified by their sudden transition from the warm hold to a cold bath.[8]

All certainly was hustle and bustle, although there appears to have been little confusion. In fact, the entire operation to get the British Army across the Channel appears to have been planned and executed remarkably well and in a relatively short space of time, given the adjustments that many regiments had made following the end of the Peninsular War. The bulk of the troops making their way across the Channel were, naturally, the infantry, many of whom had been turned around in mid-Atlantic to return to face their old foes. Elsewhere, infantry regiments prepared quickly for the campaign before they too set off for the Channel ports from where they would sail across to Ostend. Lieutenant George Simmons, of the 95th Rifles, was a veteran of countless battles and skirmishes in the Peninsula, where his regiment had formed part of the famous Light Division. Simmons left a good account of the sort of arrangements made by a typical infantry regiment, prior to departing for the continent:

> As senior officers of each rank had the refusal of going, the juniors were under the necessity of staying at home, which was a very great mortification to Joseph [Simmons' brother]. However, if we commence hostilities he will soon be wanted to fill the place of some unlucky fellow that might bite the dust. Four skeleton companies remained behind. Joseph was made adjutant of the depot. He will have to drill the recruits and young officers. He takes a delight in his duty, and I have no doubt he will fill the situation with credit...When I embarked it was nearly dark. Our boys had been stationed some time at Dover, and the people came in crowds to see us off, cheered us, and wished us success. It was at the same place that in 1809 I embarked with as fine a regiment as ever left England.[9]

Simmons' battalion sailed from Dover on 27 April, much later than some other regiments. The crossing was not a pleasant one and he was 'dreadfully sick all the way to Ostend. My throat swelled with vomiting to such a degree that I could scarcely speak for a week after.'[10] The infantry battalions did not remain long at Ostend, for such was the need for haste that they were transported by boat to Ghent where they

disembarked prior to marching towards Brussels. The peace and tranquillity of the journey along the canals was broken only by the cheers of the local people who turned out to watch as the boats glided past. As soon as they reached Ghent, the troops were turned out and placed either in billets or in encampments close to the town. It was 11 May when Sergeant David Robertson, of the 92nd Highlanders, arrived in the town with his battalion, which had originally been bound for North America before being despatched to Ostend. Soldiering was nothing new for the 38-year-old Scot, who had been in the 92nd for some fifteen years, during which time he had seen a great deal of action, none harder than the fighting in the Pyrenees and in the south of France just two years earlier. It happened to be market-day when Robertson reached Ostend, and he later described the scene as crowds of British soldiers descended on the market place:

> It happened to be the weekly market-day when we landed, and none of us ever saw such a sight before. The day was beautiful, and the people were coming in boats from all directions to the centre of the city, which caused great stir and bustle; and to add to the effect of the scene, we were disembarked at the large market-place. If the novelty of what we saw made an impression on our minds, the Belgians were no less surprised at our strange appearance, as, I believe, none of them had ever seen any clad in the Highland garb before.[11]

The kilted Scottish warriors, mixing with the scarlet and red of the other regiments, the blue of the cavalry and artillery, and the general throbbing mass of British soldiers, certainly created a wonderful spectacle, not only in Ghent but in other towns through which Wellington's men passed or in which they were billeted. Colonel Augustus Frazer, of the Royal Horse Artillery, was another who journeyed by boat to Ghent. Like Robertson, of the 92nd, Frazer was a 38-year-old Scot. He had seen service in Holland, South America and in the Peninsula and had been awarded the KCB and the Army Gold Cross with one clasp. He left a wonderful description of his journey on board a boat that must have been in stark contrast to that which ferried Robertson and his comrades of the 92nd to Ghent.

> From Ostend to Bruges by water is about twelve miles, and from Bruges to Ghent by water about twenty-one; by land the journey is two or three leagues longer. Nothing can be pleasanter than travelling in these canal boats,

which are large and commodious vessels. At either end is a cabin, nicely fitted up. In the middle is a kind of public-house; on one side an excellent kitchen, on the other, larders and storerooms for all manner of eatables. The stern cabin, which is considered the best, is fitted up with looking glasses, sofas, and chairs; and the sides, as well as ceiling, very prettily painted. There were six windows in the cabin of the boat yesterday; and at 1pm we sat down to an excellent dinner, well put on the table. For this excellent dinner and carriage from Bruges, the price is five francs, that is, 4s 2d. Wine, coffee, and liqueurs are paid for separately. We were fifteen in the stern cabin; there might be twenty people in the middle part of the boat; and there were eighteen in the fore cabin; yet there seemed no difficulty in providing good cheer for all. There were several pretty and very agreeable women, and altogether no journey could be more pleasant. The country through which we passed is rich, and in all the fresh beauty of spring. Four horses drew the boat, and were changed about halfway between this and Bruges.[12]

As they marched towards their concentration points around Brussels, many of the officers and men appear to have had mixed feelings. Many were relieved at being spared duty in Barbados or North America, whilst others were only too delighted to be handed another opportunity of having a crack at their old enemies, something which they believed had gone following their victory in the Peninsula. Others were keen to take on Bonaparte, the Emperor having paid only a fleeting visit to Spain back in the winter of 1808–9. Others were dismayed by the resumption of hostilities, as many men were looking forward to a quiet time in England or Scotland, whilst others looked forward to an end to their term of service and a return to civilian life. But the overwhelming feeling appears to have been one of tremendous excitement at the prospect of fighting under Wellington again, this time against Bonaparte. They had taken on and defeated all of the marshals whom Bonaparte had sent to the Peninsula. This time they wanted the chance to test the Emperor himself and they were eager for the test to come. 'I do not care how soon,' wrote George Simmons. 'I hope I shall see Paris before the summer is over, in a whole skin.'

John Douglas, of the 3/1st, was a veteran of several actions in the Peninsula, dating back to the Battle of Busaco in September 1810. He had been severely wounded at San Sebastian in August 1813. His battalion sailed for Ostend from Cove in May 1815.

We sailed from Cove for the Downs, where we remained just as long as to shift from one vessel to another, and away for Ostend. On arriving there we piled arms in a large piece of waste ground on the right of the town. Bales of blankets were opened, and each man served out with one, and in a good many cases more than that complement. As the old Dutch frows [sic] were serving out the Schnapps at such a rate, and at the same time were not idle in swathing themselves under the loop petticoats, in this manner a great number were carried off unnoticed. We halted for a while on the banks of the canal, waiting for boats. Here we got highly entertained in a garden very tastefully laid out with seats and arbours. The landlord of the inn pocketed the gilt in great style, while all distinction was levelled as the gin began to operate. Officers and men were all alike, while the songs went round in full chorus. The bugles called us reluctantly away, and into the boats we scrambled, and away for Ghent.[13]

Gradually Wellington's British battalions began to arrive in the Low Countries, but the commander-in-chief still considered the army at his disposal to be relatively weak, both in numbers and experience. It was certainly a much weaker army than he had commanded in the Peninsula, although he was gradually assembling many of his old veterans, though not in sufficient numbers. One of the largest contingents to fight under his command in the Peninsula was the wonderfully skilled and immensely experienced King's German Legion. The KGL – in effect the Hanoverian Army in exile – had been formed in 1803 following the French invasion of Hanover. Thousands of men subsequently made their way to England and thus the Legion was formed. The KGL gradually converted to the British system of army drill, its officers and men were paid by the British government, armed and equipped in the same way as the British Army regiments and, to all intents and purposes, was a British Army unit. It had its own artillery, infantry, cavalry and engineers, all of whom served with great distinction in the Peninsula and in other theatres of war. Wellington knew he could rely on the KGL but under an agreement drawn up between the British government and the Legion itself the KGL's period of service had expired. At the end of the Peninsular War the KGL regiments did not return to England but instead were sent to the Low Countries from where they expected to make their way home. In fact, at the time of Bonaparte's escape from Elba the men were indeed on their way back to their homes and the Legion on the verge of being disbanded. Fortunately, the KGL offered to volunteer for a further six months, an offer that was gratefully accepted by the British government in March 1815.

The King's German Legion supplied no fewer than eight battalions of infantry and four regiments of cavalry for Wellington's army in addition to three batteries of artillery. The infantry battalions were the 1st and 2nd Light, and the 1st, 2nd, 3rd, 4th, 5th and 8th Line. The cavalry regiments were the 1st and 2nd Dragoons and the 1st, 2nd and 3rd Hussars. The artillery serving under Wellington consisted of the batteries of Sympher, Kuhlmann and Cleeves, in addition to the 1st and 2nd companies under Bruckmann. Five engineer officers also volunteered. The KGL contingent numbered almost 7,000 with eighteen guns. However, the infantry battalions were not particularly strong and Wellington suggested that men from the newly raised Hanoverian militia should be allowed to fill up the vacancies. Unfortunately, the idea was rejected by the Hanoverian government and the KGL battalions were thus reduced from ten to six companies each, the officers from the 'disbanded' companies being transferred into the Hanoverian regiments. It was a plan that did not entirely meet with Wellington's approval, for it was undoubtedly wiser to mix the raw recruits with a greater number of experienced veterans, rather than distribute supernumerary officers and NCOs amongst the Hanoverian militia. It was a policy that Wellington was to extend to the army in general, with the mixing of seasoned British battalions with inexperienced Hanoverian, Dutch and Belgian troops. In the event, it was something that troubled Wellington little, for he was becoming accustomed to having to deal with the agendas of Continental governments.

What did concern him was the selection of his own staff. While the British Army units were making their way across the English Channel, Wellington was busy trying to assemble a suitable staff, and he was finding it a struggle. Many of his old Peninsular colleagues were present with him in Brussels but he still found himself surrounded by people whom he had 'never seen before', prompting him to complain to Earl Bathurst and Sir Henry Torrens, the Military Secretary. A brief perusal of Wellington's despatches clearly shows what a struggle he had assembling his own team. Doubtless there were many officers who had never served in the Peninsula and who were only too anxious not to miss out a second time. But what Wellington needed more than ever, with so many different and unfamiliar Allied contingents, was not a bunch of inexperienced 'Johnny Newcomes', eager for glory, but a group of seasoned battle-

Lieutenant Colonel Sir John Colborne, commanding officer of the 52nd Light Infantry. Colborne, a veteran of the Peninsula, was to make a telling contribution to the battle on 18 June when he wheeled his battalion round to open fire into the left flank of the Imperial Guard during its final attack.

hardened veterans who knew both the Duke's foibles and his method of waging war. Gradually, Wellington managed to rid himself of these supernumeraries, although many were still present when the first shots of the campaign were fired.

The most notable absentee was Sir George Murray, his old Quartermaster-General. Murray, a vastly underrated soldier, was Wellington's right-hand man for much of the campaign in Spain and Portugal, but when he was needed in the early spring of 1815 he was to be found in distant Canada. In his place was Sir Hudson Lowe, later called 'a damned fool' by Wellington. It was obvious from the moment Wellington arrived in Brussels that Lowe 'would not do for the Duke'. And so it proved. At the end of May Lowe departed for the Mediterranean and his place was taken by Colonel Sir William De Lancey, a man who would go on to create his own Waterloo legend. Another absentee was Sir John Burgoyne, of the Royal Engineers, who like Murray was in North America. Always a prominent figure in the Peninsula, Burgoyne had assumed a key role in Spain following the death of Sir Richard Fletcher at San Sebastian in August 1813. Fortunately, his replacement, Sir James Carmichael Smyth, was suitably able and had been present throughout the attack on Bergen-op-Zoom. Commanding the artillery was Sir George Wood, an experienced commander, and although Sir Alexander Dickson,

Major General Sir Thomas Picton, commander of the 5th British division. The fiery Welshman was never one of Wellington's 'inner circle' but was the kind of soldier you wanted when the prospect of a tough fight lay ahead. Picton suffered a severe wound at Quatre Bras on 16 June but concealed it in order to fight at Waterloo two days later. He was killed during the attack on Wellington's left centre, early on the afternoon of 18 June.

though not when it came to his uniform, as it was as flamboyant as anything ever worn by the fanciest of French officers – he was remarkably reliable and demonstrated on numerous occasions tremendous bravery in the field. He was badly wounded at Salamanca, for example, but declined the surgeon's offer to take his arm off. Instead, he asked for a second opinion, received it, and, it being a positive one, his arm remained. He returned from the Peninsula to be made a peer, Lord Combermere, and naturally sought employment when news of Bonaparte's escape from Elba broke. Wellington himself was desirous of having him in his team and duly wrote, requesting he be appointed to command the cavalry. However, both the Duke of York and the Prince Regent had other ideas. Combermere, when plain Colonel Cotton, had apparently been the source of a snippet of damaging gossip about the Prince Regent's nocturnal visits to a lady friend. The gossip led to a major scandal and, although it appears to have been either overlooked or forgotten in 1809, it certainly wasn't in 1815, for when the appointment as commander of the cavalry was being made, Lord Uxbridge was named. This came as a bitter blow to Combermere but there was little he could do. It seems as though a determined effort was being made by Horse Guards to wrest back the power that Wellington had acquired during the long years of war in Portugal and Spain. Wellington's reaction to the appointment was typical. Reminded of the affair between Uxbridge and his sister-in-law, Wellington simply remarked, 'I'll take good care he don't run off away with me!' In the event, there were no problems between the two men, despite a somewhat frosty relationship. They were simply too professional to allow personal considerations to stand in the way of the task before them. It is, nevertheless, a great pity that Uxbridge and Combermere were not allowed to serve side by side. What a sight that would have been.

Wellington's ever-reliable artillery chief in the Peninsula, was another of the North American absentees he would, nevertheless, return in time to take part in the battle on 18 June. Other prominent personalities from the old Peninsular army included Francis Larpent, Wellington's judge-advocate general, and Dr James McGrigor, his inspector-general of hospitals, neither of whom was able to take his place at his old chief's side.

It was the appointment of Henry, Lord Paget, by now Lord Uxbridge, that caused greatest comment. The dashing hussar had commanded the British cavalry during Sir John Moore's ill-fated Corunna campaign of 1808–9 with great distinction, gaining notable successes at Sahagun, Benavente and Mayorga. Upon his return to England, however, he made the mistake of eloping with Wellington's brother's wife, which, of course, made it impossible for him to return to join Wellington in the Peninsula. Instead, Sir Stapleton Cotton assumed command of the cavalry and served throughout the Peninsular War with great credit. Although he lacked much of Uxbridge's dash and flair –

Meanwhile, more and more familiar faces began to report to Wellington's headquarters in Brussels, until by the outbreak of hostilities he could call upon the services of such great fighting men as Hill, Colville, Clinton, Alten, Lambert, Barnes, Byng, Maitland, Halkett, Kempt, Ponsonby, Somerset, Vivian, Vandeleur, Pack and Picton, in addition to many fine regimental commanders.

Sir Thomas Picton, in fact, left London as late as 11 June, and arrived at Brussels barely three days prior to the Battle of Waterloo. When he left London he was leaving England's capital for the last time, for he was to become the most famous of the many who fell at Waterloo. Picton appears to have had a feeling that the coming campaign would be his last, for he made a point of saying farewell to many of his friends. Indeed, he left them with some prophetic words. 'When you hear of my death,' he said, 'you will hear of a bloody day.'[14] Picton was one of the great characters in the old Peninsular army. He had led the 'Fighting' 3rd Division to the walls of Badajoz, had thrown back the French at Busaco and had dealt the decisive blow at Vittoria when he stormed the bridge of Mendoza without orders from his chief. And yet, when the time came to hand out the rewards, Picton missed out. There were peerages for Graham, Cotton and Hill, but nothing for himself, save the thanks of a grateful country. If crowns were to be won in the breaches, he later claimed, he would have stood as good a chance as the next man. He was always a little too rough for Wellington's liking and, although the commander-in-chief knew full well his fighting abilities, he could never endear himself as did other high-ranking officers. Wellington also famously remarked that Picton gave the worst dinners in the army!

Nevertheless, Picton was in good spirits when he set sail for Ostend. With him were his old friend and aide-de-camp, Major Tyler, along with Howell Rees Gronow and Chambers, of the Foot Guards. Gronow, later to become one of the great raconteurs and diarists of the age, recalled the moment when Picton met Wellington again. They had been parted for a year since the end of the Peninsular War, in which they had shared many a glorious moment, and Picton was naturally looking forward to seeing his old chief. He found Wellington walking with Fitzroy Somerset in the park opposite his headquarters. 'Picton's manner was always more familiar than the Duke liked in his lieutenants,' wrote Gronow, 'and on this occasion he approached him in a careless sort of way, just as he might have met an equal. The Duke bowed coldly to him, and said, "I am glad you are come, Sir Thomas; the sooner you get on horseback the better: no time is to be lost. You will take command of the troops in advance. The Prince of Orange knows by this time that you will go to his assistance."' Picton appeared not to like the Duke's manner, for when he bowed and left, he muttered a few words, which convinced those who were with him that he was not much pleased with his interview.[15] Despite his cold reception, Picton did not let his commander down when the time came to the serious business of fighting the French.

Given the list of veteran commanders present in Brussels, it seems somewhat difficult to understand Wellington's notorious remark made in a letter to Charles Stewart on 8 May. 'I have got an infamous army,' he wrote, 'very weak and ill-equipped, and a very inexperienced staff.' One suspects that much of this dissatisfaction was due to the number of foreign officers and their aides with whom Wellington had to do business. In the Peninsula Wellington was used to running his own very tight ship. They were largely his men and, although Horse Guards foisted a few senior officers upon him, his 'family' was largely of his own design. Spanish and Portuguese liaison officers were few and far between, but even these were afforded both time and attention whenever they desired it and when Wellington considered it necessary. But in Brussels he had difficulty in keeping the hordes of strangers at arm's length. Ultimately, Wellington was to gather around him a mixture of many seasoned veterans and a sprinkling of raw 'Johnny Newcomes'. As on many occasions in the Peninsula he was forced to make the best of a bad situation.

Wellington's staff and, indeed, his British battalions, gradually began to muster around Brussels, but there was one important issue that still dogged and irritated him. Amazingly, it was the question of whether Britain was at peace or at war with France. On the face of it the answer was quite simple. The Royal Navy had been taking French ships since March, whilst French citizens passing through the Low Countries had been arrested, lest information about the Allied build up be passed on to Bonaparte. And yet, in England, and in the House of Commons in particular, where a sense of fair play and mischief still pervaded, the question was being asked in all seriousness. After all, Bonaparte might have been declared an outlaw of Europe but France had not. It should be remembered that, despite all of Wellington's great successes in the Peninsula, there were still those who harboured grudges against him and who enjoyed playing the game of politics to the distraction of the government. Men like Samuel Whitbread were amongst the chief protagonists who enjoyed nothing more than stirring the political pot and making life awkward for the government. The fact that Britain was suddenly plunged back into a national crisis appears to have escaped them. The peace parties were anxious for a lasting peace and the planned-for war was of course a great blow to them, coming so soon after what appeared to be an end to the Napoleonic Wars.

Thus, the question of peace or war was, to some, a very real one. In fact, it was a question that troubled the government for it prevented them from implementing one very important act that would have solved many of Wellington's problems. This was, of course, the embodiment of the Militia.

There were thousands of regular troops in Ireland and England, many of whom were being used simply to maintain law and order. If the Militia could be called out these troops would be freed from their tiresome tasks in order to join Wellington's army. The problem was that the Militia could only be called out in time of war. It remained, therefore, for the government to decide whether or not Britain was indeed at war with France, and hence the continual raising of the question by such men as Whitbread. The unfortunate answer was that Britain was not at war with France, only Bonaparte. Wellington's exasperation can well be judged from the tone of several despatches sent to the government in April and May 1815. 'In my opinion they are doing nothing in England,' he wrote to Charles Stewart. 'They have not raised a man; they have not called out the Militia either in England or Ireland; are unable to send me anything; and they have not sent a message to Parliament about the money [subsidies for foreign armies]. The war spirit is therefore evaporating as I am informed.' The British government's determination to play by the book is absolutely astonishing given the crisis rapidly developing across the Channel and little

Lieutenant General the Earl of Uxbridge, 1768-1854. After eloping with Wellington's brother's wife, Uxbridge was unable to remain with the army in the Peninsula. He returned to the fold at Waterloo, however, where he served with great distinction, particularly during the retreat from Quatre Bras on 17 June.

appears to have been done to help Wellington in his efforts to muster a satisfactory force with which he could face the might of Bonaparte. The amazing conclusion to this preposterous but complex situation came on 9 May when the government finally came to its senses and brought forward a Bill to allow the local Militia to volunteer for garrison duties and thus release the far more experienced old Militia for more important duties. The final sad comment on the matter can best be found in the date upon which the Bill was finally passed – 14 June. This was just one day before Bonaparte's men crossed the Sambre to open hostilities. Notwithstanding the timing of the new Bill, many of the old Militia regiments passed their men on to the regular army, whilst in some cases entire companies served with the regulars. Thus it was that many regiments, including the Coldstream Guards, for example, fought at Waterloo with their ranks swelled by additions from the Militia.

As May wore on British battalions continued to cross the English Channel to join Wellington, but there were simply not enough of them. The legal issue concerning the Militia annoyed Wellington immensely and he must have felt at times as though he was being asked to fight the coming campaign with one arm tied firmly behind his back. His frustration at not being able to call upon his old Peninsular army can perhaps be gauged by the fact that he went so far as to request from the Portuguese Regent a brigade of Portuguese infantry. It was a request that came to nothing. His exasperation at having to work with unfamiliar staff surfaced when, on 2 June, he tried unsuccessfully to stop his old judge-advocate, Francis Larpent, whilst he was on his way to Vienna. Wellington simply could not work with the new incumbent but Larpent had to press on to Vienna, leaving his old chief to make the best of things. All in all, one is struck by the tone and content of Wellington's despatches between his arrival in Brussels and the first week in June, for there is hardly any mention at all of the plans for the coming campaign. Instead, the despatches merely illustrate the problems facing Wellington as he sought to forge an army from the various contingents placed at his disposal by the British and Dutch governments. Fortunately, hard work was never a problem for the Duke who was used to working long hours in Spain. The hours were certainly longer in Brussels and the problems more acute and pressing. It is a testament to the man's great organisational and diplomatic skills that he was able to weld anything at all from the hotch-potch available to him, and that it would emerge with great credit at the end of the campaign.

By the beginning of June the majority of Wellington's British contingent had arrived in the Low Countries. There were thirty-nine British and King's German Legion infantry battalions, all of various strengths: the 2/1st Foot Guards, the 3/1st Foot Guards, 2/Coldstream, 2/3rd Foot Guards, 3/1st, 1/4th, 3/14th, 1/23rd, 1/27th, 1/28th, 2/30th, 1/32nd, 33rd, 2/35th, 1/40th, 1/42nd, 2/44th, 51st, 1/52nd, 1/54th, 2/59th, 2/69th, 1/71st, 2/73rd, 1/79th, 2/81st, 1/91st, 1/92nd, 1/95th, 2/95th, 3/95th, 1st and 2nd Light KGL, and the 1st, 2nd, 3rd, 4th, 5th and 8th Line KGL. Of the cavalry, there were twenty-one British and KGL regiments, again of varying strengths: 1st and 2nd Life Guards, Royal Horse Guards, 1st (Royal) Dragoons, 2nd (Royal North British) Dragoons, 1st (King's) Dragoon Guards, 6th (Inniskilling) Dragoons, 11th, 12th, 13th, 16th and 23rd Light Dragoons, 7th, 10th, 15th and 18th Hussars, 1st and 2nd Light Dragoons KGL, and the 1st, 2nd and 3rd Hussars KGL. It was a pale shadow of the old Peninsular army, but there were, nevertheless, some fine regiments present, and the British contingent was certainly not the inexperienced and raw army, 'most of whom had never seen a shot fired in anger', that some historians would have us believe.

While his army assembled Wellington no doubt allowed himself a degree of relaxation if only to forget momentarily the problems that he had to grapple with on a daily basis. In Spain there was little to do for sport and relaxation, save for hunting, but in Brussels there was a constant round of balls and parties to relieve some of the pressures that at times would have seemed almost unbearable to men of less talent and resolve. Part of the social side to life in pre-Waterloo Brussels involved interviews with numerous politicians and correspondents. It was during one conversation between Wellington and Thomas Creevey, the Radical gossip, held whilst walking in one of Brussels' numerous parks, that Wellington gave an indication that, despite the immense problems of mustering an army to face Bonaparte, he had at last begun to think that, provided he could count on the support of Marshal Blücher and the Prussians, he might yet give a good account of himself and emerge victorious. 'By God! I think Blücher and myself can do the thing,' he exclaimed, and as if to emphasise the key to success he pointed at a red-jacketed British soldier passing by. 'There, it all depends upon that article whether we do the business or not. Give me enough of it and I am sure.' But whether he had enough of 'that article' he was not sure, for on 2 June, just sixteen days before the Battle of Waterloo, he confided his anxieties to Sir Lowry Cole. 'I wish,' he said, 'I could bring everything together as I had it when I took leave of the Army at Bordeaux [in June 1814], and I would engage that we should not be last in the race.' Unfortunately, the army he had taken leave of the previous year was a thing of the past. The question remained in his mind; would this 'infamous army', the pale shadow of his all-conquering Peninsular army, be able to emulate the latter's great achievements? He was about to find out.

Miguel Alava.
One of Wellington's closest friends, Alava had fought at Trafalgar on the side of the Spaniards. He served with Wellington in the Peninsula and was the only member of Wellington's staff to dine with the Duke on the night of 18 June.

1 William Wheeler, *The Letters of Private Wheeler 1809–1828*, edited by Capt. BH Liddell Hart (London, 1951), p.158.
2 Anon, *A Soldier of the 71st*, edited by Christopher Hibbert (London, 1975), pp.104–5.
3 Lt.Col. William Tomkinson, *The Diary of a Cavalry Officer in the Peninsular War and Waterloo Campaign 1809–1815*, edited by James Tomkinson (London, 1894), pp.273–4.
4 Capt. William Hay, *Reminiscences 1808–1815 under Wellington*, edited by Mrs SCI Wood (London, 1901), p.158.
5 Haddy James, *Surgeon James' Journal 1815*, edited by Jane Vansittart (London, 1964), p.6.
6 AE Clark-Kennedy, *Attack the Colour! The Royal Dragoons in the Peninsula and at Waterloo* (London, 1975), p.88.
7 Capt. Cavalié Mercer, *Journal of the Waterloo Campaign*, edited by Sir John Fortescue (London, 1927), pp.2–3.
8 Ibid. p.7.
9 Maj. George Simmons, *A British Rifleman. The Journals and Correspondence of Major George Simmons, Rifle Brigade, During the Peninsular War and the Campaign of Waterloo*, edited by Willoughby Verner (London, 1899), p.360.
10 Ibid. p.361.
11 Sgt. David Robertson, *The Journal of Sergeant D. Robertson, late 92nd Foot, comprising the different campaigns between the years 1797 and 1818* (Perth, 1842), pp.140–1.
12 Col. Augustus Frazer, *Letters of Augustus Frazer, KCB, commanding the Royal Horse Artillery in the Army under the Duke of Wellington, written during the Peninsular and Waterloo campaigns*, edited by Edward Sabine (London, 1859), pp.487–8.
13 Sgt. John Douglas, *Douglas's Tale of the Peninsula and Waterloo*, edited by Stanley Monick (London, 1997), p.96.
14 Sir Thomas Picton, *Memoirs of Lieutenant General Sir Thomas Picton*, edited by HB Robinson (London, 1835), II. pp.339.
15 Capt. Howell Rees Gronow, *The Reminiscences of Captain Gronow*, edited by Nicolas Bentley (London, 1977), p.40.

Chapter II

LULL BEFORE
THE STORM

*There is nothing new here. We have reports of Bonaparte's joining the army and attacking us;
but I have accounts from Paris of the 10th, on which day he was still there; and I judge
from his speech to the Legislature that his departure was not likely to be immediate.
I think we are now too strong for him here.*

Wellington to Lord Lynedoch, 13 June 1815

Throughout the early spring of 1815 thousands of British soldiers continued to arrive in the Low Countries in preparation for the coming campaign against Bonaparte. For many regiments it was a new experience, whilst for the old lags from the Peninsula it was just another day's work. The common feeling amongst all, however, was one of eagerness to get to grips with the enemy combined with boredom and frustration. War has been described as long periods of boredom punctuated by periods of violent activity. April, May and early June 1815 was one of those periods. Naturally, a great deal of drilling and routine preparation work took place. Many regiments had been swollen by recruits from the Militia and by the beat of drum and these men, who had barely had time to learn His Majesty's drill in England, now found themselves flung into the middle of one of the great campaigns in history. Hence, it called for a heavy dose of daily drilling, marching and live-ball firing. A General Order, dated 9 May 1815, declared that 'General Officers commanding divisions and brigades should exercise the infantry in marching in column, of as large numbers as can be conveniently collected at half and quarter distances, with a front of one company, on the high road, from the distance of five or six miles from the point of collecting, and returning in the same order, twice or three times a week.'[1]

Apart from the endless hours of routine drill, the men's time was passed in a variety of ways. Cricket matches were played and all manner of improvised pastimes introduced. Races were very popular also, particularly amongst the officers. Digby Mackworth had served in the Peninsula with the 7th (Royal) Fusiliers and had been taken prisoner by the French before being exchanged for a French officer. He was now one of Lord Hill's aides-de-camp, and took part in one such meeting on 11 June:

We have just been having some races here which were very numerously attended. My little horse Vestris won three times, but Miss Fidget ran herself out of breath the first half mile and lagged sadly the second. I offered to run Vestris against any horse on the course, that like him was not in training, but could not get a match for him. I am quite vain of his prowess and so I think he is too, for he never was so spirited and saucy before since I had him. As for Miss Fidget she ought to be quite ashamed of herself, but like other young Ladies she will have her own way.[2]

Sightseeing was an obvious pastime. The Low Countries, and particularly Brussels, were in marked contrast to both Portugal and Spain where, apart from the major cities, there was little to interest even the most inquisitive officer. Brussels, Ghent and Bruges, on the other hand, boasted some fine architecture and museums, and during the quiet weeks before the outbreak of hostilities many a British officer found time to visit these cities. Their visits did not pass without incident, however, and during one infamous incident Wellington was moved to censure a group of high-spirited British officers who lassoed the famous Manikin Pis statue in Brussels and hauled it into the fountain in front of it. Brussels, in fact, was by far the favourite haunt of the British Army during the spring of 1815. Cavalié Mercer's troop of horse artillery had been based at Strytem, to the west of the city, for a week or two before he found time to ride over to the capital. His first impressions were not good, however:

Descending the hill, I entered this lower town by the Barrière de Grand and a long winding narrow street, bordered on either side by houses of black stone, three stories (generally) high, but of a mean appearance, without *trottoirs* for the foot passengers, and the mud above my horse's fetlocks; a little farther on I passed the fishmarket, and a fearful penance it was – for the strongest stomach, I should think, could hardly resist its noisome smell, arising from a fearful accumulation of garbage flung beneath the tables.[3]

Fortunately, things improved the farther Mercer got into the city. By the time he neared its centre the streets had become crowded with a mixture of Belgian, British and Hanoverian soldiers, who crowded around the shops which were selling 'the choicest productions of India and Europe'. The Grand Place and the Royal Park were amongst the favourite haunts. Augustus Frazer, also of the horse artillery, had little time for tourism in Brussels and instead had to return on 21 April to Ostend to supervise the landing of ordnance, stores and horses. However, on 3 May he was back in the city and the following day finished his work early in order to pay a visit to the museum which he described as resembling London's Somerset House.

Ghent was another popular place to visit. Surgeon Haddy James, of the 1st Life Guards,

was moved to remark that the entrance to Ghent was very similar to Oxford from the number and appearance of the steeples. 'On the entire route from Ostend,' he wrote, 'there was nothing to remind the traveller of the neighbourhood of armies and the state of war.' But as soon as he entered Ghent he noticed that numbers of British infantry had been placed on guard duty in key positions around the place. The business of war was quietly assuming its role although, for the majority of people, soldiers and civilians alike, there were few outward signs of the impending storm, which allowed Wellington's men to continue their leisurely introduction to this fresh theatre of war.

In the towns almost all the people speak and understand French; [wrote James] in the country the langue du pays is still in common use. The streets, the shops and the inns for the most part bear an inscription in French as well as in Dutch. The former are generally of a recent date and have been added since the country was annexed to France. At the present time it seems that some badge to designate attachment to the House of Orange is considered necessary as most of the inhabitants wear a piece of ribbon of that colour.[4]

Elsewhere, British troops were growing accustomed to their surroundings. After the hot,

The château at Strytem where Captain Cavalié Mercer spent the days leading up to the outbreak of hostilities.

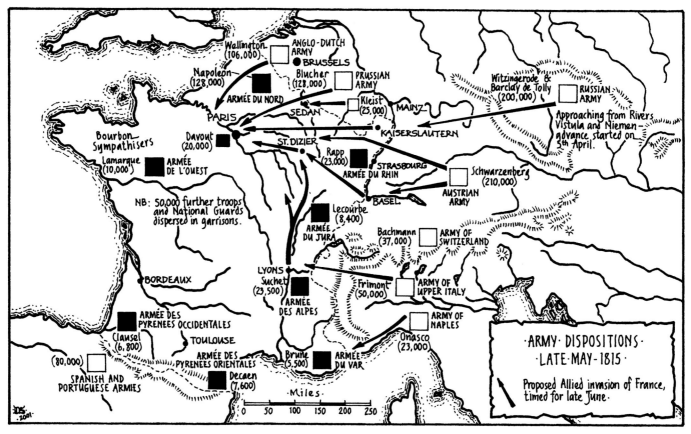

Map labels:

Wellington (106,000)
ANGLO-DUTCH ARMY
BRUSSELS
Napoleon (128,000)
Blucher (128,000)
PRUSSIAN ARMY
ARMÉE DU NORD
Witzingerode & Barclay de Tolly (200,000)
RUSSIAN ARMY
PARIS
SEDAN
Kleist (25,000)
MAINZ
KAISERSLAUTERN
Approaching from Rivers Vistula and Niemen – advance started on 5th April.
Bourbon Sympathisers
Davout (20,000)
ST. DIZIER
Lamarque (10,000)
ARMÉE DE L'OUEST
Rapp (23,000)
STRASBOURG
ARMÉE DU RHIN
Schwarzenberg (210,000)
NB: 50,000 further troops and National Guards dispersed in garrisons.
BASEL
AUSTRIAN ARMY
Lecourbe (8,400)
ARMÉE DU JURA
Bachmann (37,000)
ARMY OF SWITZERLAND
LYONS
BORDEAUX
Suchet (23,500)
ARMÉE DES ALPES
Frimont (50,000)
ARMY OF UPPER ITALY
ARMÉE DES PYRENEES OCCIDENTALES
TOULOUSE
ARMY OF NAPLES
Clausel (6,800)
(80,000)
SPANISH AND PORTUGUESE ARMIES
ARMÉE DES PYRENEES ORIENTALES
Brune (5,500)
ARMÉE DU VAR
Onasco (23,000)
Decaen (7,600)
·Miles·
0 50 100 150 200 250

·ARMY· DISPOSITIONS· LATE·MAY·1815·
Proposed Allied invasion of France, timed for late June.

dusty plains of Portugal and Spain, the rain-soaked fields and bad roads around Brussels came as a total contrast. There were hedgerows in abundance, the fields were greener, the population larger and more sophisticated, and towns bigger and more like those in England. Indeed, the close proximity of the campaign country to England not only made it far easier for supplies to be obtained but gave the countryside a certain familiarity in contrast to the far-off battlefields of the Peninsula. It was a similar type of feeling that many officers had remarked upon when Wellington's army emerged from the Pyrenees to invade southern France in late 1813. When the 1814 campaign began, more than a few officers described the countryside as reminding them of England, with hedgerows and vales which, after the past few years, came as a pleasant change.

It did not take long for Wellington's men to settle down into a routine. Even those regiments which arrived relatively late found time to settle into their billets, organise a routine of daily work and drill and begin improving their lot as regards accommodation, food and supplies, and those small comforts which made campaign life marginally more tolerable. The 1st (Royal) Dragoons, for example, arrived in mid-May, barely four weeks prior to the French invasion, but still found time to indulge in cricket matches and race meetings or go 'up to town', as Brussels was

called. Otherwise, officers simply settled down to bivouac life. In his quarters at the château at Strytem, Cavalié Mercer enjoyed a relatively relaxing stay, enlivened only by the daily parades and inspections and by the watering of his horses. Otherwise, everything was easy. 'After dinner,' he wrote,

some took a short ride previous to seeing their horses done up for the night. For my part I preferred enjoying the calm beauties of evening with my cigar under the splendid avenue of beech in rear of the château, and when night closed in, retired to my antique saloon, with a blazing fire of faggots and a couple of candles made tolerably comfortable. Here I busied myself in Madame de Genlis's *Life of Henri IV*, sometimes until midnight, tranquil and happy. At times, as I occasionally look up from my book and cast my eyes round, no sound interrupting the solemn stillness save the ticking of my watch as it lay on the table before me, the croaking of the frogs, or the moaning of the wind as it eddied round the old hall, I could almost fancy the deep-toned portraits of *ci-devant* Van Voldens, in their sombre velvet suits and stiff ruffs, actually embued with life, and frowning on my intrusion; or fixing them on the door of the chapel, damsels clad all in white, raising the tapestry, and – but then old Bal, getting up from his place before the fire to scratch himself, or the voice of the sentry in the outer court solemnly proclaiming

'All's well', would suddenly recall me from my reverie to a consciousness that it was bedtime; and so to bed I hied me, to sleep as well as the eternal frog-concert would allow.[5]

It was not just the officers who led an easy-paced existence. William Wheeler marched with his regiment, the 51st, from Brussels to Grammont on 13 April, and here they were to stay until hostilities broke out. Wheeler was quartered along with another man with a Belgian family who ran a tobacco shop.

> We eat and drink with the landlord and family, coffee stands ready for use all day long, when we get our rations we give it to the Mistress of the house, except our gin, this we take care of ourselves. We never see a bit of the bread after, if the meat should be good, it is cooked, if not, it is given with the bread to the beggars. I will tell you the manner we live. As soon as we rise a cup or two of good coffee. Eight o'clock breakfast of bread and butter eggs and coffee. Dinner meat and vegetables, dressed various ways, with beer, afterwards a glass of Holland's grog and tobacco, evening, salad, coffee, etc., then the whole is washed down by a pipe or two, then off to bed.[6]

Surgeon James was fortunate enough to stay in the Hôtel de Commerce in Bruges, which was filled with travellers from England. In Ghent, he found himself at another hotel, the Lion d'Or, which was full of French officers in the service of the exiled King Louis. Elsewhere, John Edgecombe Daniell, of the Commissariat, found himself in a farmhouse at Schendelbecke, whilst William Tomkinson, of the 16th Light Dragoons, was billeted in a farmhouse at Oyke, which was situated on the position that the French held at the Battle of Oudenarde in 1708.

The problem of billeting thousands of British soldiers in and around Brussels was partly solved by the issue of tents, something which had not become standard practice in the Peninsula until at least 1813. On 13 April 1815 a General Order was issued which 'recommended' that officers draw from the Quarter-Master General's stores one tent for each field officer, one for each officer commanding a troop or company and one for staff officers. The catch was that these were to be drawn on the condition that each officer carried his own tent. Thirty tents per British and KGL infantry battalion were to be drawn, whilst the Hanoverian Army was allowed to draw tents at a rate of sixty per brigade. Transportation was provided also,

being one wagon with two horses and a driver for each British and KGL battalion, and two wagons with four horses and two drivers per Hanoverian brigade.

In Brussels, Wellington housed himself right opposite the Rue Royale, either side of which various members of his staff took up residence. Although Wellington's hard work continued unabated throughout April and May, he still found time to attend many of the numerous balls and parties that were held in Brussels. Lady Caroline Capel wrote:

> Balls are going on here as if we had had none for a year. Nothing ever was so fine or so magnificent as the review of English cavalry 3 days ago. It was 30 miles off, and Capel thought it too great an undertaking for me or I certainly should have gone, for I could have done it free of expense, Lord Hill having offered me quarters, & General Barnes relays of horses. The day was tremendously hot, however, & part of the road bad, and as Capel was generous enough not to go himself as I did not, there was nothing to be said. Paget gave a most magnificent dinner to above 100 people, & Lord Hill a breakfast. The Duke of Wellington has not improved the morality of our society, as he has given several things & makes a point of asking all the ladies of loose character. Everyone was surprised at seeing Lady John Campbell at his house and one of his staff told me it had been represented to him her not being received for that her Character was more than suspicious. 'Is it, by God', said he, 'then I will go and ask her myself.' On which he immediately took his hat and went out for the purpose.[7]

Wellington was frequently seen in the company of 16-year-old Lady Jane Lennox, and accompanied her to a cricket match attended by members of several other aristocratic British families. Balls organised by wealthy families were certainly *de rigeur* in pre-Waterloo Brussels. The celebrated ball given by the Duchess of Richmond on the eve of the Battle of Quatre Bras is the most famous of the social functions held in Brussels during the campaign, although there was never a shortage of similar events, particularly as there were so many British ladies present in the capital. On 27 May Wellington himself gave a ball, attended by Digby Mackworth, who wrote in his diary:

> Lord Wellington gave a grand ball yesterday at which all the principal people in Brussels were present, a most magnificent supper was prepared and the gardens so well illuminated as

almost to resemble day. The Duke himself danced and always with the same person, a Lady Caroline Webster to whom he paid so much attention that scandal who is supreme Goddess here, began to whisper all sorts of stories, but we are not bound to believe all she says; not but that the well known bad private character of his Grace would warrant any suspicions whatever. When the Duke of Wellington after Lord Uxbridge's appointment to the command of the British Cavalry, was asked whether he would find it unpleasant to meet the man who had run off with his sister: why said he 'D-m him he won't run off with me too.' They did meet and appeared to be on the best possible terms.[8]

One wonders whether the relaxed atmosphere in Brussels and in the surrounding countryside was due in part to the fact that the prospects for the coming campaign were good. The journals of both officers and men reflect their eagerness to get to grips with Bonaparte, as well as a certain air of excitement. True, there was the prospect of great battles to come, but few write with an air of immediate expectancy, or of any urgency amongst Wellington's army. Some considered it unlikely that Bonaparte would ever attack and instead they looked forward to invading France. Even Wellington's own despatches are virtually devoid of anything relating to the impending campaign. Instead, they are largely concerned with administration, of his dealings with his allies and of the problems of trying to integrate the various Allied forces with his own British units. There is very little which deals directly with his strategy for the coming campaign.

Between 5 April, when he arrived in Brussels, and 14 June Wellington wrote some 273 despatches, very few of which actually refer to Bonaparte's movements. Most that do are written during May. By June Wellington appears to have been convinced that an attack upon him was unlikely and that if it ever did occur his army was now in a reasonably good condition to meet it. On 13 June he wrote to Lord Lynedoch, formerly Sir Thomas Graham, to say, 'There is nothing new here. We have reports of Bonaparte's joining the army and attacking us; but I have accounts from Paris of the 10th, on which day he was still there; and I judge from his speech to the Legislature that his departure was not likely to be immediate. I think we are now too strong for him here.'[9] In fact, many of his June despatches concern the provision for the subsistence of armies when in France, a subject upon which he was writing to Prince Metternich

as late as 14 June. However, this is not to say that he had completely ruled out the possibility of an attack upon either him or Marshal Blücher's Prussians, for Wellington did not gain the reputation of being cautious and defensive-minded for nothing.

The strange atmosphere, the 'phoney war' as it might later be called, extended to England. Sir Lowry Cole was one of the most distinguished generals in Wellington's army and was a veteran of countless campaigns in the Peninsula where he commanded the 4th Division. Indeed, he was the saviour of the Allied Army at Albuera on 16 May 1811. Naturally, he was summoned by Wellington to join him in Brussels. However, with little immediate prospect of action he decided to ask for leave in order to get married. On 30 May he wrote to Fitzroy Somerset requesting permission to remain in London for a further three weeks, which was granted, and thus he missed the great battle on 18 June.

Meanwhile, the parades and pastimes continued. Many Belgian villages took on the air of an English country village as regiments turned out to indulge in cricket matches, whilst the race meetings continued to be held. There was still the routine of daily drills, however, for the business of war was not completely pushed to the back of everyone's mind. The cavalry, in particular, were kept busy maintaining their horses and seeing to it that in the event of hostilities their precious mounts would be capable of getting them in and out of any given situation. The British cavalry had served with distinction in the Peninsula, despite the handicap of bad terrain, of the lack of a consistently good commander and of very low numbers. Now, for the first time under Wellington's command, the British cavalry arm could boast a very fine and very strong force. Between them the British and KGL cavalry could muster over 8,500 officers and men. Only at the Battle of Vittoria, two years earlier, could Wellington call upon anything like this number of cavalrymen, and on that particular occasion the ground, as usual, prevented them from being able to make as great a contribution as they might have done. Also, Wellington could call upon the services of a further 6,000 Dutch-Belgian, Hanoverian and Brunswick cavalry.

On 27 May, on the banks of the Dender river opposite the village of Schendelbeke, the majority of the British cavalry took part in one of the greatest displays of British cavalry during the Napoleonic Wars. It was an event witnessed by Cavalié Mercer, as some batteries of horse artillery took part also. Apparently, a farmer was

paid about £500 for the use of, 'the arena chosen for the review, and a more favourable one could scarcely have been chosen'.[10]

We were formed in three lines. [Mercer went on] The first, near the banks of the river, was composed of hussars in squadrons with wide intervals between them, and a battery of horse artillery (6-pounders) on either flank. Opposite the centre of this line was a bridge (temporary, I believe) by which the cortège was to arrive on the ground, descending from the village of Schendelbeke. The second line – compact, or with only the usual squadron intervals – was composed entirely of heavy dragoons, having two batteries – the one of 24-pounder howitzers, the other of 9-pounders – in front of the centre, and a battery of 9-pounders on either flank. The third was a compact line like the second, but entirely of light dragoons, supported on either flank by a battery of 9-pounders.

It was a splendid spectacle. The scattered lines of hussars in their fanciful yet picturesque costume; the more sober, but far more imposing line of heavy dragoons, like a wall of red brick; and again the serviceable and active appearance of the third line in their blue uniforms, with broad lapels of white, buff, red, yellow and orange – the whole backed by the dark wood of the declivity already mentioned – formed, indeed, a fine picture. There were, I understood, about 6,000 men on the field; and

as I looked and admired their fine appearance, complete equipment, and excellent horses, I wondered how any troops could withstand their attacks, and wished Napoleon and his chiefs could but see them as they stood.'[11]

Augustus Frazer was also present at the parade. 'It is not possible to imagine a finer sight,' he wrote the following day. 'The day was bright and hot, but with a gentle breeze. We were in meadows with grass up to the horses' knees, in a country fertile and rich, and well wooded. There were thousands of spectators, both of military men from all parts of the army, and of the people of the country for ten leagues round. The review passed off without a check, an error or an accident; one could see the cavalry had fallen into the hands of a master.'[12] The parade was intended to be for Wellington, Blücher and 'an immense cortège' but before the official party arrived the French Duc de Berri, full of self-importance and with his retinue in tow, appeared on the scene expecting to receive the due salute and respect of the British cavalry. He was to be sadly disappointed. His approach caught the British troops busy cleaning and scrubbing, most of them wearing their fatigue jackets. Suddenly, a shout went up, announcing the imminent arrival, or so they thought, of Wellington. Mercer again:

The whole line was in the midst of this business

It was in this meadow on the banks of the Dender river at Schendelbeke that the last great parade of British and KGL cavalry took place. On 29 May 1815 the entire British cavalry contingent as well as five regiments of KGL cavalry and eight batteries of Royal Horse Artillery paraded before Wellington, Blücher and 'an immense' cortege of some of the most distinguished officers in Europe.

[cleaning], many of the men even with their jackets off, when suddenly a forest of plumes and a galaxy of brilliant uniforms came galloping towards the temporary bridge. 'The Duke!' 'the Duke' 'the Duke's coming!' ran along the lines, and for a moment caused considerable bustle amongst the people; but almost immediately this was discovered to be a mistake, and the brushing and cleaning recommenced with more devotion than ever; whilst the cavalcade, after slowly descending the bridge and debouching on the meadows, started at full gallop toward the saluting point already marked out, the Duc de Berri, whom we now recognised, keeping several yards ahead, no doubt that he might be seen. At this point he reined up and looked haughtily and impatiently about him; and as we were now pretty intimate with his manner, it was easy to see, even from our distant position, that he was in a passion. The brushing, however, suffered no interruption, and no notice was taken of his presence. One of his suite was now called up and despatched to the front. What further took place I know not, but, certes! The messenger no sooner returned than his Highness was off like a comet, his tail streaming after him all the way up the slope, unable to keep pace with him, for he rode like a madman, whilst a general titter pervaded our lines as the report flew from one to the other that Monseer was off in a huff because we did not give him a general salute.[13]

It is easy to imagine the laughter in the ranks as the mischievous British cavalrymen continued their preparations for the real parade. This duly took place at 2pm when Wellington, Uxbridge and Blücher, along with their staffs and many other officers, arrived to inspect them. Blücher himself was so struck by the superb condition of the horses belonging to the horse artillery that he was moved to exclaim, 'Mein Gott, dere is not von orse in dies batterie wich is not goot for Veldt Marshal.'[14]

After the parade, Uxbridge invited all to dinner at his headquarters at Ninove. The dinner took place in a monastery, where the dining room was some one hundred feet square. The tables were laid horseshoe fashion, and Uxbridge sat in the centre with Wellington and Blücher on either side of him. Other guests included the Duke of Brunswick, the Prince of Orange, Prince Frederick, the Prussian officers Gneisenau, Zeithen and Kleist, Dornberg, Arentschild, Sir Sydney Smith, Hill, Pack, Picton, and Sir John Elley. A noble gathering indeed. Needless to say, the Duc de Berri was not present.

The balls and the parades went on, but as the social events continued the euphoria and excitement that accompanied the opening of the campaign began to give way as both officers and men started to wonder whether they would ever see action. It was almost as though a 'phoney war' had set in, with much talk and posturing but no real prospect of immediate action. The British regiments had been packed off to the Low Countries from far and wide, and in great haste, but once there the majority soon found themselves with little to do but endure the drudgery of daily drilling. The danger was, of course, that the edge might be taken off the troops and complacency would set in. There was little or no information forthcoming about enemy movements and even Wellington appears to have been in the dark as to Bonaparte's real intentions. But as May turned to June, things began to stir south of the French border. Bonaparte's men began to move slowly north away from Paris towards the Sambre river, while artillery, ammunition and supplies were collected and moved forward also. Bonaparte himself may have been staying in Paris, but while he continued to give speeches to his people his devoted legions began to collect for the final conflict. Hostilities were about to commence.

1 General Order Brussels, 9 May 1815.
2 Digby Mackworth MSS.
3 Capt. Cavalié Mercer, *Journal of the Waterloo Campaign*, edited by Sir John Fortescue (London, 1927), p.110.
4 Haddy James, *Surgeon James' Journal 1815*, edited by Jane Vansittart (London, 1964), p.10.
5 Mercer, *Journal*, p.77.
6 William Wheeler, *The Letters of Private Wheeler 1809–1828*, edited by Capt. BH Liddell Hart (London, 1951), p.162.
7 *The Capel Letters, 1814–1817*, edited by the Marquess of Anglesey (London, 1955), p.102.
8 Mackworth MSS.
9 Wellington to Lord Lynedoch, 13 June 1815, *The Despatches of Field Marshal the Duke of Wellington*, (London, 1832), XII. p.462.
10 Mercer, *Journal*, p.117.
11 Ibid. p.118.
12 Col. Augustus Frazer, *Letters of Augustus Frazer, KCB, commanding the Royal Horse Artillery in the Army under the Duke of Wellington, written during the Peninsular and Waterloo campaigns*, edited by Edward Sabine (London, 1859), pp.521–2.
13 Mercer, *Journal*, p.119.
14 Ibid, p. 119

Chapter III

COMMUNICATIONS BREAKDOWN

There was certainly something out of order in the communication
between the two armies in the middle of June.

Wellington to the Earl of Ellesmere, September 1851

While the British Army mustered to the south and west of Brussels, their Prussian allies began to gather to the east. The Prussian Army consisted of four corps under Ziethen, Pirch I, Thielemann and Bulow, and numbered around 117,000 men, including 12,000 cavalry and 312 guns. They were concentrated between Liège in the east and Charleroi in the west. This latter town lay on the Sambre river just north of the French border and was very close to the demarcation point between the Anglo-Dutch and Prussian armies. It was also through this town that one of the two main roads likely to be used by the French ran north to Brussels, the other being via Mons. It took no military genius, therefore, to see that the weak point in the Allied dispositions, and consequently the logical point of any French attack, was via the main road through Charleroi. However, as Wellington himself remarked, Bonaparte was not prone to do the obvious. Charleroi was indeed the obvious route; but what if Bonaparte attacked via Mons?

Wellington had met Blücher at Tirlemont, about twenty-five miles east of Brussels, on 3 May to discuss their joint plan for the coming campaign. It is strange that no document was ever produced or signed and we only have the barest of details as to what was said and actually agreed. Wellington himself merely said that he met Blücher, 'and received from him the most satisfactory assurances of support'. He also added that given the numerical superiority of the two Allied armies they were confident of giving 'a good account even of Bonaparte'. It is quite obvious that both men agreed to support each other should Bonaparte attack them. Apart from this there was never any written agreement. Judging from his despatches Wellington's main concern following the meeting was the condition of Blücher's Saxon troops, who had mutinied and who could not be trusted to fight during the coming campaign. Other than this the despatches betray no actual concerted plan for mutual support. They did, however, agree that the lateral line of communication between their armies should be the road running east to west from Sombreffe through the hamlet of Quatre Bras to Nivelles.

By the middle of June Wellington's Anglo-Dutch Army had grown to around 94,000 men, including 15,000 cavalry and 196 guns. The British and KGL contingent numbered around 27,000 infantry, 8,473 cavalry, 5,556 artillery and 120 guns. The ratio of guns to men was very high when we consider that at the Battle of Vittoria, for example, Wellington could boast just over 78,000 British and Portuguese troops, which happened to be the largest number he ever gathered together on a battlefield in the Peninsula and yet he had the services of just seventy-six guns. Wellington's army was organised and distributed as follows: the 1st Corps, under the Prince of Orange, numbered 25,000 men with forty-eight guns. It consisted of the 1st British Division under Cooke, Alten's 3rd Division of British, KGL and Hanoverians, and the 2nd and 3rd Dutch-Belgian divisions. Orange's headquarters were at Braine-le-Comte and his divisions were posted between Enghien and Nivelles, watching the country between the Brussels–Charleroi road and the Dender river to the west. The 1st Corps was also the farthest south of Wellington's troops and was the nearest to the Prussian 1st Corps of Ziethen.

The 2nd Corps, under the ever-reliable Rowland Hill, was the most westerly of Wellington's corps and was based between Ath, Alost and Oudenarde. It comprised Clinton's 2nd Division of British, KGL and Hanoverians, the 4th Division,

A fine study of a trooper of the 2nd (North British) Dragoons, otherwise known as the Scots Greys. Like the majority of the British cavalry contingent, the regiment spent the days prior to the opening of hostilities close to Ninove.

under Colville, consisting of British and Hanoverians, and the 1st Dutch-Belgian Division, along with the oddly-named Dutch-Belgian Indian Brigade under Anthing. Hill's corps numbered 24,000 men with forty guns.

The Reserve, under Wellington himself, numbered a further 21,000 men with sixty-four guns. Naturally, its headquarters were at Brussels. It consisted of the 5th and 6th British and Hanoverian divisions, the Brunswick corps of the Duke of Brunswick, and the Nassau contingent under General von Kruse.

Finally, there was the Allied cavalry under Lord Uxbridge. In addition to the 8,473 British and KGL cavalry there were 6,009 Hanoverian, Dutch-Belgian and Brunswick cavalry. The British and KGL contingent were stationed along the Dender river around Grammont and Ninove.

Because Wellington had no definite idea what route Bonaparte might use if he took the

offensive, his army was necessarily scattered. Too scattered, some might say. Indeed, one of the major criticisms aimed at Wellington has been the dangerously stretched dispositions of his men. However, one has to appreciate the problems facing him at the time. Just a brief glance at the Ferraris and Capitaine map of 1797, used by both sides during the campaign, is enough to show quite clearly that it was possible for Bonaparte to use several routes, although there were really only two likely ones. The first, via Charleroi, was essentially the demarcation point between Wellington's and Blücher's armies. The second, via Mons, lay farther to the west and was the route that Wellington feared most of all. After all, it was the one which, if Bonaparte attacked along it, would threaten his right flank and consequently his communications with both Ostend and Antwerp. There remained a third route, via Tournai, which would also threaten his communications. This route ran north to Ghent rather than Brussels, but it was here that the exiled Louis XVIII resided, and as Wellington was responsible for the safety of the King this third route also gave him cause for anxiety.

However, whether Wellington actually considered an offensive move by Bonaparte as a real prospect is open to debate. It is certain that throughout the spring of 1815 and, in fact, the previous year, he had made strong recommendations regarding the strengthening of the frontier towns such as Mons, Ypres and Tournai. And yet five days after meeting with Blücher at Tirlemont, he was discussing offensive operations himself with Charles Stewart.

When the British Army began to muster in the Low Countries, Colonel Colquhoun Grant was amongst the first men requested by Wellington in person. The Duke knew exactly what he needed in order to keep one step ahead of Bonaparte, and that was intelligence, and in order to gain this vital weapon he needed his top man – Colquhoun Grant. 'The first respectable spy' was how Jock Haswell described him in his biography. Grant was Wellington's head of intelligence during the Peninsular and Waterloo campaigns and it was his daring missions behind enemy lines that frequently supplied Wellington with vital information about French plans, movements and troop numbers. Indeed, it was men like Grant who gave Wellington the edge over his adversaries and enabled him to know what was happening 'on the other side of the hill'. Grant was to play an equally important role during the Waterloo campaign, although things did not turn out exactly as he would have wished.

At the time of Bonaparte's escape from Elba, Grant was sitting an entrance examination to the Royal Military College at Farnham, Surrey, and after successfully negotiating the questions he entered the college on 31 March. He barely had time to get settled before his old chief summoned him to Brussels. Wellington knew his worth and accepted his information without question. In the Peninsula Grant had spent long periods behind enemy lines and, on 15 April 1812 had even suffered the misfortune of being captured. He was subsequently taken to Salamanca where he dined with Marshal Marmont before being taken under escort to Bayonne. Here, he escaped and after several adventures made his way back to London. He then returned to join Wellington in Spain in September 1813 and served throughout the remainder of the Peninsular War. His presence in Brussels was, there-

fore, imperative to Wellington if he was to find out what Bonaparte intended to do in the coming campaign.

Grant arrived in Brussels on 12 May and after a briefing from Wellington took himself off to the French border. Soon afterwards he disappeared into France where he began making contact with agents friendly to the Allies. There were, after all, still many people who remained loyal to King Louis and who had little reason to rejoice at Bonaparte's return. And then there were those who simply couldn't care less who governed the nation; a plague on both houses. Grant had little trouble, therefore, in discovering French movements. After all, it was difficult to see how Bonaparte hoped to mask the movements of thousands of French troops heading north towards the Sambre river. Indeed, on 16 May Wellington wrote a memorandum to the King of the Netherlands and Marshal Blücher which gave a complete and very detailed breakdown of the strength and composition of the French Army, the information having come from inside France. But what Grant and Wellington could not discover was the route any invading French Army might take. Would it move via Mons or Charleroi? It was the crucial question and it was one that would effectively paralyse Wellington until it was almost too late.

Wellington's network of spies, agents and regular patrols were organised in such a way that any reports were to be sent via Mons, where Major General Wilhelm von Dörnberg had his headquarters. Dörnberg commanded the 3rd Cavalry Brigade, which consisted of the 1st and 2nd Light Dragoons of the King's German Legion, and the British 23rd Light Dragoons. The German cavalry had demonstrated on numerous occasions in the Peninsula just how valuable they were to Wellington. Their horsemanship, fighting prowess and overall professionalism were legendary and the outposts could not have been in better hands. The 23rd Light Dragoons, on the other hand, had enjoyed a short and unhappy time in Spain. Indeed, their campaign came to an abrupt end after the Battle of Talavera in July 1809, during which they charged into the midst of enemy cavalry and suffered such severe losses that they were forced to return to England to recruit. They did not return to Spain and the Waterloo campaign was their first overseas service for six years. However, they were to serve with distinction throughout the campaign. It was, in fact, Dörnberg who would prove to be the weak link in Wellington's chain of outposts at Mons, for he appears to have been negligent in his appreciation of intelligence received by him and in its distribution to Wellington's headquarters.

According to Grant's biographer, Dörnberg intercepted a courier bearing a message which appeared to indicate that Charleroi was the likely route of Bonaparte's attack. The message, apparently written by Grant, confirmed an enemy build up between Mauberge, Beaumont and Philippeville, but why Grant deduced from this that Charleroi was the intended invasion route is actually a mystery, for the three towns were far closer to Mons. Nevertheless, there were apparently good enough grounds for Grant to consider Charleroi the target. Unfortunately Dörnberg failed to realise that the source of the information was Grant. He judged the information to be of dubious value and returned it, adding that 'so far from convincing him that the emperor was advancing for battle, it assured him of the contrary'.[1] Thus, Dörnberg merely took down the information regarding troop movements but apparently omitted Grant's crucial conclusion. The returning courier was met with incredulity by Grant who had little choice but to try and deliver the message to Wellington himself, despite running the risk of being captured by one of the thousands of French troops who lay between him and his chief. The delay in getting the message through to Wellington – Grant finally delivered it to Wellington upon the field of Quatre Bras – undoubtedly prevented Wellington from concentrating his army in time for the battle on 16 June. Little is made of the story in the majority of Waterloo histories, although this is not to say that it is without foundation.[2] What it does demonstrate is Wellington's reliance on Grant and his reluctance to make any premature move to his left towards the Prussians, a move which, if Bonaparte did decide to attack via Mons, might prove fatal. He simply had to know by which route Bonaparte was advancing and the fact that reports indicated a massive build up of French troops between Mauberge, Beaumont and Philippeville did little to answer the question. After all, Mons was a mere thirteen miles from Mauberge, and only twenty-six miles from Beaumont. Given that Bonaparte had assembled 43,000 men at Solre-sur-Sambre, eight miles east of Mauberge, and a further 58,000 at Beaumont, it is little wonder that Wellington feared for his right flank. Conversely, it would not be difficult for the French to transfer their forces from Solre-sur-Sambre and Mauberge via Beaumont, north to Charleroi.

The information received by Wellington up to the evening of 14 June gave no real indication of the likely route of the French attack. There were various reported sightings of Bonaparte, whilst rumours of French activity flew everywhere. The glare of campfires seen in the night sky near Beaumont confirmed the presence of thousands of enemy troops, but there was still no definite news regarding the direction of their attack. The only reliable information was the report from Grant, and as we have seen, this vital information was being returned to him by the royalist courier whom Dörnberg had dismissed. There was little Wellington could do, therefore, except continue to await reports from his patrols or, more crucially, from Grant.

In fact, whilst Allied cavalry continued to patrol the frontier around Mons, Bonaparte's men were streaming away to the east, making for the Sambre at Charleroi. Despite all of his posturing in front of Mons, Bonaparte, who had arrived at Beaumont on 14 June, was going for Charleroi after all. It was a classic example of his so-called 'strategy of the central position', whereby he would detach a portion of his army to keep one enemy force at bay whilst he fell upon and defeated the other with his main army. He would then rejoin the detached wing and defeat the remaining enemy in turn. It was quite simple on paper but it had worked before. It almost worked during the Waterloo campaign. In this case it was Ney who would lead the detached portion to keep Wellington at bay whilst Bonaparte moved against Blücher's Prussians. Some historians have claimed, perhaps with justification, that Bonaparte knew the character of his enemies well. If he attacked Wellington, the hot-headed Blücher would almost certainly march to his comrade's aid, whereas if he attacked Blücher first of all, he doubted whether Wellington would do the same. He judged Wellington to be the more cautious of the two and reckoned that Wellington would take his time in concentrating his army before moving. In the event, he was not far wrong.

When Bonaparte struck on the morning of 15 June, he struck at the very hinge of the two Allied armies. Wellington always claimed that Bonaparte was never one to do the obvious, but here he was. The Charleroi gap yawned before him and at around 3.30am his men were flooding slowly across the Sambre, many of them using bridges which the Prussians had neglected to destroy. The fighting was brisk and sharp as Ziethen's men fought a determined rearguard action. There was no panic. The Prussians fought

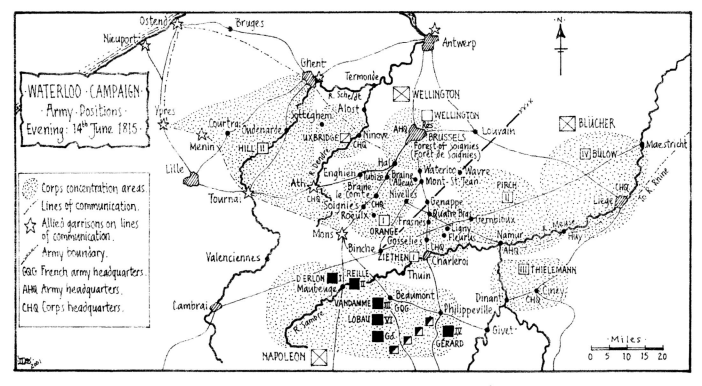

hard, delaying the passage of the Sambre and causing the French an almighty traffic jam as convoys of baggage and ammunition wagons, in addition to columns of men, were stopped in their tracks. However, Ziethen could not stop the French alone and he fell back slowly in the direction of Fleurus, after having fired the alarm guns.

The sequence of events surrounding the French attack on 15 June has been the subject of countless in-depth debates, whilst literally thousands of pages have been consumed in analysing the Allied response to the attack and in apportioning blame for the tardiness of the Allied reaction. Wellington in particular has come in for widespread criticism for his reluctance to move to Blücher's assistance and the lack of speed with which he concentrated his army. The arguments raged for years afterwards, and continue to do so today, about the timings of the various despatches written and received by those concerned. All of this only serves to demonstrate that there was an almighty breakdown in communications between the armies of Wellington and Blücher at a most critical moment of the campaign.

A year before his death Wellington wrote 'there was certainly something out of order in the communication between the two armies in the middle of June'.[3] This was putting it mildly. To this very day German historians claim messages were despatched to Wellington much earlier than he admitted, and allege that when Bonaparte finally revealed his true direction of attack

Wellington's forces were too overstretched to meet it.[4] Thus, it was in his interests to claim that he received news from the Prussians of Bonaparte's attack far later than they claim he actually did, since this provided him with the perfect excuse for his inactivity and his slow response to the French attack. Countering this, one can do no better than to quote the late Jac Weller who, in his expert analysis of the situation in his *Wellington at Waterloo*, wrote, 'There is not one shred of evidence for such a view in all the dozens of memoirs which survive. Wellington's whole life and character argue against it.'[5]

With hostilities having finally begun, and with Ziethen's Corps engaged in a skilful fighting retreat towards Fleurus, we must return to Brussels and the reaction at Wellington's headquarters. Quite simply, there was no reaction, for Wellington was blissfully unaware that the fighting had started. Whilst the opening shots of the campaign were being exchanged on the Sambre, Wellington continued to deal with the mundane tasks of the commander-in-chief of the army. Even as Prussian and French soldiers were dying, he sat in the relative calm of his Brussels headquarters penning a despatch, timed at 1pm, to Sir Henry Clinton on the re-numbering of his British divisions in response to a request that they be given their old Peninsular numbers. But while he attended to his paperwork in Brussels, other more important and urgent messages were being written by those close to the frontier away to the south.

One of the messages was from Ziethen, apparently timed at 9am, who despatched a courier to Brussels to inform Wellington of the French attack.[6] Another was from Dörnberg at Mons. Writing at 9.30am, Dörnberg wrote to Fitzroy Somerset that information had come in from Mauberge that all of the French troops there had marched towards Philippeville and that only a few National Guardsmen remained there. Also at Mons was General Behr who wrote to his corps commander, the Prince of Orange at Braine-le-Comte, reporting that General Steinmetz, who commanded the Prussians at Fontaine l'Eveque, was under attack. Steinmetz sent his report at 8am and this was duly communicated to the Prince of Orange, arriving upon his desk two hours later. Behr added that the fighting appeared to be heavy at Charleroi and that all in front of General van Merlen, who commanded the 3rd Dutch-Belgian Cavalry Brigade, south of Mons, was quiet. Unfortunately, the Prince of Orange was not at Braine-le-Comte, for he was out visiting the outposts and thus the messages from Dörnberg and Behr lay on his desk for a further four hours. At 2pm they were picked up and forwarded by General Constant Rebecque to Wellington's liaison officer at the Prince's headquarters, Sir George Berkeley, who in turn sent them on to Brussels after adding a note to say that the Prussians had evacuated Binche and were being attacked at Charleroi.

Meanwhile, the Prussians were being slowly driven back towards Fleurus, but it would only be a matter of time, surely, before Wellington moved his troops east to meet the French attack. However, it was to be some time before this came about, for in accordance with his own instructions all intelligence received was to be gathered at Mons before being transmitted via Braine-le-Comte to Brussels. Thus it was that while the Prussians continued their struggle, the report from Sir George Berkeley was labouring its way across the Belgian countryside. The distance from Mons to Braine-le-Comte is fourteen miles, and from there to Brussels a further twenty. The messenger carrying Ziethen's despatch, meanwhile, was making an even longer journey, the report having to travel from Charleroi to Mons, to Braine-le-Comte and finally on to Brussels. Ziethen had naturally reported the fighting to Blücher at Namur, twenty-eight miles away, and the Prussian commander in turn ordered Gneisenau to inform Wellington. The journey from Namur to Brussels is forty-two miles and this done at a pace which one could best describe as painfully slow. Matters were not helped by the fact that Blücher, in Wellington's words, 'picked the fattest man in the Prussian Army' to deliver the despatch. Indeed, the journeys from Mons and Namur to Brussels appear to have taken a remarkably long time to accomplish, a fact that remains one of the great mysteries of the campaign.

In Brussels the British Army continued to pass the time partying and sightseeing. The talk amongst many of Wellington's officers in the capital was the ball to be hosted by the Duchess of Richmond. Throughout 15 June officers preened themselves whilst servants groomed the full dress uniforms of their masters in preparation for the evening's event. The guest list included countless officers, senior and junior, as well as Wellington himself. Elsewhere, officers continued with their normal activities, seemingly unaware of what was happening just thirty-four miles away to the south. As late as 10pm Augustus Frazer sat down to write a letter describing the last few days of sightseeing and dinner parties. His letter gives an indication of just how relaxed things were in Brussels. It also demonstrates just how inaccurate Allied intelligence was:

> I have this moment returned from dining with Hawker to celebrate his promotion to a lieutenant-colonelcy. He lives in a very large and comfortable house at the village of Lenniche St Quentin…We were a jolly party of a dozen, the cheer was excellent, but the roads detestable. On returning I find Ross here, he has dined at General Kempt's, and has learned in the course of the evening that the enemy has moved upon Mons, and that in consequence we are to move during the night. Sir George Wood has just been here to say the same thing…I find on my table an invitation to dine with Delancey tomorrow; his lady is here; this will be a pleasanter way of passing the day than marching to Mons.[7]

Frazer went on to describe a visit to see a collection of paintings, before going on to record some pertinent observations on the situation late on 15 June:

> It seems that Bonaparte is at Mauberge, that he has about 120,000 men there, that he has advanced in the direction of Binch, leaving Mons to his left and rear; that Blücher with 80,000 Prussians has moved from Namur to Sombreffe (on the road from Namur to Nivelles), that we shall concentrate our force in

front of Braine l'Aleud (near Hal). Admitting this to be true, we may have a battle the day after tomorrow. The Duke has gone to a ball at the Duchess of Richmond's, but all is ready to move at daybreak. Of course, all depends on the news which may arrive in the night. By way of being ready, I shall go to bed, and get a few hours' sleep. It is now half-past 11.[8]

Given the events unfolding around him at the time Frazer appears to have been remarkably relaxed about the whole situation. No signs of undue worry or anxiety here, just an acknowledgement that the campaign had finally opened and of the need to get some sleep, for he knew that once the orders came for him to move it might be some time before he would be able to rest again.

Meanwhile the scattered British regiments had yet to hear of developments at Charleroi. Indeed, the talk amongst many of the officers was the coming Duchess of Richmond's ball. At Strytem, Cavalié Mercer had little to do but enjoy the pleasures of an evening walk.

> Most of the other officers had gone to the ball at Brussels, and I remained quite alone. The balmy softness of the air, the beauty and repose of scenery, were, I thought, more exquisite than ever; and I continued in the avenue until the increasing obscurity of the evening drove me in to enjoy an hour or two with The Hermit of the Chaussée d'Antin ere I retired for the night.[9]

Elsewhere, Surgeon Haddy James, of the 1st Life Guards, enjoyed an afternoon with the 2nd Life Guards. 'A very jolly afternoon' was had, and he returned to Ninove replete with an excellent dinner. Lord Edward Somerset reviewed the Household Brigade the same day. William Lawrence, of the 40th Regiment, had an uneventful day, as did David Robertson, of the 92nd. Both simply endured yet another routine day of drilling and inspections. It appeared as if 15 June was going to be just another day spent waiting for something to happen.

Back in Brussels, however, things were stirring, for news had been received of the French attack and something was indeed definitely happening. John Kincaid, of the 95th Rifles, was one of the most celebrated diarists of the Peninsular and Waterloo campaigns. Kincaid, who was 28 years old, had come through the Peninsular War unscathed, which is quite remarkable considering his regiment was one of those which made up the Light Division, a force that was usually in the thick of the action. He was also

one of the leaders of the storming parties that took Ciudad Rodrigo in January 1812. Kincaid was with the 1st Battalion of his regiment on the afternoon of the 15th:

> We were, on the whole of the 15th, on the most anxious look out for news from the front; but no report had been received prior to the hour of dinner. I went, about seven in the evening, to take a stroll in the park, and meeting one of the Duke's staff, he asked me, en passant, whether my pack-saddles were all ready? I told him that they were nearly so, and added, 'I suppose they won't be wanted, at all events, before tomorrow?' to which he replied, in the act of leaving me, 'If you have any preparation to make, I would recommend you not to delay so long.' I took the hint, and returning to quarters, remained in momentary expectation of an order to move. The bugles sounded to arms two hours after.[10]

In fact, things had begun to stir at about 3pm, when the first reports of the French attack were received. The Prince of Orange, it will be recalled, had left his headquarters at Braine-le-Comte at about 5am in order to visit the outposts. Whilst on his rounds he heard firing from the direction of Thuin, to the south-west of Charleroi. Instead of returning to his headquarters he rode directly to Brussels, arriving there at around 3pm. He had been invited to the Duchess of Richmond's ball in any case and he intended to remain in Brussels for the evening. It was a stroke of good fortune that he was able to report first-hand to the Duke of the firing at the Prussian outposts, although it was still a relatively vague report. However, at about the same time Ziethen's report finally arrived at Müffling's quarters having taken almost six hours to reach Brussels. The report was immediately taken by Müffling to Wellington, but despite the news of the French attack at Charleroi, Wellington was still not convinced that it was the main enemy attack and until he received word from Mons he was reluctant to move any of his troops. 'If all is as General von Ziethen supposes,' he said, 'I will concentrate on my left wing, i.e. the corps of the Prince of Orange. I shall then be à potrée to fight in conjunction with the Prussian Army. Should, however, a portion of the enemy's forces come by Mons, I must concentrate more towards my centre. For this reason I must positively wait for news from Mons before I fix my rendezvous.'[11]

It was becoming increasingly clear that the attack upon the Prussians at Charleroi had been made in strength and that the reports from Dörnberg and Behr indicated that few if any French troops remained in front of Mons. But despite this evidence Wellington remained unconvinced, for he had yet to hear anything from his chief of intelligence, Colquhoun Grant, and the silence from this quarter gave him great cause for concern. His reliance on Grant is understandable, given the latter's record in the Peninsula, but his faith in this single source of information, despite the increasing evidence that suggested that Charleroi was the real invasion route, would appear to have been misplaced. Of course, had the Grant despatch not been returned to him by Dörnberg, Wellington would already have received the information he needed. But such is history. Dörnberg apparently fumbled the chance to apprise Wellington of the situation and instead the Duke remained anxiously waiting for news from Grant.

Accounts differ as to what actually prompted Wellington to issue orders for the movement of his army. Some say it was Ziethen's report, received at about 3pm, coupled with the Prince of Orange's report, that forced Wellington's arm. Others claim that it was the arrival of the reports from Dörnberg and Behr, which reached Wellington at about 5pm, that prompted the move. What is clear is that at some time between 5pm and 7pm, Wellington issued his first set of orders for the concentration of his army, in order that it could be held in readiness to march and block any French attack that might come via Mons or Charleroi. The exact wording was as follows:

> General Dörnberg's brigade of cavalry, and the Cumberland Hussars, to march this night upon Vilvorde, and to bivouac on the high road near to that town.
>
> The Earl of Uxbridge will be pleased to collect the cavalry this night at Ninove, leaving the 2nd hussars looking out between the Scheldt and the Lys.
>
> The Ist division of infantry to collect this night at Ath and adjacent, and to be in readiness to move at a moment's notice.
>
> The 3rd division to collect this night at Braine le Comte, and to be in readiness to move at the shortest notice.
>
> The 4th division to be collected this night at Grammont, with the exception of the troops beyond the Scheldt, which are to be moved to Audenarde.
>
> The 5th division, the 81st Regiment, and the Hanoverian brigade of the 6th Division, to be in readiness to march from Bruxelles at a moment's notice.
>
> The Duke of Brunswick's corps to collect this night on the high road between Bruxelles and Vilvorde.
>
> The Nassau troops to collect at daylight tomorrow morning on the Louvrain road, and to be in readiness to move at a moment's notice.
>
> The Hanoverian brigade of the 5th division to collect this night at Hal, and to be in readiness at daylight tomorrow morning to move towards Bruxelles, and to halt on the high road between Alost and Assche for further orders.
>
> The Prince of Orange is requested to collect at Nivelles the 2nd and 3rd divisions of the army of the Low Countries; and, should that point have been attacked this day, to move the 3rd division of British infantry upon Nivelles as soon as collected.
>
> This movement is not to take place until it is quite certain that the enemy's attack is upon the right of the Prussian army, and the left of the British army.
>
> Lord Hill will be so good as to order Prince Frederick of Orange to occupy Audenarde with 500 men, and to collect the 1st division of the army of the Low Countries, and the Indian brigade at Sotteghem, so as to be ready to march in the morning at daylight.
>
> The reserve artillery to be in readiness to move at daylight.[12]

Despite the news from Charleroi that Bonaparte was attacking in some strength, Wellington still refused to risk everything on the belief that it was the main attack. Indeed, Wellington's orders simply allowed for the collection of his scattered forces but did not actually go so far as to say in which direction any subsequent move would be made. The only allowance he made for a move to the east was the instruction to the Prince of Orange to move the 3rd British Division, which he had originally ordered to be collected at Braine-le-Comte, to Nivelles in the event of the place being attacked. Otherwise, there was still no firm order for his army to march east to either Nivelles or beyond. Thus Wellington's men were placed in such dispositions as would allow them to parry any French thrust via Mons, Nivelles or Charleroi. The major drawback of having his men so dangerously dispersed over such a wide area was the time it would take to collect them in order to face the French whenever the main direction of attack was finally determined. Along with these orders Wellington also sent a despatch to Dörnberg requesting the immediate reporting of any enemy movement at Mons.

Meanwhile in Brussels, Wellington and

many of his senior officers were preparing for the ball to be given by the Duchess of Richmond on the night of 15 June. At the same time, to the south and south-west of Brussels, bugles and trumpets blared across the countryside calling Wellington's British divisions to arms. At last a sense of urgency descended upon the various camps and billets of the men scattered across the land. But while they prepared to move in accordance with Wellington's orders, transmitted earlier in the evening at about 5pm, one of the most significant and important acts of the entire Waterloo campaign was being played out, not by any of Wellington's British troops but by some of his Dutch allies. Whilst Colquhoun Grant was trying desperately to deliver his report, which it is believed gave the true direction of Bonaparte's attack, Prince Bernhard of Saxe-Weimar, commanding the 2nd Brigade of the 2nd Dutch-Belgian Division, was discovering the direction for himself. For, even as Wellington was writing his orders, Prince Bernhard was being attacked at Quatre Bras, a small hamlet situated at the vital crossroads at the main junction of the Charleroi–Brussels and Sombreffe–Nivelles roads.

The Prince's commanding officer was Baron de Perponcher, whose headquarters were at Nivelles. At around 9pm Perponcher received a despatch from Prince Bernhard in which he reported the French attack, adding that he thought it unlikely that he would be able to hang on for much longer owing to a shortage of ammunition. It was just as well that darkness came down to put an end to the day's fighting, otherwise the French might well have pushed on and taken the crossroads. Perponcher immediately communicated Prince Bernhard's report to General Constant Rebecque, the Prince of Orange's Chief of Staff at Braine-le-Comte, and the two men wisely decided to ignore Wellington's order for them to concentrate at Nivelles and instead reinforce Quatre Bras. This was sound reasoning, for had they complied with Wellington's order to move west to Nivelles the important crossroads at Quatre Bras would have been left unoccupied and it is unlikely that the French would have spurned such a gift. Thus, the vital lateral east–west communication between Blücher's Prussians, now concentrating around Sombreffe, and Wellington's troops, who had been ordered to collect in anticipation of a

Wellington inspects his troops in the forest of Soignies at the beginning of the campaign.

possible move to Nivelles, would have been left in French hands.

The Prince of Orange it will be remembered was in Brussels, having ridden there earlier in the day to report having heard firing away at Thuin. He remained in order to attend the Duchess of Richmond's ball. Therefore, Perponcher and Rebecque were not in a position to involve the Prince in their decision to remain at and reinforce Quatre Bras. They did, however, send one of the Prince's aides, Lieutenant Henry Webster, galloping off to Brussels to inform him of their decision, a report that was sent at 10.30pm.

While Webster was galloping the twenty or so miles north from Braine-le-Comte to Brussels, further intelligence arrived at Wellington's headquarters. At about 8pm Gneisenau's report of the French attack reached Wellington, having taken about seven hours to travel the forty miles from Namur. It did little to enlighten the situation for Wellington, however, other than to confirm that the Prussians had been engaged at Charleroi and that Blücher was now concentrating his forces at Sombreffe, north of Fleurus. Wellington refused to alter his plans and reiterated to Müffling, the Prussian liaison officer, that until he received positive information from Mons he would not order the concentration of his forces. At some time just before 10pm, however, Wellington received word from Mons, when Dörnberg sent in a report that there were no French troops in front of him but that they had turned off towards Charleroi. This prompted Wellington to issue a further set of movement orders, the 'After Orders', timed at 10pm. They ran:

The 3rd division of infantry to continue its movement from Braine le Comte upon Nivelles.

The 1st division to move from Enghien upon Braine le Comte.

The 2nd and 4th divisions of infantry to move from Ath and Grammont, also from Audenarde, and to continue their movements upon Enghien.

The cavalry to continue its movement from Ninhove upon Enghien.

The above movements to take place with as little delay as possible.[13]

Even now, these orders do not allow for any concentration of Wellington's troops farther east than Nivelles. He still appears to have believed that, despite the overwhelming weight of evidence arriving at his headquarters in the Rue Royale, there remained the possibility that Bonaparte might yet attack via Mons. Was this Wellington being ultra-cautious – even on 18 June he would leave 17,000 troops away to the west at Hal and Turbize – or was it he just placing too strong a reliance on information from his head of intelligence, Colquhoun Grant? Whichever it was, the After Orders only allowed for the concentration of his army around Nivelles, leaving Prince Bernhard and his men to await reinforcements while the number of French troops steadily increased in front of them.

Looking back over the years it seems quite absurd that with Brussels rapidly becoming the scene of great turmoil, and at the very moment that Bonaparte's men were pouring across the Sambre and marching north, Wellington, the commander-in-chief of the Anglo-Dutch Army, decided to play Drake, and took himself off to the Duchess of Richmond's ball.

1 Jock Haswell, *The First Respectable Spy: The Life and Times of Colquhoun Grant, Wellington's Head of Intelligence* (London, 1969), p.220.

2 See David Hamilton-Williams, *Waterloo: New Perspectives* (London, 1993), p.148, who quotes Dörnberg's MSS.

3 Francis Ellesmere, *Personal Reminiscences of the Duke of Wellington* (London, 1904), p.185.

4 These allegations were begun as long ago as 1880 by Hans Delbruck in his biography of Gneisenau, *Das Leben des Feldmarschalls Grafen Reithardt von Gneisenau*.

5 Jac Weller, *Wellington at Waterloo* (London, 1967), p.46.

6 The timing of this message has long been the subject of much heated and in-depth discussion. See Ropes, *The Campaign of Waterloo*, for more on the subject.

7 Col. Augustus Frazer, *Letters of Augustus Frazer, KCB, commanding the Royal Horse Artillery in the Army under the Duke of Wellington, written during the Peninsular and Waterloo campaigns*, edited by Edward Sabine (London, 1859), pp.533–4.

8 Ibid. p.535.

9 Capt. Cavalié Mercer, *Journal of the Waterloo Campaign*, edited by Sir John Fortescue (London, 1927), p.126.

10 Capt. John Kincaid, *Adventures in the Rifle Brigade* (London, 1830), pp.308–9.

11 Carl von Müffling, *Passages from my Life* (London, 1853), p.229.

12 *Wellington's Despatches*, Memorandum for the Deputy Quarter Master General, Brussels 15 June 1815.

13 *Wellington's Despatches*, Movement of the Army After Orders, 10pm Brussels 15 June 1815.

Chapter IV
HUMBUGGED!

The whole place is in a bustle. Such jostling of baggage, of guns, and of waggons.
It is very useful to acquire a quietness and composure about all these matters;
one does not mend things by being in a hurry.

Augustus Frazer, Royal Horse Artillery, 6am, 16 June 1815

On reflection, there was probably little Wellington could do on the night of 15 June except attend the Duchess of Richmond's ball. The ball had been well advertised and he did not wish to see it cancelled, lest it cause panic in the streets of Brussels and give Bonaparte's supporters grounds for optimism. He needed to demonstrate in the eyes of the watching guests that he was in full control of the situation and that there was no cause for alarm. But beneath the calm exterior of the cool aristocrat, one suspects that there must have been a certain degree of anxiety. Wellington had dealt with many a dangerous situation in the Peninsula; close battles such as Talavera and Fuentes de Oñoro, the storming of Badajoz, which came close to bloody failure, and the long, agonised retreat from Burgos were just a few. Indeed, rarely a month had passed without some crisis or other rearing its head, whether it be military or political, but he dealt with them all. The crisis unfolding throughout 15 June 1815 was possibly the greatest he had yet to face, but he was doing his utmost to remain in control of the situation. Events elsewhere, however, were dictating the pace. He was still labouring under the impression that Bonaparte's thrust north from Charleroi might yet be a feint and that Mons was the true point of attack. Wellington had still not heard from Grant and, despite the news from Dörnberg that all was in fact quiet in front of Mons, the ever-cautious commander still refused to commit his forces to the march east.

While the Duke of Wellington was preparing to leave for the Duchess of Richmond's ball, Lieutenant Henry Webster was pounding along the Brussels road from Braine-le-Comte, bearing the report from Constant Rebecque, written at 10.30pm, that the French had attacked the Allied outposts at Frasnes, just to the south of Quatre Bras. Webster was aided by a bright moon and by having the use of two horses, one of which had been sent on ahead to meet him halfway. Meanwhile Wellington made his way to the Duchess of Richmond's house in the Rue de la Blanchisserie. Never one to pass up an invitation to a ball or dinner party, Wellington may, nevertheless, have felt slightly peeved and upstaged as he passed along the Brussels streets, for he had intended to mark the anniversary of his great victory at Vittoria, on 21 June 1813, with a similar function six days later. Nevertheless, the Duchess could be relied upon to host a first-rate event. It was also to prove one of the most famous balls in history.

Artists and writers have long since portrayed the Waterloo ball as a classic regency affair; a magnificent ballroom complete with huge drapes, chandeliers of all sizes, fine furniture, sweeping staircases and dazzling lights. Byron's lamps may well have 'shone o'er fair women and brave men', whilst the music 'arose with voluptuous swell', but the reader should not be deluded by visions of grandeur. In fact, the ball was held in the depot of a Brussels coachbuilder, from whom the Duke and Duchess of Richmond had rented the house for the season. Strenuous efforts had been made to transform the room from a bare, wooden-floored hall into a ballroom worthy of Brussels' finest. The guest list read like a who's who of Brussels society and encompassed social, military and political figures. Naturally, the majority of the guests were British officers in Wellington's army and so the room was awash in scarlet, gold and white. When the officers were called away to join their regiments many could not find their campaign uniforms and fought the next day still wearing their silk stockings and fine dancing pumps. But for now, all thoughts of war were set

This painting by Hillingford depicts a sumptuous evening at the Duchess of Richmond's ball on 15 June. In fact, contrary to popular belief, the ball was held in the large workshop of a Brussels coachbuilder. The costume worn at the ball, however, would have been very similar to that depicted here by the artist.

aside, though not without difficulty, for rumours of a French attack had been rife throughout Brussels ever since the first reports began to filter through from about 3pm.

At the top of the guest list were, naturally, HRH the Prince of Orange and HRH Prince Frederick of Orange. Then there was the Duke of Brunswick, the Prince of Nassau, the Duc d'Aremberg, and a host of counts and countesses. Numerous aides-de-camp were invited as well as the cream of Brussels society, including aristocratic English families who were spending the season in the city. The list of British officers ran to over eighty. It must have been about 11pm when Wellington himself arrived, having issued his 'After Orders' at 10.30. He was as relaxed as ever at the ball, and spent long periods locked in conversation with various guests, both civilian and military. He was seen seated upon a sofa, deep in conversation with Lady Hamilton Dalrymple, one of many who later wrote of her experiences on that memorable night:

Although the Duke affected great gaiety and cheerfulness, it struck me that I had never seen him have such an expression of care and anxiety on his countenance. I sat next him on a sofa a long time, but his mind seemed pre-occupied; and although he spoke to me in the kindest manner possible, yet frequently in the middle of a sentence he stopped abruptly and called to some officer, giving him directions, in particular to the Duke of Brunswick and Prince of Orange, who both left the ball before supper. Despatches were constantly coming in to the Duke.[1]

Digby Mackworth, aide to Lord Hill, was another of those present at the ball who wrote an account of it in his journal:

We had heard during the day that the French had begun to advance and we know that Bonaparte had joined them; still it was thought that as the Prussian Army was nearer to them than we were, we should have quite sufficient notice of their approach to make the necessary preparations to give them a warm hearty reception. About 11 o'clock however, while the dancing was yet going on with great spirit we learned from the Duke that the Prussians had suffered severely that same evening, and that our Belgian outposts had given notice that the enemy was in sight of them. It was consequently necessary to start immediately and rejoin as quick as possible our several corps. In vain did the charms of music the persuasions, and in some instances, the tears of beauty tempt us to remain, in vain did the afflicted Duchess of Richmond, placing herself at the entrance of the ball room pray and entreat that we should not 'go before supper', that we would wait 'one little hour longer' and 'not spoil her ball'. Ungentle hearted cavaliers we resisted all and departed. Ladies, beware of all fair young knights, they dance and they ride away. In our ball costume, brilliant with gold lace and embroidery, exulting in the assurance that our long tiresome days of inactivity were at an end, and that we were on the point of meeting this celebrated military Loup-garon Bonaparte, so long our anxious wish, we spurred our chargers and soon covered the thirty miles which separated us from our corps. Some had already marched and the whole arrived this evening at Enghien where it now is. The firing towards our left is at present heavy and we are just going to mount fresh horses and start off to see what it is. Vive la Guerre.[2]

The scene was as gay as Byron's famous poem would have us believe, but those present could not help but notice that Wellington appeared preoccupied. A series of nods and quiet words were exchanged here and there between him and some of his officers who slowly began to depart. Once again, Waterloo lore has made it difficult to pin down with any degree of accuracy the sequence of events and the timings of various messages that arrived while the ball was in progress. One eye-witness account will have a message arriving at one given point whilst another will have it arriving at a different time. What we can be certain of is that the situation was growing more serious by the hour. Everywhere, British troops were being called to arms in response to Wellington's orders issued earlier in the afternoon, at around 5pm, whilst away to the south Prince Bernhard's Dutch-Belgian brigade, the only troops in the Anglo-Dutch Army yet to be engaged, held their positions at Quatre Bras. All of this was happening while Wellington and many of his senior officers continued to linger at the Duchess of Richmond's ball.

Presently, Wellington left the ballroom with

Lady Charlotte Greville upon his arm, and sat down to dinner with several other guests. It was apparently well past midnight, possibly even 1am, when the Prince of Orange appeared and, approaching the Duke, leaned over and whispered something in his ear. Captain George Bowles was a well connected officer in the Coldstream Guards. He had seen a great deal of service, in Germany, Copenhagen and throughout the Peninsular War. He had received an invitation to the ball and was a witness to the most significant event of the entire evening:

> At the Duchess of Richmond's ball at Brussels the Prince of Orange, who commanded the 1st Division of the army, came back suddenly, just as the Duke of Wellington had taken his place at the supper table, and whispered some minutes to his grace, who only said he had no fresh orders to give, and recommended the Prince to go back to his quarters and go to bed.
>
> The Duke of Wellington remained nearly twenty minutes after this, and then said to the Duke of Richmond, 'I think it is time for me to go to bed likewise;' and then, whilst wishing him goodnight, whispered to ask him if he had a good map in his house. The Duke of Richmond said he had, and took him into his dressing-room, which opened into the supper-room. The Duke of Wellington shut the door and said, 'Napoleon has humbugged me (by G—), he has gained twenty-four hours' march on me.' The Duke of Richmond said, 'What do you intend doing?'
>
> The Duke of Wellington replied, 'I have ordered the army to concentrate at Quatre Bras; but we shall not stop him there, and if so I must fight him here' (at the same time passing his thumb-nail over the position of Waterloo). He then said adieu and left the house by another way out...The conversation in the Duke of Richmond's dressing-room was repeated to me, two minutes after it occurred, by the Duke of Richmond, who was to have had the command of the reserve, if formed, and to whom I was to have been aide-de-camp. He marked the Duke of Wellington's thumb-nail with his pencil on the map, and we often looked at it together some months afterwards.[3]

No sooner had Wellington left the ball than Brussels was thrown into turmoil. Numerous British officers had left the ball while it was in progress, whilst other more senior officers summoned aides and issued orders for the movement of their regiments before leaving also. Wellington himself returned to his headquarters to take a couple of hours' sleep. As he rode through the streets he would have heard the wailing of pipes and blast of bugles that rang out through the night across the city as sleepy British soldiers were roused from their billets and ordered to arms in preparation for the march south. Some regiments had begun to muster before the ball, even though no orders had actually been issued. The Reserve, under Sir Thomas Picton, was billeted at various places in and around Brussels. John Kincaid and the 95th Rifles were among them:

> To the credit of our battalion, be it recorded, that, although the greater part were in bed when the assembly sounded, and billeted over the most distant parts of that extensive city, every man was on his alarm-post before eleven o'clock, in a complete state of marching order; whereas, it was nearly two o'clock in the morning before we were joined by the others...Waiting for the arrival of the other regiments, we endeavoured to snatch an hour's repose on the pavement, but we were every instant disturbed, by ladies as well as gentlemen; some stumbling over us in the dark – some shaking us out of our sleep, to be told the news – and not a few, conceiving their immediate safety depending upon our standing in place of lying.[4]

Sir James Kempt, commanding the 8th British Brigade of Wellington's reserve, had received an invitation to the Duchess of Richmond's ball but, like several others, such as Lord Hill, elected to stay with his men. Whilst the ball was in progress, Sir James was dining with several British officers, amongst whom was 37-year-old Harry Ross-Lewin, of the 32nd Regiment. Ross-Lewin was no stranger to battle and had been wounded late in the day at the Battle of Salamanca on 22 July 1812. He wrote in his journal:

> That day I dined with Sir James Kempt. Coffee and a young aide-de-camp from the Duke of Wellington came in together. This officer was the bearer of a note from the Duke, and while Sir James was reading it, said, 'Old Blücher has been hard at it; a Prussian officer has just come to the Beau [Wellington], all covered with sweat and dirt, and says they have had much fighting.' Our host then rose, and addressing the regimental officers at the table, said: 'Gentlemen, you will proceed without delay to your respective regiments, and let them get under arms immediately.'
>
> On my way I found several of our officers sitting at a coffee-house door, and told them Sir James Kempt's orders. They seemed at first to think that I was jesting, being hardly able to credit the tidings of so near and so unexpected

an approach of the French; but they soon perceived that I spoke seriously, and dispersed each to his own quarters. In a few minutes, however, the most incredulous would have been thoroughly undeceived, for then drums began to beat, bugles to sound, and Highland pipes to squeal in all quarters of the city. The scene that ensued was of the most animated kind: such was the excitement of the inhabitants, the buzz of tongues, the repeated words of command, the hurrying of soldiers through the streets, the clattering of horses' hoofs, the clash of arms, the rattling of the wheels of waggons and gun-carriages, and the sounds of warlike music.[5]

Sergeant David Robertson, of the 92nd Highlanders, had just lain down to sleep when he was roused by the din outside:

> On the evening of the 15th of June, the sergeants on duty were all in the orderly room until ten o'clock at night; and no orders having been issued, we went home to our quarters. I had newly lain down in bed when the bugle sounded the alarm, the drums beat to arms, bagpipes played, and all was in commotion – thus stunning the drowsy ear of night by all kinds of martial music sounding in every street. Upon hearing this, sergeants and corporals ran to the quarters of their respective parties to run them out. I went to the quarter-master for bread, and four days' allowance was given out of the store, which was soon distributed among the men – every one getting his share and speedily falling into rank. So regular and orderly was the affair gone about, that we were ready to march in half an hour after the first sound of the bugle.[6]

The British regiments were quickly assembled and very soon they were marching south, leaving Brussels by the Porte de Namur, bound for Waterloo. Meanwhile the British troops to the south-west of Brussels were only just receiving the first set of orders issued by Wellington earlier that evening. Cavalié Mercer was sound asleep in his 'tranquil abode' at Strytem when he was rudely awakened by his servant who brought a note delivered a moment or two earlier by an orderly hussar. The message, without time or date, simply directed Mercer to assemble his troop and make directly for Enghien:

> That we were to move forward, then, was certain. It was rather sudden, to be sure, and all the whys and wherefores were left to conjecture; but the suddenness of it, and the importance of arriving quickly at the appointed place,

rather alarmed me, for upon reflection I remembered that I had been guilty of two or three imprudences. First, all my officers were absent; secondly, all my country waggons were absent; thirdly, a whole division (one-third of my troop) was absent at Yseringen. 'Send the sergeant-major here,' was the first order, as I drew on my stockings. 'Send for Mr Coates' (my commissariat officer), the second, as I got one leg into my overalls. 'William, make haste and get breakfast,' the third, as I buttoned them up. The sergeant-major soon came, and received his orders to turn out instanter, with the three days' provisions and forage in the haversacks and on the horses; also to send an express for the first division. He withdrew, and immediately the fine martial clang of 'boot and saddle' resounded through the village and courts of the château, making the woods ring again, and even the frogs stop to listen.[7]

At length, Mercer assembled his men, but only two thirds of his troop was present and so he was forced to wait for the others to come in. The delay allowed Mercer to cook a hearty breakfast and, uncertain as to when he would be able to eat another, he and his fellow officers stowed away a double portion of eggs. Finally, the absentees arrived at Strytem, the 'animating and soul-stirring notes of the turnout again awoke the echoes of the hills and woods', and, with his old dog, Bal, barking and jumping at the horses' noses, Mercer was able to hold a hastily arranged inspection before his troop set off for Enghien.

The problem was, as Mercer quickly discovered, that finding the road to Enghien was not as simple as he thought, for once he got beyond the area in which he had been billeted for the last few weeks, he became lost. It wasn't easy to find the way, even in the early morning, as one bad track looked much like the next. The map he carried in his sabretache, presumably the Ferraris and Capitaine map of 1797, did not help him much either, but he rode on regardless. He was already somewhat anxious for he had divided his troop into three columns, and so while Mercer pushed on with his guns, the ammunition and supply waggons remained behind for a while with orders to follow on as soon as they were ready. Eventually, he came across the 23rd Light Dragoons with whom his troop rode until they finally reached Enghien where he discov-

British officers bid their farewells to their ladies early on the morning of 16 June after leaving the Duchess of Richmond's ball. The officer on the left wears silk stockings and dancing pumps. With their baggage stuck in the rear many British officers fought at Quatre Bras still wearing their costume of the night before.

ered Sir John Vandeleur's brigade of light dragoons dismounted and feeding their horses. With no further orders, Mercer was left with little choice but to await the arrival of Major MacDonald, commanding the horse artillery.

Augustus Frazer, also of the horse artillery, penned a letter at 6am on the morning of 16 June, which illustrates just what a confusing situation some British units found themselves in:

> I have just learned that the Duke moves in half an hour. Wood thinks to Waterloo, which we cannot find on the map: this is the old story over again. I have sent Bell to Delancey's office, where we shall learn the real names, etc. The whole place is in a bustle. Such jostling of baggage, of guns, and of waggons. It is very useful to acquire a quietness and composure about all these matters; one does not mend things by being in a hurry.[8]

The timing of Frazer's letter illustrates the lateness of the British concentration. He had already received the Duke's first order, for he said in an earlier letter, timed at 11.30pm on the 15th, that all was ready and that his men were ready to move at daybreak. However, 6am would seem a very late hour to be setting off towards Nivelles, considering the French were poised to strike at Quatre Bras. It also seems quite remarkable that neither Wood nor Frazer could find Waterloo on the map.

Like Frazer and Mercer, Captain Webber-Smith did not march until daybreak on 16 June, leaving Haltert, near Alost, and finally arriving at Quatre Bras at 10am on 17 June. Fortunately, some batteries of Royal Artillery did manage to make it in time, amongst them the batteries of Lloyd and Cleeves, attached to Alten's 3rd Division. The division formed part of the Prince of Orange's 1st Corps and, having been situated at Braine-le-Comte, were not too far from Quatre Bras.

Wellington's reserve, marching south from Brussels, had no trouble at all finding and following the road towards Waterloo. It was the route which Wellington himself would take when he left Brussels on the morning of the 16th. It is no coincidence, therefore, that Picton's division bore the brunt of the fighting later that day at Quatre Bras, it being the first British division to arrive at the battlefield. Elsewhere, things were not proving as easy. Wellington's first set of orders, it will be remembered, allowed for the collection of his troops only, rather than their actual movement. This was just as well, for the 'After Orders', issued much later, appear to have reached their various destinations at different times on the morning of 16 June. The Coldstream Guards, for example, received their orders to march from Enghien to Braine-le-Comte at 3am, whereas the 52nd Light Infantry at Quevaucamps, thirteen miles west of Mons, did not receive their orders to march until 10am. Indeed, the regiment had only just formed in a meadow ready for drill when orders came to form up on the road to Ath. Little wonder, therefore, that the regiment took no part in the fighting of 16 June. In fact, it was not until 7am on the 17th that the 52nd reached Nivelles, where it remained for a further four hours until being ordered north to Mont St Jean.

The British cavalry, billeted along the Dender river at Ninove, had a similarly anxious time getting forward in response to Wellington's order to move to Enghien. William Tomkinson, of the 16th Light Dragoons, wrote:

> Soon after daylight my servant came into my room saying there had arrived an order to march directly, and that the whole army was moving. We were ignorant of the cause, and heard rumours that it was occasioned by an attack the enemy had made on the Prussian outposts. We marched about 5, moving on the Enghien road. On our arrival at Enghien, we found the Guards had left it, and it was said we were to remain in the neighbourhood for the purpose of watching the road from Enghien to Mons. We halted for a considerable time near the town waiting for orders, when we moved upon Braine-le-Comte. This we passed, and when we had got about a mile on the other side, and at, I think, about 2pm, we began to hear some firing beyond Nivelles, on which we were moving.[9]

Captain Thomas Taylor, of the 10th Hussars, was in Brussels on the night of 15 June and upon returning to his billet at Vivorde found orders waiting for him for a field day the next morning. Taylor retired for the night but had only been asleep for a few hours when he was awoken by his servant:

> On the 16th, at about half-past four a.m., my servant called me and said the regiment was ordered to turn out in full marching order to change quarters. The Brigade assembled on the road from Vivorde to Grammont. We waited some time for the 18th Hussars. When assembled we commenced our march (I think) about seven. We proceeded through Grammont and Enghien, falling in with other corps of cavalry on the march. At Enghien, Lieut. Parsons of my Troop joined, having come from Brussels, where I had left him the day before; he

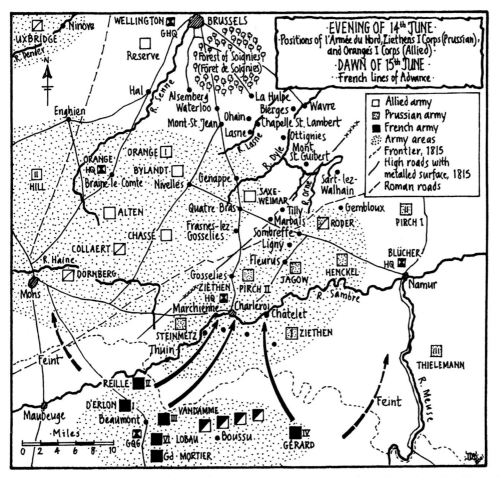

informed me of the advance of the French, that the troops had turned out from Brussels, and that there would probably be an action in the course of the day.[10]

It is quite clear that many regiments did not receive Wellington's first set of orders until very late at night on 15 June or early on 16 June. Nevertheless, throughout the morning of the 16th thousands of British soldiers began moving as a result of the orders issued the previous night.

By all accounts, 16 June was a beautiful day, and the image of a fine misty morning with regiment upon regiment of red-jacketed soldiers heading along leafy country lanes is easy to imagine. It was certainly a contrast to the years of marching through the dusty wastes of Spain, despite the poor quality of the roads in many places. It was also a morning full of anxiety, for rumours that the French had already attacked were rife, fuelling speculation of an impending great battle. The anxiety must also have increased when the noise of firing began to become audible during the afternoon as the fighting began at Quatre Bras.

Surgeon Haddy James, of the 1st Life Guards, had been roused from his sleep shortly after dawn on 16 June. After a breakfast of coffee and eggs he gathered his medical valise and other equipment and was ready for the day's march:

By four o'clock the first regiment was ready, and the baggage in its place, but we were obliged to wait until past eight o'clock before the brigade was collected. Had it been known at that time what urgent occasion there would be for cavalry in the progress of that day, 16th June, I imagine we should have been dispatched the moment we were formed. But at this time we knew nothing of what had occurred nor what was likely to. We were only informed that our route was to Enghien, a village about twelve or fourteen miles off, and it was generally thought that it was only intended to concentrate the army…At Enghien the brigade received a fresh route, to proceed further to a place called le-Comte [sic]. It became then very obvious that their assistance would almost certainly be speedily required.[11]

The assistance of the British cavalry at Quatre Bras would indeed have been of great value, but what chance had they of arriving in time if, as James states, they did not march to Enghien until past 8am? The same scenario was being played out all over the Belgian countryside as brigade after brigade made its way towards Braine-le-Comte and then Nivelles, the men knowing hardly anything at all of the events rapidly unfolding away to the east at Quatre Bras and Ligny, where the Prussians were deploying to face Bonaparte himself.

John Banner was a lieutenant with the 23rd Light Dragoons, whom Mercer had met on the morning of 16 June. The 23rd had been stationed about seven miles from Brussels, with detachments billeted in various places. At 2am the various detachments had been ordered to collect in order to march to regimental headquarters. The regiment moved off shortly after daybreak and presently came across the various other cavalry regiments. Despite efforts to reach the battlefield of Quatre Bras the 23rd failed to arrive in time to take part in the battle. Banner's account of the march to Quatre Bras reflects the growing anxiety experienced by the British cavalry as they neared the scene of the action:

> When we arrived within a few miles of Nivelles a brisk cannonading was plainly heard, which indicated that a general engagement was going on; the cavalry had to proceed through bad roads, which retarded their progress exceedingly, but they trotted whenever the road admitted of their moving at that pace, and pressed forward with the greatest alacrity to participate in the glories of the Field of Action.
>
> On reaching Nivelles it was in the greatest possible state of excitation and confusion, the inhabitants from distant parts of the neighbourhood having come there for security; every house was filled with ladies and well-dressed females, who crowded to the windows, waved their handkerchiefs, and cheered the troops as they passed along the streets, in the most enthusiastic manner; the spectacle was encouraging beyond description.
>
> Never was a sight more touching than that on approaching nearer to the Field of Battle. The road sides close to Quatre Bras were covered with the slain, and a vast number of gallant fellows in their last dying moments of agony.
>
> The British cavalry having a long march from their cantonments did not reach Quatre Bras until near six o'clock in the afternoon of the 16th June, about the close of the action.[12]

Wellington himself had not been idle since receiving Rebecque's report at the Duchess of Richmond's ball. After leaving the ball he made the short journey back to his headquarters where, despite the clamour in the streets outside, he managed to sleep for two or three hours.

While he was asleep further messages arrived, brought in by breathless gallopers. The situation was becoming much clearer, although nothing had worsened. Indeed, the main aim for Wellington now was to move his troops towards Nivelles. He was comforted by the fact that his orders of 5pm had already begun the concentration, but he knew it would be a close thing to get his men to Nivelles in time before matters became serious.

The story of the momentous night of 15 June and the morning of the 16th has been told and retold countless times, and still the sequence of events is unclear and shrouded in mystery. Much of the controversy surrounds the timing of Wellington's decision to march to Quatre Bras. According to Müffling, the Prussian liaison officer at Wellington's headquarters, Wellington said he had ordered his army to concentrate at Nivelles and Quatre Bras prior to leaving for the ball. The problem is that, as the American historian Ropes explained, 'not a single order of Wellington's, directing any troops, except those belonging to the Reserves, upon Quatre Bras, has ever been brought to light'.[13] Indeed, the only surviving orders issued from Brussels on 16 June are those given to Lord Hill, and these merely order a concentration of the 2nd Division and the cavalry at Braine-le-Comte. Further orders were subsequently issued on 16 June, also to Lord Hill, requested him to order Prince Frederick of Orange to move the 1st Dutch-Belgian Division to Enghien. Thus, we have no orders for a concentration at Quatre Bras.

There were, however, a further set of orders issued to Lord Hill, this time from Genappe, ordering him to move the 2nd Division from Nivelles to Quatre Bras and the 4th Division to Nivelles. However, these orders stated that Hill was to move 'tomorrow morning', that is, the 17th. There is still the possibility that orders to concentrate at Quatre Bras were issued by Wellington, and that they were amongst the papers of Sir William De Lancey that were lost when that officer was carried mortally wounded from the field of Waterloo on 18 June. However, this still does not account for the subsequent orders to Hill, issued on 16 June, none of which ordered a movement upon Quatre Bras. George Bowles quoted the Duke of Richmond as having stated that Wellington had ordered his army to concentrate at Quatre Bras but this may have been the reserve only. We know that when Wellington left Brussels on the morning of 16 June he rode to Waterloo. It states as much in the first of the 16 June orders to Lord Hill. This proves nothing, however, for the roads from Nivelles and Quatre Bras meet to the south of Waterloo. It is almost certain, therefore, that Wellington decided to move his army towards Quatre Bras only on the morning of 16 June, probably after he left the Duchess of Richmond's ball. It is even possible, although unlikely, that when he rode out of Brussels at dawn that day, he was still undecided.

Further evidence of the timing of his decision came from Sir Hussey Vivian. Six weeks short of his 40th birthday, Vivian had lost the use of his right arm at the Battle of Toulouse on 10 April 1814, but that did not stop him continuing to serve in Wellington's army. During the Waterloo campaign he found himself commanding the 6th Brigade Light Cavalry Brigade, consisting of the 10th and 18th Hussars and the 1st KGL Hussars. On the evening of 15 June he dined with Lord Uxbridge before departing for the Duchess of Richmond's ball:

> It was only during the ball that the Duke called several of those who commanded Divisions or Brigades together, and told us to be prepared to move in the morning, and it was during the night only that orders were issued for the actual march of the British troops from the right towards Nivelles, and it was on the march that we received orders to continue our march on Quatre Bras.[14]

The evidence is confused and conflicting as to when Wellington finally decided to concentrate his army at Quatre Bras. What we do know is that throughout the morning of 16 June all of Wellington's British divisions had begun to shift to their left, that is, to the east, save for the Reserve, which made its way south from Brussels. By concentrating at Nivelles it would be a relatively easy march from there to Quatre Bras for those divisions coming from the west. For the Reserve, coming south from Brussels, the order to march to Waterloo simply gave them the opportunity to march either to Nivelles or Quatre Bras, for the road from Brussels separated at Waterloo before running south and south-west to Quatre Bras and Nivelles respectively.

The British divisions, so dangerously scattered, were finally on the march, and they were now on the march to Quatre Bras. The confusion during the night of 15 June and early morning of 16 June ensured that a great number of Wellington's British troops would not make it in time, but those who did would not let their leader down and would fight in the greatest traditions of the British Army.

1 Sir Herbert Maxwell, *The Life of Wellington; the Restoration of Martial Britain* (London, 1899), II. p.13.

2 Digby Mackworth MSS.

3 Capt. George Bowles, *A Series of Letters to the First Earl of Malmesbury, his family and friends, from 1745 to 1820*, edited by his grandson, the Earl of Malmesbury (London, 1870), II. pp.445–6.

4 Capt. John Kincaid, *Adventures in the Rifle Brigade* (London, 1830), pp.310–11.

5 Harry Ross-Lewin, *With the 32nd in the Peninsula and other campaigns*, edited by John Wardell (London, 1914), p.253.

6 Sgt. David Robertson, *The Journal of Sergeant D. Robertson, late 92nd Foot, comprising the different campaigns between the years 1797 and 1818* (Perth, 1842), p.141.

7 Captain Cavalié Mercer, *Journal of the Waterloo Campaign*, edited by Sir John Fortescue, (London, 1927), pp. 127–8.

8 Col. Augustus Frazer, *Letters of Augustus Frazer, KCB, commanding the Royal Horse Artillery in the Army under the Duke of Wellington, written during the Peninsular and Waterloo campaigns*, edited by Edward Sabine (London, 1859), p.536.

9 Lt.Col. William Tomkinson, *The Diary of a Cavalry Officer in the Peninsular War and Waterloo Campaign 1809–1815*, edited by James Tomkinson (London, 1894), p.278.

10 Lt.Col. T. Taylor, quoted in *Waterloo Letters*, edited by Maj.Gen. HT Siborne (London, 1891), p.165.

11 Haddy James, *Surgeon James' Journal 1815*, edited by Jane Vansittart (London, 1964), p.14.

12 Maj. John Banner, quoted in *Waterloo Letters*, pp.92–3.

13 John Cadman Ropes, *The Campaign of Waterloo* (New York, 1893), p.81.

14 Maj.Gen. Sir Hussey Vivian, quoted in *Waterloo Letters*, p.151.

Chapter V
THE BATTLE
OF QUATRE BRAS

If Waterloo had not occurred forty-eight hours later,
Quatre Bras would be remembered as one of the great days of the British Army.

Jac Weller, in *Wellington at Waterloo*

The morning of 16 June 1815 dawned with thousands of British and Allied troops making their way towards Quatre Bras. Many would arrive in time to fight. Many more would not. The battle itself was one of the most desperate Wellington ever fought, with his troops arriving piecemeal throughout the late morning and afternoon before being flung straight into the conflict. Not since Fuentes de Oñoro, in May 1811, had he fought such an unsatisfactory battle with so much resting upon its outcome.

The Battle of Quatre Bras, fought on 16 June, was desperate enough, but it is the events of the morning, before the fighting had even begun, that cause heated debate even today. The controversies centre upon the so-called 'Delancey

Disposition', a document apparently drawn up for the Duke of Wellington by William De Lancey, the Deputy Quartermaster General, although it was not signed by him. In fact, the document was signed by no one and only came to light when Sir De Lacy Evans was going through his papers many years later. De Lacy Evans was aide-de-camp to Major General Sir William Ponsonby, served on the staff of the British cavalry during the retreat from Quatre Bras on 17 June and was, by his own account, with Delancey when the orders on 15, 16 and 17 June were issued. Years later he forwarded the Disposition to Colonel Gurwood, who at the time was compiling the second edition of Wellington's *Despatches* – it was not included in the first edition. The Disposition ran as follows:

1st Division	Braine-le-Comte	Marching to Nivelles and Quatre Bras
2nd Division	Braine-le-Comte	Marching to Nivelles
3rd Division	Nivelles	Marching to Quatre Bras
4th Division	Audenarde	Marching to Braine-le-Comte
5th Division	Beyond Waterloo	Marching to Genappe
6th Division	Assche	Marching to Genappe and Quatre Bras
5th Hanoverian Brigade	Hal	Marching to Genappe and Quatre Bras
4th Hanoverian Brigade	Beyond Waterloo	Marching to Genappe and Quatre Bras
2nd and 3rd Divisions (Army of the Low Countries)		At Nivelles and Quatre Bras
1st Division, Indian Bgde	Sotteghem	Marching to Enghien
Major General Dörnberg's Brigade and Cumberland Hussars	Beyond Waterloo	Marching to Genappe and Quatre Bras
Remainder of Cavalry	Braine-le-Comte	Marching to Nivelles and Quatre Bras
Duke of Brunswick's Corps	Beyond Waterloo	Marching to Genappe
Nassau Corps	Beyond Waterloo	Marching to Genappe

Evans added a note to the effect that the paper had been drawn up by Delancey for the benefit of the commander-in-chief. He also added an explanation as to what the document actually meant. The document was set out in three columns and gave the positions of the various

Allied divisions as of 7am as they marched towards Quatre Bras, the place at which the troops had arrived or were moving on, and the place to which they had been ordered to proceed at 7am. To say the document was inaccurate and a poor piece of staff work is putting it mildly.

However, given the confusion in Brussels and the haste with which Wellington's two sets of orders were issued it is little wonder, with them arriving piecemeal at their destinations and at different times of the night of 15 June and morning of 16 June, that De Lancey – supposing him to be the author – was incorrect in his placement of the Allied divisions. As one author on the campaign wrote, 'the fog of war does not lift at one's pleasure.[1]

The 1st Division, for example, did not reach Braine-le-Comte until 9am, where it halted for three hours before continuing on to Quatre Bras, arriving there late in the afternoon. The 2nd Division, stated in the Disposition as being at Braine-le-Comte, did not even receive orders to march until 10am on the 16th. In fact, the division did not arrive at Braine-le-Comte until midnight. As for the British cavalry, they were still miles from the battlefield and would not arrive at Quatre Bras until the battle was over. All in all, the Disposition was a poor piece of work, for very few of the locations of the divisions were accurately given. Faulty staff work is nothing new, of course, and the De Lancey Disposition would probably have been consigned to the back pages of history had it not been for the fact that it was upon this very document that Wellington gave assurances of support to Marshal Blücher. These assurances, whilst not inducing the Prussian commander to fight at Ligny on 16 June, certainly gave him great encouragement and a belief that he could fight in the expectation of receiving assistance from Wellington, assistance that ultimately failed to materialise. It is upon this basis that German historians have sought to tarnish Wellington's character and accuse him of deceit. There is little doubt that Wellington's troops were dangerously scattered, but to suggest that he induced Blücher to fight at Ligny in order to gain time for himself to concentrate his forces is nonsense. As the great historian of the British Army, the Hon. JW Fortescue, put it, when referring to the 16 June letter from Wellington to Blücher, 'the insinuations of German writers, that he wrote this letter with the deliberate purpose of deceiving Blücher and making him fight to cover the concentration of the Anglo-Netherlandish Army, deserve nothing more than contempt'.[2]

The translation of the actual letter from Wellington to Blücher – the original was written in French – runs as follows:

> Upon the heights behind Frasnes,
> June 16th, 1815, at half-past ten.

My Dear Prince,
My army is situated as follows. Of the corps of the Prince of Orange, one division is here and at Quatre Bras, the remainder at Nivelles. The reserve is on the march from Waterloo to Genappe, where it will arrive at noon. The English cavalry will be at the same hour at Nivelles. Lord Hill's corps is at Braine-le-Comte.

I do not see any great force of the enemy in front of us, and I await news from Your Royal Highness, and the arrival of troops to decide upon my operations for the day.

Nothing has appeared in the direction of Binche, nor on our right.

This tree-lined road at Quatre Bras was the vital communication between there and Ligny. It was along this stretch of the road that Picton's veteran battalions deployed after marching south from Brussels on the morning of 16 June. During the battle the fields in the foreground were covered in tall crops, into which French lancers thrust their lances in order mark the position of Wellington's men.

The locations of most of Wellington's troops set out in the above letter are clearly inaccurate, but the Duke wrote in good faith and based it upon the Disposition given to him, apparently, by De Lancey. The charges of duplicity on the part of Wellington towards Blücher are understandable when we consider the reliance the Prussian commander placed upon Wellington's letter. However, it should not be forgotten that Wellington himself was preparing to do battle with the French, and that he was expecting his troops to arrive very soon. It is inconceivable that Wellington would have allowed himself to be exposed to such a risk, of concentrating piecemeal in the face of a strong enemy and fighting him, just to deceive the Prussians. It goes against everything that he had done in the Peninsula. Wellington adopted his position at Quatre Bras and prepared for battle there on 16 June having based his decision upon the expectation of his troops arriving throughout the day, an expectation born of the Disposition. If Blücher felt anxious throughout 16 June, imagine how nervous Wellington must have been, hourly watching the road from Nivelles for his troops to arrive, many of whom did not.

Wellington had arrived at Quatre Bras at around 9am and found the vital crossroads safe in the hands of Prince Bernhard of Saxe Weimar. Nevertheless, there were still relatively few Allied troops present, only 6,500 in fact, with just eight guns. After a ride round the position with the Prince of Orange and Perponcher, Wellington sat down and wrote the controversial letter to Blücher, the contents of which are given above. A further inspection of the position followed, and as he gazed to the south towards Frasnes he could see no great enemy force before him and no signs of enemy activity. Therefore, he took himself off to see Blücher whose army had deployed for battle between the villages of St Amand, Ligny and Sombreffe, a few miles to the east of Quatre Bras.

Wellington, accompanied by Sir Alexander Gordon and two orderlies, was met by Henry Hardinge, the British liaison officer at Prussian headquarters. Wellington found the Prussian commander at Brye, just north of Ligny, from where the two old friends surveyed the dark masses of French in front of them. The meeting, under the hot summer sun, was as cordial as one would expect between the two men even if Wellington was moved to remark upon the formation of the Prussian troops. There is no record

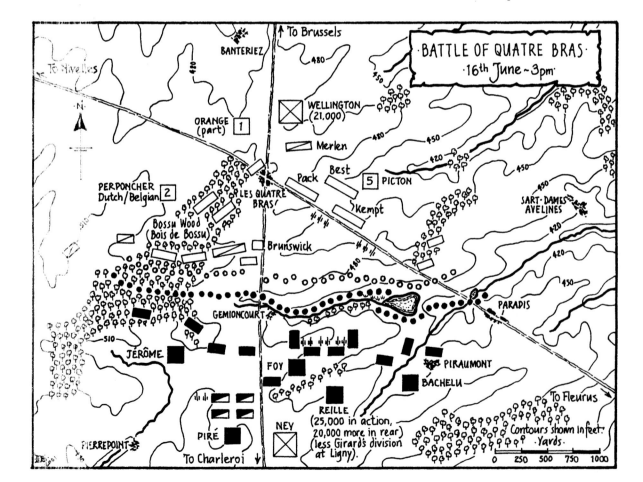

of what was actually said at the meeting, although one or two points were recalled later. According to Müffling, Wellington promised to march east and come to Blücher's assistance at about 4pm, but only if he were not attacked himself. As we shall discover, it was a promise that he was unable to keep. The other point concerns the Prussian dispositions, which Wellington considered dangerously exposed. Wellington later recalled his observations in a conversation with Lord de Ros:

On the morning of the 16th I left Brussels and rode forward about five miles beyond Quatre Bras to see the Prince of Orange's outposts. After that, I went over to the Prussians about seven miles to our left from Quatre Bras, and found them drawn up on the slope of the ground with their advanced columns close down to the rivulet of Ligny, the banks of which were so marshy that the French could only cross it at the bridges of three or four villages that lie along its course. I told the Prussian officers, in the presence of Hardinge, that, according to my judgement, the exposure of the advanced columns and, indeed, of the whole army to cannonade, standing as they did displayed to the aim of the enemy's fire, was not prudent. The marshy banks of the stream made it out of their power to cross and attack the French, while the latter, on the other hand, though they could not attack them, had it in their power to cannonade them, and shatter them to pieces, after which they might fall upon them by the bridges at the villages. I said that if I were in Blücher's place with English troops, I should withdraw all the columns I saw scattered about in front, and get more of the troops under shelter of the rising ground. However, they seemed to think they knew best, so I came away very shortly. It all fell out exactly as I feared – the French overwhelmed them, as they stood, by a prodigious fire of artillery, and I myself could distinguish with my glass from Quatre Bras a general charge of the French cavalry on their confused columns, in which charge it was that Blücher was ridden over and near killed.[3]

Many years later, the Duke dined with Henry Hardinge, who recalled the meeting at Brye. 'When you had examined the Prussian position,' said Hardinge, 'I remember you much disapproved of it, and said to me, if they fight here they will be damnably mauled.' 'I told them myself,' replied Wellington, 'but of course in different terms. I said to them, everybody knows their own army best; but if I were to fight with mine here, I should expect to be beat.'[4]

The Battle of Ligny, fought on the afternoon of 16 June, was a bloody affair involving 68,000 French troops with 210 guns, under Bonaparte, against Blücher's 87,000 Prussians, with 224 guns. The battle involved a series of French attacks against the Prussian-held villages between Wagnalee and Sombreffe. The fighting was particularly bloody at St Amand and Ligny, both of which changed hands several times during the afternoon. The battle of attrition stretched Prussian resources to the limit until finally Bonaparte launched his decisive attack that effectively split the Prussian Army in two. Blücher himself led a charmed life for his horse was killed during a cavalry charge and he was fortunate not to be killed or taken prisoner. By 9.30pm the battle had ended in a complete victory for the French and it was only the onset of darkness that saved the defeated Prussian Army from destruction. Prussian casualties numbered around 12,000 with the French losing 11,000 themselves. It was an awesome day's fighting that ought to have seen the Prussian Army eliminated from the campaign. Indeed, Gneisenau, Blücher's chief of staff, advocated a retreat towards Namur, away from Wellington, a move that would almost certainly have prompted a retreat by Wellington towards the safety of the Channel ports. Fortunately, Blücher, a man of great honour, persuaded him that a retreat north was the only realistic option if the Allies were to defeat Bonaparte. Thus, the order was given to retreat north and, as we shall see, the Prussians lived to fight another day. But we must return to matters at Quatre Bras.

Quatre Bras was, and still is, a small hamlet situated at the junction of the Namur–Nivelles and Charleroi–Brussels roads. Its importance lay in the fact that it commanded the road along which Wellington would march east should he be able to join Blücher. There were a few houses dotted around the crossroads with another, called La Bergerie, a short way down the road towards Frasnes, the next village south of Quatre Bras. To the east of the Brussels road the ground was open, undulating and covered with high standing crops. The only landmark on an otherwise open field on this side of the road is the Materne Lake, situated about 200 yards in front of the Namur road and about 1,200 yards from the Brussels road. To the west of the lake, and situated close to the Brussels road itself, is the Gemioncourt Farm, a typically high-walled structure, solid and tough enough to withstand artillery. The Allied line ran along the Namur road as far as the hamlet of Thyle, about 600 yards east of the Materne Lake. Beyond this lay the farm of Pireaumont, and Hutte Wood, beyond which the battlefield of Ligny was visible. To the west of the Brussels road there stood an extensive wood, the Bois de Bossu, which extended a mile and a half south from Quatre Bras towards the farm of Grand Pierrepont. About another 800 yards from this farm lay a second, Petit Pierrepont. The Bois de Bossu ran from Quatre Bras in a south-westerly direction, leaving an area of open ground about 500 yards wide between it and the Brussels road. However, at the point at which the wood reached level with Gemioncourt Farm, the wood drew back farther, leaving an open area of about a mile between it and the Brussels road. The position was not a strong one, for it had no real reverse slope behind which Wellington could shield his men from enemy artillery fire. However, the slope was deep enough to prevent prying French eyes from seeing what lay in front of them, and of course there were the high-standing crops, which completely hid Wellington's men from the enemy. It was a small, compact battlefield, around two miles from east to west, which is just as well given the relatively small number of troops which Wellington possessed at the start of the battle.

The Battle of Quatre Bras was a confusing and desperate action for Wellington and his men, from which they emerged with great credit. Brigades and divisions were thrown into the thick of the action as soon as they arrived upon the field, without even the comfort of settling down into any given position. Unlike the Battle of Waterloo, two days later, which can be conveniently divided into distinct phases, Quatre Bras is one long blurred struggle, which lasted from about 2pm until 9pm. Timings are, however, as confusing as the action itself, for the opening shots, the return of Wellington from Brye, the arrival of Picton and the timings of the French attacks vary enormously depending upon which account one follows.

Advancing against the Prince of Orange's 6,500 men were some 42,000 French troops, of whom 7,000 were cavalry, under the command of Marshal Ney, 'the bravest of the brave'. In addition, he could call upon ninety-two guns. However, not all of these were sent forward against the Allies straight away. The Dutch-Belgian troops holding Quatre Bras were deployed in forward positions as far south as Gemioncourt, which itself was held in strength. Other troops held the Bois de Bossu and the Hutte Wood, whilst troops were also deployed along the Brussels road itself from Quatre Bras to Gemioncourt. In all, Wellington's Dutch allies had done a very creditable job in maintaining a strong front in the face of a far superior enemy.

A ragged square of 42nd Highlanders is attacked by French lancers at Quatre Bras. During the action the regiment lost its commanding officer, Macara, who was speared by enemy lancers. Several of the battalion's other officers were either killed or wounded by enemy lancers, the battalion getting off relatively lightly considering its perilous position.

Despite this, the French were still far too strong in numbers and an attack by Ney before the British arrived might have reaped great dividends. But at this point, the French delayed their attack. The great psychological advantage which Wellington had built up over the years in Portugal and Spain returned to haunt the French and provide Wellington with a stroke of good fortune, if only a small one, that would allow his British troops to get ever nearer to the battlefield before too much fighting had passed.

In order to examine the reason for the French delay we must return to the Peninsula. Wellington's adoption of the reverse slope as a vital tactic did not win him the majority of his victories. Busaco, Vimeiro and Sorauren were the three notable examples, his other victories being either offensive or won without having to resort to the use of the reverse slope. However, there were many other significant instances of his adoption of the tactic, notably at Fuenteguinaldo in September 1811. Here, Marmont, with a vastly superior army, refused to attack Wellington whose numerically weaker army lay hidden out of sight on a reverse slope. The French commander, unaware of the advantage he held, feared a repeat of the disaster at Busaco, did not attack and thus a great chance went awry. Wellington's reputation as a defensive-minded general stood him in good stead at Salamanca in July 1812, when Marmont over-extended his troops, thinking that the overly cautious Wellington would not dare to attack him. Sadly for him he was mistaken, to which a massive French defeat bears testimony. And now, on 16 June 1815 General Reille, a veteran of many a Spanish campaign, urged Ney to be cautious and pleaded with him to send forward troops in greater numbers. He had spotted the dreaded red jackets along the low horizon in front of him, and the memories of many a bitter defeat came flooding back to halt him in his tracks. After all, it had been Ney himself who had come to grief in classic style at Busaco in September 1810. Was he willing to risk disaster a second time?

We cannot be sure of the length of the delay Ney experienced in getting his troops forward after listening to Reille's warning, although some accounts put it at up to two hours. Whatever it was, the delay demonstrated the moral ascendancy Wellington had gained over the French and gave him much-needed breathing space before the arrival of his Peninsular veterans. It also allowed Wellington himself to return from his meeting with Blücher at Brye before too much action had passed. Once again, accounts vary as to the timing of Wellington's return; some say he arrived as early as 1.30 whilst others have him arriving back at Quatre Bras at 3pm.

It was not until 2pm that Ney finally deployed his divisions for the attack, by which time the Dutch-Belgian troops were ready and waiting to receive them. The days of waiting and watching on the French border were finally over, and at last it was time to get to grips with the enemy. Ney's first attack consisted of about 6,000 infantry, supported by 2,000 cavalry, who crunched their way through the crops to the south of Gemioncourt and to the east of the Brussels road. The crackle of muskets heralded the first contact between the two sides as Dutch-Belgian skirmishers engaged their French counterparts. As the main French columns pushed forward the Dutch-Belgians were slowly driven back and were forced to relinquish their control of Gemioncourt, which fell to the French during the first attack. Elsewhere, French cavalry galloped up the Brussels road to inflict damage on the retiring defenders, whilst other French columns came forward to begin clearing the Bois de Bossu. Progress was slow owing to the density of the undergrowth, but slowly and steadily the defenders in the wood began to draw back in the face of the French advance. Meanwhile to the east of the Brussels road the Prince of Orange's artillery opened fire on the other French columns, inflicting casualties on them as they moved slowly forward through the crops. Wellington himself had by now returned from his meeting with Blücher but already found a rapidly deteriorating situation awaiting him. The French were advancing, the Dutch-Belgians had fallen back, and the advanced post of Gemioncourt had fallen, as had the farm of Pireaumont, on his left flank. All was not well, therefore, and with the battle only just begun Wellington must have wondered how long it would be before his British battalions arrived on the scene.

Fortunately for the Duke, he did not have to wait long, for soon after the Dutch-Belgians had retired towards the Namur road the leading elements of Picton's British division came hurrying down the road from Brussels, along with Van Merlen's brigade of Dutch-Belgian cavalry and the Duke of Brunswick's legion of infantry and cavalry. No sooner had they appeared than Wellington was ready to launch a counter-attack in order to thrust back the French. The leading British troops were the 1st Battalion 95th Rifles who were immediately ordered to try and recover the farm of Pireaumont on Wellington's left flank, of which the French had taken possession. Captain John Kincaid, having ridden from Brussels, was a little less breathless than his men, who were given only a fleeting chance to compose themselves before they entered the fray. Kincaid wrote later:

> We halted for a moment on the brow of the hill; and as Sir Andrew Barnard galloped forward to the headquarter group, I followed, to be in readiness to convey any orders to the battalion. The moment we approached, Lord Fitzroy Somerset, separating himself from the duke, said, 'Barnard, you are wanted instantly; take your battalion and endeavour to get possession of that village,' pointing to one on the face of the rising ground, down which the enemy were moving; 'but if you cannot do that, secure that wood on the left, and keep the road open for communication with the Prussians.' We instantly moved in the given direction; but, ere we had got half-way to the village, we had the mortification to see the enemy throw such a force into it, as rendered any attempt to retake it, with our numbers, utterly hopeless; and as another strong body of them were hastening towards the wood, which was the second object pointed out to us, we immediately brought them into action, and secured it. In moving to that point, one of our men went raving mad, from excessive heat. The poor fellow cut a few extraordinary capers, and died in the course of a few minutes.[5]

The 95th were too late to prevent the French from consolidating their position at Pireaumont but they did, nevertheless, secure the Cherry Wood situated on the northern side of the Namur road, just north of the Materne Lake. The riflemen advanced through the wood and deployed along the Namur road, pushing on towards the village of Thyle. Thus, communications with the Prussians via the Namur road were maintained.

While the 95th settled in Cherry Wood the rest of Picton's division, being the brigades of Kempt and Pack, all' veterans of the Peninsula, arrived and began to deploy at Quatre Bras. There was no time for them to become acquainted with the battlefield and they, like everyone else, were simply thrown into the battle as soon as they arrived. The 92nd Highlanders held the crossroads themselves, while the 42nd, 44th, 1st, 32nd and 79th continued east along the Namur road until the length of it as far as the Cherry Wood was lined with red-jacketed British veterans. Rogers's battery of artillery was positioned on the extreme left-hand end of the line.

The remaining battalion, the 28th, was sent forward to support the attempt by some Dutch militia to recapture Gemioncourt. The 28th, commanded by Sir Charles Belson, advanced in support of the Dutch and watched as they surged around the walls of Gemioncourt, driving the French from it. Unfortunately, they barely had time to settle before another French column attacked the farm and in turn drove the Dutch out, leaving the 28th with little option but to return to the Namur road. Meanwhile, in the Bois de Bossu, Prince Bernhard's men advanced once more, driving the French back and maintaining possession of this important position. Wellington's counterattack had not achieved any great gains but it did buy valuable time which allowed the Duke of Brunswick to get forward and deploy his troops to the west of the Brussels road. In the meantime, the Prince of Orange led Van Merlen's cavalry in a charge down the Brussels road against a column of French infantry but in turn were attacked by enemy cavalry, forcing them to retreat headlong towards the crossroads. Here, the Dutch-Belgian cavalry came under fire from the two Scottish regiments, the 92nd and 42nd, who were positioned closest to the crossroads, and took severe casualties from their allies before the mistake was realised. Sadly, it was symptomatic of the situation in Wellington's army, with so many British units never having even seen their Netherlands allies before. Moreover, one of Van Merlen's regiments, the Belgian 5th Light Dragoons, had green uniforms with yellow facings and shakos very similar to French Chasseurs à Cheval.

The opening phase of the battle ended with Wellington's men pushed back to the Namur road, save for Prince Bernhard's troops who still held the Bois de Bossu. Picton's division was present but no other British troops had as yet arrived. Even as the first French artillery shots began to fall amidst the Allies, Alten's and Cooke's divisions were hurrying along the road from Nivelles to Quatre Bras in a state of some anxiety, for as they neared the battlefield the sounds of gunfire became all the more audible. Lieutenant Harry Powell, of the 1st Foot Guards, and a veteran of Walcheren and the Peninsula, was amongst the troops marching to the battlefield. His battalion had started out at from Enghien at 4am and had arrived at Braine-le-Comte five hours later. Here the 1st Foot Guards were joined by the Coldstream Guards and 3rd Foot Guards:

> We halted on the eastern side, having had great difficulty in getting through the town in consequence of the numberless waggons and bag-

After attempting to rally some retiring Dutch-Belgian cavalry, Wellington found himself caught up in their retreat and was in danger of being taken prisoner or even killed by enemy cavalry. A proficient horseman, he was forced to ride for safety by leaping into the middle of a square formed by the 92nd Highlanders.

gage confusedly huddled together in the street. About twelve, General Cooke returned from a reconnaissance to the southward, and (as said at the time) on his own judgement ordered the Division to move to the left towards Nivelles. The heat was excessive, and the men suffered much from the weight of their packs. At about 3pm the Division arrived within half a mile of Nivelles, and took up a position looking over the town, supposing our day's work was done. We were, however, scarcely halted, and the men disencumbered of their loads, when an Aide-de-camp brought the order to advance immediately.

The Division were under arms in a minute, and started double quick down the hill into Nivelles, supposing that the enemy were entering it at the other side, for the firing had by this time become very heavy, and apparently very close. We continued our march through the town to Hautain-le-Val, where we halted to collect the stragglers and to let the Artillery pass to the head of the column. We then continued along the chausee from Nivelles to Namur. On the march the order was given to untie ten rounds ammunition and to see the flints in order, then for the Officers to join their companies and fix the bayonets [ammunition was issued in bun-

Wellington at Quatre Bras, 16 June 1815. With his men arriving piecemeal, the battle was one of the closest fought contests of his career. He is pictured here looking far more relaxed than he probably was on the day.

dles of ten paper cartridges tied together with pack thread]. On the road we met many wounded, and Major Jessop, of the 44th (QMG Department) shot through the foot; who urged us to get on as the action was going badly.[6]

It would be some time yet, however, before Cooke's division reached Quatre Bras. In front of Cooke was Alten's division, but it too was still some way from the battlefield when the action commenced. In the meantime, the French had brought forward forty-two guns and had arrayed them between the farms of Pireaumont and Gemioncourt. The British troops may not have seen them deploy for action, owing to the tall crops, but they certainly felt their power as shot and shell began to rain down upon them as a prelude to another French infantry attack.

Once again the French directed their main effort against the section of the Namur road which lay to the east of the crossroads, for it was here that their columns would find space to manoeuvre, although other French divisions advanced along the Brussels road while a single brigade attacked the Bois de Bossu. The French advanced steadily through the crops before coming up against Picton's skirmish line which lay lurking amongst the rye. In fact, French cavalry frequently charged forward and darted lances into the ground in order to mark the position of the British. Wellington watched from his position at the crossroads and decided

not to wait for the French but instead ordered Picton's division to rise and charge. The French, instead of enjoying an expected success, found their confident advance halted by the unexpected appearance of Picton's Peninsular veterans, an apparition that would, even on the best of days, have been a fearsome sight. James Anton was with the 42nd when they advanced through the crops against the oncoming French columns:

We were all ready and in line, – 'Forward!' was the word of command, and forward we hastened, though we saw no enemy in front. The stalks of rye, like the reeds that grow on the margin of some swamp, opposed our advance; the tops were up to our bonnets, and we strode and groped our way through as fast as we could. By the time we reached a field of clover on the other side, we were very much straggled; however, we united in line as fast as time and our speedy advance would permit. The Belgic skirmishers retired through our ranks, and in an instant we were on their victorious pursuers. Our sudden appearance seemed to paralyze their advance. The singular appearance of our dress, combined no doubt with our sudden debut, tended to stagger their resolution: we were on them, our pieces were loaded, and our bayonets glittered, impatient to drink their blood. Those who had so proudly driven the Belgians before them, turned now to fly, whilst our loud cheers made the fields echo to our wild hurrahs.[7]

Major Felix Calvert was with the 32nd Regiment, and he too recalled the moment when Picton's division hurled back the French attack:

> When this attacking force had crossed both hedges lining the meadow in the bottom, and had commenced ascending our position, the 32nd poured in upon it a heavy fire succeeded by a charge. This the enemy did not wait to receive, but retired with precipitation, and getting entangled in the hedges on returning to their position must have suffered considerable loss. We halted and reformed at the first hedge, when Sir Thomas Picton desired the regiment to retire to its original position.[8]

Picton's men followed up their attack and sent the French tumbling back in confusion. They then returned to their original positions, save for the 79th who remained at one of the hedges, firing at the French until Wellington ordered their recall. To the west of the Brussels road, however, things went much better for the French. In the Bois de Bossu the Dutch defenders watched as the enemy came on in dense columns. They had been joined in the wood by two battalions of Brunswickers but their joint fire could not stop the French who were soon amongst them, driving the Dutch and Brunswickers from their positions and sending them reeling back through the wood. The Duke of Brunswick's hussars, who had been brought forward, were driven back also, forcing the Duke himself to lead a squadron of his lancers against the French in order to cover the retreat of his men. This also ended in bloody failure, for his lancers could make no impression on the mass of French infantry, supported as they were by artillery and cavalry. The Duke, a brave man, rallied his men and led them a second time, but this too was brought to a swift end when he was mortally wounded by a musket ball. His men were shaken by the sight of their beloved leader being carried away, but to their credit they made a third charge, this time supported by Van Merlen's Dutch-Belgian cavalry, but again they were halted by French cavalry and fled back up the Brussels road with the French in hot pursuit.

Watching the progress of the fight from just south of the crossroads, Wellington was sitting upon his horse, Copenhagen, surrounded by his staff, when suddenly the mass of Dutch, Brunswick and French cavalry came surging up the road, leaving him with no choice but to beat a hasty retreat to safety of his British infantry, the nearest of whom were the 92nd Highlanders. The Duke, an accomplished horseman, galloped

towards them with some French chasseurs behind him, and, shouting, 'lie down, 92nd!' he leapt his horse over them to save himself. It was not the first time that Wellington had come close to being taken prisoner, wounded or even killed. At Talavera he escaped by the skin of his teeth, riding through French voltigeurs to make good his escape, whilst at Castrejon he had to draw his sword to protect himself from French cavalry. At Sorauren he rode out of one end of the village whilst French dragoons were entering the other; and, finally, at Orthes he was actually wounded by a spent ball that prevented him from riding for a few days. The history of the Waterloo campaign might have been very different had he not been able to vault his way out of trouble at Quatre Bras.

The French chasseurs were greeted by the 92nd in the traditional manner, and when the smoke rolled away more than a few enemy horses were minus their riders. The chasseurs, in fact, were roughly treated, not only by the Highlanders but also by the Brunswick infantry to the west of the Brussels road. Having run the gauntlet of fire they emerged on the northern side of the Namur road where, after setting about some stragglers and some of the many supernumeraries behind the main firing line, they turned and attempted to regain their own lines. Not many managed to, however, for the fire upon them was extremely destructive. Many rode in and about the buildings at Quatre Bras desperately trying to find a way through, but most were shot down and few lived to make it unscathed back to the French lines.

Charging behind the chasseurs came two regiments of French lancers. It is possible that these green-jacketed horsemen were able to reach the Namur road unscathed because of the fact that the chasseurs in front of them drew the Allies' fire. Whatever the reason, they suddenly appeared behind the Namur road in rear of the British infantry, having swept through the gap between the 92nd and 42nd. It is also possible that they were so close behind the Dutch and Brunswick cavalry – some had even got amongst them – that the British failed to realise they were French until it was too late. In an attack that bore a strong resemblance to the devastating charge by Polish lancers at Albuera, just over four years earlier, the French lancers swept down amongst the British infantry while they were still in their two-deep lines. It was to prove the most devastating attack on the British of the whole battle.

The French came on suddenly out of the crops and were met by a weak fire from some of the 42nd who recognised them as enemy cavalry. Denis Pack, a Peninsular veteran, apparently reproached his men for firing on them, assuming them to be friendly. After all, he had already seen Van Merlen's cavalry suffer at the hands of British infantry by mistake. Unfortunately, on this occasion they were distinctly unfriendly and, lowering their lances, the French charged forward against the 42nd and the 44th, who were situated on the left of the 42nd. The 42nd, in fact, realised they were French at the very last moment and in an instant hastily changed formation from line to square. This was not easily done, however, with the French so close at hand, and as the rear ranks tried to close up, there ensued an almighty collision as the lancers charged home. A Memorandum, printed in Siborne's *Waterloo Letters* recalled the moment when the French lancers crashed into the 42nd:

> The 42nd were not a quarter of an hour in the field before they were charged by the lancers. They must have been at the time a little in advance of the Namur road, expecting the remainder of the brigade to form upon them. The 44th moved up to the left instead of the right of the 42nd, its proper place. A few skirmishers were out in front. Lancers appeared approaching as if reconnoitring.
>
> Sergeant McEween said to his commanding Officer, 'Those are French lancers.' The latter replied, 'No, they belong to the Prince of Orange!' Sergeant McEween said he was sure they were the 3rd French lancers, whom he had seen when formerly a prisoner-of-war. [He] proposed to fire at them to see what notice they would take of the shot. He fired, and they immediately advanced upon the 42nd. The skirmishers ran in with the cry, 'Square, Square, French cavalry!'
>
> The lancers overtook two companies in the act of completing the square. Several of the 42nd were cut off, but a portion of the lancers became hemmed inside the square by the remainder of those two companies, and were instantly bayoneted.[9]

The confusion was tremendous. The lancers crashed into the square before it was fully formed and in no time at all scores of kilted Highlanders had fallen, including Colonel Robert Macara, who was badly wounded. He was being carried away by four privates when the lancers got in amongst them and all were speared mercilessly. Macara, in fact, was killed by a lance thrust which entered his chin and

continued upwards, piercing his brain. Under normal circumstances an infantryman could throw himself on the ground in order to escape the worst an enemy cavalryman could give, but against lancers even this was futile. A lancer, armed with a nine-foot lance, simply had to lean over and thrust down in order to deliver a killing blow against his powerless enemy. Such was the case at Albuera in May 1811, and here, at Quatre Bras, it was being repeated, although with less dramatic results. Indeed, the Highlanders took a heavy toll of their mounted adversaries but not before they too had suffered heavy casualties. Once again, the cause of this minor disaster was partly the confusion in trying to distinguish friend from foe. James Anton again:

> I think we stood with too much confidence, gazing towards them [the French] as if they had been our friends, anticipating the gallant charge they would make on the flying foe, and we were making no preparative movement to receive them as enemies, further than the reloading of the muskets, until a German orderly dragoon galloped up, exclaiming, 'Franchee! Franchee!' and, wheeling about, galloped off. We instantly formed a rallying square; no time for particularity; every man's piece was loaded, and our enemies approached at full charge; the feet of their horses seemed to tear up the ground. Our skirmishers having been impressed with the same opinion, that these were Brunswick cavalry, fell beneath their lances, and few escaped death or wounds: our brave colonel fell at this time, pierced through the chin until the point of the lance reached the brain. Captain (now Major) Menzies fell, covered with wounds, and a momentary conflict took place over him; he was a powerful man, and, hand to hand, more than a match for six ordinary men. The grenadiers, whom he commanded, pressed round to save or avenge him, but fell beneath the enemies' lances.[10]

Captain Archibald Menzies had given his horse to a drummer boy, preferring to fight on foot. During the French attack he fell wounded, close to a private soldier named Donald Mackintosh, who was also wounded. The drummer happened to be a friend of the latter soldier and rushed to help him. At this point, a French lancer tried to snatch Menzies' horse, at which an outraged Mackintosh screamed, 'Hoot, man, ye manna tak that beast, 't belangs to our captain here!' A French cavalry officer rode up and tried to finish off Menzies with his sword but as he leant over his saddle the Scottish officer reached up and pulled him from his horse. Seeing his officer in trouble, another French lancer rode up and thrust down with his lance. Fortunately, the quick-thinking Menzies managed to thrust the French officer between himself and the lance, which ripped into the Frenchman's body which fell on top of him. Menzies then lay beneath the dead body of the Frenchman for some time before he was pulled clear by some of his men. It was then discovered that Menzies had sustained no fewer than sixteen wounds.

The fight in the square was furious and confused, with those at the front continuing to fire whilst hoping that those behind would see to the enemy lancers in their midst. At length, the square was closed when the flank companies wheeled in, penning like sheep those lancers who had been unable to ride out before the square closed. All were then either killed or taken by the enraged Highlanders around them. With the last of the French lancers having been taken or dispatched the men of the 42nd were able to see to their wounded and regroup. It had been a desperate fight. Colonel Robert Dick had assumed command of the 42nd upon the death of Macara, but he too was wounded, as was Major Davidson who succeeded him. By the time the French retired, the 42nd were commanded by Brevet-major Campbell, the regiment's fourth commanding officer of the day.

The 42nd had not been the only regiment to be charged by the French lancers, for as they swept past the right flank of the Highlanders, many lancers continued their charge east and in so doing hit the 44th. This battalion was also caught in line, but like their kilted comrades to their right, they were experienced soldiers. Indeed, the regiment had captured an Imperial Eagle from the French on the hot and dusty battlefield of Salamanca on 22 July 1812. The regiment's commanding officer, Lieutenant Colonel John Hamerton, realised there was little time to get his men into square and so he calmly and confidently ordered the rear rank to face about, just as the 28th had done at Alexandria in 1801 when they saw off French attacks from both front and rear. The French lancers were almost upon the 44th when Hammerton gave the word to open fire, at which dozens of enemy saddles were emptied. The volley certainly took the momentum out of the French charge but it did not stop the lancers from crashing into the 44th's precariously formed line. Bayonets were thrust and lances darted as the two sides set about each other in a furious scrap which saw the red-jacketed British fighting desperately to retain their

formation. Officers calmly called out above the roar, ordering their charges to keep firing, whilst the French closed time and again, looking for any signs of disorder in the British line.

While the fight rolled back and forth around the 44th, a group of French lancers attacked the centre of the line where the regiment's colours fluttered above the smoke. Proudly holding the regimental colour was 16-year-old James Christie, who had been with the regiment just over eighteen months. The colours were always guaranteed to draw the unwanted attention of any enemy troops and this occasion was no different. As he stood there holding the colour, Christie was attacked by an enemy lancer who charged forward and thrust down his nine-foot long lance. We can only imagine the pain Christie must have suffered as the lance entered his left eye and penetrated as far as the lower jaw. Despite the pain, he managed to retain possession of the colour, even though part of the silk was torn away by the Frenchman. The latter, however, paid for his bravery with his life, for he was shot dead on the spot by one of Christie's comrades. Christie himself survived the battle and if gallantry awards had been in existence in 1815 he surely would have been awarded one.

When the smoke rolled away from the 44th's lines, the men could look out and congratulate themselves on a fine job, for they had beaten off a potentially disastrous attack by the French lancers. The 42nd, however, were not so lucky, and when the 44th looked away to their right they would have seen the Highlanders in a sorry state having been roughly handled by the enemy. Elsewhere, the 92nd Highlanders had played their part in seeing off the French cavalry, wheeling back to pour in a destructive fire against the right flank of some chasseurs as they rode past. The French attack had failed, and as the cavalry and infantry retreated to their staging positions, the artillery resumed its bombardment of Wellington's line. Indeed, apart from the French cavalry attacks during the afternoon, the main damage inflicted upon Wellington's men was done by the French artillery which continued to shell the Namur road throughout the afternoon, ceasing only when the cavalry attacked the Allied line.

Away to the left of the 42nd and 44th were the 1st. Sergeant John Douglas later recalled the strain of standing in line under cavalry attack and artillery fire throughout the afternoon, without having any cavalry with which to hit back:

We were rather awkwardly placed, not being able to destroy the enemy until close at hand. Their cavalry being numerous, whereas we had none, we were obliged to form square against cavalry, and after sending them to the four winds, form line against infantry. Thus for want of cavalry we were kept forming squares and lines between 2 and 3 o'clock in the afternoon until dark. When in square they plied us with round shot, and in line with grape, so that the rye was prematurely cut down by an invisible hand, as between the 2 fires and the trampling of men and horses it was laid low in a short time. In one charge of the cuirassiers, we were so short taken, not being aware of the advance of the cavalry, that the 28th Regiment and we had to form one square, with Picton in the centre. On came the lancers full charge but the murderous fire they received swept them off their saddles in great style. Thus they persevered in breaking the square, making a trial at each face, until very few of them were left to carry the intelligence to their comrades. On the defeat of the cavalry, Sir Thomas Picton returned thanks to the two regiments, saying he could not desire it better done (and it must be allowed he was a pretty well experienced judge in such matters), adding that he would recommend them to the government to wear feathers, but he fell on the 18th of June and with him fell the feathers.'[11] [i.e. a special plume in commemoration. British regiments set great store by such tribal distinctions.]

Apart from the French cavalry attacks the main fighting during the mid-afternoon took place in the Bois de Bossu where French infantry continued to press on through the wood, driving back Prince Bernhard's men towards its northern end. The fight here was as fierce as on any other part of the battlefield on 16 June. Prince Bernhard himself wrote to his father, three days after the battle:

I kept my ground a long time against an enemy thrice my number, and had only two Belgic cannons to protect myself with. The enemy took the point of a wood opposite me, and incommoded my left flank. I, without loss of time, took some volunteers, and two companies of Dutch militia, and recovered my wood at the point of the bayonet; I was at the head of the storming parties, and had the honour to be one of the first in the wood. In cutting away some branches, I wounded myself with my sabre very slightly in the right leg, but was not a moment out of the battle.[12]

Otherwise, the French were making little progress. In the centre, Picton's division held firm despite intense pressure, whilst on Wellington's left, the 95th Rifles continued to hold back and thwart French attempts to drive them from the Namur road at Thyle.

The cessation of French artillery heralded yet another cavalry attack, and as Wellington looked south he could see squadrons of French cavalry forming once again on the low ridge north of Gemioncourt. There were about 800 cuirassiers, in fact, arrayed in a dense formation astride the Brussels road, with the majority to the east of it where they had more room to manoeuvre. Despite the earlier cavalry charges, the crops evidently remained standing sufficiently high for the British infantry to be unaware of this latest French charge. Indeed, it was only when the skirmishers of the 42nd and 44th came rushing back that the two battalions became aware of yet another enemy cavalry charge. The order was given immediately to form square, and once again the British battalions prepared to face up to yet another French cavalry charge. The cuirassiers had seldom been seen in the Peninsula, the bulk of the work in Spain and Portugal being done by dragoons, hussars and chasseurs. In fact, there was much discussion amongst British officers as to whether the cuirasses of both the cuirassiers and, indeed, the carabiniers, whom they would meet at Waterloo, could withstand a musket shot. They were about to get their answer.

The British squares waited until the French cuirassiers had got to within about thirty yards of them before they opened fire, their controlled volleys bringing scores of horses crashing to the ground. Then, as the cavalry swirled between the squares, the British opened up a rolling fire which inflicted great damage on their enemies. To the right of the 42nd and 44th, the 92nd Highlanders braced themselves to receive the cuirassiers who had charged directly up the Brussels road. With them was Wellington himself, who assumed command. '92nd, don't fire until I tell you,' he shouted, and of course they didn't. The Gordons had served with distinction in the Peninsula, and barely two years before had stormed the heights of Puebla to open the Battle of Vittoria. The following month half a battalion of them had defended the pass at Maya against an entire French division. They were, therefore, veterans in every sense of the word. Indeed, so confident was he that Wellington had the regiment remain in line, rather than form square. Lieutenant Robert Winchester was one of those waiting for the French to come on at the crossroads:

The French cuirassiers soon after this, under cover of their guns, came charging up the fields in front of the Regiment, which still remained in line. Lord Wellington, who was by this time in rear of the centre of the Regiment, said, '92nd, don't fire until I tell you,' and when they came within twenty or thirty paces of us, his Grace gave the order to fire, which killed and wounded an immense number of men and horses, on which they immediately faced about and galloped off.[13]

The effect that four lines of British musketry had upon the French cavalry was spectacular. Men and horses rolled upon the ground whilst others tried desperately to pick their way through and over those in front. There was simply nothing the cuirassiers could do to break the 92nd, who continued firing away until eventually the French retreated down the Brussels road, leaving the Gordons to see to their wounded, to reload, check their ammunition and prepare for the next attack.

The cuirassiers enjoyed no success at all during the charge but they were not easily discouraged. They reformed to the south of Gemioncourt and, supported by lancers and chasseurs, they charged yet again up the slopes towards the Namur road and along the Brussels road itself.

The result was as predictable as it was deadly, with wave after wave of French cavalry breaking upon the squares of the 42nd and 44th and around the four-deep line of the 92nd. An officer of the 92nd later described the effect the British musketry had on the charging cavalry:

> The volley was decisive. The front of the French charge was completely separated from the rear by the gap which we made, and nothing was seen but men and horses tumbling on each other; their rear retreated, and the front dashed through the village, cutting down all stragglers; our assistant surgeon, dressing a man behind a house, had his bonnet cut in two and a lance run into his side.[14]

Lieutenant Robert Winchester also recorded this latest French cavalry charge:

> Shortly afterwards they formed again, and, accompanied by a body of Light Dragoons, charged up again in our front. They were all allowed to come within about the same distance as before, when we fired as formerly, and the same result was effected, causing great loss to them in killed and wounded. At this time a French officer of Light Dragoons, thinking his men were still following him, got too far to be able to retire by the way he had advanced, galloped down the road in the rear of our

A Highland regiment in action at Quatre Bras. Despite the well documented mishap to the 69th Regiment, the 79th (Cameron) Highlanders sustained far heavier casualties during the battle, over twice as many in fact.

regiment. The Duke of Wellington observing him, called out, 'damn it, 92nd, will you allow that fellow to escape?' Some of the men turned immediately round, fired and killed his horse, and a musket ball at the same time passed through each foot of the gallant young officer. I was afterwards billeted with him in the same house at Brussels for six months, and then went with him to Paris, where I received much kind attention from him – Monsieur Burgoine – and his family.[15]

The majority of the French cavalry who swept beyond the British line found it extremely difficult to regain their own lines and were shot down in the attempt. Many actually found themselves in the courtyard of the farm of Quatre Bras itself. These too paid for their folly with their lives. Others were attacked by the Brunswick cavalry who had been in position on the reverse slope behind the British infantry. One may well imagine the relief felt amongst Wellington's men as they peered through the smoke to see the French cavalry riding away once more to the safety of their own lines. Then, as before, they saw to their wounded, dusted themselves down, and regrouped, ready for the next French move.

Watching the masses of French cavalry swirling around the three British battalions immediately to the east of the Brussels road was the divisional commander, Sir Thomas Picton. The fiery Welshman was growing increasingly impatient, waiting for Allied cavalry to support his beleaguered infantry. Unfortunately, the British cavalry regiments were nowhere near the battlefield, and would not reach it until well after the fighting had ended on 16 June. Therefore, it fell to the various Dutch-Belgian and Brunswick regiments to support the infantry but little help was forthcoming at the time. Tired of waiting, an exasperated Picton took the step of ordering his other battalions forward from the Namur road into the fields beyond, from where they could pour a flanking fire into the French cavalry.

The 28th and 1st had been standing in column at the time of the French cavalry attacks when Picton ordered them into the fields south of the Namur road. Picton apparently led them in person, along with Sir James Kempt, one of his two brigade commanders. The 79th and 32nd did the same until all four battalions were arrayed in echelon with the 28th and 1st on the right, followed by the 32nd and, finally, the 79th, who were farthest forward. Beyond them the 95th remained in control at Thyle. Meanwhile,

the sorely tried 42nd and 44th were formed into a single square to the right of the 28th, with the 92nd remaining on the right of the line at the crossroads. Behind Picton's men came Best's Hanoverian brigade, who advanced to the Namur road in support.

The respite was short-lived for Wellington's men, for no sooner had the steel-clad cuirassiers departed than the French artillery barrage resumed, this time with increased intensity for the French gunners were now positioned just north of Gemioncourt at a range of about 500 yards from the British line. French skirmishers also caused havoc, creeping forward amidst the crops to keep up a constant and damaging fire on the British squares. At length, the artillery fire ceased and the skirmishers pulled back as more cavalry swept forward to attack the squares, but the latter again met with little success. In fact, the cavalry charges, trying as they were, proved a welcome relief for the British infantry who were freed of the punishment being handed out to them by the French artillery. The squares had only to maintain their discipline and formation and, in theory, they would be safe from the cavalry. It would take either a stroke of extreme good fortune or an outstandingly brave act on the part of a French cavalryman to break one of the squares. At Garcia Hernandez, in July 1812, Wellington's heavy dragoons of the King's German Legion had broken three French squares but only after a dying horse had plunged headlong into the first, creating a breach through which the remaining dragoons charged. The sight of the square disappearing beneath a welter of heavy cavalry swords had been enough to cause panic in the other squares which were collapsed like packs of cards in the face of further charges. At Quatre Bras, however, the French were to be denied a similar slice of luck and so the squares remained, stoic and unflinching, as wave after wave of enemy cavalry broke up around them.

There was little the French cavalry could do except hope for a sign of disorder in any of the squares, but none was forthcoming. The red-jacketed infantry continued to hold their ground and blaze away at their enemies, jeering at them and waving their fists while the cuirassiers buzzed angrily around them. At length the tide of horses receded and the French cavalry galloped off once more to the south, with the cheers of the defiant British soldiers resounding behind them, the men waving their shakos above their heads as they shouted themselves hoarse.

With the French cavalry driven back it was the turn of their skirmishers to resume their battle. They were a real nuisance to the British, firing apparently unseen from forward positions amidst the crops that lay in front of them and from the enclosures to the north of Gemioncourt. Officers were picked off and scores of men killed and wounded by these experienced French soldiers, causing Picton to send forward his own light troops to drive them back. Whether it was because they had expended most of their ammunition during the French cavalry attacks, or whether they simply used plenty of it during the skirmishing is not clear, but before too long the British skirmishers ran out of ammunition. Indeed, the French enjoyed a marked superiority over their British counterparts during this phase of the battle and were able to pick off Picton's skirmishers without too much difficulty, mainly due to the fact that the latter simply ran short of ammunition. The British light troops were commanded by Lieutenant Alexander Riddock, of the 44th Regiment:

It became my duty to command the party in advance (the regiment and brigade being in squares), not thirty yards from the French, and I continued in that position until my ammunition was totally exhausted; the French picking my men off as fast as they could load and fire, and our ammunition being intercepted by the frequent and daring charges of the French cavalry, round and round, and in the rear of our little squares. I deemed it proper to call the attention of the General, Sir Denis Pack, to the awkward situation my men and I were in; his orders were to close my men to the centre and join my regiment.

I did so in so far, but ere this time a number of squadrons of French cuirassiers and lancers were sweeping the field in the rear, round and round every square, showing no mercy, dashing at and sticking the helpless wounded officers and men that unfortunately lay without the protection of the square. I could compare them to nothing but a swarm of bees.

At this time I and my men were cut off from the regiment. I instantly formed four deep and charged bayonets, the rear rank with ported arms, and fought my way through the French cavalry until I reached the south side of the square of my regiment. But so hot and hard pressed was the regiment on all sides, that I could obtain no admittance, and my ammunition being gone, as before mentioned, we had no other alternative than to lie down close to a square, and crave their friendly protection.[16]

Riddock was unable to enter his regiment's square simply because of the men's discipline. They dared not open up even to admit their own comrades, lest the French manage to charge home through the gap. The consequences for the regiment would be disastrous. Fortunately, Riddock survived beneath the bayonets of his regiment and at length he and the majority of his men were able to regain the safety of their square.

The time now was about 4.30pm, and still no more British troops had arrived at Quatre Bras, save for those who had been battling away for the last hour or so. Picton's men had driven off successive French cavalry attacks but this could not go on forever. The 44th, for example, had been reduced to a skeleton, whilst the 42nd had suffered similarly heavy casualties. Meanwhile, Picton had formed the 28th and 1st into a single square which came under renewed attack from French cavalry, who assaulted three of the square's sides simultaneously. The pressure was intense but the square remained rock solid, the men in front presenting their bayonets to the French whilst those behind unloaded their muskets into the faces of their would-be assailants outside the square. Inside the square sat Sir Thomas Picton, unmoved and unimpressed by the French cavalry. He had seen it all before and their efforts to break in worried him not one jot. After all, this was the man who had led his men to the castle walls at Badajoz, had thrown back the French at Busaco and who had broken the back of King Joseph's army at Vittoria. No, the French would have to do a lot better if they were to impress this rough, foul-mouthed, fighting Welshman. 'Twenty-eighth,' he cried out, 'Remember Egypt!' And so they did, and once again the French cavalry, the 'old grey-headed devils' as Riddock described them, were flung back having suffered heavy casualties, but not before they had ridden down one of Best's Hanoverian battalions that had been caught in line.

French pressure on Wellington's line was unrelenting. Successive cavalry charges had begun to wear down the defenders whose ammunition was beginning to run dangerously low. Indeed, the 92nd Highlanders were barely able to reply to their adversaries, so low were they. The French cavalry attacks seemed endless, with wave after wave sweeping forward, but in an increasingly haphazard fashion. There was no real order to their attacks, whilst an ever-increasing number of dead and wounded men and horses rendered it almost impossible to get

*The Battle of Quatre Bras.
Wellington's close fought
victory prevented Marshal
Ney's wing of the French Army
from seizing the vital crossroads
and from falling upon the right
flank of the Prussian Army at
Ligny. However, the fight also
prevented Wellington from
marching to assist Blücher,
whose army was badly mauled
by Napoleon. This painting
shows the fighting at the
crossroads, with an emphasis
on the rear area behind the
main fighting line.*

within a sabre cut of the squares. Nevertheless, with the combination of cavalry, artillery and skirmishers taking its toll, Wellington's situation grew desperate. To the west of the Brussels road, Dutch and Brunswick infantry were just about managing to hold on to the Bois de Bossu, whilst in the centre and to the east of the road his British infantry were being sorely pressed. Away to the east, on his left flank, things were also deteriorating. The 95th Rifles had been thrown out of Thyle and with Kempt's brigade having been drawn farther west, away from them, there was a very real danger that a French thrust north from Pireaumont across the Namur road would cut them off altogether. In the event, they pulled back to the Cherry Wood, where they hung on grimly in the face of strong French pressure. It was now past 5pm and Wellington must have wondered where the hell the rest of his men were. After all, had not De Lancey informed him that the majority of his divisions would arrive at Quatre Bras soon after noon?

Wellington's position was desperate indeed, but, even as Picton's men endured yet another cavalry attack, the high piercing shrill of British bugles could be heard playing 'The British

Grenadiers', and there, hurrying along the road from Nivelles, came Colin Halkett's British brigade, followed close behind by a Hanoverian brigade under Kielmansegge, both of which formed part of Sir Charles Alten's 3rd Division. It was a tremendous relief to see the column of 2,000 red-jacketed infantry high-tailing it along the road, their officers riding in front, and their colours flying proudly in the midst of them. Halkett's brigade hardly constituted a veteran brigade, for only the 2/30th had seen service in the Peninsula where, as part of the 5th Division, they had scaled the walls of Badajoz and, three months later, helped devastate the centre of the French Army at Salamanca. The other three battalions, the 33rd, 2/69th and 2/73rd, were not Peninsular veterans although they had formed part of Graham's force that attacked Bergen-op-Zoom. It mattered little to Wellington, however, for in the late afternoon of 16 June 1815 any troops in red jackets were a welcome sight.

Immediately on getting there [wrote Lieutenant Frederick Hope Pattison, of the 33rd] orders were given for the brigade to move forward to the right, and support the right of Picton's division. A movement agreeably to this order took place, each regiment advancing in open column of companies, preserving their respective distances, so as to deploy into line when necessary. The ground through which he had to advance was much undulated, and in full crop of rye, which in that rich and luxuriant country grows excessively high, and on this account obstructed observation.[17]

Whilst Halkett's brigade deployed to the west of the Brussels road, the batteries of Major Lloyd and Captain Cleeves came trundling up the road to join in the action, providing Wellington with much needed artillery. Wellington, in fact, took himself off towards Thyle and his left flank, taking with him Kielmansegge's brigade and leaving Picton in command at the crossroads to supervise the deployment of Halkett's brigade. Picton duly ordered Halkett to lead his men into the Bois de Bossu to attack the French left, to support the Brunswickers who were holding on there, and to try and drive back the French who were rapidly gaining control of it. Halkett had barely entered the wood when a messenger arrived from Denis Pack informing him that his men were desperately short of ammunition and that he needed assistance urgently if he was to maintain his position. Halkett's men had already begun to filter into the wood and the timing of Pack's request could not have been worse. Nevertheless, he decided to send the 69th to the Brussels road to support Pack's right flank. Picton, in fact, ordered the battalion to be deployed immediately to the east of the Brussels road from where they could support Pack. And so the regiment, under its commander, Charles Morice, strode out across the field, little knowing that in a few minutes it was to fall victim to an almighty blunder, traditionally ascribed to the Prince of Orange. Closer examination, however, reveals the true cause to be nearer to home.

Halkett's arrival in the Bois de Bossu came not a moment too soon, for the Brunswickers were apparently on the point of breaking. Indeed, some accounts have them streaming away from the field at this point. The arrival of fresh British troops evidently strengthened their resolve, however, and Halkett was able to move out of the wood and deploy according to Picton's original instructions. He duly moved his remaining three battalions, the 33rd, 30th and 73rd, out into the field beyond the wood, moving them in echelon.[18] As he did so he sent word to Morice that the 69th should form square as he had seen French cavalry massing for another attack, but kept his own battalions

formed in open column of companies for ease of movement. Twenty-two years later Halkett recalled the sequence of events that led to one of the most notorious incidents of the battle.

> I, with one of my ADCs galloped to the front so as to clear the farm covered by wood which Pack occupied, perceived a large corps of cavalry forming by detachments, moved forward under the appearance of going to water their horses. I immediately, however, made my mind up as to their intention of moving forward almost immediately. I had hardly returned to my brigade when a heavy artillery fire commenced upon the road, and having sent Lieut. [?Kelsey] one of my ADCs to the 69th Regiment to inform them and Pack that I expected cavalry to advance, and I supposed the guns indicated that intention, and that the 69th Regiment should, forthwith, prepare to receive cavalry, I received an answer from the Commanding Officer of the 69th Regiment (Colonel Morice) that my order had been received and that he had attended to my instructions. Unfortunately, in the act of forming square an Officer of high rank came up to the 69th Regiment, and asked what they were about. The reply was the directions they received from me, on which he said [there was] no chance of the cavalry appearing, and ordered them to form column and to deploy into line, which of course was complied with, and during this very movement the cavalry did attack, rode through the 69th Regiment, but situated as they were, the enemy suffered a heavy loss.[19]

Despite the onrush of French cavalry, the 69th were still in line, having been ordered to deploy in that manner by the Prince of Orange. The young Prince, nominally second-in-command to Wellington, resented the interference of both Halkett and Picton who, despite their massive experience, were actually junior to him within the Anglo-Dutch Army. Riding up to Morice, he asked him what he thought he was doing. The 69th's commanding officer stated the obvious, that he was preparing to receive cavalry. The Prince of Orange, however, was nonplussed, for he could see no cavalry. Furthermore, he was led to believe that the whole point of having the 69th deployed to the east of the Brussels road was to give fire support to Pack's beleaguered brigade. The 69th would be no good to them if they were in square, he reasoned. The bravery of the Prince of Orange was never in question. He had served under Wellington at a young age in the Peninsula, where he had seen for himself the effectiveness of the two-deep British line. Now, at Quatre Bras, he needed to see it again in order to afford Pack the sort of support he had requested. Unfortunately the prince had yet to master the simplest forms of battlefield strategy and tactics. 'Get in line, sir!' he bellowed, at which Morice, reluctantly and presumably in a state of some anguish, gave the order for his men to deploy from the safety of their square into line.

Right on cue, hundreds of heavily armed French cuirassiers came thundering towards the 33rd but saw they had formed square and were prepared to receive them. Away to the right, however, the 69th stood like statues, in line, and a very inviting target for the cuirassiers who had suffered severe casualties themselves during the afternoon. At the last moment Morice realised what was about to hit him and immediately the order was given to form square. The battalion duly began to form square but were on the point of closing ranks when three companies were halted in the act of doing so. Although it would undoubtedly have been prudent for the Prince of Orange to have allowed the 69th to remain in square, it appears that the real cause of the disaster to the 69th was due to one of its own officers, Captain Henry Lindsay, who commanded No.1 company. According to Lieutenant Brooke Pigot, also of the 69th, Lindsay halted the grenadier company and companies 1 and 2 in the act of forming square in order to face about and open fire at the cuirassiers. 'But for that we should have got into square, as it was these companies [that] were really cut down,' he later wrote, adding, 'Poor man, to the day of his death he regretted having done so, but at the time he did it for the best.'[20]

The French cuirassiers were amongst the 69th in an instant, thrusting and hacking at the hapless infantrymen with their long, straight Klingenthal swords. The cuirassiers were huge, steel-clad warriors, mounted on large black horses, and the red-jacketed infantrymen were helpless in the face of their onslaught. Small groups banded together to defend themselves as best they could and, amazingly, the majority of the battalion survived the attack. In fact, the episode is usually represented as being a disaster of the greatest magnitude, but only 150 of the 516-strong battalion became casualties at Quatre Bras, and not all of these were suffered at the hands of the French cavalrymen. The battalion suffered just one officer and thirty-four other ranks killed. But these figures are nowhere near as fearful as those suffered by the battalions of John Colborne's brigade at Albuera, for exam-

ple, where 1,300 of the 1,600-strong brigade were lost. The 69th, to their immense credit, must have put up a great fight to prevent a similar disaster occurring. The casualty figures were bad enough but they might have been far worse. In the event, both officers and men fought like devils in the true tradition of the British Army. In the middle of the fight was Christopher Clarke, a cadet from the Military College, one of the so-called 'gentleman volunteers'. Clarke defended himself furiously and managed to kill three cuirassiers before he himself fell, covered with no fewer than twenty-two sabre wounds, but he survived to tell the tale. Captain Lindsay himself was badly wounded during the attack, as was Ensign Henry Keith, carrying the King's Colour. He was ridden down and had to suffer the agony of seeing the precious Colour being carried away by the enemy. Gradually, the survivors of the attack made their way to the safety of the nearby square of the 42nd and 44th, whilst the mounted officers made their escape by riding off to the north of the Namur road.[21]

Having dispersed the 69th the French cuirassiers looked to continue their trail of destruction and crossed to the west of the Brussels road where Halkett's other three battalions lay in wait. Sergeant Thomas Morris, an abrasive Londoner, was standing with his regiment, the 73rd, when the cavalry appeared:

We continued to advance, the glittering of the tops of our bayonets, guided us towards a large body of the enemy's cuirassiers, who, coming so unexpectedly upon us, threw us in the utmost confusion. Having no time to form a square, we were compelled to retire, or rather to run, to the wood through which we had advanced.[22]

Frederick Hope Pattison, of the 33rd, also recalled the moment when the French cavalry appeared:

Advancing in open column of companies, a voice was heard calling aloud, 'Cavalry, cavalry, form square, form square!' The leading companies of the regiment halted immediately, and we soon were in a position to receive them. Having accomplished this important movement (we being then on an elevated part of the field), a large body of French cuirassiers were seen approaching at great speed. Perceiving, however, that we were ready to receive them, and that the 69th (which was to our left) was still in open column of companies, they brought their left shoulders forward, and passing by us at full gallop, dashed in amongst them, when a terrible sabring ensued...The 33rd were not left long to indulge the self-complacent feeling of defying cavalry. Infantry, if cool and collected in square, are invulnerable to cavalry. They might as well try to ride over St Paul's, as to break them. We laughed them to scorn.[23]

Unfortunately, by forming square the 33rd presented a very respectable target to the French gunners a few hundred yards to the south, and soon enough the shells began to rain down on them in their exposed position. Hope Pattison again:

The two French batteries which had stealthily advanced at point-blank distance, opened fire simultaneously on our helpless square, cutting down the men like hay before the scythe of the mower. At this juncture Lieutenant Arthur Gore of the Grenadier company, who was standing close by me (an exceedingly handsome young man; like Saul, from his shoulders and upwards, he was higher than any of his compeers), was hit by a cannon ball, and his brains bespattered the shakos of the officers near him. In the twinkling of an eye he fell, like a stately oak from the last blow of the hewer, a lifeless corpse on his mother earth...In a few minutes, if not a more awful, certainly a more touching catastrophe ensued. Captain Haigh perceiving that the front of the square facing the artillery was bending inwards, left his place much excited, and, flourishing his sword, called aloud vehemently with an oath, 'Keep up, keep up; I say keep up.' The words were vibrating on his lips, when a cannon ball hit him on the abdomen, and cut him nearly in twain. He fell on his back; the separation between body and soul was most appalling. His eyes strained as if they would leap from their sockets, and the quiver of the lip with the strong convulsion of his whole frame, showed unquestionably how unwilling his spirit was to be driven in this ruthless way from her clay tenement.[24]

Haigh's brother was standing nearby and witnessed his death, shedding tears over the corpse. He himself was mortally wounded at Waterloo, two days later. The 33rd risked virtual destruction if they remained in square, and so was forced to deploy once again into line and moved to a less exposed position. However, the regiment had hardly taken up this new position when French cavalry reappeared, forcing the 33rd to make for the relative safety of the Bois de Bossu, to which the 73rd retreated also. The 73rd, in fact, had been under artillery fire also,

and the men ordered to lie down. Sergeant Thomas Morris again:

Not having any enemy immediately before us, at this particular time, we were ordered to lie down, to avoid the shots, which were flying thickly around us. The colonel ordered two companies out skirmishing; the light company, and the company to which I belonged, were detached on this duty, but not together. Our company was unfortunately commanded by a captain, sixty years of age; who had been upwards of thirty years in the service, but was never before in action. He knew nothing of field movements, and when going through the ordinary evolutions of a parade, the sergeant was obliged to tell him what to say and do. He now led us forward, and we fired a few shots at a portion of the enemy who were within reach. Presently we saw a regiment of cuirassiers making towards us, and he was then at his wits' end, and there is no doubt we should all have been sacrificed, had we not been seen by the adjutant of our regiment, a fine spirited fellow, who had been our regimental surgeon, but through the interest of the colonel, exchanged to ensign and adjutant. On seeing us in this perilous position, he immediately rode up, and exclaimed, 'Captain Robinson, what are you about? Are you going to murder your men?' He directly ordered us to make the best of our way to the regiment, where we arrived just in time to form square; and on the cuirassiers coming up, and finding us so well prepared, they wheeled off to the left, receiving from us a volley as they retired.[25]

Only the experienced veterans of the 30th remained in the open. The battalion had formed square well before the French cavalry charged, forming up on some rising ground, and never appear to have been in danger.

By now Wellington had returned from surveying the scene on his left flank. The French greeted his return with a renewal of their artillery barrage and by more cavalry charges against Picton. Once again the attacks were beaten off, as were those directed against Halkett's only battalion in the open, the 30th. With the 69th recovering amidst the relative protection of Picton's men, Halkett was left with just the 33rd and 73rd, along with the Brunswickers, with which to try and stem the French advance through the Bois de Bossu. The situation here, in fact, had grown serious for Wellington, with increasing numbers of French troops infiltrating through it. Halkett's men were left on the fringes of the wood, too shaken by the cavalry to enter the wood but reluctant to leave the safety of the trees lest they be attacked once more by cavalry.

The French persisted with their cavalry charges, but by this time the British squares were supported by the guns of Lloyd's battery, and Cleeves' and Kuhlmann's KGL batteries, which brought Wellington's artillery to a respectable strength. Despite the failure of the French cavalry to break Wellington's centre, the Allies were in a sorry state. To the east, the 95th Rifles and Kielmansegge's brigade continued to hold on at the Cherry Wood, whilst Picton's British infantry maintained the centre. But the threat now, at about 6.30pm, was to Wellington's right flank, for the French had all but secured the whole of the Bois de Bossu. It needed just one final successful advance to take themselves out of the wood and across the Nivelles road. Thus, Wellington's right would be turned. But, at this most important moment, Cooke's 1st Division arrived, with the 2/1st Foot Guards leading the way. Behind them came the 3rd Battalion of the regiment, both battalions forming Maitland's brigade, whilst the second battalions of the Coldstream and 3rd Foot Guards followed close on their heels along with two battalions of Brunswickers.

The Guards could not have arrived at a more crucial time, but they still had to endure a moment of stupidity from the Prince of Orange who, impatient to get the Guards into the wood, rode up to Lord Saltoun, who commanded the light companies, and ordered him to attack it immediately. Naturally enough, Saltoun needed to know where exactly the enemy were. After all, only a complete idiot would take his men into such a situation without first having ascertained their whereabouts. The young Prince replied sternly, 'If you do not undertake it, I'll find someone who will.' One can well imagine just how the Peninsular veteran must have felt at this unwanted and ill-timed tirade, coming from the young man with far less experience, but with great restraint Saltoun repeated the question. He evidently found the reply to be more like that which he expected from a corps commander and so formed his light companies into skirmishing lines and entered the wood, followed close behind by the remainder of the two battalions.

No sooner had the Guards Division begun clearing the Bois de Bossu, than a large French column began to emerge from its southern end, making for the Brussels road.[26] As it moved across the ground between the Bois de Bossu and the road, another enemy column began to appear in support of the first, which, once at the

Brussels road, began to advance towards the Allied position. Having established itself on the road, the leading French column occupied a house called La Bergerie, situated just a few hundred yards from the crossroads, entering the large house and taking over the garden. The occupation of La Bergerie was too close for comfort for the Allies, something that did not go unnoticed by the Adjutant General, Sir Edward Barnes, nor indeed by Wellington himself. Barnes, known as 'the fire-eating adjutant general', was an old friend of the 92nd. He had saved the regiment at the pass of Maya on 26 July 1813, when he arrived in the nick of time with his brigade to stop a French attack in its tracks, an attack that had already overrun the 92nd's camp. He later commanded the 92nd when it formed part of his brigade. Colonel John Cameron, commanding the 92nd Highlanders, was evidently impatient to get to grips with these French columns and drew a rebuke from Wellington. 'Take your time, Cameron, you'll get your fill of it before night.' Shortly afterwards he shouted, 'Now, 92nd, you must charge these two columns of infantry!'

The grenadier company of the 92nd and the 1st Company led the way, advancing directly down the Brussels road whilst the other companies advanced on their right against the house, its garden and the hedges around it. Lieutenant James Hope was with the 92nd, and left a most detailed account of the fighting:

> Before the order to charge was given, the enemy had occupied a house of two storeys, which stands on the left of the highway to Charleroi, at the distance of 200 yards from the village [Quatre Bras]. On the opposite side of the road, there was a large garden, surrounded by a thick thorn hedge, having a little gate on the side nearest the road, and another of a similar size immediately opposite to it. Between the two, there was a gravel walk, of about a yard in breadth. On the left of the house there was another hedge, which the enemy had also taken possession of. The order to charge had scarcely been given, when every man in the regiment appeared in front of the bank, and, amidst one of the heaviest fires of musketry I have ever witnessed, advanced to dislodge the enemy from the house, garden and hedge. Colonel Cameron, with the right companies of the regiment, and accompanied by General Barnes, advanced by the highway, the other companies, by making an oblique movement to their right, threw the whole strength of the regiment against the enemy at the house and garden. The enemy continued to resist the High-

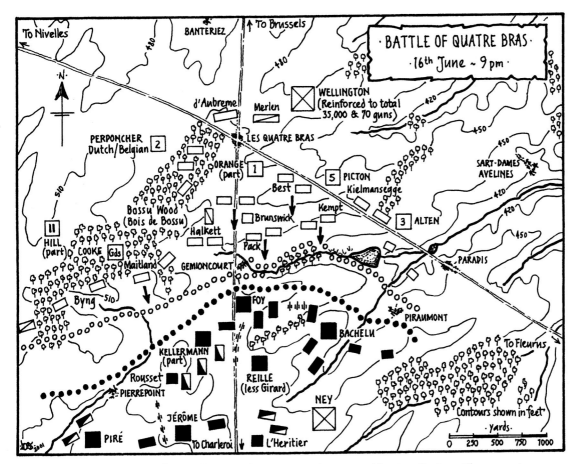

landers for some time with great bravery. Our brave Colonel, Cameron, was mortally wounded close to the garden, and retired from the field, regretted by the whole corps. After a terrible conflict, we succeeded in wresting the house from them. The garden, which had never been occupied by the enemy, was now the only obstacle between us and them. But as they were formed, ready to receive us at a few paces only from the rear hedge, there appeared some little danger in attempting to charge them in that position, as they were greatly superior in numbers to us, and as the space between the garden hedge and the wood of Bossu would not permit us to advance with the whole of our troops in line. Thus situated, we were under the necessity of hazarding something, or of giving up what we had already gained. As there was little time to be lost, part of the regiment moved round the garden by its right, and another part by the left. It was proposed to enter by the little gate, fronting the road, and, advancing across the garden, break open the one opposite to it, whence the troops, employed on this service, were to sally, and, in conjunction with those on their right and left, attack the enemy with the bayonet. To the centre party I attached myself. We accomplished the task allotted to us, of forcing the gates, with ease, although the enemy kept up a dreadful fire of small arms during these operations, which, from the nature of the

service, we could not well return. The rear gate having been speedily opened, we moved out of the garden, and quickly formed in front of the hedge. The right and left columns, seeing us ready, moved round the corners of the garden, in order to try the metal of the enemy. The signal having been made, every man joined in three hearty cheers, and then, with the irresistible bayonet in their hands, advanced to the work of death.[27]

With pipes squealing and the men cheering, the Highlanders went to work right enough with their bayonets, hunting down the French and driving them from the house and its gardens. Sadly, John Cameron, 'old Fassiefern' as he was affectionately known, did not see his men's triumph, for he was shot and mortally wounded during the attack. Cameron was the hero of several actions in the Peninsula, not least at the bridge of Almaraz, the pass at Maya and at St Pierre. It is a great shame that he never lived to see his beloved Highlanders in action at Waterloo two days later. Cameron was wounded by a musket ball in the groin, and as he reared backwards his horse turned and galloped back to the crossroads where Cameron's groom was waiting with his master's second horse. Cameron's horse stopped suddenly and he was pitched

La Bergerie as it looks today. It was during the charge of the 92nd Highlanders, led by Sir Edward Barnes, that the 92nd's commanding officer, John Cameron, was killed. The brick construction to the right has obviously been added since the battle of Quatre Bras was fought.

headlong on to the ground. He was not the only officer to be struck down, for the officer carrying the 92nd's Regimental Colour was shot through the heart and the staff of the Colour shattered in six pieces by three balls, and the King's Colour by one. Having seen Cameron fall, the men went about the business with a vengeance. One private soldier wrote later:

> It was hot work then. They were in the hoose like as mony mice, an' we couldna get at them wi' oor shot when their fire was ca'in' doon mony a goot man among us; but we had seen Cameron fall, an' oot o' that they had to come, or dee where they were; so we ower the hedge an' through the garden till the hoose was fair surrounded, an' they couldna get a shot oot where we couldna get ane in. In the end they were driven oot, an' keepit oot. Ay, but the French were brave men, an' tried again an' again to take it from us, but they only got beaten back for their pains, and left their dead to fatten the garden ground.[28]

Some Highlanders pursued the enemy south towards Gemioncourt but suffered from the fire of French artillery and were thrown back upon

La Bergerie, which remained in British hands for the remainder of the day. The attack by Barnes and the 92nd had the desired effect of driving back the French infantry from in front of Wellington's centre. Thus, Wellington could feel relatively satisfied with affairs in his front.

Meanwhile the Guards set about securing Wellington's right flank. The arrival of Cooke's division marked the turning point in the Battle of Quatre Bras, for with Wellington's men holding their own on his left and centre, it only needed his right flank to be restored before he could finally consider counter-attacking. The Foot Guards were known as 'The Gentlemen's Sons', for they had an extremely high concentration of titled officers as well as sons of the landed gentry and the professional classes. These men were paid more than the ordinary line regiments. They also spent more, their mess bills being quite amazing. They were the King's men, who would stand guard at St James's Palace and at Windsor, and who would provide the pomp and circumstance at many a state pageant in early nineteenth-century England. They were also men not to be trifled with, and despite a large number of militia which had been absorbed into their ranks immediately prior to the campaign, they were considered to be the most disciplined in the British Army. It was with great relish, therefore, that they swept into the Bois de Bossu, hardly having time to catch their breath after their long hot march from Enghien.

It was no easy business for the Guards to clear the wood, as they found it difficult to see their opponents. Gold and scarlet against dark blue amidst a world of deep green and brown was hardly beneficial to them. Nor was it particularly easy to distinguish friend from foe. Indeed, there were numerous instances of what we would now call 'friendly fire' with several British units firing at each other through the dense brushwood. There were, however, several 'rides' through the wood, which made access slightly easy, although these became killing grounds for both sides. Many men were killed or wounded by flying timbers, thrown through the air as a result of French artillery which shelled the wood. While Saltoun led his men through the wood, the remaining companies, under Colonel Henry Askew, followed. These battalion companies had halted, but as soon as they heard firing in front of them – which happened to be Saltoun's men engaging the enemy – the Prince of Orange sent Askew forward and ordered him to open fire, assuming those in front to be the enemy. Unfortunately, they were not, and Saltoun was forced to send back one of his officers, Charlie Ellis, to tell them to stop firing. The Guards then continued amidst a rain of shot and shell. Amongst them was Private William Blake:

> Our regiment marched into the wood without the slightest suspicion, when we were attacked on all sides by the enemy who had lain in the ditches on each side of the wood where hundreds of brave fellows fell without an opportunity of defending themselves as they [the French] opened a heavy fire from their guns which were posted on a hill about half a mile distant, which threw the whole of our men into confusion, some running one way and some another.[29]

The Guards gradually began clearing the Bois de Bossu of Frenchmen, until after two hours of hard and difficult fighting they reached the southern edge of the wood. From here they could see the guns that had been creating so much havoc amongst them. The Guards, tired, hungry and thirsty, and irritated after stumbling their way through the wood, immediately decided to attack them. In the attempt, Colonels

Askew and Stuart, commanding the 2nd and 3rd Battalions of the 1st Foot Guards respectively, were wounded and command devolved upon Edward Stables and Francis D'Oyly. The attacks were unsuccessful, however, and the Guards were forced back into the wood.

By now Byng's brigade of Guards had joined Maitland's brigade, although only the light company of the Coldstream Guards, under Lieutenant Colonel James MacDonell, four battalion companies, under Lieutenant Colonel Daniel Mackinnon, and the light company of the 3rd Foot Guards, under Lieutenant Colonel Francis Home, were engaged at Quatre Bras. They fought their way through the Bois de Bossu and emerged in the open, ready to attack the farm of Grand Pierrepoint. With the light company of the 3rd Foot Guards was Private Matthew Clay:

> We loaded our muskets and very hastily advanced up the rising ground in the open field; (the shots from the enemy now whizzing amongst us) we quickly attained the summit, and bringing our left shoulders forward, the enemy retiring before us. We had now arrived near to a building against the walls of which the shots from the guns of the enemy (intended for us) were freely rebounding, being just within range of their guns, our skilful commander led us through an enclosed yard, (where several bodies of the enemy's cavalry lay, slain previous to our arrival). We immediately formed in the field into which we had entered and were at the same time joined by our light artillery guns.[30]

The five companies of Foot Guards from Byng's brigade immediately became embroiled in a sharp struggle at the farm, with the fighting swaying back and forth until the Guards gradually established the upper hand. Then, when the French appeared to be preparing for another charge, Lieutenant Colonel Dashwood, of the 3rd Foot Guards, turned to his men and shouted, 'Now men, let us see what you are made of!' at which they cheered, charged, and forced the French back at bayonet point. In fact, Dashwood would have led his men even farther, had it not been for the presence of enemy cavalry, as Matthew Clay later wrote:

> We continued pursuing the enemy over the slain, which were thickly spread around us. By this time our commander found it necessary to form us into squares to oppose the enemy's cavalry, who were constantly menacing us on our advance, our square being compactly formed and prepared to receive cavalry. Their cavalry

now bearing off, the enemy's artillery would alternately annoy us with their shells which were skilfully directed...Their cavalry now menaced us more daringly and prevented our taking fresh ground until their artillery had thrown their shells amongst us. By this means we had a more narrow escape than before, being compelled to remain longer in our position to resist cavalry. I being one of the outward rank of the square, can testify as to the correct aim of the enemy, whose shells having fallen to the ground and exploded within a few paces of the rank in which I was kneeling, a portion of their destructive fragments in their ascent [would] pass between my head and that of my comrade next in the rank; its force and tremendous sound causing an unconscious movement of the head, not to be forgotten in haste.[31]

The French cavalry forced the Foot Guards, both Saltoun's men and the five companies of Byng's brigade, back from the farm and back to the safety of the Bois de Bossu. As they returned to the wood Lord James Hay, acting as adjutant to Saltoun and described by the Prince Regent as the most handsome man he'd ever seen in the uniform of a British officer, tried to leap a fence but his horse refused and reared up. As Hay struggled to control it he was shot dead by a French cavalryman. His body remained sitting in the saddle until Saltoun himself came riding up, at which the body fell across the neck of Hay's horse and rolled off on to the ground. Another Guards officer killed during the fighting was Lieutenant Colonel William Miller, of the 1st Foot Guards. He was mortally wounded and was carried from the field by four privates. As he lay wounded, he sent for his friend, Charles Thomas, and said he would like to see the Colours of the regiment for one last time. The Colours were brought forward to him by Ensign Robert Batty and waved above him, and as he was carried from the field, smiling, he declared himself 'satisfied'. Miller was later taken to Brussels where he died on 19 June. Captain Robert Adair, also of the 3/1st Foot Guards, was killed at Quatre Bras when a cannon ball shattered his thigh near the hip towards the end of the day. Ensign Howell Rees Gronow, the famous diarist, later wrote that Adair suffered terribly during the amputation as the shot had torn away the flesh, and the bones were sticking out in splinters near the hip. A gruesome but not unusual sight on a battlefield. Nevertheless, Adair, in the true style of a gentleman officer, managed to joke with the surgeon throughout the operation, saying, 'take your time, Mr Carver'. He later died through loss of blood.

With the Bois de Bossu finally secured, Halkett's brigade was able to push forward against Gemioncourt which was taken by two companies of the 30th under Captain Thomas Chambers.[32] Chambers and his men charged into the courtyard of the farm but were driven out, but they reformed immediately in the orchard outside and a second attack proved successful and the farm was taken and held. All along the entire Allied line, in fact, from the Bois de Bossu to Gemioncourt and to Pireaumont in the east, Wellington's position had stabilised, and by 9pm he was in a position to drive the French back completely.

When darkness fell on the night of 16 June, the French found themselves driven back beyond Frasnes, where they had started the day. It had been a bloody and confused day that had cost Wellington 2,205 British casualties, including over 300 dead. Heaviest casualties had been amongst the 42nd, 92nd, 79th and the two battalions of the 1st Foot Guards. These figures testify to the fact that the 'disaster' to the 69th Regiment has become blown out of all proportion. Indeed, the 79th Highlanders, for example, suffered twice the number of casualties suffered by the 69th. The loss of the Colours by the 69th and the interference by the Prince of Orange, which is open to doubt, has simply become part of Waterloo folk lore. A further 2,600 casualties were suffered by the other Allied units, which bears testimony to the part played by them at Quatre Bras. French casualties were put at just over 4,000.

Wellington's force had grown throughout the day to around 30,000 infantry and 2,000 cavalry, all of the latter being either Dutch, Belgian or Brunswick, for none of the British cavalry regiments arrived in time to fight. By the end of the day Wellington's force outnumbered Ney's by just over 10,000 men, and as the size of the Allied Army grew, so did the enormity of the task expected of Ney, whose job it was to drive Wellington away before falling upon the right flank of the Prussians. In the event, Ney was unable to achieve his part of Bonaparte's strategy and thus the Allies lived to fight – and combine – another day.

If the Battle of Waterloo was, in Wellington's words, 'a close run thing', one wonders how he rated Quatre Bras. Perhaps it was even closer, for never before had Wellington been forced to fight under such difficult and ill-prepared conditions. In the event, it was the great tenacity on the part of all of his troops, particularly Picton's division, which held the centre of Wellington's position in the face of tremendous pressure and which won the day. But we should not forget the wisdom and bravery shown by Prince Bernhard and Perponcher in ignoring Wellington's order to march west, even before the battle had begun, a decision which proved to be of vital importance. The part played by the Dutch, Belgian and Brunswick troops was also crucial, to which the casualties they suffered testified. But this is not their story. To end this particular chapter, we can do little better than quote the words of Jac Weller, whose own study of Wellington and Waterloo is one of the best to appear in recent years. 'If Waterloo had not occurred forty-eight hours later,' he wrote, 'Quatre Bras would be remembered as one of the great days of the British Army.'[33]

1 Maj.Gen. CW Robinson, *Wellington's Campaigns 1808–1815* (London, 1906), III. p.509.

2 Sir John Fortescue, *History of the British Army* (London, 1920), X. p.290.

3 Sir Herbert Maxwell, *The Life of Wellington; the Restoration of Martial Britain* (London, 1899), II. pp.19–20.

4 Philip Henry, Earl Stanhope, *Notes of Conversations with the Duke of Wellington* (London, 1888), p.109.

5 Capt. John Kincaid, *Adventures in the Rifle Brigade* (London, 1830), pp.315–6.

6 Capt. HW Powell, quoted in *Waterloo Letters*, edited by Maj.Gen. HT Siborne (London, 1891), pp.250–1.

7 James Anton, *Retrospect of a Military Life* (Edinburgh, 1841), pp.191–2.

8 Lt.Col. F Calvert, quoted in *Waterloo Letters*, pp.353–4.

9 Sgt. Alexander McEween, quoted in *Waterloo Letters*, p.377.

10 Anton, *Retrospect*, pp.192–3.

11 Sgt. John Douglas, *Douglas's Tale of the Peninsula and Waterloo*, edited by Stanley Monick (London, 1997), p.98.

12 Prince Bernhard of Saxe Weimar, in J Booth (*A Near Observer*), *The Battle of Waterloo* (London, 1815), p.lxxv.

13 Maj. R Winchester, quoted in *Waterloo Letters*, p.386.

14 Lt.Col. C Gardyne, *The Life of a Regiment* (Edinburgh, 1929), p.354.

15 Maj. R Winchester, quoted in *Waterloo Letters*, pp.386–7.

16 Lt. A Riddock, quoted in *Waterloo Letters*, p.381.

17 Lt. F Hope Pattison, quoted in *Waterloo Letters*, p.334.

18 The exact formation of Halkett's battalions has eluded even the best historians, Fortescue included. I do not intend to speculate but merely state which side of the road the battalions were on.

19 Lt.Gen. Sir Colin Halkett, quoted in *Waterloo Letters*, p.322.

20 Capt. B Pigot, quoted in *Waterloo Letters*, pp.337–8. Pigot calls Lindsay a major, but he appears on the roll as a captain.

21 The position of the 69th has often been open to debate. The fact that the survivors ran to the 42nd and 44th indicates that the battalion was almost certainly attacked whilst to the east of the Brussels road.

22 Thomas Morris, *The Napoleonic Wars*, edited by John Selby (London, 1967), p.68.

23 Lt. Frederick Hope Pattison, *Personal Recollections of the Waterloo Campaign*, edited by Bob Elmer (London, 1997), pp.6–7.

24 Ibid. pp.8–9.

25 Morris, *The Napoleonic Wars*, pp.68–9.

26 Both Weller and Fortescue have this particular episode much later in the day. I prefer to follow Siborne here, supported by the evidence of David Robertson of the 92nd, an eye-witness.

27 Lt. James Hope, *Letters from Portugal, Spain and France, during the memorable campaigns of 1811, 1812, & 1813, and from Belgium and France in the year 1815* (Edinburgh, 1819) pp.230–2.

28 Gardyne, *Life of a Regiment*, p.355.

29 Ian Fletcher, *Gentlemen's Sons: The Foot Guards in the Peninsula and at Waterloo* (Speldhurst, 1992), p.197.

30 Matthew Clay, *A Narrative of the Battles of Quatre Bras and Waterloo, with the Defence of Hougoumont* (Bedford n.d.), pp.2–3.

31 Ibid. pp.3–4.

32 Siborne mistakenly cites Chambers' regiment as being the 36th, which took no part in the Waterloo Campaign. Chambers was killed two days later at Waterloo.

33 Jac Weller, *Wellington at Waterloo* (London, 1967), p.70.

Chapter VI
THE PRETTIEST FIELD DAY
The Retreat from Quatre Bras

We were received by the Duke of Wellington upon entering the position of Waterloo, having effected the retreat with very trifling loss. Thus ended the prettiest Field Day of Cavalry and Horse Artillery that I ever witnessed.

The Marquis of Anglesey (Lord Uxbridge at Waterloo) writing to Siborne in 1842

A battlefield is not a pleasant sight once the fighting has ended, and when night cast its shadow over Quatre Bras on 16 June it hid many a horrific sight. Although the numbers involved at Quatre Bras were not particularly great, especially when compared to Ligny, for example, the battlefield itself was a relatively small one and the casualties were concentrated in small areas. James Anton, of the 42nd, wrote:

> The night passed off in silence: no fires were lit; every man lay down in rear of his arms, and silence was enjoined for the night. Round us lay the dying and the dead, the latter not yet interred, and many of the former, wishing to breathe their last where they fell, slept to death with their heads on the same pillow on which those who had to toil through the future fortunes of the field reposed.[1]

The low murmur of the living and the moaning of hundreds of wounded and dying men was only interrupted during the night by the belated arrival of the British cavalry. Lord Uxbridge's cavalry had covered a great distance during the day but, despite their efforts to reach the battlefield, they arrived too late to share in the day's fighting. They would, however, have their turn the following day. Wellington himself remained with his men at Quatre Bras for news of events farther east, where the sounds of battle had remained audible even after the fighting at Quatre Bras had died down. He was naturally concerned about the lack of information coming from his allies, but he need not have worried. Blücher's crucial decision to retreat towards Wavre and not Namur meant that, all being well, he would be in a position to march and join Wellington in a day or two, which as we know was exactly

what happened. True, it meant that Wellington would have to retreat himself on 17 June, but at least he could do it in the knowledge that the Prussians were retreating parallel to him. It also meant that Bonaparte had failed to separate the two Allied armies. It would now depend upon whether the Prussians would be able to join Wellington in the next few days. Nevertheless, it was a somewhat anxious Wellington who rode back to Genappe, a few miles north of Quatre Bras, where he spent a comfortable night at the inn called the Roi d'Espagne.

Many a wounded man died during the night as a result of not being able to receive treatment. Indeed, with the onset of darkness there was little the living could do but to see to themselves. Surgeons managed to work by candlelight in the houses around Quatre Bras, working on those lucky enough to have been brought in during the hours of daylight, but for many help would come too late. Down at the house of La Bergerie, the 92nd Highlanders stood down after their efforts to take the place at the close of the battle. Lieutenant James Hope wrote:

> About 10 o'clock, the piper of the 92nd took post behind the garden hedge in front of the village, and, tuning his bag-pipes, attempted to collect the sad remains of his regiment. Long and loud blew Cameron; and although the hills and the valleys echoed the hoarse murmurs of his favourite instrument, his utmost efforts could not produce above one-half of those whom his music had cheered in the morning, on their march to the field of battle. Alas! Many of them had taken a final leave of this bustling world. Numbers of them were lying in the fields, and in the woods, and not a few of them in the farmyard of Quatre Bras, weltering in their blood. The yard, I have been assured by a

surgeon, who dressed a number of the wounded, at one time contained upwards of 1000 soldiers of the 3rd and 5th Divisions. The ground, inside of the yard, was literally dyed with blood, and the walls very much stained. In short, the interior of that place presented to the eye a scene of unparalleled horror. From the garden, the 92nd regiment retired behind the houses of Quatre Bras, and then bivouacked.[2]

Whilst many men sank into a deep sleep others found it impossible to rest. Thomas Morris, of the 73rd, was one of many who awoke in the night to relive the events of the day:

I was awakened about midnight, and was sitting meditating on the occurrences of the past day, and thinking of the poor fellows we had lost, and wondering whose turn it would be on the morrow. The corn, which had covered the field in the day-time, was now all trodden down, and we had an uninterrupted view across the plain; and such a scene by moonlight, was grand but awful![3]

The Foot Guards spent the night in the open close to the edge of the Bois de Bossu. Matthew Clay, of the 3rd Foot Guards, found it almost impossible to sleep:

We were extended in line and lay down on our arms amongst the trampled corn. All being quiet, and diligently watching during the night, the only sounds we heard arose from the suffering wounded (in their different languages) who lay as they had fallen, some in the adjoining wood, others distant, and others nearer to us. In different parts of the plain or cornfield where we were posted, the deep and heavy groans of the more faint and expiring [mixed] with the loud calls for water from others less exhausted, whilst many hundreds of slain lay on every side, and a very formidable and watchful enemy before us.[4]

Those on duty had no choice but to remain awake, of course. Ensign Charles Short, of the Coldstream Guards, was on picquet duty during the night, close to the Bois de Bossu:

The night passed off rather well, though the groaning of the wounded was rather disagreeable or so, for the first time. I was very hungry the next morning, having had nothing to eat since ten o'clock the day before, but a ship biscuit. I was called in about four o'clock. I then went to sleep and awoke about half past five, when I found Whitaker had sent me some bread and meat and a bottle of brandy, which I assure you was a great comfort, not being able to draw rations.[5]

By now the British cavalry had arrived, the regiments coming in after the last shots had been fired on 16 June. They must have been particularly galled at not having arrived in time to take part in the action. Hence, their outlook on the day was somewhat different to those who had endured the day's hard fighting. Curiosity was the order of the day among some British officers. Colonel Frederick Ponsonby, of the 12th Light Dragoons, had served with great distinction in the Peninsula. He had been with the 23rd Light Dragoons when they met with their infamous mishap at Talavera. He subsequently joined the

In order to prevent congestion on the main Brussels road, part of Alten's division marched from Quatre Bras along this track that runs north parallel to the main road.

12th, with which he enjoyed many successes. He had fought chasseurs, dragoons and hussars, but had yet to face carabiniers or the more famous cuirassiers, and here at Quatre Bras he found the answer to a question that had evidently puzzled him for some time. Captain William Hay was with him as he wandered over the corpse-strewn battlefield on the night of 16 June:

> I was rendered speechless with wonder, when the voice of Colonel Ponsonby called me to my senses by telling me to look at a cuirass he had taken from one of the dead bodies – it was perforated with three balls. He said; 'I wanted to find out if these cuirasses were ball proof or not, this plainly shows they are not.' On looking closely I pointed out several others with one or two balls through them.[6]

Wellington rose well before daylight on 17 June, as was his habit, and was soon riding back to the scene of the previous day's fight. Earlier, he had sent Alexander Gordon along with a troop of 10th Hussars to Ligny to find out what had happened there, as earlier patrols to Sombreffe, where Blücher had mustered on the 16th, had discovered nothing but French troops. The Prussians were nowhere to be found.

The day dawned cold, grey and misty, and Wellington dismounted by a group of 92nd Highlanders who were standing around close to the farm of Quatre Bras. James Hope was with them, and he later penned a beautiful description of the drama that unfolded in a makeshift hut made from the branches of a tree:

> The morning being cold, and rather inclined to rain, his Grace, on alighting, came up to some of our men, and said, 'Ninety-second, I will be obliged to you for a little fire.' The request had no sooner been made, than every man flew to the village, to procure the necessary materials. In a very short time they returned, lighted the fire opposite to the door of a small hut, constructed of boughs of trees, which they repaired in the best manner they could. For their attention, particularly the latter part of it, his Grace expressed himself truly grateful. In this splendid mansion, the Field Marshal received the Prince of Orange, Lord Hill, and a great many officers of other rank; in that hut, he received the melancholy tidings from Prince Blücher, communicating the disasters that had befallen his army at Ligny, and in that place, he arranged the order of retreat to the famed position at Waterloo.[7]

Another view of the lane along which part of Alten's division retreated from Quatre Bras. This sunken lane runs down to Bassy-Ways, half a mile east of Genappe.

Captain George Bowles, of the Coldstream Guards, was also at Quatre Bras on that momentous morning. Bowles had been present at the Duchess of Richmond's ball before he departed to join his regiment for the march to Quatre Bras. Like many others, therefore, he must have felt pretty exhausted after the events of the previous eighteen hours. As he stood by the crossroads, Wellington, who knew Bowles personally, came over to talk with him. According to Bowles, the conversation lasted about an hour, and the Duke expressed great surprise at not having heard anything from Blücher. At length, a staff officer galloped up, 'his horse covered with foam', and whispered a few words to Wellington who promptly dismissed him. 'He then turned round to me,' said Bowles, and said, 'Old Blücher has had a damned good licking and gone back to Wavre, eighteen miles. As he has gone back we must go too. I suppose in England they will say we have been licked. I can't help it, as they are gone back we must go too.'[8]

The decision by Blücher to move on Wavre, rather than Namur, was one of the most crucial decisions of the campaign, for it would allow Blücher and Wellington to reunite on 18 June at Waterloo to drive the final nail in Bonaparte's coffin. But the decision had not been an easy one, for there were those on Blücher's own staff who advocated a withdrawal to the east. Gneisenau was particularly strong in his views, and trusted Wellington not one jot. Fortunately, Blücher was a man of greater honour and so his bruised and battered army began the retreat towards Wavre.

It took Wellington and his staff some time to even find Wavre on the map. When they saw where it was they expressed some shock that Blücher had been forced to retreat so great a distance. There were even suggestions that Blücher had purposely hidden the magnitude of the defeat that had befallen them in order to keep Wellington at Quatre Bras to cover their own retreat. But once the picture became clear, Wellington simply focused on the task ahead of him. 'Nothing whatever escaped him,' wrote Hope, and here, in his miserable hut, he was his usual self, a picture of concentration as he scanned the map laid out before him.

We have already noted, in an earlier chapter, how during the previous year Wellington had ridden south from Brussels in the company of two Royal Engineer officers, and how he made copious notes on suitable defensive positions along the way. Waterloo was one of them. Now, nine months later, he was to reap the benefits of his reconnaissance. The position – actually Mont St Jean – lay astride the Brussels road at its intersection with the Nivelles road, thus blocking the French advance upon Brussels. But more important, it lay just seven miles from Wavre. If Blücher could manage to send just a single corps across to Waterloo, then Wellington would stand and fight. It was, realistically, a calculated risk, expecting the Prussians to recover in time to march and fight again at Waterloo. In the event, they would fight two battles on 18 June, at Wavre and at Waterloo itself. It says much for Wellington's faith in the abilities of his old Prussian friend that he was prepared to stand and fight, but he almost certainly had greater belief in his own abilities as a soldier. After all, he had defeated all of the much-vaunted French marshals whom Bonaparte had sent against him in the Peninsula. Jourdan, Kellerman, Masséna, Marmont, Victor, Mortier, Soult, Victor and Ney had all tried their luck against Wellington but none had succeeded. Bonaparte represented the ultimate test of his prowess but, in the event, the French Emperor fared no better than his lieutenants.

At around 9am a Prussian officer reined in at Quatre Bras to confirm Blücher's intention to march towards Wavre. It was at this point that Wellington in turn communicated to the Prussian officer his own intention of standing at Mont St Jean, provided he could count upon the assistance of at least one Prussian corps. And with that, the officer galloped off to inform Blücher. In the meantime, Wellington had given orders for his men to cook their breakfasts, for apart from a popping of muskets at the piquets there were no signs of enemy activity. If all went to plan, Wellington hoped to get his army away in good time before the French were ready to move.

By now the majority of Wellington's men had stirred from what sleep they had managed to get during the night. Whilst many saw to their breakfast, others, particularly those who had not taken part in the battle the previous day, wandered off to look over the battlefield. James Gibney, surgeon to the 15th Hussars, was one of them:

> Before daybreak on the 17th, we were up and in the saddle, waiting for orders in little anxiety, as the firing to our right had become louder and more continuous [this was largely the skirmishers of both sides, clearing their weapons]; but nothing came of it. The regiments stood on the ground where they had bivouacked, ready for action, and some rations were served. Seeing hour after hour pass away, and evidently neither party very willing to try their strength, I took the opportunity of riding over the field of battle, so far as circumstances would permit. It was a painful sight, and exhibited only too distinctly the horrors of war. Dead men and horses, mixed up indiscriminately, were scattered about the field. Clotted blood in small pools, and corpses besmeared with blood, their countenances even now exhibiting in what agonies many had departed. Caps, cuirasses, swords, bayonets, were strewn everywhere. Houses, fields, roads, cut up and injured by artillery; drums, waggons, and parts of uniforms lying about; whilst every house or cottage near was full of wounded and dying; and this was only the commencement of the war.[9]

The battlefield of Quatre Bras presented a strange sight on the morning of 17 June. Captain Mercer, whose horse artillery had arrived towards the end of the battle, noticed that amidst the dead and wounded men who lay about in their hundreds, other men cooked their breakfasts, laughed with each other and amused themselves, whilst others cleaned their arms or just lay about.

While his men cooked their breakfasts, Wellington issued his orders for the retreat to Waterloo. The bulk of his troops had now arrived at Quatre Bras, and the majority of these were to retreat north using the main road itself. However, in order to avoid congestion, he ordered part of Alten's 3rd Division to use a minor road, more of a track, which ran parallel to and east of the main road, running through Ways before continuing on towards Waterloo. The 2nd Division, part of the 4th Division and the 3rd Dutch-Belgian Division were to march on Waterloo from Nivelles, and the 2nd Dutch-Belgian Division from Quatre Bras. The remainder of the 4th Division were to halt at Braine-le-Comte and were to move to Hal on the morning of the 18th. Prince Frederick of Orange's corps was ordered to retreat from Enghien to Hal.

Having issued his orders for the retreat, Wellington was left to contemplate a situation that he had not expected to be in just a few days before. Only a week or so earlier he had been discussing the probability of offensive movements in co-ordination with the other coalition powers. But now, barely thirty hours after he had enjoyed himself at the Duchess of Richmond's ball, he found himself on the back foot at Quatre Bras, separated from his Prussian

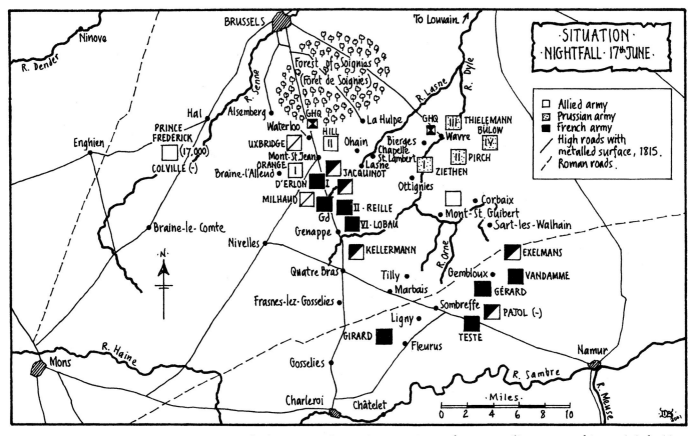

allies and with the full might of the French Army in front of him. It was certainly a situation that would have tried lesser men. But Wellington had been on the defensive for many a year in the Peninsula and this situation was nothing new to him. Nevertheless, he was deep in thought when he emerged from his hut at Quatre Bras on the cold morning of 17 June, as James Hope later recalled:

> The moment that the retreat of Blücher was made known, our spirits were as much depressed as they were elated before. A gloom stole over the countenances of all. Every soldier was more or less affected. The breast of none was more agitated than of our illustrious General. For some time after he had received the unwelcome news, his Grace remained closely shut up in the hut. Having issued the necessary orders for the retreat of the army, he came out of his airy residence, and for an hour walked alone in front of it. Now and then his meditations were interrupted by a courier with a note, who, at the moment he had delivered it, retired some distance to wait his General's will. The Field Marshal had a small switch in his right hand, the one end of which he frequently put to his mouth, apparently unconscious that he was doing so. His left hand was thrown carelessly behind his back, and he walked at the rate of three and a half to four miles in the hour. He was dressed in white pantaloons, with half

boots, a military vest, white neckcloth, blue surtout, and cocked hat.[10]

If 16 June was a great day for British infantry, the 17th was a day when the British cavalry took centre stage to demonstrate that, despite their reputation for being ill-disciplined and uncontrollable, they were more than a match for anything the French could throw at them. Indeed, it was a day of high drama, when even the heavy dragoons, including the inexperienced Scots Greys, skirmished in the best syle.

The retreat from Quatre Bras began just before 10am, when the infantry put out their fires, gathered their arms and equipment, and fell in for the march. The sun had begun to burn away the morning mist and its rays soon began to warm many a chilled bone and ease aching limbs. Despite the presence of a large French Army there were no outward signs of anxiety on the part of Wellington's men. Disengaging from an enemy was a hazardous business at the best of times but the French showed no signs of activity whatsoever. Instead, they simply lit their fires and saw to their breakfasts, seemingly oblivious to the fact that their enemies were walking away from them.

And so Wellington's men made their retreat. It was vital that they put good mileage between themselves and the French before the latter began their pursuit, which they would surely do. Hence, the retreat quickly became a kind of race, the men growing in excitement during the first hour or so. The retirement from Quatre Bras was planned and executed with precision, and while the thousands of Allied troops streamed quietly away, the French remained totally unaware that they were doing so. Wellington deployed a screen of light troops out in front of his line, with their supports behind them. Behind these troops the main bulk of the army began to slip away unseen. The 1st and 5th Divisions, the Brunswickers and the 2nd Dutch-Belgian Division made their way along the Brussels road, passing through Genappe and, crossing the Dyle by the tiny bridge in the town, continued unhindered to Waterloo. It was not until 11am when Alten's division, which had been covering the retreat, finally moved off, unnoticed by the enemy, with the bulk of the division marching via the main road. The light troops of Alten's division were the last infantry to retire, slipping to the rear at around noon, and falling back upon Christian Ompteda's KGL brigade, which then joined them. They then began marching north via the minor road to the east, which ran parallel to the main road, and which took them across the Dyle at Bassy-Ways and continued on to Waterloo.

When the last of the infantry had departed, only the cavalry and some horse artillery remained, keeping up a screen to prevent prying French eyes from observing the departing redcoats. As the last few companies sloped away from behind the crossroads, Wellington is reputed to have said, 'Well, there is the last of the infantry gone, and I don't care now.' Nor need he have done: noon had come and gone and still the French showed no inclination to pursue the retreating Allied Army. Instead, Wellington just sat himself down behind the crossroads at Quatre Bras and, with the cavalry and horse artillery watching out on either side of the road, he produced a newspaper and commenced reading it, sometimes laughing aloud as he did so. Every now and then he got up and, putting his telescope to his eye, scanned the ground to the south in anticipation of enemy movement. But still nothing stirred.

Captain Mercer's horse artillery had been standing idle to the east of the Brussels road, with the right of the battery resting on the farm of Quatre Bras. Colonel Augustus Frazer had ridden over to see Mercer and had relieved him of most of his ammunition, so as to facilitate his flight should it be necessary to retreat in a hurry.

Mercer was left with just fifty rounds per gun, which, as he later wrote, 'nearly led to very disagreeable results'. It was past 1pm when Lord Uxbridge and his aide came riding over to join him. The two cavalrymen dismounted and, along with Mercer, sat themselves down on the ground. The afternoon had grown hot and sultry, the cold morning having given way to a fine summer's day. Uxbridge took out his telescope and began scanning the French lines for signs of movement, but still nothing moved. 'It will not be long now before they are on us,' said the aide-de-camp, 'for they always dine before they move; and those smokes seem to indicate that they are cooking now.'[11] Sure enough, another aide-de-camp came galloping up and reported that a large column of cavalry was moving towards them. However, the column was initially thought to be friendly, as Mercer later recalled:

> At the same moment we saw them distinctly; and Lord Uxbridge, having reconnoitred them a moment through his glass, started up, exclaiming in a joyful tone, 'By the Lord, they are Prussians!' jumped on his horse, and, followed by the two aides, dashed off like a whirl-wind to meet them.[12]

Unfortunately, they were not Prussians but French. One can well imagine Mercer's shock as the commander of Wellington's cavalry charged off with just two aides towards the large enemy column. Fortunately, the error was realised before it was too late and Uxbridge and his two aides came galloping back as fast as their horses would carry them. Elsewhere, British hussars were galloping in from all directions with French lancers chasing after them. The French had finally stirred themselves from their inactivity. The great 'fox hunt', as Mercer put it, was about to begin.

Instructions for the retreat of the British cavalry had already been issued and it was now simply a case of implementing them, albeit somewhat hurriedly. The cavalry would retreat north using three different routes. The two brigades of heavy cavalry, the Union and Household, would retire along the main road itself, through Genappe and on to Waterloo. Dörnberg's brigade would take a more westerly route, crossing the Dyle river at Barriere, whilst Vivian and Vandeleur's British and KGL light cavalry would make a sweep out to the east, retreating along narrow lanes to Thy, east of Genappe, where they would cross the Dyle before continuing on towards Waterloo.

The cavalry brigades of Vivian and Vandeleur marched along this lane which runs north from the village of Sart D'Avelines. Both brigades were followed by French cavalry as far as Thy, where Vivian was forced to turn and fight. View looking south.

British cavalry piquets had engaged their French counterparts throughout the morning – Hugh Trainer of the 18th Hussars, for example, had killed a French lancer early on – but this was different, this time it seemed as though the entire mass of French cavalry was bearing down upon the Allied position. Captain William Tomkinson, of the 16th Light Dragoons, was amazed by the large numbers moving towards him:

I saw the French cavalry when moving out of their bivouac, and thought from their numbers we must either bring all our force to oppose them and keep our ground, or that, if a retreat was determined on, the sooner we moved the more prudent. They advanced in very large bodies, and Lord Uxbridge soon saw that so far from having any chance afforded of charging he had nothing left but to get his troops away with the least delay. They came out in column after column, and in greater force than I ever recollect seeing together at one point.[13]

Not far from Tomkinson was Captain William Hay, of the 12th Light Dragoons. His regiment was posted on the forward slope, looking out over the Quatre Bras battlefield. Hay noticed that black thunderclouds were gathering overhead, indicating a coming thunderstorm. He also noticed something rather more sinister:

At a great distance in the wood, on each side of these roads, clouds of dust began to spread over the trees. That dust appeared thicker and thicker, and dead silence pervaded our ranks. I thought even the horses were more still than usual, no champing of bits, no clattering of swords. Every eye was directed anxiously to what was passing in front.

In a moment, as if by magic, debouched from the dark green foliage, which had hitherto kept them from our sight, by the three roads, the gorgeous uniforms of the French cavalry, composed of the cuirassiers, lancers, and brass-helmeted dragoons. On they came at a gallop, those from the right-hand road forming on the plain to their left, the centre to their front, and the left to their right, until three lines fronting our own were drawn up. There were now in front of us, waiting, twenty-two thousand cavalry – double our number – and these supported by fifty guns of artillery, all ready for action.[14]

The alarm and excitement amongst the British cavalry can best be imagined. Even the most experienced Peninsular veterans had never seen such an array of French cavalry and orders were quickly given for an immediate retirement according to the pre-arranged plan. Meanwhile to the east of the Brussels road Captain Mercer prepared to give the fleeing Lord Uxbridge some cover, and after retiring across a dip in the ground behind the crest unlimbered his guns. Fortunately, the French halted and deployed the massive array as described above by William Hay. This gave Uxbridge the chance to regain his line without danger. In the meantime Mercer found himself embroiled in an ill-timed argument with Sir John Vandeleur, who appears to

It was down this lane that a squadron of the 1st Hussars KGL was forced to gallop to safety after being cut off from the rest of Vivian's brigade during the fight south of Thy on 17 June. A small bridge crosses the Dyle at the end of the lane.

have been prepared to charge the French mass. 'What are you doing here, sir?' Vandeleur demanded. 'You encumber my front, and we shall not be able to charge. Take your guns away, sir; instantly, I say – take them away!' An astonished Mercer tried to explain what he was doing, but a furious Vandeleur continued to demand the guns be removed from his front. He was just preparing to obey when Uxbridge came riding up and asked whether he was loaded, to which Mercer replied that he was. Uxbridge ordered Mercer to wait until the French cavalry had reached the top of the crest before firing into them, after which he was to retreat as quickly as possible. It was at this point that Mercer saw 'that mighty man of war' – Bonaparte. He also noticed the change in the appearance of the sky:

> Large isolated masses of thundercloud, of the deepest, almost inky black, their lower edges hard and strongly defined, lagging down, as if momentarily about to burst, hung suspended over us, involving our position and everything on it in deep and gloomy obscurity; whilst the distant hill lately occupied by the French Army lay bathed in brilliant sunshine. Lord Uxbridge was yet speaking, when a single horseman, immediately followed by several others, mounted the plateau I had left at a gallop, their dark figures thrown forward in strong relief from the illuminated distance, making them appear much nearer to us than they really were. For an instant they pulled up and regarded us, when several squadrons, coming rapidly on the plateau, Lord Uxbridge cried out, 'Fire! – fire!' and, giving them a general discharge, we quickly limbered up to retire, as they dashed forward supported by some horse artillery guns, which opened upon us ere we could complete the manoeuvre, but without much effect, for the only one touched was the servant of Major Whinyates, who was wounded in the leg by a splinter of a howitzer shell.[15]

The single horseman was Bonaparte, who personally led the pursuit for some distance. It is tempting to consider how history might have been changed had one of Mercer's shells struck him down. In the event, Mercer let loose his brief barrage before limbering up and retreating. As he did so, the heavens opened. In one of the most vivid passages in Waterloo literature, Mercer described the opening phase of his retreat and of his narrow escape south of Genappe:

> The first gun that was fired seemed to burst the clouds overhead, for its report was instantly followed by an awful clap of thunder, and lightning that almost blinded us, whilst the rain came down as if a waterspout had broken over us. The sublimity of the scene was inconceivable. Flash succeeded flash, and the peals of thunder were long and tremendous; whilst, as if in mockery of the elements, the French guns still sent forth their feebler glare and now scarcely audible reports – their cavalry dashing on at a headlong pace, adding their shouts to the uproar. We galloped for our lives through the storm, striving to gain the enclosures about the houses of the hamlets, Lord Uxbridge urging us on, crying, 'Make haste! – make haste! For God's sake, gallop, or you will be taken!' We did make haste, and succeeded in getting amongst the houses and gardens, but with the French advance close on our heels. Here, however, observing the chaussée full of hussars, they pulled up. Had they continued their charge we were gone, for these hussars were scattered about the road in the utmost confusion, some in little squads, others singly, and, moreover, so crowded together that we had no room whatever to act with any effect – either they or us.[16]

Presently, French cavalry began to surround the gardens in which Mercer found himself, at which point Lord Uxbridge called to him and told him to bring two of his guns along a narrow lane. Mercer had no idea why but obeyed anyway. The sunken lane ran for about two hundred yards out into a field. Mercer, Uxbridge and the two guns with their limbers, got to within fifty yards of the end of the lane when a large group of French chasseurs suddenly appeared there waiting for them. In his journal Mercer likened it to a dream; there he was, stuck fast with two guns in the narrow lane, accompanied by the commander-in-chief of the entire Allied cavalry! After exclaiming 'By God! We are all prisoners,' Uxbridge leapt up one of the banks, cleared it and dashed off, leaving Mercer to it. Amazingly, the French cavalry sat motionless upon their horses, probably too astonished to act. In the meantime Mercer's men unlimbered their guns and ran them slightly up the bank, allowing the limbers to reverse back past them, before limbering up once more and galloping off back to the chaussée. Here they were met by Uxbridge who had, in fact, ridden off to collect a group of British hussars with the intention of acting as rescuers. The retreat then continued.

> Heavy as the rain was and thick the weather, yet the French could not but have seen the confusion we were in, as they had closed up to the entrance

of the enclosure: and yet they did not at once take advantage of it. Things could not remain long in this state. A heavy column of cavalry approached us by the chaussée, whilst another, skirting the enclosures, appeared pushing forward to cut us off. Retreat now became imperative. The order was given, and away we went, all mixed *pêle-mêle*, going like mad, and covering each other with mud, to be washed off by the rain, which, before sufficiently heavy, now came down again as it had done at first in splashes instead of drops, soaking us anew to the skin, and, what was worse, extinguishing every slow match in the brigade. The obscurity caused by the splashing of the rain was such, that at one period I could not distinguish objects more than a few yards distant. Of course we lost sight of our pursuers altogether, and the shouts and halloos, and even laughter, they had at first sent forth were either silenced or drowned in the uproar of the elements and the noise of our too rapid retreat; for in addition to everything else the crashing and rattling of the thunder were most awful, and the glare of the lightning blinding. In this state we gained the bridge of Genappe at the moment when the thundercloud, having passed over, left us in comparative fine weather, although still raining heavily.[17]

Having reached Genappe Mercer crossed the tiny bridge in the centre of town before passing through its narrow streets which appeared deserted, 'nothing disturbing its deathlike stillness save the iron sound of horses' feet, the rumbling of the carriages, and the splashing of water as it fell from the eaves, – all this was stillness compared with the hurly-burly and din from which we had just emerged.'[18] Mercer passed through the town and emerged on the high ground to the north of the town where he found British cavalry drawn up on either side of the road. The story of Mercer's dramatic dash to avoid capture ranks as one of the finest pieces of military literature, as indeed does his entire journal. However, there were similar stories of close shaves and anxious moments during a momentous day full of incident. The British cavalry drawn up on the rising ground to the north of Genappe were the heavy cavalry brigades of Ponsonby and Somerset. A single detachment of the 11th Light Dragoons, plus the 23rd Light Dragoons, also passed through the town and formed up in front of the heavies. The 7th Hussars, meanwhile, were deployed to the south of Genappe to act as the rearguard. Once the skirmishers were drawn in the 7th would likewise retire through the town.

Genappe presented a great problem to both armies in 1815, for the main road from Brussels to Charleroi passed through it. Consequently, armies faced the problem of crossing the small bridge over the Dyle river that was situated at the southern end of the town. 22-year-old Edmund Wheatley was an ensign in the 5th Line Battalion KGL. He had seen service with his battalion during the closing stages of the Peninsular War, and on 17 June 1815 found himself in the midst of the traffic that clogged the narrow streets in Genappe.

> At Genappe [he wrote] I found sufficient employment for my whole Regiment. The town was choked up with wounded, and crowds and crowds of cavalry poured in [from Quatre Bras] each man leading his horse by the bridle with a wounded foot soldier laying across the saddle. A thought instantly suggested itself that instead of driving off the Commisarry carts of beef and liquor, I would empty them in the ditches and put the wounded in them, which my men suceeded in doing with considerable opposition. I had seized a covered wagon belonging to the train of the Duke of Brunswick and was assisting some wounded Belgians in when the Brunswick Sergeant of the escort galloped up, and had I not parried with my sword [he] would have laid my skull open. The fellow instantly perceived my wings and before I could return the compliment was out of sight.[19]

Uxbridge's retreating cavalry would need to put a good distance between themselves and the French if they were to pass through Genappe without being caught in the congestion that would inevitably occur at the bridge. Fortunately, both Ponsonby and Somerset had already passed but there were still a number of British cavalry skirmishers engaged with the enemy south of Genappe. The 7th Hussars, under Major Edward Hodge, were engaged to the south of the Dyle river , his men skirmishing in the muddy fields, holding back the French advance guard. Lieutenant Standish O'Grady, was present with them:

> We threw out the right troop to skirmish, and Major Hodge went with them. I held the high road with the left troop, and had from time to time to send them assistance, and frequently to advance to enable them to hold their ground, as their movements were difficult through ploughed fields so soft that the horses were sunk up to their knees always, and sometimes to their girths.
> Whilst I was so employed Sir William Dörnberg joined me. Thus we continued to dispute every inch of the ground until we

The Dyle river at Thy runs along the small ditch in the foreground before flowing under the road at the foot of the telephone pole. A small bridge, today scarcely noticeable, stands here. In the background, behind the trees, is the bank where the 10th Hussars dismounted and, using their Baker rifled carbines, kept the pursuing French cavalry in check, allowing Vivian's force to get away relatively unscathed.

came within a short distance of the town of Genappe. Here Sir William Dörnberg told me that he must leave me; that it was of the utmost importance to face the enemy boldly at this spot, as the bridge in the town of Genappe was so narrow we must pass it in file; that I should endeavour if possible to obtain time for the skirmishers to come in, but that I was not to compromise my Troop too much. Sir William had been riding with me some hours, and when he bid me farewell he shook my hand, and I saw plainly he never expected to see me again.

I then called in the skirmishers and advanced at a trot up the road. The troops opposed to me went about, and as I followed them they did not stop as soon as I did. I continued advancing and retiring alternately, until I saw all my right Troop safe on the road in my rear, and then I began to retire at a walk, occasionally halting and fronting until I turned the corner of the town of Genappe. I then filed the men from the left, and passed through the town at a gallop, no enemy in sight. When I arrived at the opposite entrance of the town I found the 7th drawn up on the road in a column of divisions, and having re-formed our Squadron we took our place between those already formed and the town.[20]

Despite the appalling weather Wellington's infantry made good time and put a good few miles between themselves and the oncoming French. However, Lord Uxbridge still thought it

necessary to defend the defile at Genappe and delay the French advance further. It was the perfect position for a rearguard action, for although the French were vastly superior numerically the narrow streets, not to mention the tiny bridge over the Dyle, would prevent them from deploying in strength. It was a classical example of a position that could be held by a few against the many.

Uxbridge deployed his cavalry on a low ridge about six or seven hundred yards from the northern entrance to Genappe. Somerset's Household Brigade and the artillery were placed astride the main road whilst Ponsonby's Union Brigade was positioned in a field away to their right. About three hundred yards in front of these were the 7th Hussars with the 23rd Light Dragoons in support. Thus, the exit from the town was covered in some strength.

Uxbridge and his men had sat waiting for about twenty minutes when, suddenly but not unexpectedly, loud shouts announced the approach of the French cavalry, at which point a handful of them came charging up the street, straight into Major Hodge's squadron of the 7th Hussars. They were apparently drunk and were duly taken prisoner. Not long afterwards, the main French force appeared, lancers leading the way. The column halted at the exit of the town facing the British light cavalry who sat motionless two hundred yards from them. Fifteen minutes

A 'fox hunt' was how Captain Cavalié Mercer described the retreat from Quatre Bras. It was certainly a close call with the French pursuers snapping away at the heels of the British rearguard until the latter reached the safety of the ridge at Mont St Jean. Here, Bonaparte himself is seen at the head of the chasing pack.

passed before they showed any signs of advancing, but during this time thousands more French came across the Dyle to cause a massive jam in the town. Apparently, those at the rear continued to cross into the town unaware that those at the head of the column had halted. Thus, the front of the French column was fixed in position, with nowhere to go but up the hill against the waiting British hussars. Standish O'Grady described what happened next:

> In this state of affairs Lord Anglesey [Uxbridge] gave us orders to charge them, which we immediately did. Of course, our charge could make no impression, but we continued cutting at them, and we did not give ground, nor did they move. Their commanding Officer was cut down, and so was ours (Major Hodge), and this state of things lasted some minutes, when they brought down some Light Artillery, which struck the rear of the right (the charging) Squadron and knocked over some men and horses, impeding the road in our rear. We then received orders to go about from Lord Anglesey, who was up with us, but not on the road during all this time. The lancers then advanced upon us, and in the mêlée which ensued they lost quite as many as we did, and when at last we were able to disengage ourselves they did not attempt to pursue us.[21]

The fight 'see-sawed' back and forth for some minutes but, unable to make any real impression on the lancers, the 7th Hussars drew back, passing through the 23rd Light Dragoons who had been drawn up behind them. It is difficult to see what the hussars, with their much shorter reach, could have done in the circumstances. The French lances were nine feet long, and it was impossible for the sabre-wielding hussars to close with them with any great effect. Nevertheless, the lancers were hampered by the fact that they were jammed in between the buildings of the town and had nowhere to go. A similar situation had occurred at Usagre, in May 1811, when Lumley's cavalry had trapped a French cavalry force against a narrow bridge on the outskirts of the town. Their escape was blocked when one of the supporting French regiments came up and the British heavy dragoons went about their deadly work with relish, cutting and hewing and inflicting a severe reverse on their adversaries. The difference at Genappe was that the French were armed with lances, which gave them a marked advantage, and despite the bravest of efforts by men like Edward Hodge, who was cut down, and Captain Elphinstone, who was wounded and captured, the 7th Hussars were forced to withdraw.

With the 7th Hussars forced back, Uxbridge rode to the 23rd Light Dragoons and ordered them to prepare to charge. His address evidently did not go down too well with the regiment, who showed a marked lack of resolve, as Uxbridge himself later recalled:

> My address to these Light Dragoons not having been received with all the enthusiasm that I expected, I ordered them to clear the chaussée, and said, 'The Life Guards shall have this honour,' and instantly sending for them, two squadrons of the 1st Regiment, gallantly led by Major Kelly, came on with *right good will*, and I sent them in to finish the lancers. They at once overthrew them, and pursued into the town, where they punished them severely.[22]

Captain William Siborne, in his history of the campaign, records that the lancers had 'abandoned the secure cover to which they had been indebted for their temporary success', and had begun to advance up the road when they were hit by the charge of Kelly's Life Guards. It is certainly the only way to explain the success of the British cavalry against the lancers, for had the latter remained where they were, with their flanks protected, it is difficult to see how the Life Guards could have succeeded. But succeed they did. One eye-witness wrote that the Life Guards scattered the French lancers in all directions, at which they continued driving them back into the streets of Genappe, inflicting great damage upon them. Once the French lancers had turned their backs to the Life Guards they were at their mercy, and some accounts mention the Life Guards driving the French completely out of the town, although this must be considered doubtful given the large number of French cavalry present at Genappe. Uxbridge himself said that the affair ended 'at the gates of Genappe', although it is not clear whether he meant the southern or northern entrance to the place.

The charge had the desired effect of checking the pursuit and from here on the retreat along the main Brussels road continued at a slow, unhurried pace. The French had been given a bloody nose, and in the appalling weather conditions evidently showed a marked lack of enthusiasm for the pursuit. They continued to follow behind Uxbridge, and even skirmished, but nothing serious occurred on the main Brussels road between Genappe and Waterloo. As Uxbridge himself later wrote:

> Having thus checked the ardour of the enemy's advanced guard, the retreat was continued at a slow pace, and with the most perfect regularity. Assuredly this *coup de collier* had the very best effect, for although there was much cannonading, and a constant appearance of a disposition to charge, they continued at a respectful distance.[23]

The French pursuit was not totally thwarted, however. Indeed, for the next few miles the British heavy cavalry demonstrated that the art of skirmishing was not the exclusive domain of light cavalry. The British cavalry frequently draw criticism for their wild behaviour and for their inexperience, particularly the Scots Greys and Inniskillings, but here, on the muddy slopes above Genappe, and indeed, for the next few miles or so, they skirmished in the finest style, frustrating all attempts by the French to pass round their flanks and cut them off. 'The Royals, Inniskillings and Greys,' wrote Uxbridge,

> manoeuvred beautifully, retiring by alternate squadrons, and skirmished in the very best style; but finding that all the efforts of the enemy to get upon their right flank were vain, and that by manoeuvring upon the plain, which was amazingly deep and heavy from the violent storm of rain, it only uselessly exhausted the horses. I drew these regiments in upon the chaussée in one column, the guns falling back from position to position, and from these batteries, checking the advance of the enemy.
>
> We were received by the Duke of Wellington upon entering the position of Waterloo, having effected the retreat with very trifling loss.
>
> Thus ended the prettiest Field Day of Cavalry and Horse Artillery that I ever witnessed.[24]

Although the threat from the French cavalry had momentarily receded, the British cavalry still remained under fire from French artillery, the enemy having managed to get some guns into the meadow close to the bridge from where they shelled the British lines. It was with no little effort that Mercer heaved his own guns into a field opposite in order to return the fire, although ammunition was in short supply, Alexander Frazer having relieved the troop of much of it at Quatre Bras earlier that morning. Fortunately, along came Major MacDonald with some of the notorious Rocket Troop in tow. The Congreve rocket was a peculiar weapon and was prone to inflict as much damage on those who fired it as on the intended target. It was scorned by many, including Wellington himself, who ordered Captain Edward Whinyates to rid

Columns of British infantry and cavalry disappear into the distance as Wellington salutes from the roadside during the retreat to Mont St Jean on 17 June. The initial lethargy on the part of the French, coupled with atrocious weather during the afternoon, conspired to make Wellington's retreat much easier than it might have been had the French showed more energy during the morning.

himself of his rockets and get some guns instead. 'It will break poor Whinyates' heart,' interjected Sir George Wood, commanding the artillery at Waterloo, to which Wellington characteristically replied, 'Damn his heart! Let my order be obeyed.' Despite their reputation, rockets had been used to some effect in the Peninsula, particularly at the crossing of the Adour, on 14 February 1814. When the French tried to interfere with the crossing a couple of rockets were sent fizzing into their midst to send them fleeing in panic. The rocketeers were as surprised as they were delighted.

Here, at Quatre Bras, they prepared for action, setting up a triangular frame in the road upon which the rockets with their long sticks were placed. The first of these giant fireworks was then set off and with a mighty whoosh it went flying off down the road towards the French guns, a line of thick grey smoke trailing behind. The rocket recorded a direct hit on one of the French guns, the crew falling dead and wounded all around, whilst the crews of the other guns fled in terror at this astonishing result. More rockets were launched, and the sky was filled with spluttering, fizzing missiles, but none of them achieved the same results. Indeed, Mercer recorded that one of the rockets came whizzing back towards the British line. The French gunners soon saw that there was little to fear from these unpredictable

weapons and returned to their pieces to resume firing on the British rearguard. At length, Mercer, along with Uxbridge's cavalry, retired from above Genappe and continued their retreat towards Waterloo, the French never pressing them too closely.

Whilst the main column of the British cavalry was retreating along the road to Brussels, the brigades of Vivian and Vandeleur experienced a similar close call just south of Thy, a small hamlet on the Dyle river, east of Genappe. Vivian's brigade consisted of the 10th and 18th Hussars, and the 1st Hussars KGL, whilst Vandeleur had with him the 11th, 12th and 16th Light Dragoons and the 2nd Hussars KGL. The latter brigade was a formidable force with years of experience, whilst even the British hussars of Vivian's brigade, which had only seen service at the beginning and end of the Peninsular War, could still boast a fine record. The two light cavalry brigades held the left flank of Wellington's position at Quatre Bras during the morning of 17 June, before they began to retreat north through the village of Sart Dame Avelines.

Earlier in the morning Vivian had sent off Lieutenant William Swabey, of the Royal Horse Artillery, to reconnoitre the passages of the Dyle river. The main road, being used by the bulk of Wellington's army, was out of the question, as was the road immediately to the east of it, which Alten's 3rd Division was using. However, there remained a third route, which ran from Sart Dame Avelines to Bassy-Thy and on to Thy itself, where a small stone bridge crossed the river. The Dyle here is no more than a stream but to cavalry and, more importantly, artillery, even the smallest stream can represent quite an obstacle. With the infantry having got off, and with the other cavalry brigades having set off along the main road, the two light cavalry brigades duly began to retire, skirmishing all the while with enemy cavalry as they went.

The hussars and light dragoons passed along cobbled lanes from where they could see other British and Allied troops retreating away to the west, whilst above them the skies grew ever darker. When Vandeleur's brigade passed through Bassy-Thy, it turned and took up a position on a plateau, with the valley of the river Dyle in their rear, whilst Dyneley's horse artillery careered down the narrow lane to the bridge. Meanwhile Vivian's brigade came on, skirmishing with the enemy and coming under fire from their horse artillery. As he passed through Bassy-Thy, Vivian saw Vandeleur's brigade drawn up about six hundred yards away and expected it to remain there whilst his own brigade passed through it. Thus, Vandeleur would then become the rearguard. However, it

did not work out as he intended, for no sooner had Vivian got to within fifty yards of Vandeleur, than the latter turned his brigade around and off it went, galloping down the narrow road to the bridge at Thy, leaving Vivian to stand and continue as rearguard. Meanwhile French shells continued to fall and explode amongst the British and German hussars, whilst the skirmishing continued. Presently, Lieutenant Colonel Thornhill, Uxbridge's aide, came galloping up to ask Vivian how things were.

> I told him that I had enough upon my hands, but that I hoped to get my people all well off, and I sent an ADC to Sir J. Vandeleur to desire he would as fast as possible get his brigade over the bridge, in order that I might have no interruption in my retreat in case I was hard pressed.
>
> About this time the most tremendous storm I ever witnessed came on, and in a very short time rendering the ground so deep that the horses had some difficulty in moving through it. To this I am persuaded I am in a very great degree indebted for the little loss I experienced in the retreat to the bridge. The enemy began to relax in their preparations for enveloping me, which considerable bodies assembling on my left appeared preparing to do; those in my front were contented with simply skirmishing.[25]

Wellington salutes his men during the retreat from Quatre Bras. The officer on the right is still wearing his silk stockings and dancing pumps, his field uniform having been packed away in the baggage train, stuck somewhere in the rear.

In this painting by Ernest Crofts, Wellington and some of his staff are halted beneath a tree as Highlanders and horse artillery make their way north to Waterloo after having retreated from Quatre Bras.

downpour was having on the fight, Vivian ordered the 10th and 18th Hussars to fall back to the bridge, whilst he remained behind with the 1st Hussars KGL.

The 10th and 18th Hussars duly turned and, leaving their German comrades to act as rearguard, they galloped for the bridge. Presently Vivian ordered the KGL hussars to follow, but no sooner had they turned than the French darted forward, cutting off the squadron at the extreme left-hand end of the line. This squadron had been fighting about a quarter of a mile from the road and had no realistic chance of reaching it, with large numbers of French cavalry charging across their front. Fortunately, a sunken lane was discovered which led down to a second small bridge, about three hundred yards from the first, and so the hussars galloped down this lane before crossing the bridge to safety. The French then charged towards the first bridge, cheering, and took a wounded sergeant prisoner, but when they arrived at the bridge they came under heavy fire from the some of the 10th Hussars who had dismounted and were lining a bank which overlooked it. The hussars were armed with Baker rifled carbines, an accurate weapon even in the hands of the cavalry, and the concentrated fire brought down against the bridge stopped the enemy cavalry in their tracks. 'From that moment,' wrote Vivian, 'no attempt was made to molest us.' It is not clear whether any French cavalry followed the single squadron of the KGL hussars across the second bridge but even if they did it appears that they too made no effort to attack Vivian further.

With the north bank of the Dyle having been gained, both Vivian and Vandeleur continued their retreat, passing to the east of Mont St Jean and arriving at the hamlet of Verde Cocou, where they bivouacked for the night.

By the evening of 17 June Wellington's army had arrived at the position astride the Brussels road at Mont St Jean. It had been a terrible and fatiguing day for all concerned. The infantry were exhausted after their march, the more so since the majority of them had marched many miles on 16 June to reach Quatre Bras. The weather had not helped matters either, beginning extremely cold, turning hot and sultry and ending in a storm which was likened to a tropical rainstorm. The only positive aspect of the conditions, at least from the Allied point of view, was that the weather helped hinder the French pursuit. It had been a close call for Wellington, and it was just as well that the French failed to stir until his infantry had put many a good mile between them and the enemy. Otherwise, the retreat might well have ended in very different circumstances.

The rain did indeed have a great impact on the fight at Thy, as it did at various other places during the retreat. Whilst Vivian's men skirmished with the French, the skies opened to unleash torrents of rain that not only made the ground very difficult, but rendered carbines ineffective, the priming pans of flintlock weapons being far from waterproof. Blue-jacketed hussars resorted to cutting and slashing at their enemies whenever they closed, whilst others tried to work their carbines. The British and KGL hussars were holding their own, but only just, and as the French grew in numbers the situation facing Vivian grew desperate. He knew that just a single bridge lay behind him, and he knew it was a narrow one, and crossing it with the enemy so close behind would be difficult. He must have prayed that Vandeleur had got his own men across and that the bridge would be free of traffic. The rain certainly dampened the ardour of the French, and having seen the effect that the

Amongst the last Allied troops to drag themselves up on to the ridge at Mont St Jean were Mercer's troop of the Royal Horse Artillery. Mercer, it will be remembered, had endured several narrow escapes during the day, and had only just managed to elude capture. After having passed through Genappe, Mercer continued along the main Brussels road, driving his gun teams on through the appalling weather as day began to give way to evening. He inevitably caught up with some of the infantry who had begun to straggle, including some Brunswick infantry who had thrown away much of their equipment in their haste to make good their retreat. Eventually he halted on a good position on the northern side of a valley, where a large gravel pit lay gaping by the roadside, with a long hedge behind it. He unlimbered his guns and turned them around to fire once more on the French who had begun to appear on the heights to the south. By now the Allied cavalry regiments had begun to arrive also, driving the last of the infantry along the road before them. When they were clear of his guns Mercer ordered his men to open fire at a range of about twelve hundred yards, his guns hurling large iron balls across the valley at the French troops massing opposite.

The echo of our first gun had not ceased [he wrote] when to my astonishment, a heavy cannonade, commencing in a most startling manner from behind our hedge, rolled along the rising ground, on part of which we were posted. The truth now flashed on me; we had rejoined the army, and it is impossible to describe the pleasing sense of security I felt at having now the support of something more staunch than cavalry.[26]

It was true. Without realising it, Mercer had caught up with Wellington's army which had halted astride the Brussels road just south of the farm of Mont St Jean. The gravel pit, as he called it, was the sandpit where, the following day, the 95th Rifles would fight, whilst the hedge in front of which he had stopped would prove to be the high tide of the great French infantry attack to the east of the main road.

A few more rounds followed, during an exchange of artillery fire, but at such extreme range casualties were few. At length the firing died down and with the onset of darkness the soldiers destined to fight on the morrow settled down amidst more heavy rain. For the survivors it would be the most momentous night of their lives – and almost certainly one of the most miserable. But for thousands more, the night of 17 June 1815 would be their last.

1 James Anton, *Retrospect of a Military Life* (Edinburgh, 1841), p.201.

2 Lt. James Hope, *Letters from Portugal, Spain and France, during the memorable campaigns of 1811, 1812, & 1813, and from Belgium and France in the year 1815* (Edinburgh, 1819), pp.235–6.

3 Thomas Morris, *The Napoleonic Wars*, edited by John Selby (London, 1967), p.71.

4 Matthew Clay, *A Narrative of the Battles of Quatre Bras and Waterloo, with the Defence of Hougoumont* (Bedford n.d.), p.5.

5 Ensign Charles Short, NAM (GS 202).

6 Capt. William Hay, *Reminiscences 1808–1815 under Wellington*, edited by Mrs SCI Wood (London, 1901), p.165.

7 Hope, *Letters*, pp.236–7.

8 Captain George Bowles, *A Series of Letters to the First Earl of Malmesbury, his family and friends, from 1745 to 1820*, edited by his grandson, the Earl of Malmesbury (London, 1870), II, p.447.

9 Dr Thomas Gibney, *Eighty Years Ago, or the Recollections of an old Army Doctor*, edited by his son, RD Gibney (London, 1896), pp.180–1.

10 Hope, *Letters*, pp.237–8.

11 Capt. Cavalié Mercer, *Journal of the Waterloo Campaign*, edited by Sir John Fortescue (London, 1927), p.146.

12 Ibid. p.146.

13 Lt.Col. William Tomkinson, *The Diary of a Cavalry Officer in the Peninsular War and Waterloo Campaign 1809–1815*, edited by James Tomkinson (London, 1894), p.284.

14 Hay, *Reminiscences*, pp.168–9.

15 Mercer, *Journal*, pp.147–8.

16 Ibid. p.148.

17 Ibid. p.150.

18 Ibid. p.151.

19 Edmund Wheatley, *The Wheatley Diary*, edited by Christopher Hibbert (London, 1964), pp.60–1.

20 Lt.Col. S O'Grady, quoted in *Waterloo Letters*, edited by Maj.Gen. HT Siborne (London, 1891), pp.132–3.

21 Ibid. p.134.

22 Lt.Gen. the Earl of Uxbridge, quoted in *Waterloo Letters*, p.6.

23 Ibid. p.7.

24 Ibid. p.7.

25 Maj.Gen. Sir Hussey Vivian, quoted in *Waterloo Letters*, p.156.

26 Mercer, *Journal*, p.155.

Chapter VII
THE EVE OF WATERLOO

'What would such as you have done in the Pyrenees?'
'Oho, my boy! This is but child's play to what we saw in Spain.'

Peninsular veterans to the Johnny Newcomes, on the wet and stormy eve of Waterloo

The night of 17–18 June 1815 was as dark, stormy and wet as any veteran of the Peninsular War could remember. There had been dramatic thunderstorms before. Indeed, the eve of Salamanca, on 21 July 1812, was marked by a tremendous thunderstorm, with bolts of lightning that sent frightened horses stampeding in all directions. And when Wellington arrived at Sorauren on 27 July 1813, his men greeted him with shouts of 'Douro! Douro!', before he set himself down in his cloak on the open hillside whilst the heavens thundered and roared above him. There were numerous occasions, in fact, when Wellington's men had spent the night before a battle huddling under their blankets or in miserable hovels, waiting for the rain to stop. Six years of fighting the French had taught them many things, one of which was that if there was a storm on the eve of a battle then Wellington would emerge as victor. Waterloo was to be no different. The unceasing rain, the roar of thunder and the flashes of lightning were truly miserable, but for the veterans of Spain and Portugal they were an omen of victory. William Wheeler, of the 51st, wrote:

Night came on, we were wet to the skin, but having plenty of liquor we were to use an expression of one of my old comrades 'wet and comfortable'. The bad weather continued the whole of the night, we had often experienced such weather in the Peninsula on the eve of a battle, for instance the nights before the battles of Fuentes d'Onor, Salamanca and Vittoria were attended with thunder and lightning. It was always a prelude to victory.[1]

Wellington's headquarters at Waterloo. Frantic and dramatic scenes ensued throughout the night of 17 June and morning of the following day as aides sought to discover Blücher's whereabouts and plans for the day. Wellington's headquarters were in the building on the left. On the right stands the church of St Joseph's, where many wounded British soldiers were brought after the battle.

Men of the 6th (Inniskilling) Dragoons gather round a cooking pot on the eve of Waterloo. The regiment had not been present in the Peninsula but, like other 'Johnny Newcome' regiments, would distinguish themselves at Waterloo on 18 June.

The omens may have been good for Wellington's men, but this was small comfort to them as they tried to light fires, stay dry or simply find somewhere to sleep or something to eat. Nevertheless, many of them welcomed the chance to sleep. After all, they had marched many miles on 16 June, had fought a battle the same day, and had marched back to Mont St Jean on 17 June during the retreat. After such an exhausting ordeal many found it easy to sleep. Augustus Frazer, of the Royal Horse Artillery, woke refreshed on the morning of 18 June as a result of a few hours of sleep. But thousands more were not so lucky. Surgeon Haddy James, of the Life Guards, was one of those lucky enough to eventually find a billet on the eve of Waterloo:

It was quite dark but the soldiers lighted some fires amidst the trees; as I found myself cold, chilly and wet to the skin, and I had given almost my last drop of gin to Kelly which I now regretted, I thought my only chance to avoid being utterly benumbed was to slip off all my clothes and put on a flannel jacket and a pair of worsted stockings that I had in my valisse. It was all I had, as I had not the least idea when we left Ninove on the 15th that we should so soon have been separated from all kinds of conveniences.

It seemed a cruel thing to strip naked under a pouring rain, but it was the best thing I could do. Just after I had accomplished this feat Haywood came to tell me that there was a cottage near in which I could get shelter and a fire, and he also kindly offered to take care of my horses. This offer I was thankful to embrace, and although I could not get more than a corner of a chair this was infinitely better than lying in the mud with the rain pouring upon me as the majority of my unfortunate comrades had to do.

The room was mostly filled with soldiers, who, giving way to the influence of the occasion, and notwithstanding the presence of some officers, talked freely and fully over the business of Genappe among each other, and related many anecdotes of great exploits, heroic stands, and indeed even comical occurrences in the heat of battle, which passed away a weary night in a situation in which no one could sleep. I was so wet I did not leave the fire to lie down; sleep was out of the question in any case and I was glad when the first light of dawn began to lighten the crowded and airless room.[2]

The cavalry and horse artillery had the added responsibility of seeing to their horses before they themselves could look to their own food and shelter. Cavalié Mercer and his men were fortunate to have found a large sack of corn discarded on the road from Genappe, which they hastily put aboard an ammunition waggon. This was served out to the horses as they stood tethered together, some remaining in their harnesses in case of emergency. Having seen to the horses, the artillerymen tried to make the best of a bad situation themselves. Many of the gunners lay down beneath the gun carriages, draping canvas sheets over them for added protection, whilst Mercer and some other officers erected a small tent in an attempt to escape the rain which was by now heavier than ever. Judging from eye-witness accounts, the night before Waterloo was one of the worst experienced by Wellington's men, but the Peninsular veterans tried to put a brave face on it with the usual bravado, as Mercer recalled in his journal:

> We set up a small tent, into which…we crept, and rolling ourselves in our wet blankets, huddled close together, in hope, wet as we were, and wet as the ground was, of keeping each other warm. I know not how my bedfellows got on, as we all lay for a long while perfectly still and silent – the old Peninsular hands disdaining to complain before their Johnny Newcome comrades, and these fearing to do lest they should provoke some such remarks as, 'Lord have mercy upon your poor carcass! What would such as you have done in the Pyrenees?' or 'Oho, my boy! This is but child's play to what we saw in Spain.' So all who did not sleep (I believe the majority) pretended to do so, and bore their suffering with admirable heroism.[3]

The miserable night was only made bearable for Mercer by a Hanoverian soldier, wet through and shivering with cold, who stopped to smoke his pipe. When he got up to leave he thanked the artillerymen and took out a half-starved chicken, which was immediately plunged into the pot and boiled. Mercer's own share was a leg, although it amounted to a single mouthful only. It was the first food he had eaten since the night of 16 June.

All along the ridge at Waterloo British and Allied soldiers tried to kindle fires, which was not easy, given the heavy rain and the lack of dry firewood. Nevertheless, fires were lit, and plenty of them too. Thousands of troops on both sides of the battlefield shared the miseries of the night, wondering what might happen to them on the morrow. Wills were written and exchanged, letters handed to friends and handshakes freely given between friends and brothers, lest they be struck down during the battle.

Away to the west of the battlefield the Foot Guards did what they did best; they made the best of a thoroughly bad situation. The weather was bad enough; the rain was incessant and heavy, but they had experienced similar bad weather in southern France in December 1813. Indeed, the Guards had drawn a stern rebuke from Wellington when he found them by the main road just outside Bayonne, skulking beneath umbrellas. Lord Hill came riding over to tell them that, 'Lord Wellington does not approve of the use of umbrellas during the enemy's firing, and will not allow the Gentlemen's Sons to make themselves ridiculous in the eyes of the enemy.' A few days later came a further warning from Wellington. 'The Guards may in uniform, when on duty at St James's, carry them if they please; but in the field it is not only ridiculous but unmilitary.'[4]

The two brigades of Guards, Byng's and Maitland's, were up on the ridge, sitting beneath their blankets. Each blanket had six button holes along the edges and small loops of cord at each corner. The companies were told off in fours and lots were drawn to see which two men out of each four was to unpack his knapsack and pitch his blanket. Muskets were then placed perpendicular at each end of the blanket, passing the knob of the ramrod through the two button holes at the corresponding corner of each blanket. Then, by tying the cords round the muzzles of the muskets and pegging out the blankets at the lower corners, a sort of crude tent was fashioned, large enough for four men to crawl under. This shelter was normally sufficient to keep the rain off, but at Waterloo it came down in such torrents that the blankets were quickly soaked. Not long afterwards, an order came for the four light companies to march down to a large château which lay just in front of them. This of course meant that the men whose blankets had been used for the tents now had to wring them out as best they could and pack them away again. This was not easy, as the blankets were not only extremely wet but the straps of the knapsacks became very slippery, leaving them difficult to pack and slip over the shoulders. Matthew Clay, of the light company of the 3rd Foot Guards, was one of the unlucky ones chosen to unpack his blanket and he now had great difficulty packing it again. He took so long about it that by the time he had done so his company had filed off towards a large orchard close to the château. Clay eventually put his pack on and hurried after his comrades. It was a dark night and Clay couldn't see where his company had gone, save for the fact that they had marched down the hill to the large orchard. Presently, he came across an opening in a fence, beyond which he saw his company. On the other side of the fence lay a ditch, fall of muddy rainwater, and in his attempt to jump it he slipped and fell in, and quickly found himself up to his neck in water. At length, he managed to crawl out and rejoin his comrades, wet through,

This atmospheric painting shows British infantry gathered round a camp fire on the night before Waterloo. Dark rain clouds roll overhead whilst a bolt of lightning issues from the sky in the distance. Even Peninsular veterans agreed that the night was one of the most uncomfortable of their lives. Many, however, drew comfort from the fact that such a storm was an omen of victory, such storms having preceded several of Wellington's major victories in the Peninsula.

muddy, cold and hungry. The château was, of course, Hougoumont, and Clay was to be one of the participants in its epic defence, one of the great episodes of the Battle of Waterloo. Another of Hougoumont's defenders was Ensign Charles Short, who was just a few months past his 16th birthday:

> We were under arms the whole night expecting an attack and it rained to the degree that the field where we were was half way up our legs in the mud. Nobody of course could lie down and the ague got hold of some of the men. I with another officer had a blanket, and with a little more gin, we kept up very well.
>
> We had only one fire and you cannot conceive the state we were in. We formed a hollow square and prepared to receive cavalry twice but found it was a false alarm both times. Soon after daylight, the commissary sent up with the greatest difficulty some gin and we found an old cask full of wet rye loaves which we breakfasted upon. Everybody was in high spirits. We broke up the cask and got some dry wood and made some fine fires, got some straw and I went to sleep for a couple of hours.'[5]

The weather certainly exposed the frailties of British Army equipment. Like Matthew Clay, Corporal Knight, of the 95th Rifles, also found his equipment falling apart:

> Such a tempest of thunder, lightning, and rain came on, that from the slippery state of the ground our men were constantly falling, and our gaiter-straps breaking, the low shoes we

had came off, and many of us had to walk in our stockings. Our beds this night were a cornfield, and our covering blankets soaked with wet; but some of us, setting out to forage, picked up wood, and making a blazing fire, we threw ourselves down beside it. Whilst foraging I got into a barn, and getting up to the loft, pitched down bundles of straw to my comrades. Oh, how comfortable I felt I could have made myself there, instead of going back to lie down in a splashing wet blanket on the ground[6]

Clay and Knight were typical of thousands of troops who spent the night of 17 June stumbling around in the dark, trying to find their comrades, or attempting to light fires, find food and shelter and generally enduring a completely miserable night as the rain continued to fall and thunder boom overhead. Thomas Morris, whom we last saw at Quatre Bras, was with his regiment on the forward slope of the ridge, halfway between Hougoumont and the Brussels road:

> As the storm continued, without any signs of abatement, and the night was setting in, orders were given to pile arms, but no man was on any account to quit his position. Under such circumstances our prospect of a night's lodging was anything but cheering; the only provision we had, being the remnant of the salt provision, served out on the 16th. Having disposed of that, we began to consider in what way to pass the night; to lie down was out of the question, and to stand up all night was equally so. We endeavoured to light some fires, but the rain soon put them out, and the only plan we could adopt was, to gather arms-full of the standing

A nineteenth-century photograph of the farm at Mont St Jean, looking south towards the crossroads. The farm was used as a hospital during and after the battle.

corn, and, rolling it together, make a sort of mat, on which we placed the knapsack; and sitting on that, each man holding his blanket over his head to keep off the rain, which was almost needless, as we were so thoroughly drenched:– however, this was the plan generally adopted and maintained during the night.[7]

William Gibney, of the 15th Hussars, was one of the minority who managed to find some food and drink, if only in tiny quantities, to offset the miseries of the night. And despite the storm and the terrible conditions he managed to pass the night sound asleep:

A wretched bivouac it was, far worse than on the previous night. Officers, men, and horses were completely done up with the long march of the day before and the continuous moving on this day, having very little to eat during the whole time. We were up to our knees in mud and stinking water, but not a drop of drinking water was to be found in the villages. We were half famished. We had marched and starved from our quarters in the village to Quatre Bras, and now had added a little fighting to starving and marching. There was no choice; we had to settle down in the mud and filth as best we could, and those having any provisions about them were fortunate. As I had obtained a bit of tongue (but whether cooked, or only smoked and salted, I know not) in the morning, and had a thimbleful of brandy in my flask, I was better off than many, and finishing the somewhat queer tasting food, with others I looked about for a drier place to lie down on and rest weary limbs. It was all mud, but we got some straw and boughs of trees, and with these tried to lessen the mud and to make a rough shelter against the torrents of rain which fell all night; wrapping our cloaks round us, and huddling close together, we lay in the mud and wooed the

drowsy god, and that with tolerable success. For, notwithstanding pouring rain, mud, and water, cold, and the proximity of the enemy, most of us managed to sleep. As for myself, I slept like a top, but I had become seasoned to the work, and was young and strong.[8]

The 92nd Highlanders had marched from Quatre Bras and upon arrival at Mont St Jean were greeted with an order to bivouac in a newly ploughed field. The regiment had already endured the miseries of the march, along roads knee-deep in mud and water. It was enough to try even the most experienced campaigner, as Lieutenant James Hope wrote:

When we took up our ground on the position of Waterloo, not one of us had a dry stitch on our backs, and our baggage was no one knew where. To add to our miseries, we were ordered to bivouac in a newly ploughed field, in no part of which could a person stand in one place, for many minutes, without sinking to the knees in water and clay; and where, notwithstanding the great quantity that had fallen, not one drop of good water could be procured to quench our thirst...Fancy yourself seated on a few twigs, or a little straw, in a newly ploughed field, well soaked with six hours heavy rain; your feet six or eight inches deep in the mud; a thin blanket your only shelter from the surly attacks of the midnight hurricane – cold, wet, and hungry, without a fire, without meat, and without drink. Imagine yourself placed in such a situation, and you will have a faint idea of what we suffered on the night of the 17th, and morning of the memorable 18th of June. A sound sleep was a luxury which none of us could expect to enjoy. The men were seated in pairs, with their backs to the storm, and their blankets between it and them; some of them were recounting their former sufferings in Portugal, Spain, and

France; others their deeds of arms in the same countries; and not a few were humming a verse of some warlike song; all were attempting to pass away the dreary hours in the best manner they could, in hopes that the morning would present them with something comfortable.[9]

It was, in short, one of the worst nights Wellington's men could recall in their long years of fighting under him. But what of the commander-in-chief himself? Wellington had ridden along the Brussels road during the afternoon and evening of 17 June until he finally reached the ridge at Mont St Jean, where his army had halted. We know that during his reconnaissance of the area in 1814 Wellington had earmarked five or six good defensive positions along the main road, his favourite being the position at Rossomme. This, ironically, was the very position upon which Bonaparte would draw up his troops on the evening of 17 June. For some reason, however, De Lancey, the Quartermaster General, passed through the position and had the men halt on the next ridge, which was the position at Mont St Jean. Looking at the position at Rossomme today, one cannot help but notice how very strong it is. It affords a much steeper glacis than the one at Mont St Jean and there are even a couple of farms that would have provided useful forward bastions for the Allies. But it was not to be, and so Wellington's men drew up on the position at Mont St Jean and it was here that the battle would be fought the following day.

With his men having halted for the night, Wellington and his staff rode off to the village of Waterloo, a couple of miles to the north, where quarters had been found for him in an inn opposite the church of St Joseph's, on the Brussels road. Here, Wellington waited anxiously for news from Blücher. And an anxious wait it must have been. We know that Müffling had already given him a vague, verbal assurance that Blücher would march to Waterloo, whilst the two had been staying at the Roi d'Espagne the night before, but as yet nothing official had arrived at Wellington's headquarters. At some time between 10pm and 11pm, however, a messenger arrived bearing a despatch from Blücher, timed at 6pm, assuring Wellington that the Prussian Army would march to join him on 18 June. Wellington had requested from Blücher a single Prussian corps, but here, the old warrior was promising to march with his entire army and that, should the French not attack on the 18th, then he and Wellington would attack them on the 19th. It was an extravagant promise, particularly given the mauling the Prussians had been given at Ligny, but it was a promise that Blücher, to his immense credit, would keep. A further message arrived from Blücher at 2am on 18 June, in which Gneisenau set out details of how the Prussians would arrive, with Bulow's corps in the lead, followed by Pirch I.

Despite these promises, Wellington was evidently feeling decidedly anxious about the outcome of the battle which now seemed inevitable. He wrote to Sir Charles Stuart, British Ambassador in Brussels, on the need for him to, 'keep the English quiet', lest the large British population in the city begin to panic, especially with Bonaparte barely twenty miles away. If they really felt it necessary they were to prepare to move to Antwerp, but this should not be done in any manner which may arouse alarm in the

A nineteenth-century photograph of La Haye Sainte, looking north towards the crossroads. The farm was defended by Major George Baring and light infantry of the King's German Legion.

capital, 'as all will yet turn out well'. He also wrote to the Duc de Berry, informing him that he was to prepare to move the French royal family, also to Antwerp, if things went against him. Other letters were sent, including one to Lady Frances Webster, in which Wellington advised her to prepare to move to Antwerp 'at a moment's notice'.

As the rain beat down upon the windows of his quarters, Wellington looked out on to the road outside as artillery cantered past, staff officers galloped up and down, and orderlies splashed through the puddles. Wellington was not a man to be easily distracted from the task ahead of him, but on the early morning of 18 June he must have reflected upon his past triumphs, and upon how his men had never let him down. But he had never faced Bonaparte himself. One wonders whether he relished the challenge and whether, in his mind, he went over the strategy he would employ later in the day. Wellington was far too professional to care who he fought, although it is evident throughout the Waterloo campaign that he was certainly wary of what Bonaparte might do next. As to his own plans, he didn't really know what he would do. When Uxbridge enquired as to what he intended doing, Wellington simply replied, 'Well, Bonaparte has not given me any idea of his projects: and as my plans depend upon his, how can you expect me to tell you what mine are?' The relationship between the two men was often strained; after all, Uxbridge had eloped with Wellington's brother's wife. It was probably for this reason that he received the somewhat sarcastic reply, even though it was true. But Wellington did give Uxbridge some reassurance, by putting his hand on his shoulder and saying, 'There is one thing certain, Uxbridge, that is, that whatever happens, you and I will do our duty.' Of that, he could be sure.

Wellington tried to sleep but there was far too much activity going on for him to do so. He may have managed some sleep after midnight but we know he was up again between 2am and 3am, almost certainly as a result of having received Blücher's message of support. It is doubtful whether he managed any afterwards, which was unusual for him, as he had developed the knack of being able to sleep in the most unpleasant and trying circumstances. Upon being asked how he could sleep at such moments, Wellington simply replied, 'When I cast off my clothes, I cast off my cares.'

The morning continued, dark and stormy, and the candles in Wellington's headquarters burned low. Two miles to the south his men shivered beneath the rain which continued to fall unabated. The odd shot was exchanged between piquets, but for the most part the men on both sides huddled quietly beneath their blankets, besides fires, on muddy straw mats, or they simply stood or sat around in small groups in the open. For Wellington's Peninsular veterans, the coming battle represented their final examination. They had beaten a dozen French marshals and had defeated their armies in countless bloody battles. They had stormed fiery breaches and crossed countless rivers, until they had swept the French over the Pyrenees and back on to the 'sacred soil' of France. Yet they had never faced Bonaparte.

But Boney had not faced them either, and he was about to discover what his much-vaunted marshals had discovered in the Peninsula, at places like Albuera, Talavera, Salamanca, Vittoria, at Badajoz and at the Nivelle. The lads from the shires of England, from Scotland, Wales and from Ireland cared little for reputations. These were the lads who, when they had dried themselves off, and had scraped the mud from their uniforms, would make good a line from one of their favourite songs. Yes, these were the lads who would 'kick Boney's arse'.

1 William Wheeler, *The Letters of Private Wheeler 1809–1828*, edited by Capt. BH Liddell Hart (London, 1951), p.170.

2 Haddy James, *Surgeon James' Journal 1815*, edited by Jane Vansittart (London, 1964), pp.28–9.

3 Capt. Cavalié Mercer, *Journal of the Waterloo Campaign*, edited by Sir John Fortescue (London, 1927), p.157.

4 Capt. Howell Rees Gronow, *The Reminiscences of Captain Gronow*, edited by Nicolas Bentley (London, 1977), p.23.

5 Ensign Charles Short, MSS, NAM GS213.

6 Cpl. Knight, *British Battalion at Oporto* (London n.d.), pp.19–20.

7 Thomas Morris, *The Napoleonic Wars*, edited by John Selby (London, 1967), p.74.

8 Dr Thomas Gibney, *Eighty Years Ago, or the Recollections of an old Army Doctor*, edited by his son, RD Gibney (London, 1896), pp.183–4.

9 Lt. James Hope, *Letters from Portugal, Spain and France, during the memorable campaigns of 1811, 1812, & 1813, and from Belgium and France in the year 1815* (Edinburgh, 1819), pp.240–2.

1. The 44th (East Essex) Regiment in action against French cavalry at Quatre Bras, 16 June 1815. Painting by Vereker Hamilton.

2. Colonel Sir Robert Macara, commanding officer of the 42nd Highlanders, is killed by enemy lancers whilst being carried wounded from the field at Quatre Bras, in this painting by Richard Simkin.

3. Arthur Wellesley, 1st Duke of Wellington, 1769–1852. Waterloo was to prove the crowning glory of a magnificent military

career that included the remarkably successful Peninsular War, from 1808 to 1814. Painting by Chris Collingwood.

4. Trooper, 6th (Inniskilling) Dragoons. By Alix Baker.

5. Private, 79th Highlanders. By Alix Baker.

6. Officer and Corporal, 92nd Highlanders. By Alix Baker.

7. Officer, 6th (Inniskilling) Dragoons. By Alix Baker.

8. Officers, Royal Horse Guards (Blue), and 1st Life Guards. By Alix Baker.

9. Corporal, Royal Sappers and Miners. By Alix Baker.

10. Corporal, 27th (Inniskilling) Regiment. By Alix Baker.

11. Gunner, Royal Horse Artillery. By Alix Baker.

12. 'The British Army at Waterloo'. A montage of British troops, painted by Chris Collingwood.

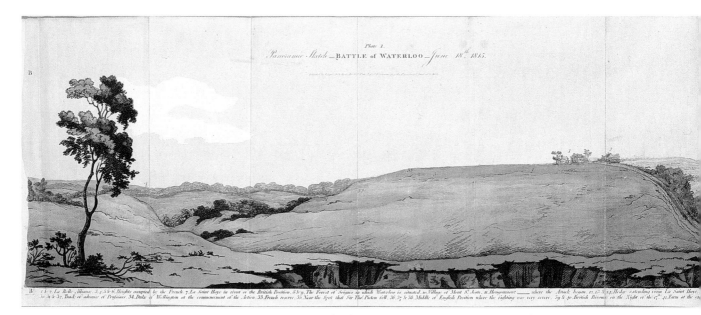

13. A panoramic sketch of the field of Waterloo, as printed in *Booth's Battle of Waterloo*, published shortly after the battle. The panorama extends from Papelotte and La Haye, to the left, to La Belle Alliance and La Haye Sainte in the centre, and to Hougoumont on the right.

14. A contemporary view of the field of Waterloo, looking south from Wellington's position. La Haye Sainte is visible on the left. The cutting through which the main Brussels road runs is visible also.

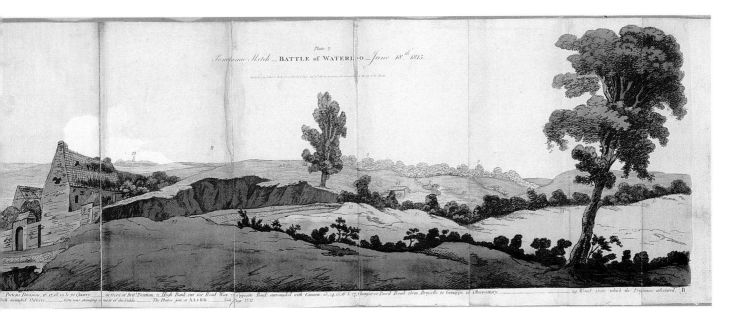

15. A view south from the crossroads, looking down the Brussels road towards La Haye Sainte.

16. Another contemporary view of the battlefield of Waterloo, again from Wellington's position, looking down towards Hougoumont which is obscured by the trees.

17. The Duke of Wellington, mounted upon Copenhagen, outside his headquarters in the village of Waterloo. Painting by Hillingford.

18. British infantry in action against French hussars during the Waterloo Campaign.
The ability of British infantry to remain firm against enemy cavalry attacks, both at Quatre Bras and Waterloo,
was a major factor in Wellington's success during the campaign. Painting by Dighton.

19. 13th Light Dragoons on patrol, keeping a watchful eye on French troops in the distance.

The 13th was one of the most experienced cavalry regiments in Wellington's army. Painting by Chris Collingwood.

20. The Duke of Wellington inspects some of his troops at Hougoumont on the morning of Waterloo, 18 June 1815.

The artist, Hillingford, was obviously no expert on military uniforms and equipment, but his series of Waterloo paintings are amongst the most atmospheric of all Waterloo art.

21. Sergeant Charles Ewart, of the Scots Greys, achieves immortality by capturing the Imperial Eagle of the French 45th Ligne Regiment at Waterloo during the great charge of the British heavy cavalry.

22. Captain Clark-Kennedy and Corporal Styles, of the 1st (Royal) Dragoons, in action at Waterloo capturing the Imperial Eagle of the 105th Ligne.

23. Wellington's Foot Guards – the 'Gentlemen's Sons' – are pictured here by Ernest Crofts during their epic defence of the château of Hougoumont, a position which they held throughout the Battle of Waterloo against repeated French attacks.

24. The 13th Light Dragoons in action on the afternoon of 18 June against French chasseurs and cuirassiers.

Wellington's cavalry provided vital support for the infantry during the mass attacks by French cavalry, making several effective and controlled charges. Painting by Chris Collingwood.

25. The epic defence of La Haye Sainte by Major George Baring and the King's German Legion is captured superbly here in this painting by Adolf Northen.

Of the original garrison of almost 400 men, just over forty, including Baring himself, escaped from the farm when it fell on the evening of 18 June.

26. Sir John Colborne and the 52nd Light Infantry in action at Waterloo,
capturing a battery of French artillery during the closing stages of the battle. Painting by Ernest Crofts.

27. Wellington raises his hat at Waterloo as the signal for the general advance following
the defeat of the Imperial Guard by Allied infantry. Painting by Atkinson.

28. 'The Whole Line Will Advance'. Granville Baker's painting captures the moment when Wellington's embattled infantry descended from their ridge to drive Bonaparte's army from the field of Waterloo.

29. Another of Hillingford's Waterloo paintings, 'After Waterloo', showing some of the survivors enjoying some well-earned rest in an inn after the battle.

30. 'The Reading of the Waterloo Despatch', by Sir David Wilkie. Delighted Chelsea Pensioners read Wellington's *Waterloo Despatch*, published in *The Times* on 22 June 1815.

31. The inhabitants of Waterloo had little difficulty in finding tourists eager to purchase souvenirs of the battle. Indeed, such was the vast amount of debris left on the battlefield that it took months to clear.

Chapter VIII
A WET MORNING AT WATERLOO

The water ran in streams from the cuffs of our jackets, in short, we were as wet as if we had been plunged over head into a river. We had one consolation, we knew the enemy were in the same plight.

William Wheeler, 51st Light Infantry

It was 6am on 18 June when the Duke of Wellington buckled on his sword, straightened his coat and mounted his faithful chestnut horse, Copenhagen, who had carried his master through many a campaign in the Peninsula. Waterloo was to prove their final battle. They passed beneath the arch of the inn at Waterloo and made their way to join the Allied Army which waited, drenched through, on the ridge at Mont St Jean.

It was still raining when Wellington arrived at Mont St Jean to begin his inspection of his 'infamous army'. If the sight of Bonaparte's hat on a battlefield was said to have been worth 10,000 men, the same can surely be said of Wellington, whose aristocratic figure quickly stirred the soaked redcoats on the ridge, whilst instilling some sort of belief in the other Allied contingents. At Sorauren, in the Pyrenees, the sight of Wellington riding up towards them prompted his Portuguese troops to begin cheering, 'Douro! Douro!', the name by which he had been known to them since 1809. The shout was taken up by the British troops and it quickly rolled along the entire length of their position,

much to the dismay of Marshal Soult who sat despondently across the ravine separating the two armies. There was no such cheering at Waterloo, but there is little doubt that the sight of Wellington riding along the ridge was enough to boost his men's confidence. 'Atty', as they called him, was with them, and for a moment the miserable weather was forgotten as he rode amongst them. The sight of his long hooked nose, as one veteran put it, was indeed worth a few thousand extra men.

Wellington's men had stirred from whatever sleep they could manage, and found themselves packed tightly into a small battlefield of not more than three square miles. On Wellington's right flank lay the strong outpost of the château and farm buildings of Hougoumont, which were masked from enemy view by an extensive wood which lay to the south. The buildings were enclosed by walls, in the centre of which was the château itself. Behind it was the farmyard which was protected on the other three sides by walls and farm buildings, including the Great Barn on the western side of the yard. The entrance to Hougoumont was by the great north

The centre of Wellington's position at Waterloo, as seen from the top of the Lion Mound. The farm of La Haye Sainte can just be seen on the right of the photo, illustrating just how perilous Wellington's position became following its capture by the French on the evening of 18 June. The vast majority of Wellington's men were hidden from view on the reverse slope of the ridge, which can be seen to the left of the road in the centre. The level of the ground to the south, or right, of the road was dramatically reduced following the construction of the mound in 1825. The bank on the north, or left, of the road, resembles the original level of the ground. The buildings at the crossroads are post-1815.

gate. There was another gate at the south of the farm and a smaller gate in the western side. To the east of the buildings there was a large garden surrounded by a wall and beyond this an orchard, which was in turn protected on its south side by a large hedge and on the north by a long ditch, known as 'the hollow way'.

It was close to the hollow way that Matthew Clay had spent the night. In fact, he had fallen into it. It was a quiet morning, and so Clay and his comrades took themselves off to look for firewood. They found some in the château, and lit fires and tried to warm themselves.

> The sergeant of each section gave a small piece of bread (about an ounce) to each man and enquiry was made along the ranks for a butcher; one having gone forward, he was immediately ordered to kill a pig, there being cattle at the above named farm house; which having been slaughtered, was divided amongst the company. A portion of the head (in its rough state) being my share, and having placed it upon the fire, the heat of which served to dry our clothing and accoutrements, and to cook our separate portion of meat, which having become warmed through and blackened with smoke, I partook of a little, but finding it too raw and unsavoury (having neither bread nor salt), I put the remainder in my haversack, and taking my musket to put in order for action (which having been loaded the previous day and the enemy not having disturbed us during the night), I discharged in the bank where I had purposely placed it as a target.[1]

Clay then set to work, as a good soldier should on the morning of a battle, cleaning his musket and preparing his equipment. He examined the state and amount of his ammunition and put his musket into fighting trim, well oiled and flinted. Although the famous 'Brown Bess' flintlock musket had proved itself on scores of battlefields, its cheap construction exposed flaws dur-

ing the bad weather. Clay thought it to be a 'sad bore', from the effects of the wet, the springs at the lock becoming wood-bound, with the result that it would not work correctly. In action, the clumsy flints became useless also. According to Clay, the best way to correct this fault was simply to take flints from the dead lying around. Clay wandered into the courtyard at Hougoumont and found some straw to sit on. Other Foot Guards were already inside, sitting around, whilst others had been busy making loopholes in the strong walls.

The Foot Guards, in fact, had only just managed to occupy Hougoumont the night before, beating off an attempt by the French who had also tried to take it. Some French cavalry tried likewise, but these also failed. When Wellington arrived at Hougoumont he found the two light companies from the two battalions of the 1st Foot Guards, under Lord Saltoun, preparing to march into the orchard. In addition, the light company of the Coldstream Guards, under Henry Wyndham, would occupy the farm and château itself. Elsewhere, the light company of the 3rd Foot Guards, under Charles Dashwood, would defend the garden and the grounds surrounding the farm. Except for Saltoun's men, the garrison of Hougoumont was placed under the command of James Macdonnell, of the Coldstream Guards.

Soon after the Foot Guards had marched into the orchard, a staff officer arrived with a battalion of Nassau infantry, 300 Hanoverian Jaegers, and 100 Luneberg infantry. These troops were to relieve Saltoun's men, who in turn were to rejoin the other companies of the regiment positioned on the main ridge. As Saltoun marched back to the ridge, Wellington appeared, along with his Military Secretary, Fitzroy Somerset. 'Hello. Who are you? Where are you going?' he asked, at which Saltoun halted his men and ordered them to lie down. He explained to Wellington

A similar view of the reverse slope to the east of the Brussels road. This was Picton's sector. It was also from here that the Union Brigade began its famous charge. Once again it is possible to gauge the angle of vision to which Wellington's men were limited. Apart from the great French infantry attack at 2pm it is doubtful whether any Allied troops saw any of the enemy until late on in the day. The reverse slope may well have hidden Wellington's men from view but it did not completely shelter them from enemy artillery which swept this field throughout the day.

his new orders, to which the commander-in-chief expressed his surprise. 'Well, I was not aware of such an order. However, don't join your brigade yet. Remain quiet where you are until you receive further orders from me.' Then, turning to one of his aides, Wellington remarked, 'That was one of my old Peninsular officers. See how he made his men lie down.'

Wellington continued his inspection of Hougoumont, allowing the Hanoverians, Nassauers and Lunebergers to pass into the woods south of Hougoumont, relieving the 3rd Foot Guards, whilst a section of the light company of the same regiment took up a position by the haystack, just outside the farm's south-western perimeter. Saltoun was then moved into the orchard, the light company of the Coldstream into the château, and the remainder of the light company of the 3rd Foot Guards into the lane to the west of the farm. This comprised the initial garrison of Hougoumont, but as we shall see, it increased dramatically as the day wore on.

Later on that morning Wellington returned to Hougoumont to make his final inspection. With him was the Prussian liaison officer, Müffling. The two men were greeted by James Macdonnell, commanding at Hougoumont, who was told by Wellington that Hougoumont must be defended 'to the last extremity'. When Müffling expressed doubts as to whether 1,500 British Foot Guards could defend the post, Wellington replied simply, 'Ah, but you do not know Macdonnell.'

Elsewhere along the ridge, other British troops were trying to ease their aching limbs after the uncomfortable night. Those who had been lucky enough to have slept for a while awoke to find it still raining. The horses, according to Radclyffe, of the 1st (Royals), 'were fetlock deep in mud; no baggage for the officers, and neither provisions nor water for the men, though some stray cattle had been killed and

eaten, and a small supply of spirits had a short time before been found on the road. So we might be said to go "coolly" into action.'[2]

William Wheeler, of the 51st, awoke to find himself drenched, 'benumbed and shaking with the cold', and thought that had he not had a good stock of tobacco he would have, 'given up the ghost'. Johnny Kincaid, of the 95th, was also drenched with rain, but had been able to sleep soundly through the night. His immediate concern was for his horse, which had disappeared, and it was about an hour before he found him again, nestling between two artillery horses about a mile and a half away. Despite the close proximity of the enemy, Kincaid was confident that no action would take place that day, and so put his arms in order and began to dry himself. Some of his brother officers made for the small hovel which lay behind the crossroads. It was here that Sir Andrew Barnard had made his headquarters:

> We made a fire against the wall of Sir Andrew Barnard's cottage, and boiled a huge camp-kettle full of tea, mixed up with a suitable quantity of milk and sugar, for breakfast; and as it stood on the edge of the high road, where all the big-wigs of the army had occasion to pass, in the early part of the morning, I believe every one of them, from the Duke downwards, claimed a cupful.[3]

Lieutenant James Hope, of the 92nd, also managed to get some breakfast on the morning of the 18th:

> About nine, the Commissary issued beef to the division, but very few seemed inclined to eat it. From the hind quarter of a bullock, I cut a steak, which I fastened to a ramrod and held over a fire, till it was tolerably warm; then putting it to my mouth, I swallowed the delicious morsel with more than common avidity. But, to tell

you the truth, I was extremely hungry, having had very little of anything to eat for two days before. Soon after, an allowance of grog was given to each man, which tended to keep our drooping spirits from sinking under our accumulated load of misery.

From our bivouac in the clay puddle, we were moved to a dry one, a little in rear of the other. There we lighted fires, pulled off our jackets, shoes, and stockings, dried them, and endeavoured to make ourselves as comfortable as the existing circumstances would admit. In hopes of getting a little repose, we had begun to construct huts; some, indeed, were finished; three of us were asleep in one of these, when the bugle's shrill sound called on us to battle.[4]

There was plenty of meat dished out during the morning but very little of it was cooked and even less eaten, despite the hunger of the men who had had little to eat during the past two days. A swig of gin or rum was enough to revive many of the men, Ensign Edmund Wheatley, of the 5th Line Battalion KGL, included, who took his allowance of rum after having first ordered his men to clean out their muskets. Captain Mercer and his men were luckier than most. A bombardier had been despatched to Langeveldt to pick up a supply of ammunition. On his return he found scores of waggons abandoned by the roadside, many of which contained food and drink.

With the providence of an old soldier, he had picked up and brought on a considerable quantity of beef, biscuit, and oatmeal, of which there was abundance scattered about elsewhere. Casks of rum, etc., there were, and having broached one of these – he and his drivers – every one filled his canteen – a most considerate act, and one for which the whole troop was sincerely thankful. Nor must I omit to remark that, amidst such temptations, his men behaved with the most perfect regularity, and returned to us quite sober!

The rum was divided on the spot; and surely if ardent spirits are ever beneficial, it must be to men situated as ours were; it therefore came most providentially. The oatmeal was converted speedily into stirabout, and afforded our people a hearty meal, after which all hands set to work to prepare beef, make soup, etc.[5]

Mercer's troop of the Royal Horse Artillery certainly enjoyed a better breakfast on the morning of Waterloo than the majority of Wellington's men. Not to be outdone, however, were the officers of the 1st Foot Guards, who, in typical fashion, managed to conjure up some genuine St James's fare and turn what was a wet Sunday morning into something resembling a picnic in the country. The sun was just breaking through when Howell Rees Gronow joined his fellow dandies:

I was now greeted by many of my old friends (whom I had not time to speak to the day before, when I was sent off to the village of Waterloo) with loud cries of 'How are you, old fellow? Take a glass of wine and a bit of ham? It will perhaps be your last breakfast.' Then [Ensign] Burgess called out, 'Come here, Gronow, and tell us some London news.'

He had made himself a sort of gypsy tent, with the aid of some blankets, a sergeant's halberd and a couple of muskets. My dear old friend was sitting on a knapsack, with Colonel Stuart (who afterwards lost his arm), eating cold pie and drinking champagne, which his servant had just brought from Brussels.[6]

William Wheeler, with the 51st, perhaps summed up the situation on the morning of 18 June as well as anybody in Wellington's army:

A French view of Wellington's ridge at the sector held by Picton's men. The march to the top of the crest is deceptively steep and, given the boggy nature of the ground, would have been a real slog for the French infantry who attacked here during the early afternoon. This photo was taken from the easternmost end of the spur running east-north-east from just south of La Haye Sainte, and upon which the French guns were positioned prior to the great infantry assault. It was somewhere in this valley that Sergeant Ewart, of the Scots Greys, captured the Eagle of the 45th Ligne. It was also here that so many officers and men of the Union Brigade were either killed or wounded.

It would be impossible for any one to form any opinion of what we endured this night. Being close to the enemy we could not use our blankets, the ground was too wet to lie down, we sat on our knapsacks until daylight without fires, there was no shelter against the weather: the water ran in streams from the cuffs of our jackets, in short, we were as wet as if we had been plunged over head into a river. We had one consolation, we knew the enemy were in the same plight.[7]

It was not until around 9am that the rain finally stopped, by which time the majority of Wellington's men had stirred from their slumbers or else were beginning to feel the effects of no sleep at all. The sight of the sun's rays burning their way through the clouds cheered them and as the day began to warm up so their spirits rose too. There was still the prospect of a severe action ahead of them, but their immediate concern was to dry themselves, their arms and their accoutrements.

The Waterloo battlefield was, by contemporary standards, relatively small. From Hougoumont in the west to the farms of Papelotte, La Haye and Frischermont in the east, was barely 3,500 yards. The first two of these farms lay about 800 yards in front of the Chemin d'Ohain, a small road which ran along the ridge and which effectively marked Wellington's front. The chemin, in fact, divided about 800 yards east of the main Brussels road, with the road to Ohain continuing on in a north-easterly direction, and the road to Wavre running south-east to Papelotte. Frischermont lay another 500 yards to the south-east of La Haye and marked the eastern end of Wellington's position. From Papelotte and La Haye, the road ran west diagonally up towards the main ridge before continuing until it reached the Brussels road. This was the crossroads. From here, the lane ran west along the ridge for about 500 yards before it divided, running south-west and north-west. Both roads joined the Nivelles road, which ran north-east to Mont St Jean. The area 500 or so yards beyond the Nivelles road effectively marked the western end of Wellington's position. The areas to the north or rear of the ridge were shallow in comparison with some of the Peninsular battlefields but the ridge afforded Wellington's men suitable protection from enemy observation and from artillery fire.

In addition to the farms of La Haye, Papelotte and Frischermont, and Hougoumont, there was one other important forward bastion, which was to become the scene of violent struggles. Barely 250 yards south of the crossroads, and situated on the Brussels road itself, was the farm of La Haye Sainte, consisting of high farm buildings with walls on its eastern side and an orchard to its south. From the Allied ridge Wellington was able to look out over a low, shallow valley, which was deceptively undulating, full of dips and folds, within which it was easy to conceal troops. 1,500 yards to the south was the main French position, with a small inn called La Belle Alliance at its centre. From here the French position ran north-east towards Frischermont and north-west towards the wood that lay to the south of Hougoumont. Behind the right flank of the French position was the village of Plancenoit, where Blücher's Prussians would make their telling contribution to the battle. It was a small, compact battlefield which would fit onto the field of Fuentes de Oñoro, for example, four times over. It was for this reason that, given the casualties, the battlefield presented such an horrific sight when the fighting was over.

Wellington, meanwhile, was putting the finishing touches to his dispositions. Despite their positive performance at Quatre Bras, Wellington

A view from the same spot looking west towards La Haye Sainte and the centre of Wellington's position. Trees mark the Brussels road. The Lion Mound can be seen in the background.

was still not entirely convinced about the majority of the Dutch troops. Therefore, he decided to place the 'foreign' brigades at intervals between his British troops. This ensured that he would not need to gamble upon them holding any extensive sector of his line.

Wellington's army at Waterloo numbered around 68,000 men, including 12,000 cavalry. He also had the services of 156 guns. In his first line, beginning with the right flank, Wellington deployed Mitchell's brigade immediately to the north-west of Hougoumont. Then continuing along the line from the right, were Byng's and Maitland's brigades, Colin Halkett's brigade, Kielmansegge's Hanoverians, and Ompteda's KGL brigade, which had its left flank resting upon the crossroads. To the east of the Brussels road were Kempt's brigade, Bylandt's Belgians, Pack's brigade, Best's and Vincke's Hanoverian brigades, and, finally, Vandeleur's and Vivian's brigades of light cavalry, the latter occupying the left-hand end of Wellington's line. In front of Vivian were Prince Bernhard's men, occupying the farms of Papelotte and La Haye. The only other Allied troops to the east of the Brussels road were Ponsonby's Union brigade of cavalry

and, farther back, De Ghiny's Dutch and Belgian cavalry. Lambert's British brigade were even farther back, beside the farm of Mont St Jean. Otherwise, the bulk of Wellington's men were placed to the west of the main road. In the second line were the cavalry of Grant, Dörnberg, Hake, Kruse, Somerset, Arentschildt, Van Merlen and Tripp, whilst farther east, on the other side of the Nivelles road, were Du Plat's KGL brigade and Adam's British brigade. The farm of La Haye Sainte was occupied by the 2nd Light Battalion of the KGL, under Major George Baring. The garrison of Hougoumont, we have already dealt with. Wellington's concern for his right flank is reflected in the fact that he maintained a large detachment of 17,000 men, under Prince Frederick of the Netherlands, ten miles to the west of the battlefield, at Hal and Tubize, to guard against any possible outflanking move. Of these, 2,400 were British troops from Johnstone's division. They were to play no part in the battle at all

Thus, the morning of 18 June 1815 wore on. The rain had stopped, the sun shone and Wellington's 68,000 men braced themselves for the expected onslaught. And yet, as at Quatre

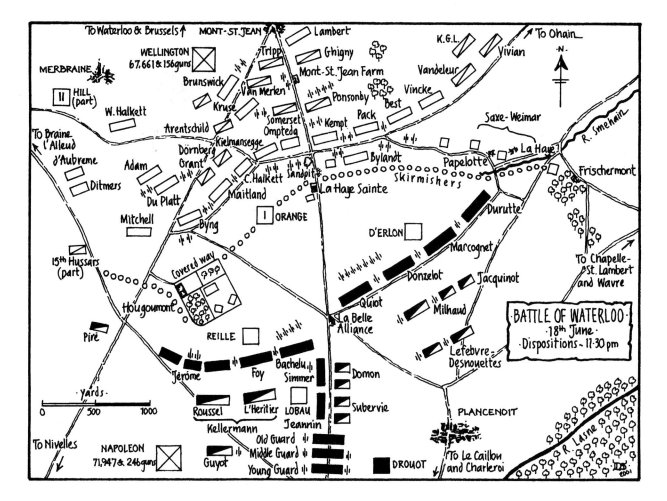

Wellington and his staff at Waterloo on the morning of 18 June. By the end of the day, many of them would be either dead or wounded. Wellington himself escaped without a scratch, prompting him to say, 'The finger of Providence was upon me.'

Bras, there was little sign of any enemy offensive. Instead, the men upon the Allied ridge were treated to the distant spectacle of thousands of French troops parading before their beloved leader as they took up their positions. It was the last great parade by the French Army of the Napoleonic Wars. Then, with 72,000 French troops and 68,000 Allied troops in position, all fell silent, and for a moment both armies stood motionless, looking out at each other, waiting for the battle to begin.

Wellington, of course, was in no hurry. Indeed, every minute that passed without activity meant that another precious few yards were gained by the Prussian Army as it marched closer towards him. The French, meanwhile, needed to attack before Blücher could intervene, but the condition of the ground prevented it. The overnight storm had given the ground such a thorough soaking that it was impossible for artillery to be moved without the most incredible effort. 10am came and went without any attack, as did 11am. The ground began to dry but not fast enough. And so Wellington's men continued to watch and wait.

Above Papelotte, Sir Hussey Vivian waited with his cavalry. Only fourteen months earlier a French musket shot at the Croix d'Orade, prior to the Battle of Toulouse, had cost him the use of his right arm, but here he was, gazing out over the valley, towards the French guns and the mass of enemy lancers that sat motionless beside them. Farther along the Chemin d'Ohain, Denis Pack sat upon his horse, reflecting, possibly, on a long career, on his capture at Buenos Aires in 1807, and on the long campaign in the Peninsula which he had shared with many of those who now stood patiently in their ranks behind him. Away to his right was Sir Thomas Picton, dressed from head to foot in his black civilian clothes. His uniform had been stowed away in the baggage and he had not had time to change since leaving the Duchess of Richmond's ball, three days earlier. Unknown to anyone but his servant, Picton was nursing a serious wound, caused by an enemy ball at Quatre Bras that had broken three of his ribs. Any other officer would have returned to Brussels to have it treated, but not Picton. One of the heroes of Busaco, Badajoz and Vittoria, the rough, foul-mouthed Welshman was not

about to let the wound prevent him from leading his men into battle. To the men of the Scots Greys and the Inniskilling Dragoons the whole thing must have seemed quite novel, for neither of the regiments had taken part in the Peninsular War. They would make up for all those lost years in dramatic style. Another veteran, Christian Ompteda, waited with his two nephews, close to the crossroads. He commanded a brigade of KGL infantry, one of the best units in Wellington's army. Like Picton, Ompteda was to die a hero's death later in the day. Behind Hougoumont, Grant's cavalry brigade waited. Amongst them was Levi Grisdale. Seven years earlier he had claimed the capture of General Lefevre-Desnouettes at Benavente. Little did he know that across the valley, just a thousand yards away, that same French general was there again with the cavalry of the Imperial Guard. Down at Hougoumont itself, the Foot Guards simply waited. They had spent the last few hours making loopholes in the garden walls, in creating firesteps and in turning the place into a veritable fortress. Despite Müffling's earlier doubts about their ability to hold the place, the 'Gentlemen's Sons' would not let their country nor their commander-in-chief down. In fact, they would play one of the most crucial parts in the entire battle.

Wellington surveys the field of Waterloo on the morning of 18 June, accompanied by some of his staff. He had seen the battlefield the previous year and was familiar with the position, its strengths and weaknesses.

All along the Allied ridge, Wellington's men waited for the battle to begin, for there was little they could do now except wait for the French. And wait for the Prussians too. The rumours had it that Blücher was making his way west to join them, but nobody quite knew when he was expected, not even Wellington, who had only a vague idea. The commander-in-chief himself sat amidst his entourage, which numbered about forty officers, most of whom were dressed in their best but somewhat damp military finery. But not Wellington. As usual he was immaculately and soberly dressed in a dark blue civilian coat, with white breeches and a dark blue cloak. His mameluke sword at his side and telescope in hand, he was a picture of concentration, riding slowly up and down the line, checking small details and exchanging words with his officers. His men saluted him as he passed, and drew comfort from his presence. 'Old Nosey' was with them, and as long as he was there they felt confident of adding further laurels to those gained on the bloody fields of the Peninsula.

The clock continued to tick away until, shortly before 11.30am, an anonymous French gunner put his match to his gun and away went the first shot of the Battle of Waterloo. As the smoke cleared, cheers, bugles and the beat of drums away to the south indicated that the game was at last afoot. Dark columns lumbered into motion, horses stirred and more guns were dragged slowly into position. The waiting was finally over. The Battle of Waterloo had begun.

Men of the Scots Greys are roused from an uncomfortable night's sleep by trumpeters on the wet morning of 18 June 1815. The Waterloo Campaign was the first time the regiment had been overseas for twenty-five years. They would mark their return to the Continent in fine and dramatic style.

1 Matthew Clay, *A Narrative of the Battles of Quatre Bras and Waterloo, with the Defence of Hougoumont* (Bedford n.d.), pp.10–11.
2 AE Clark-Kennedy, *Attack the Colour! The Royal Dragoons in the Peninsula and at Waterloo* (London, 1975), p.97.
3 Capt. John Kincaid, *Adventures in the Rifle Brigade* (London, 1830), p.329.
4 Lt. James Hope, *Letters from Portugal, Spain and France, during the memorable campaigns of 1811, 1812, & 1813, and from Belgium and France in the year 1815* (Edinburgh, 1819), pp.242–3.
5 Capt. Cavalié Mercer, *Journal of the Waterloo Campaign*, edited by Sir John Fortescue (London, 1927), p.159.
6 Capt. Howell Rees Gronow, *The Reminiscences of Captain Gronow*, edited by Nicolas Bentley (London, 1977), p.42.
7 William Wheeler, *The Letters of Private Wheeler 1809–1828*, edited by Capt. BH Liddell Hart (London, 1951), p.170.

Chapter IX
THE FIGHT FOR HOUGOUMONT

No troops but the British could have held Hougoumont, and only the best of them at that.

Wellington to Thomas Creevey

According to Ensign Gronow, there were few men, no matter how brave, who could listen to the French *pas de charge* without experiencing 'a somewhat unpleasant sensation'. He had heard it many times before in Spain and here it was again. There were others, however, who had served in the Peninsula for a great deal longer than Gronow and who now listened to it with disdain. 'Old Trousers' they called it. The bands of several French regiments were heard away to the south beyond the woods that shielded Hougoumont from enemy observation. As usual they were accompanied by the wild shouts of 'Vive l'Empereur!' as French officers tried to whip their men into a frenzy. Offi-

cers on foot ran backwards, their shakos held high above their heads, balancing on their swords. If it was intended to put fear into the hearts and minds of Wellington's men it failed. Indeed, most of the British had heard it all before and were suitably unimpressed. 'The most profound silence prevailed,' wrote Gronow, and while the French columns advanced the defenders of Hougoumont simply waited whilst officers made a final check of their arrangements for the defence of the place.

The noisy French advance did not trouble James Macdonnell, commanding at Hougoumont, who instead found himself issuing a stern rebuke to some of the Coldstream

The château of Hougoumont in all its glory, prior to being partially destroyed during the battle. The formal garden stands in the foreground, with the château itself, now gone, in the centre. Only the chapel remains of this part of the château. Note the balustrade lining the garden. At least one painting, featured in this book, suggests that the French entered the garden here, only to be shot down by Foot Guards from behind the balustrade.

The north gate at Hougoumont, photographed in the late nineteenth century, a view which would not have changed much since the battle was fought.

Guards who were busy plucking cherries from the trees. 'You scoundrels,' he roared, 'if I survive this day I will punish you all.' But, as one of the defenders wrote, 'before the close of the murderous struggle how few of the cherry stealers were left for punishment in this world.'[1]

Before long the French began to drive forward into the wood occupied by the Nassauers and Lunebergers, who gave a good account of themselves, disputing every foot of the ground. Meanwhile Sandham's battery and Cleeves's KGL battery were brought forward onto the ridge above Hougoumont, with Bull's horse artillery following soon after, all three throwing shot and shell deep into the wood to cause heavy casualties amongst the French. It was not easy for the attacking troops, for no matter how dense their columns they were unable to deploy in their traditional manner. Instead, they simply threw every man forward, their attack gradually forcing the defenders out of the wood and back to the orchard which lay to the east of the walled garden.

Julian Paget, in his book on Hougoumont, described its defence as, 'the key to victory at Waterloo', and he was surely right, for it is difficult to see how Wellington could have remained upon the ridge at Mont St Jean had the château fallen to the French. It took the enemy about thirty minutes to clear the wood, beyond which lay the walls of Hougoumont. But if they thought they were in for an easy morning they

were sadly mistaken, for there, waiting for them in silence behind the walls and in the windows of the farmhouse, were hundreds of King George's finest troops. The defenders of Hougoumont had worked feverishly throughout the night, making loopholes in the walls, constructing firing platforms and clearing away branches to create clear fields of fire. Now came the test.

One can well imagine the excitement and anxiety inside Hougoumont as the sounds of skirmishing echoed through the woods and grew ever closer. Then, as the Nassauers and Lunebergers pulled back, the Foot Guards loaded their muskets and waited for the enemy to appear. Officers stood ready, sword in hand, whilst their men waited, their fingers on their triggers. No sooner had the French begun to emerge from the edge of the wood than the order rang out, 'fire!', at which the Foot Guards opened up a withering fire which sent the French reeling back. Scores were dropped, and the open space in front of the south gate soon became a killing ground which the French would have to cross if they were to attempt to break open the barred gate. Scores of them braved the Guards' fire to rush at the gate, smashing at it with the butts of their muskets and hacking at it with their bayonets, but the Guards simply fired over the top of the adjoining wall and shot them down. Others attempted to climb over the wall but these too were cut

A slightly later view of the north gate, showing the extensive wood to the west and south of the buildings, trees which no longer exist.

down. After all, those who managed to get up on to the walls could only do so in ones and twos, and they were no match for Macdonnell's men who dispatched them with a quick bayonet thrust or a musket shot at close range.

The initial French attack upon Hougoumont itself was driven off with little difficulty, but to the east of the château their efforts met with some success. The Nassau and Luneberg troops in the orchard were driven out, back to the covered way behind the garden. However, up on the ridge were the light companies of the 1st Foot Guards, under Saltoun, which had been waiting there ever since Wellington ordered them out of the orchard barely an hour before. The men fixed bayonets and, with Saltoun at their head, they charged down the forward slope to the orchard and drove the French clean out of it. The light companies then re-occupied the position they had held before they were recalled to the main ridge. With the orchard in Saltoun's hands and with the French having been completely driven off, Macdonnell's men saw to their wounded, checked their ammunition and prepared to face the next attack which they knew would not be long in coming.

Sure enough, the French tried again, this time from the west. Outside the farm, to the southwest of the buildings, the light company of the 3rd Foot Guards, under Charles Dashwood, prepared to meet the attack. There ensued a fierce firefight between the two sides, Dashwood's men keeping up a brisk fire on the French before them. In the midst of the fighting, Lieutenant Standen waved his hat in the air and, brandishing his sword, led a group of Guards in a charge which forced the French back. But before long, the pressure began to tell and the light company was forced back down the lane which ran along the western wall of the buildings. Matthew Clay was with the light company, and as he continued to fire and load from beside a large haystack he failed to notice that his comrades had retired.

Being earnestly engaged, the intervening objects were the cause of our not perceiving the movements and retreat of our comrades. Now left to ourselves as we imagined by not seeing any one near us, and the enemy's skirmishers remaining under cover, continued firing at us, we likewise kept firing and retiring up the road, up which we had advanced.

We now halted. I unwisely ascended the higher part of a sloping ground on which the exterior wall of the farm was built, thinking of singling out the enemy's skirmishers more correctly, but very quickly found that I had become a target for them, my red coat being more distinctly visible than theirs; remaining in this position I continued to exchange shots with the enemy across the kitchen garden, they having the advantage of the fence as a covering, their shots freely struck the wall in my rear.

The south wall of the garden of Hougoumont. This wall would have been lined by men of the Coldstream and 3rd Foot Guards during the battle. French troops attacking this sector became exposed to the defenders after debouching from the wood which once lay to the south. This photo was taken in the nineteenth century

Our company from which we were separated had now opened fire from within. My musket now proving defective was very discouraging, but casting my eyes on the ground, I saw a musket which I immediately took possession of in exchange for my old one. The new musket was warm from recent use, and proved an excellent one, it having belonged to the light infantry of the 1st Foot Guards.[2]

Clay eventually managed to enter the farm and rejoin his comrades who had been hard pressed by the French. Indeed, a group of the leading French regiment had almost managed to force their way into the courtyard through the north gate but were met with a flurry of fists, bayonets and swords before they were driven off. During the fight, Sergeant Ralph Frazer, a veteran of Egypt and the Peninsula, ran out from the gates and made for a French colonel who sat upon his horse, directing his men. Frazer made at thrust at him with his pike and as the officer slashed at him Frazer dragged him from his horse and rode it triumphantly back through the gates and into the courtyard, his comrades cheering as he did so. The French colonel, meanwhile, lay on the ground at the mercy of the Guards but they declined to fire at him and he was able to make good his escape. Matthew Clay rejoined his comrades just after this and described the scene in the courtyard.

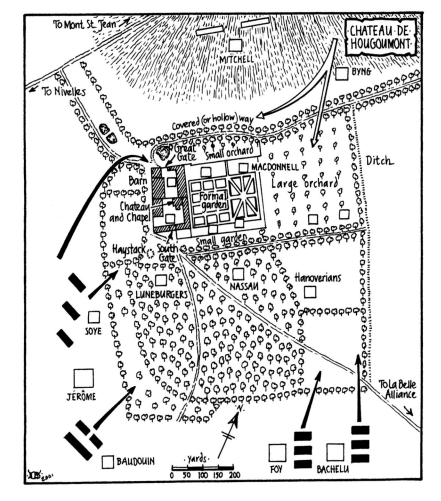

The south gate of Hougoumont, as it looked in the nineteenth century. Despite being attacked throughout the day, the gate was never forced. This picture should be compared with the painting by Ernest Crofts (below), showing the French attack on the gate.

The attack on the south gate of Hougoumont. British Foot Guards line the walls and windows to open fire on the French. After the battle, the area here was covered in dead and wounded soldiers. A huge bonfire was lit afterwards and scores of bodies burned upon it.

On entering the courtyard I saw the doors or rather gates were riddled with shot holes, and it was also very wet and dirty; in its entrance lay many dead bodies of the enemy, one I particularly noticed which appeared to have been a French officer, but they were scarcely distinguishable, being to all appearance as though they had been very much trodden upon, and covered with the mud; on gaining the interior I saw Lieutenant Colonel Macdonnell carrying a large piece of wood or trunk of a tree in his arms (one of his cheeks marked with blood, his charger lay bleeding within a short distance) with which he was hastening to secure the gates against the renewed attack of the enemy, which was vigorously repulsed.[3]

It was somewhere around 12.30pm that the most serious French attack came at Hougoumont. The north gate had not long been closed and the defenders just finished filling their ammunition pouches when a French shell burst upon them, following which a large group of French infantry rushed forward, a lieutenant leading the way brandishing a pioneer's axe. The officer swung the axe against the gates and before long he and his comrades had pushed them open and were pouring through. It was the most critical point of the action, for unless the gates could be closed Hougoumont was in danger of falling, and Wellington's right flank seriously compromised.

At first the Guards fell back upon the château, from where they opened up a galling fire on the French in the courtyard. But their fire alone would not drive the French out. There were about forty or fifty Frenchmen in the courtyard and unless they were driven out quickly their numbers would increase. The situation was not lost on Macdonnell who hastily formed a group of Coldstreamers and 3rd Foot Guards, and led a bayonet charge against the French. Macdonnell and his men charged down the slope from the château to the gate, driving back the French and cutting down all those who stood in their way. Others fired down from the windows of the château and from its doorways, and after a brief struggle all but a single drummer boy were either killed, wounded or taken. Richard MacLaurence was with Macdonnell, and he left a vivid account of the fighting in the courtyard:

> Once the French broke into the courtyard, and such a scene of bayonet work I never before or since beheld. It was fairly a trial of strength – the French grenadiers were not to be trifled with and we looked like so many butchers, red with gore, or rather like so many demons rioting against fire, for the shells had set two haystacks in a blaze and many a poor fellow lying bleeding and wounded, being unable to get out of the way, was burnt to death.[4]

But even as the Guards finished off the last of the French trespassers, more of them tried to get in. Macdonnell shouted to three other Coldstream Officers, Henry Wyndham, James Hervey and Henry Gooch, and, throwing himself at the gate, he heaved his shoulder against it, followed by his three colleagues who had been joined by two brothers, Corporals James and Joseph Graham, and four men of the 3rd Foot Guards, Sergeants Ralph Fraser, Bruce McGregor and Joseph Aston, and Private Joseph Lester. MacLaurence again:

> 'Shut the courtyard gates!' roared out our Sergeant Major Fraser, 'and keep them out', and a rush was instantly made to the gates, the French without and the Guards within. Life and death was in the struggle, for Ney was at hand with a force that threatened destruction to the post, but the English physical strength overcame the French ardour and the gates were closed by the powerful shoulders of Major Macdonnell and the giant of the Sergeant Major, with as many of ours as could get to them.
>
> The French thus enclosed in the courtyard, surrendered by throwing down their firelocks and were ordered to fall back, but they forgot the duties of prisoners. Their countrymen again charged Hougoumont with horse and foot and partly overpowered the Nassau troops and caused them to reel a bit; and then it was that the few Frenchmen we had taken, again seized their

The light companies of the Guards in action outside the south gate of Hougoumont. The wood changed hands several times, as did the orchard to the east of the château. The château itself, however, remained firmly in British hands. It was the key to Wellington's victory at Waterloo.

arms, and attacked from the rear. Fortunately, the post was not carried and now vengeance stern and dreadful awaited the prisoners. They had grossly violated the articles of war by taking up their arms after surrendering as prisoners and the consequence was that every man of them was put to death, some by the bayonet, and some were thrown into the blazing haystacks by our infuriated men.

Though now 27 years have rolled away since that dreadful scene took place, yet it is fresh in my mind's eye, and my ears yet tingle with the yells of these misguided Frenchmen as they were tumbled in the fiery furnace.[5]

The courtyard presented a bloody scene afterwards. Lying scattered about were around forty or fifty dead Frenchmen, including the tough, axe-wielding officer who had smashed his way through the gates. Others had perished in the flames of the haystacks after picking up their previously surrendered arms. Several Foot Guards lay about also, whilst others saw to their wounds. Even whilst the Guards shored up the defences at the back of the gate, the danger was not over, for as the defenders surveyed the scene a French soldier was hoisted up above the wall by one of his comrades and levelled his musket at Colonel Wyndham. The Coldstreamer hurriedly passed a musket to Corporal Graham who took aim and sent the Frenchman tumbling backwards with a bullet in his brain.

Macdonnell and his men could not have known it at the time, but the repulse of this latest French attack was to prove a pivotal moment in the Battle of Waterloo. There were several hours of extremely heavy fighting still to come, both at Hougoumont and elsewhere, but one of the most important acts on 18 June had already been played out. Indeed, Wellington was later to declare that the outcome of the battle depended upon the closing of the gates at Hougoumont.

Shortly after this latest and most serious French attack had been repulsed, Sir John Byng, commanding the 2nd Brigade of Guards, ordered three more companies of the Coldstream to make a counter-attack to drive the French away from the north gate. Soon after, he decided to send down the remaining companies of the Coldstream Guards, save for companies 7 and 8 which remained behind guarding the Colours. Led by the battalion's commanding officer, Alexander Woodford, the Coldstreamers made their way down the forward slope of the ridge and drove away the hordes of French infantry that still swarmed around the north gate. Commanding the grenadier company was Daniel Mackinnon. One of the great characters in Wellington's army, he was a dandy, a close friend of Beau Brummel, and a joker who would do anything for a bet. He once impersonated the Prince Regent in Spain and on another occasion climbed into a convent disguised as a nun, just when Wellington himself happened to be paying a visit. A veteran of the Peninsular War, he had lost an uncle, Henry Mackinnon, at the storming

Robert Gibbs' depiction of the closing of the north gate at Hougoumont is amongst the most famous battle paintings. During the incident, when a few dozen French troops entered the courtyard, James Macdonnell, commanding officer at Hougoumont, managed to close the gate literally with brute force, after gathering several other Guardsmen who charged and, putting their shoulders to it, closed the gate after a fierce struggle. All those enemy who had managed to remain inside were put to the sword, save for one drummer boy who was spared.

By early evening, Hougoumont had become a blazing furnace in many places. The heat inside was suffocating, but the garrison held on, as this painting by Hillingford shows. Despite his usual inaccuracies as regards uniforms and weapons, the artist has done a fine job in depicting the atmosphere inside Hougoumont during the battle.

of Ciudad Rodrigo in January 1812. A joker he may have been but he took his soldiering seriously. Indeed, his horse was shot beneath him at Hougoumont, whilst he himself was badly wounded in the knee by a musket ball. Mackinnon, who later wrote the first history of the Coldstream Guards, wrote to his brother after the battle:

> The grenadiers and the other companies of the Coldstream under my command were ordered to charge the enemy who had surrounded the house. I was wounded in the act [and] also had a beautiful grey horse shot. However, I did the best that lay in my power and succeeded in repulsing them till relieved by the remainder of the battalion. The whole were then obliged to fortify ourselves in the farmyard which we were ordered to defend…The ball struck me on the cap of the knee so you may suppose the pain is most excruciating, the inflammation is now very great therefore they cannot tell exactly what injury has been done but I trust in God and my good luck, a few days will make me quite easy about it.[6]

With the French driven off, Woodford led his men into the farmyard by a door in the western wall of Hougoumont. Woodford, in fact, was now the senior officer inside, but as Macdonnell had been there ever since the Guards had occupied the place, he generously declined to take command. Woodford would have been well suited to the job, as he had commanded the light

companies of the Foot Guards at Salamanca in July 1812, where they had held the village of Los Arapiles against French attacks.

Back on the ridge, the two remaining companies of the Coldstream, destined not to play a part in the defence of Hougoumont, lay down to shelter from French artillery fire. Although they missed the epic action at the château they were not spared the ordeal of enemy fire, as Ensign Charles Short, of No.7 company recalled:

> We were ordered to lie down in the road; the musket shots flew on over us like peas. An officer next to me was hit on the cap but not hurt as it went through, and another next to me was also hit on the plate of the cap, but it went through without hurting him. Two sergeants that lay near me were hit in the knapsacks, and were not hurt, besides several other shots passing as near as possible. I never saw such luck as we had.[7]

At some time around 1pm the French launched another attack on Hougoumont, this time against the orchard. Once again they came on in their hundreds, driving the defenders from the wood and from the orchard until Byng ordered Francis Home, at the head of two companies of the 3rd Foot Guards, to charge them.

> The command was given up to me by Lord Saltoun, on my reaching the near hedge of the orchard, where there was a hollow way, which served us as a rallying point more than once during the day.

Lieutenant Colonel Daniel Mackinnon was one of the defenders of Hougoumont, and was badly wounded in the knee. A veteran of the Peninsular War, Mackinnon was known as a great joker in Wellington's army and was reprimanded on several occasions following high profile pranks in Spain and Portugal. He later wrote the first regimental history of the Coldstream Guards.

Sergeant Ralph Fraser, of the 3rd Foot Guards, topples Colonel Cubieres from his horse during the fighting at Hougoumont. Fraser then mounted the horse himself and rode it back inside Hougoumont to the cheers of his comrades.

After some time we advanced, crossed the orchard, and occupied the front hedge, which I considered my post, driving the enemy through a gate at the corner of the garden wall into the wood.[8]

The combination of Hepburn's charge and the fire of the Coldstreamers lining the garden wall was enough to beat off this latest French attack. Saltoun's men then re-occupied the orchard whilst Hepburn's two companies were added to the garrison. Once again the Guards took time to shore up the defences, bring in the wounded, check their ammunition and prepare for the next French attack. It seemed as though the French were determined to take the château at any cost

and it would take all of the Foot Guards' fighting prowess to stop them.

One of the major disadvantages of Hougoumont being so far in front of the main ridge was that ammunition was difficult to procure. With French infantry swarming around the place it was never going to be easy getting ammunition through. In fact, the defenders' supply began to run low very quickly. Fortunately, Berkeley Drummond, of the 3rd Foot Guards, and Horace Seymour, of the Staff, managed to procure an ammunition tumbril with the aid of Joseph Brewster, of the Royal Wagon Train. Apparently, Drummond mentioned the shortage to Seymour, who later described what happened:

Late in the day of the 18th, I was called to by some Officers of the 3rd Guards defending Hougoumont, to use my best endeavours to send them ammunition. Soon afterwards I fell in with a private of the Wagon Train in charge of a tumbril on the crest of the position. I merely pointed out to him where he was wanted, when he gallantly started his horses, and drove straight down the hill to the farm, to the gate of which I saw him arrive. He must have lost his horses, as there was a severe fire kept on him. I feel convinced to that man's service the Guards owe their ammunition.[9]

The fight at Hougoumont was to continue unabated throughout the rest of the day. Indeed, it became a battle in itself with the defenders fighting on, completely unaware of what was happening elsewhere on the battlefield. But here we must leave Hougoumont, for the time being at least, for the French were massing their guns a few hundred yards to the east. 'The Emperor's daughters,' as Bonaparte lovingly called his guns, were about to open fire in preparation for the main French infantry attack, an attack that would be twice as large as anything the British had experienced in six long years in the Peninsula.

Caton Woodville's version of the defence of Hougoumont shows British Foot Guards repulsing a determined attack by French infantry upon the north gate, which appears to have been broken down.

1 Pte. Richard MacLaurence, *The Newcastle Journal*, 12 January 1843.
2 Matthew Clay, *A Narrative of the Battles of Quatre Bras and Waterloo, with the Defence of Hougoumont* (Bedford, n.d.), pp.13–14.
3 Ibid. pp.14–15.
4 See Daniel Mackinnon's *Origin and History of the Coldstream Guards* (London, 1837), II, p.216, for his version of the defence of Hougoumont, with interesting comments on the timings of the attack, the arrival of the ammunition wagon, etc.
5 MacLaurence, *The Newcastle Journal*, 12 January 1843.
6 Mackinnon, MSS, RHQ Coldstream Guards.
7 Ensign Charles Short, MSS, NAM GS219.
8 Maj.Gen. F Hepburn, quoted in *Waterloo Letters*, edited by Maj.Gen. HT Siborne (London, 1891), p.266.
9 Col. H Seymour, quoted in *Waterloo Letters*, pp.19–20.

Chapter X
AN URGENT STATE
OF AFFAIRS

*Napoleon did not manoeuvre at all. He just moved forward in the old style,
in columns, and was driven off in the old style.*
Wellington to Beresford, 2 July 1815

*If Lord Wellington had been at the head of his old Peninsula army, I am confident that
he would have swept his opponents off the face of the earth immediately after their first attack.*
John Kincaid, 95th Rifles

The rumble of gunfire around Hougoumont was nothing more than a distant distraction to the majority of Wellington's men on the ridge at Mont St Jean. The fight there was developing into a battle within a battle, and apart from those who were called upon to support the defenders of the château the rest of the Allied Army would fight on, largely unaware of what was happening out in front on Wellington's right flank.

It was shortly after 1pm when things began to take on a decidedly sinister aspect for those positioned in the centre of Wellington's line. As they looked out across the valley they saw scores of French gun teams moving into position, dragging their guns through the thick mud, and establishing a huge battery on a spur about 500 yards south of La Haye Sainte. The spur, which runs slightly north-east to south-west, straddles the Brussels road, the longer length being to the east of the road. It was on this spur that the French established a grand battery of around seventy-four guns, although some estimates put this figure as high as eighty-four. The guns themselves were 6-, 8- and even 12-pounders, and when the gunners had finished putting the finishing touches to their arrangements, the British troops on the ridge looked out on the largest array of enemy guns they had seen since the Battle of Vittoria, almost two years earlier.

At 1.30pm the French guns opened fire to begin softening up the Allied line prior to the great infantry attack. Those Allied troops to the west of the Brussels road were afforded a measure of cover by the reverse slope, upon which they lay down as the large iron balls went skimming and bouncing over them. Every now and then, however, an enemy shot bounced into their ranks, killing and maiming anyone in its path. Common shell was also used – hollow iron balls filled with gunpowder which exploded when the fuse ran down. Often, a unit of soldiers would wait anxiously as the fuse burned, each of the men wondering whether he would be dealt a piece of the casing which was capable of tearing into the body and inflicting fearful wounds. It was also possible, if a man was brave enough, to pull the fuse from a shell or extinguish it before the shell exploded. Men were even known to have thrown shells back, as Captain Colquitt, of the 1st Foot Guards, would famously do later in the day. But it was the solid iron balls, round shot, that cause by far the majority of wounds. It was possible for a single ball to mow down an entire rank of twenty or thirty men at one go. Even when it appeared that the ball had run its course, it was dangerous to try to stop it, either with the foot or by hand, as, even at a seemingly low speed, the ball was still liable to cause death or damage.

The men to the east of the Brussels road, in particular Kempt's and Pack's brigades, were afforded little protection from enemy artillery, as the reverse slope here was nothing like that on the other side of the road. True, there was a slight degree of protection, but one had to be positioned well back from the Chemin d'Ohain – which lay along the forward slope – in order to escape the worst effects of the shelling, and even here the dreaded iron balls would come fizzing, skimming and bouncing along to cause severe casualties amongst the Allied troops. Standing with his men in close column was James Hope, of the 92nd Highlanders, who described the ordeal:

> At first we did not mind it much, but in a few minutes it became so terrible, as to strike with awe the oldest veteran in the field. The spirits of our men were very low indeed during the whole

It was down this slope that the Lüneburg battalion marched to help assist the defenders of La Haye Sainte. Unfortunately, they were attacked by French cuirassiers who caught them still in line. Although the battalion suffered heavily, the casualty figures do not bear out the sort of disaster which is usually attributed to the battalion. Later in the day, Christian Ompteda would lead his men down this same slope, only to be met by French 1cavalry in the same manner.

of the morning, and although they had been considerably raised before the commencement of the battle, yet there was something wanting to restore their wonted daring, when opposed to the enemies of their country.[1]

Hope relates that that 'something' came when the Duke of Richmond, who was present at Waterloo, rode up and let slip that the Prussians were advancing upon Waterloo with 40,000 men. One can well imagine the effect this good news had on the wavering Highlanders, and indeed on all those who heard it.

It wasn't just the infantry that suffered from the French guns. Ponsonby's Union Brigade sat waiting behind the infantry on the reverse slope. They too were a good deal harassed by the fire that grew in intensity in preparation for the French infantry attack, which they knew would surely follow. Sir Thomas Picton had seen it all before, but he had never experienced such a heavy bombardment as this, and he too must surely have winced now and then as the shot and shell flew around him. Down in the sandpit opposite La Haye Sainte, Johnny Kincaid and his riflemen were building an abatis across the road when suddenly a round shot came flying in amongst them, taking off the head of the right-hand man. The intensity of the French bombardment was particularly felt amongst a brigade of Belgian troops, under the Count de Bylandt, who found the strain too much. Harry Ross-Lewin, of the 32nd, watched as they began to buckle:

As soon as the above mentioned portion of the enemy's artillery were in position, the limbers were removed to the rear; a few men remained at each gun, and they began to throw their shot into our columns with great precision. Their practice was undoubtedly very good, and the Belgians adopted a perfectly intelligible, although not very soldier-like method of expressing the high opinion they entertained of its excellence; for only one or two shot had passed through them when they faced about, and went in a body to the rear, artillery and all. This little circumstance did not encourage us to place excessive reliance on the support to be expected from our new allies, *les braves Belges*.[2]

In fact, Bylandt's brigade had been ordered to pull back behind the Chemin by the Prince of Orange via Perponcher. There were others, however, like James Hope of the 92nd, who thought that Bylandt's men behaved nobly and, when the French later advanced, 'returned the enemy's fire with great spirit'. The French artillery bombardment reached a crescendo, until at about 1.45pm small dark specks began to filter out into the muddy fields in front of the guns, and behind them came huge, dark masses of French infantry. The attack had finally begun. Jonathan Leach and John Kincaid, of the 95th Rifles, had spent most of their army lives fighting the French, and in particular their skirmishers, and now, from the sandpit on the Brussels road, they watched once again as enemy light troops, voltigeurs, fanned out in front of them. The enemy guns continued to roar as the French columns made their way across the boggy undulating fields, up to the ridge where Wellington's men waited for them. As usual, the French came on noisily, cheering and shouting, the officers making a great show of themselves to encourage their men. Leach, watching with disdain from the sandpit wrote later:

> Under cover of this cannonade several large columns of infantry, supported by heavy bodies of cavalry, and preceded by a multitude of light infantry, descended at a trot into the plain, with shouts and cries of, 'Vive l'Empereur!' some of them throwing up their caps in the air, and advancing to the attack with such confidence and impetuosity, as if the bare possibility of our being able to withstand the shock was out of the question, fighting as they were under the eyes of the Emperor. But Napoleon was destined, in a few minutes after the commencement of this hubbub, to see his Imperial Legions recoil in the greatest confusion, with a dreadful carnage, and with a great loss in prisoners.[3]

Leach got it entirely right. In six years of war in the Peninsula, the French had hardly got close to the British line, let alone break it, and they were not about to do it now, not even with Bonaparte himself watching them. It was all a matter of mathematics, timing and use of the ground. French infantry attacks against the British between 1808 and 1814 virtually always came on

in column, dense formations which prevented only those at the front and on the flanks from firing. The larger the column, in fact, the more useless it was, as it only served to lock up an even greater number of Frenchmen. The British, on the other hand, fought in a two-deep line, in which every single musket could be fired. It took no mathematical genius, therefore, to predict the outcome between the two formations, supposing the troops in line to be steady and determined. And Wellington's men certainly were that. The French had often intended to deploy into line when they reached the British line, but because of Wellington's use of the reverse slope they rarely knew where that line was. And even when they did manage to try and deploy, the steady, controlled volleys pouring out from the red-jacketed infantry forced them back into their tightly packed formation. Then, after a couple more volleys and a great cheer, the British would charge bayonets and in an instant would be chasing the French back the way they had come. It all sounds so simple, but it happened on umpteen different occasions in Portugal and Spain. Only at Sorauren, in the Pyrenees, did the French actually reach and break Wellington's line, and even then it was only a fleeting success.

Why Bonaparte thought he could succeed where countless marshals and generals had failed heaven only knows, but here he was, sending his men forward in their masses to try yet again. And, at Waterloo, the French almost

Sir Thomas Picton had barely shouted the words, 'Charge! Charge! Hurrah!' before he fell from his horse with a bullet through his temple. Waterloo was the final chapter in the long, distinguished and often controversial career of the fiery Welshman. Here, he lies in the arms of a British drummer boy, close to the crossroads above La Haye Sainte.

succeeded. Tired of being beaten time after time, the French appear to have tried a different formation, much wider than normal, as if to compensate for their usual lack of firepower. Their columns presented a tremendous frontage, even with the spaces between them, and this would, in theory, have given them far greater firepower than usual. They were also coming on in overwhelming strength. For example, when the brigades of Colborne, Houghton and Abercrombie stood and died hard at Albuera on 16 May 1811, they did so facing the largest single attack of the Peninsular War, of around 8,000 French troops. But here at Waterloo, the French were sending forward twice this number. It was a massive attack.

The approach to Wellington's ridge was not an easy one. The ground appears to be relatively gentle, but anyone who has stood opposite La Haye Sainte at the bottom of the valley, will know just how steep the approach to the ridge actually is. The mud at Waterloo is extremely viscous, and as the French advanced over the boggy ground their boots must have grown heavier and heavier with each muddy step. The advance was also hindered by Allied artillery fire. Never one to indulge in counter-battery fire, Wellington ordered his artillery to concentrate their fire on the attacking columns for it was these that represented the greatest danger at times like this.

The French mass extended from about a hundred yards west of the Brussels road, all the way to Papelotte, albeit with gaps in between the various columns. At the western end of the French line squadrons of steel-clad cuirassiers came on at the trot, whilst their artillery continued to pound away over their heads, keeping up their fire until the last minute. The first troops to come into contact with the French were the green-jacketed riflemen of the 95th, who crept out forward from the sandpit to engage the enemy voltigeurs and to pick off as many officers as they could. Johnny Kincaid was in the sandpit and he recalled seeing Bonaparte and his staff take post by the side of the road, the French columns cheering as they passed him. They continued shouting as they advanced towards the riflemen who remained passively unimpressed by the noise, as Kincaid later recalled:

> Backed by the thunder of their artillery, and carrying with them the rubidub of drums, and the *tantara* of trumpets, in addition to their increasing shouts, it looked, at first, as if they had some hopes of scaring us off the ground; for it was a singular contrast to the stern silence reigning on our side, where nothing, as yet, but the voices of our great guns, told that we had mouths to open when we chose to use them. Our rifles were, however, in a few seconds, required to play their parts, and opened such a fire on the advancing skirmishers as quickly brought them to a stand still; but their columns advanced steadily through them, although our incessant *tiralade* was telling in their centre with fearful exactness.[4]

It wasn't long, however, before the 95th were forced back by sheer weight of numbers, retiring to the Chemin d'Ohain and passing through Kempt's brigade. With the 95th having been forced back there remained only the garrison in La Haye Sainte forward of the main ridge. The farm, situated just 250 yards from the crossroads, was not as strong as Hougoumont. Although it was surrounded by walls and had tall buildings on three sides, the walls adjoining the road were not particularly high. An orchard lay to the south of it and a garden to the north, beyond which was some open ground and beyond that again was the Allied position. The Brussels road had been barricaded just outside the farm, loopholes had been cut in the farmhouse walls and riflemen placed in the most advantageous defensive positions. Apart from this, little had been done to fortify the place, partly owing to the fact that KGL engineers had been sent away to Hougoumont to help fortify the château. The gate in the western wall, meanwhile, had been used for firewood the night before, leaving an almighty opening that would have to be defended extremely well if the French were not to gain access. Fortunately, the farm was blessed with an excellent garrison consisting of about 370 men of the 2nd Light Battalion KGL, under Major George Baring. Baring himself was not unfamiliar with the problems of defending a forward post. At Albuera, in May 1811, he had taken part in the defence of the village in the face of several French attacks and was, in fact, wounded there. La Haye Sainte, however, presented an entirely different proposition. The attacking troops were vastly more in number, and of better quality, whilst the farm was isolated from the main Allied position and proved difficult to support both in terms of manpower and, more crucially, ammunition.

Baring initially placed three weak companies in the orchard, one in the garden, and the other two under Lieutenants Carey and Graeme, and Ensign Frank, in and around the buildings and

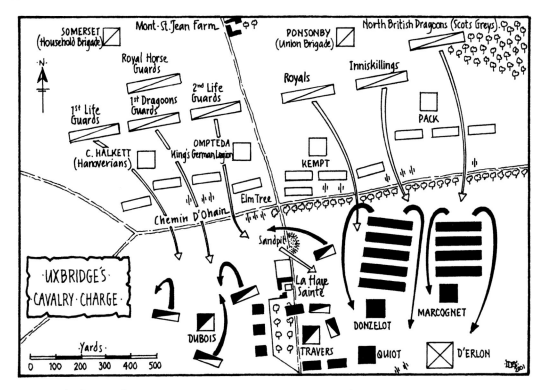

courtyard. The French appeared to be advancing in two columns, one against the orchard and the other against the buildings themselves. Watching from the orchard was George Baring, whose men lay waiting for the French to advance within range. 'Shortly after noon, some skirmishers commenced the attack,' he wrote:

> I made the men lie down, and forbad all firing until the enemy were quite near. The first shot broke the bridle of my horse close to my hand, and the second killed Major Boswiel, who was standing near me. The enemy did not stop long skirmishing, but immediately advanced over the height, with two close columns, one of which attacked the buildings, and the other threw itself in mass into the orchard, showing the greatest contempt for our fire. It was not possible for our small disjointed numbers fully to withstand this furious attack of such a superior force, and we retired upon the barn, in a more united position, in order to continue the defence: my horse's leg was broken, and I was obliged to take that of the adjutant.[5]

Baring and his men retreated to the barn where they were joined by two companies of the 1st Light Battalion KGL, under Captains Wynecken and van Groeben, as well a company of Hanoverians under Major von Sporken, all of whom were busy skirmishing to the west of the farmhouse. Watching the fight from the main ridge was Count Kielmansegge, commanding the 1st Hanoverian Brigade, and the Prince of Orange. As the two men watched, Wellington rode up and ordered a battalion of Lüneburgers, under Colonel von Klenke, forward to support Baring. The battalion, 595-strong, duly marched down the slope to La Haye Sainte where they joined Baring, Wynecken, Groeben and von Sporken, who were directing their men in the face of the French advance.

Initially things went well and the combined force began to drive the French back, but as Baring neared the orchard he noticed with alarm a long line of cuirassiers forming behind it. At the same time, one of his officers, Captain Meyer, rushed up to him to report that the French had surrounded the rear garden and that it was not possible to hold it any longer. Faced with a threat from both front and rear, Baring ordered his men to fall back once again. Unfortunately, some confusion set in. The Lünebergers outnumbered Baring's own men considerably and he had difficulty in getting his voice heard above the noise. Before he knew it the entire German force was falling backwards at speed, many of the Lünebergers apparently running for the safety of the main Allied line. At this point the cuirassiers charged and were soon in amongst the fleeing infantry. The Lünebergers were duly ridden down by the heavy French cavalrymen, as were many of Baring's men, who were caught running for the shelter of the barn.

The episode was nowhere near the disaster many historians would have us believe. Traditionally, the Lünebergers are cut to pieces, or butchered, but their casualty figures tell a very different story. Indeed, of 595 officers and men of the Luneberg battalion, only three officers and twenty-nine other ranks were killed, whilst 142 were wounded. A further forty-eight were recorded as missing. Total casualties were, therefore, 222, and these, it should not be forgotten, were for the entire day. We will never know just how many became casualties at this point of the battle, but it is difficult to believe that all of them were, and that no other casualties occurred throughout the remainder of the day. A high casualty rate, yes, but a major disaster, perhaps not.

The second myth surrounding the Lünebergers' attack concerns the Prince of Orange, who is frequently cited as being responsible for sending the Hanoverians to their deaths. Recent historians include Jac Weller, who states quite categorically that it was the Prince who sent them forward, although there is scant evidence to prove it. Siborne actually says it was Wellington himself who ordered the Lünebergers forward, whilst Kielmansegge is another suspect. The Prince of Orange will seriously blot his copybook later in the day, but it would appear that he has certainly had a raw deal over the business with the Lünebergers, as he has had over the episode concerning the 69th at Quatre Bras.

As well as the Lünebergers, the 8th Line Battalion KGL also suffered at the hands of the French cuirassiers. Ompteda's brigade had been busy driving back the French infantry to the rear of La Haye Sainte, when a body of cuirassiers returning from an unsuccessful assault on Kielmansegge's infantry squares appeared and caught the 8th Line KGL as they were charging in line. The regiment was ridden through and their greater part either cut down or dispersed. Colonel von Schroeder, seven officers and 110 rank and file were casualties and the 8th's Kings Colour was taken.

With the Lünebergers having been severely mauled by the French cuirassiers, Baring and his men were temporarily cut off, leaving the French to swarm around the buildings, although they were unable to break in. The collision outside between the KGL and Hanoverian infantry had been costly to both of them. In addition to the Luneberg casualties given above, Baring himself lost, in his own words, 'a considerable number of men, besides three officers killed, and six wounded'. One of the dead officers was Captain Gottlieb Thilo Holtzermann. When the KGL had been stationed at Bexhill-on-Sea a few years ear-

lier, Holtzermann had fallen in love with the daughter of the local customs officer and they were married in the pretty local church. It is entirely possible that whilst Gottlieb Holtzermann was lying dead on the bloody field of Waterloo on that momentous Sunday in June 1815, his wife was attending a service in that very same church. Another of the dead officers was Captain Frederick Schaumann, the brother of the author of the celebrated memoir, *On the Road with Wellington*, Auguste Schaumann.

Having come in sight of the sunken Ohain road, the French cuirassiers halted and reformed, upon which Kielmansegge and Ompteda duly took the opportunity to form their brigades into squares. But the French cuirassiers were not the only threat to the Allied line, for in addition to the troops attacking La Haye Sainte, thousands more continued to close upon the Dutch and Belgian troops in front of and at the hedge at the Ohain road. Behind the hedge and lower down on the reverse slope of the ridge lay the Peninsular veterans of Picton's division who waited in silence as their allies bore the brunt of the French advance. The crash of musketry signalled the arrival of the French in front of the hedge, and despite a brave fight by the Dutch and Belgian troops, they were driven back by sheer weight of numbers. Many ran to the rear in panic, and even British gunners, who had been firing until the very last moment into the packed ranks of the enemy, darted backwards towards their red-jacketed comrades. In the course of the entire Peninsular War Wellington had lost just one gun, at Maya, in July 1813, but here, during the first major French infantry attack, he was in danger of losing more. Indeed, a sergeant in Rogers' battery panicked and hastily spiked one of the guns before running to the rear. The performance of the Royal Artillery at Waterloo so irked Wellington that he later raised the issue in a letter to the Earl of Mulgrave:

> To tell you the truth, I was not very pleased with the Artillery in the battle of Waterloo...In some instances they [the French] were in actual possession of our guns. We could not expect the artillerymen to remain at their guns in such a case; but I had a right to expect that the officers and men of the Artillery would do as I did, and as all the staff did, that is, to take shelter in the squares of the Infantry till the French cavalry should be driven off from the ground, either by our Cavalry or Infantry. But they did no such thing; they ran off the field entirely, taking with them limbers, ammunition, and everything.[6]

With everything crumbling in front of him, and with the French beginning to close on the hedge, Picton ordered Kempt and Pack to bring their brigades forward to stop the French advance. Scores of letters were written afterwards by British officers belonging to the two brigades, and although some contradict others, and those written by cavalry officers positioned farther behind them, it would appear that although the French breached the hedge in some places, in others they did not even reach it. After all, theirs was an extremely wide formation and it is clear that the various columns did not arrive in front of the hedge at the same moment. Whatever the case, it is quite clear that a crisis was rapidly developing along the front of Picton's sector.

The men ordered to 'arrest the torrent' were Peninsular veterans, but they had been severely tried two days earlier at Quatre Bras. Kempt's brigade, being the 1/28th, 1/32nd and 1/79th, scrambled to their feet and hurried forward, whilst Pack's men, the 3/1st, 1/42nd, 2/44th and 1/92nd, did likewise. Between them, they had served in scores of actions in Spain and Portugal and here, on the muddy slopes of Mont St Jean, they were to lock horns again with some of their old French friends. For example, away to the right of Charles Belson's 28th Regiment was the French 54th Ligne Regiment. Just over four years earlier, at Barrosa, Belson had ordered his men to fire at these very same gentlemen, telling them to fire low in order to 'spoil their dancing'. And here they were again, with thousands of other Frenchmen, getting ever nearer to Wellington's redcoats.

With the Dutch and Belgian troops pushed aside, the French could be forgiven for thinking they were on the verge of a rare triumph against Wellington, but just as they began to sense victory, a bad dream in the shape of Sir Thomas Picton and a few hundred British infantry returned to haunt them. Unknown to anyone but his servant, the brusque Welshman was suffering from a severe wound which he had received at Quatre Bras. He was dressed in his black civilian garb and was wearing a top hat. He was anything but the image of a British soldier, but he was just the man to stop the French advance in its tracks. Picton twisted about in the saddle as he sat upon his horse, frantically getting his men forward, shouting, 'Charge, charge, hurrah!' when suddenly he tumbled to the ground, a French musket ball lodged in his forehead. It was a tragic if fitting end to the long, distinguished and controversial career of this fighting Welshman.

Picton's eyes had barely closed upon the scene when his enraged men came hurrying forward to the hedge and found the French deploying on their side of it. The drill was simple enough for the British, for it was something they had done time and time again in the Peninsula and on numerous bland drill grounds. They deployed into their lines, made ready and fired. Volley after volley rolled out from their lines, but on this occasion there was one difference. The French refused to budge. In fact, they stood there and returned fire, trading volley for volley with their British adversaries. Kempt's brigade fought close to the crossroads with Pack's fighting away to their left. Lieutenant Robert Belcher was with the 32nd when they reached the hedge. The ensign carrying the Regimental Colour was shot down and Belcher grabbed it until another ensign could be found to carry it. He later wrote:

> Almost instantly after, the Brigade still advancing, and the French infantry getting into disorder and beginning to retreat, a mounted [French] Officer had his horse shot under him. When he extricated himself we were close on him. I had the Colour on my left arm and was slightly in advance of the division. He suddenly fronted me and seized the staff, I still retaining a grasp of the silk (the Colours were nearly new). At the same moment he attempted to draw his sabre, but had not accomplished it when the Covering Colour Sergeant, named Switzer, thrust his pike into his breast, and the right rank and file of the division, named Lacy, fired into him. He fell dead at my feet. Brevet-Major Toole, commanding the right centre division at the moment, called out, 'Save the brave fellow', but it was too late.[7]

Along with the 32nd and 79th, the 28th got stuck into the enemy with a vengeance. At Albuera, in May 1811, a handful of British battalions had taken on and defeated two French divisions after the most intense firefight of the Peninsular War. The 28th, 'The Slashers' as they were known, had taken part in that fight and here they were again, in a firefight of much shorter duration but of similar intensity.

To the left of Kempt's brigade, Pack's men were enduring a similar hard fight, in which the French appeared to be getting the better of things. The 3/1st, 1/42nd and 2/44th were no slouches, but even they were hard pushed to halt the French advance. Indeed, at least two officers of the 92nd claim they were forced back before their own regiment was brought forward. James Hope was one of them:

Sir Denis Pack, who had remained with the

Royals and 44th, till they retired from the ridge, perceiving the urgent state of affairs, galloped up to the 92nd, and, with a countenance denoting the importance of the communication he was about to give, said, 'Ninety-second, you must charge! All the troops in your front have given way.' The regiment answered the call with cheers.[8]

Lieutenant Robert Winchester was with the 92nd, and he tells a very similar story:

Previous to this the 92nd had been lying down under cover of the position when they were immediately ordered to stand to their arms, Major General Sir Denis Pack calling out at the same time, '92nd, everything has given way on your right and left and you must charge this column,' upon which he ordered four deep to be formed and closed in to the centre. The Regiment, which was then within about 20 yards of the column, fired a volley into them. The enemy on reaching the hedge at the side of the road had ordered arms, and were in the act of shouldering them when they received the volley from the 92nd.[9]

The 92nd suffered heavy losses from the enemy's fire, which was poured into them at a very short range, possibly twenty yards or so. The unusually long French formation was beginning to pay dividends. No longer were they at a numerical disadvantage, and they were slowly beginning to drive the Highlanders back. Picton was dead,

and the expected victory of the British line over French columns had not materialised. All along the Ohain road, from the crossroads as far east as the fork in the road which led to Wavre, French infantry were pushing forward, cheering as they slowly began to establish themselves on the crest of the Allied position.

Meanwhile Wellington's heavy cavalry, the Union and Household Brigades, had sat watching anxiously from the foot of the reverse slope as the infantry tried to hold back the tide of French infantry which swept up to the Ohain road to the east of the crossroads. The Household Brigade was positioned to the west of the Brussels road and so had no infantry action in front of them. Instead, they looked up at Ompteda's and Kielmansegge's brigades who sat in square formation to protect them from a possible attack by the French cuirassiers that had already mauled the Lünebergers. The Union Brigade, however, had a much more active scene before them. Their situation, at the bottom of the slope, did not allow them to see too much of the French who were fighting on the other side of the ridge, but they did see the Dutch and Belgian troops fall back, Picton's men advance to the hedge, and, finally, the clash of musketry at the hedge itself. It was a fight they viewed with a growing anxiety.

The commander of the Allied cavalry, the Earl of Uxbridge, had been over at Hougoumont, where he had been supervising

The Duke of Wellington sits astride his horse, Copenhagen, as Somerset's brigade of heavy cavalry sets off on its charge to the west of the Brussels road. The charge, made in conjunction with Ponsonby's brigade to the east of the road, remains one of the most famous in military history.

the positioning of some of his hussars. He returned to the crossroads to find a crisis looming in front of him. A hasty appraisal of the situation was made before he sped off to the respective brigade commanders to issue his orders. On the face of it, he was left with little option but to order a charge, otherwise it looked as if the French might break through. With few reliable troops between the battlefield and Brussels the significance of his next move was not lost on him.

Uxbridge rode to Somerset, commanding the Household Brigade, and ordered him to prepare to charge, with the Life Guards and the King's Dragoon Guards in the first line and the Horse Guards in support. He then galloped across the Brussels road to Ponsonby, and ordered him to charge also, with the 1st (Royals) and the Inniskillings in the first line and the Scots Greys in support. Satisfied with his arrangements, he returned to the west of the Brussels road and, as he later wrote, he 'put the whole in motion'.

In fact, it was 16-year-old John Edwards, of the 1st Life Guards, and Somerset's field trumpeter, who set the charge in motion, his high-pitched shrill being heard by all as the signal to move forward to the crest. Then, with a cheer, and with their long, straight-bladed swords drawn from their scabbards, the Household Brigade thundered up to the crest, whilst on the other side of the Brussels road, the Union Brigade did likewise. The Household Brigade swept past the squares of Ompteda and Kielmansegge and charged down the slope towards La Haye Sainte. Coming slowly up the slope were squadrons of cuirassiers, fresh from their triumph over the Lünebergers, along with French infantry who had been attacking the farm. Lieutenant Samuel Waymouth was with the 2nd Life Guards and recalled seeing Ponsonby's brigade charging parallel to them on the other side of the Brussels road. Waymouth himself was knocked down and taken prisoner during the charge, but was later told by Captain Edward Kelly that the Household Brigade and the cuirassiers, 'came to the shock like two walls, in the most perfect lines he ever saw'. Waymouth himself wrote:

A short struggle enabled us to break through them, notwithstanding the great disadvantage arising from our swords, which were full six inches shorter than those of the cuirassiers, besides its being the custom in our Service to carry the swords in a very bad position whilst charging, the French carrying theirs in a man-

ner much less fatiguing, and also much better for either attack or defence. Having once penetrated their line, we rode over everything opposed to us.[10]

The British cavalry smashed into the French cuirassiers, scattering them to the wind and setting about them with their swords that clattered upon the breastplates of the French cavalry. Indeed, walking over the field in 1842, Edward Somerset remarked to Sergeant Major Cotton, 'You might have fancied that it was so many tinkers at work.' The cuirassiers were broken and pursued past La Haye Sainte as far as a cutting in the Brussels road, south of La Haye Sainte, where the French became hopelessly jammed. Here, the cuirassiers were helpless against the Life Guards and the King's Dragoon Guards who set about their enemies, cutting, slashing and thrusting at the tightly packed Frenchmen. During the fight Edward Kelly killed the colonel of the 1st Cuirassiers, after which he calmly dismounted and cut off the dead officer's epaulettes as a souvenir before riding off.

While Edward Kelly was busy carrying off his newly won trophies, another Life Guard, 25-year-old Corporal John Shaw, was setting about his enemies with even more gusto. Shaw was a well-known pugilist, who had defeated many an opponent with his bare fists. A giant of a man, he was unmistakable on the field of Waterloo. During this first charge Shaw encountered a cuirassier who appeared eager to tackle him in single combat. The challenge was eagerly accepted by Shaw who parried the Frenchman's low thrust before cutting through his helmet and splitting the skull down to the chin. In the words of an eye-witness, the Frenchman's 'face fell off like a bit of apple'. Two of Shaw's comrades, Hodgson and Dakin, were likewise keen fighters. Dakin was set upon by two cuirassiers but, 'with the prowess of a Paladin', he dealt them two mighty blows to split open both their heads. Hodgson, meanwhile, rode as far as a French battery and when trying to return, found his escape blocked by a unit of French infantry. With bullets whizzing round his head Hodgson rode straight through them to make good his escape, only to find a cuirassier blocking his way. The enemy cavalryman startled Hodgson by shouting, 'Damn you, I'll stop your crowing', in a Irish accent. The two men jostled each other before the cuirassier aimed a lunge at Hodgson's throat. Rather than parry the stroke Hodgson swung his sword and lopped off the Irishman's hand before plunging his own sword into the

The 6th (Inniskilling) Dragoons charging at Waterloo. The regiment are reputed to have captured a French Eagle during the charge, only to have seen it retaken by the French.

Corporal Styles, of the 1st (Royal) Dragoons, holds aloft the Eagle of the French 105th Ligne. The circumstances surrounding the capture of the bird have long since been the subject of controversy, with Captain Alexander Clark-Kennedy claiming its actual capture, the Eagle then falling across the neck of Styles' horse.

cuirassier's throat. He then turned it round and round until the man fell dead from his horse. He was next challenged by a cuirassier officer, but a mighty blow brought both horse and rider crashing to the ground. Apparently, Hodgson would have spared the officer, a 'grey-headed old man', but saw a group of enemy lancers riding up and so was obliged to finish him off before turning and riding off to rejoin his comrades.[11]

So far, the charge of the Household Brigade had been a devastating success but it had not been achieved without heavy loss. Whilst the Life Guards were cutting and hewing at the French who were jammed in at the cutting south of La Haye Sainte, scores of French infantrymen advanced to the banks overlooking it, and opened fire, killing and wounding many British cavalrymen. With Somerset's brigade having thrown back the French to the west of the Brussels road, we must turn our attention to events to the east of the road.

When Somerset's brigade began their charge they found little to obstruct their path, save for the brigades of Ompteda and Kielmansegge. The situation was very different, however, for Ponsonby and the Union Brigade. They had sat watching the fight at the Chemin d'Ohain when Uxbridge galloped over to Ponsonby with orders to charge. Thus, by

the time they began to move forward the situation at the hedge had become critical, with hundreds of French troops beginning to pour forward in places having driven the British troops back. 33-year-old Captain Alexander Clark-Kennedy, of the 1st (Royal) Dragoons, considered the timing of the charge to have been not a moment too soon:

> The heads of the French columns, which appeared to me to be nearly close together, had no appearance of having been repulsed or seriously checked. On the contrary...they had forced their way through our line – the heads of the columns were on the Brussels side of the double hedge. There was no British infantry in the immediate front that I saw, and the line that had been, I presume, behind the hedges was wheeled by sections or divisions to the left, and was firing on the left flank of the left column as it advanced. In fact, the crest of the height had been gained, and the charge of cavalry at the critical moment recovered it. Had the charge been delayed two or three minutes, I feel satisfied it would probably have failed.[12]

The Union Brigade had formed with the 1st (Royals) on the right and the Inniskillings on the left. The Scots Greys were supposed to have remained behind them in support, but owing to the heavy French bombardment they had moved

Another version of Clark-Kennedy, running through the French officer carrying the eagle of the 105th Ligne. In his account of the incident, Clark-Kennedy did indeed say that he ran his sword into the right side of the French officer.

forward to take advantage of some shelter afforded them by a group of trees. Thus, they inadvertently brought themselves into line with the other two regiments. With arrangements made, De Lacy Evans, of the Staff, waved his hat in the air as the signal for the charge to begin. Then, with trumpets blaring, the 1,100 heavy dragoons went thundering up the slope towards the hedged lane where Pack and Kempt were locked in close combat with the mass of French infantry.

With the French having begun to push across the Chemin d'Ohain and establish themselves on the crest of the Allied position, cries of 'Victoire!' went up all along their line. But at the very moment when they believed their cursed luck had finally changed, their shouts of victory were well and truly rammed down their throats in the most violent of fashions. For when the French drove across the Ohain road they believed they had broken through Wellington's line and expected to see an army falling back in disorder. But instead, coming on at full pelt towards them were the splendidly mounted British heavy dragoons of the Union Brigade.

The infantry at the crest wheeled back to let the dragoons through. Scores of the 92nd are reputed to have grabbed hold of the stirrups of the Scots Greys and bounded forward with them, shouting, 'Scotland for ever!', although it is doubtful whether this actually occurred. The three regiments crashed into the French infantry,

who appeared stunned to find British cavalry hacking at them from all sides. Hundreds of them threw down their arms, others were rooted to the spot and were simply cut down, whilst even more were ridden down or, as an officer of the 92nd wrote, 'walked over'. Neither the Greys nor the Inniskillings had been in the Peninsula. Indeed, the Greys had not been overseas for some twenty-five years. Only the 1st (Royals) could claim recent active service in Portugal and Spain where they had served with great distinction. But now, on these muddy slopes, the Peninsular absentees made up for lost time in the most dramatic manner, cutting their way through the French masses and sending hundreds of them running for their lives, 'like a flock of sheep'. Others continued to stand and fight, however, as Sergeant Major Dickson, of the Scots Greys, later wrote:

A young officer of Fusiliers made a slash at me with his sword, but I parried it and broke his arm...The French were fighting like tigers. Some of the wounded were firing at us as we passed; and poor Kinchant, who had spared one of these rascals, was himself shot by the officer he had spared. As we were sweeping down a steep slope on the top of them, they had to give way. Then those in front began to cry out for 'quarter', throwing down their muskets and taking off their belts. The Gordons at this point rushed in and drove the French to the rear.[13]

The long swords of the British heavy dragoons were clumsy and unwieldy, but they were also capable of inflicting terrible wounds. The sword was essentially a cutting weapon with a hatchet point, although Smythies, of the 1st (Royals), said he and his comrades were ordered to grind down the backs of their swords to make 'spear points'. One mighty Scotsman, now to be found cutting and slashing at the French infantry, was Sergeant Charles Ewart, of the Greys. Six feet four inches tall, he was a giant of a man, and with a 1796 heavy cavalry sword in his hand he was a truly fearsome warrior. In the midst of the turmoil he spotted an officer carrying one of the much-prized Imperial eagles, blessed by the hand of Bonaparte himself and borne proudly into battle by his adoring soldiers. The gilt-covered bird in question sat upon a box bearing the number 45 whilst the silk beneath it bore the words, 'Austerlitz, Jena, Friedland, Essling and Wagram', not that Ewart cared. He was more concerned with plucking the bird from its owners although, naturally enough, he found them reluctant to part with it:

> It was in the first charge I took the Eagle from the enemy – the bearer and I had a very hard contest for it; he thrust for my groin; I parried it off and cut him down through the head; after which I was attacked by one of their lancers, who threw his lance at me, but missed the mark, by my throwing it off with my sword by my right side – then I cut him from the chin upwards, which cut went through the teeth. Afterwards I was attacked by a foot soldier, who, after firing at me, charged me with his bayonet, but he very soon lost the combat, for I parried it, and cut him down through the head; so that finished the combat for the Eagle. After which, I presumed to follow my commander, Eagle and all, but I was stopped by the General saying to me, 'You brave fellow, take that to the rear; you have done enough till you get quit of it.' which I was obliged to obey.[14]

It remains a bit of a mystery where the lancer came from, as the infantry to the east of the Brussels road appear to have attacked unsupported. Indeed, the lancers themselves counter-attacked only after the Union Brigade reached the French guns. Is it possible that Ewart took the eagle much later than traditionally given, whilst the French were retreating in disorder, and when Ewart himself was looking to return to the Allied ridge? It is of little importance, but the presence of the lancer at this point is puzzling.

Whilst Ewart was carving a place for him in the annals of British military history, his comrades continued to deal death all around them. Far away to Ewart's right, the 1st (Royals) were in action, punishing the French infantry as they got amongst them. Alexander Clark-Kennedy had been engaged for about five minutes when he saw two French Colours, one of which was topped with an eagle, about forty yards to his left. He later estimated him to be 300 yards east of La Haye Sainte and 270 yards south of the Ohain road. The officer carrying the eagle had evidently become separated from the main column and was attempting to push his way 'back into the crowd'. Without a moment's hesitation, Clark-Kennedy shouted to his men, 'right shoulders forward, attack the Colour!' before leading his men towards the eagle:

> On reaching it, I ran my sword into the officer's right side a little above the hip joint. He was a little to my left side, and he fell to that side with the eagle across my horse's head. I tried to catch it with my left hand, but could only touch the fringe of the flag, and it is probable it would have fallen to the ground, had not it been prevented by the neck of Corporal Styles' horse, who came up on my left at that instant, and against which it fell...on running the officer through the body I called out twice together, 'Secure the Colour, secure the Colour, it belongs to me.' This order was addressed to some men close to me, of whom Corporal Styles was one. On taking up the eagle, I endeavoured to break the eagle from off the pole with the intention of putting it into the breast of my coat, but I could not break it. Corporal Styles said, 'Pray, sir, do not break it', on which I replied, 'Very well, carry it to the rear as fast as you can, it belongs to me.'[15]

One of the first officers Styles met when taking the eagle to the rear was a Lieutenant Bridges, who naturally thought that Styles himself had captured the bird. He duly put Styles' name against it and it sparked off a controversy that raged for years afterwards. The issue may not seem particularly important, but only six of these eagles had been taken in six years in the Peninsula, only three of which were actually captured on the field of battle, the others being found in a river and in a barracks in Madrid. Thus, they were something of a rare species at Horse Guards. There was even talk of a third eagle being captured. Certainly, the French admitted afterwards to losing the eagle of the 55th Regiment, but they took it back soon afterwards.

The British cavalry charge had so far been a spectacular success. Memories of Salamanca, where just over a thousand of Le Marchant's heavy dragoons demolished eight battalions of French infantry, must have come flooding back to those who had been there on that hot July day in 1812. But at the point at which Uxbridge should have sounded the recall he watched instead, helpless, as the old failing of the British cavalry came back to haunt him. The British cavalry in the Peninsula had acquired the unenviable – and undeserved – reputation of 'galloping at everything', to use Wellington's own words, a reputation gained after a few very high-profile misadventures, such as Vimeiro and Maguilla. They had tarnished their initially successful charges by failing to halt and reform, with the result that on more than one occasion, they were in turn roughly handled by enemy cavalry. Uxbridge had not been present in the Peninsula after January 1809, but he would certainly have known what had gone on there. His charge at Waterloo had achieved great results, but by placing himself at the head of the Household Brigade he was unable to control the charge or to prevent the disaster which was about to happen. 'After the overthrow of the cuirassiers,' he wrote,

> I had in vain attempted to stop my people by sounding the Rally, but neither voice nor trumpet availed; so I went back to seek the support of the second line, which unhappily had not followed the movements of the heavy cavalry. Had I, when I sounded the Rally, found only four well-formed squadrons coming steadily along at an easy trot, I feel certain that the loss the first line suffered when they were finally forced back would have been avoided, and most of these guns might have been secured, for it was obvious the effect of that charge had been prodigious, and for the rest of the day, although the cuirassiers frequently attempted to break into our lines, they always did it mollement and as if they expected something more behind the curtain.[16]

The second line of the Household Brigade consisted of just 200 men of the Royal Horse Guards, the 'Oxford Blues', as they were known, and these, in fact, provided the only support enjoyed by the first line. It is curious that Uxbridge should have criticised them, for they held themselves in check as they ought to have done and were ready to support the first line and assist in bringing them off. The support was needed too, for the Life Guards and the King's Dragoon Guards charged as far as the French batteries, getting in amongst the gunners, cutting them down and putting a number of guns out of action. Uxbridge later estimated the number of guns put out of action by the heavy cavalry to have been as high as forty. But these units fell victim to a counter-attack by a mass of French cuirassiers who found the exhausted British cavalrymen easy prey. The Household Brigade also suffered from the fire of French infantry battalions positioned close to the guns. So it was that an initially successful charge turned into a fight for survival as the Household Brigade fought to regain their own lines.

The situation of the Union Brigade was even worse. They had cut their way through the massed ranks of French infantry to find themselves looking up at the French batteries, situated on the spur running east from just south of La Haye Sainte. The guns had been inflicting steady casualties on the brigade during the charge and now, with the infantry scattered, they presented a wonderfully tempting target, as Sergeant Major Dickson, of the Scots Greys, later recalled:

> We now reached the bottom of the slope. There the ground was slippery with deep mud. Urging each other on, we dashed towards the batteries on the ridge above, which had worked such havoc on our ranks. The ground was very difficult, and especially where we crossed the edge of a ploughed field, so that our horses sank to the knees as we struggled on. My brave Rattler [his horse] was becoming quite exhausted, but we dashed ever onwards. At this moment Colonel Hamilton rode up to us crying, 'Charge! Charge the guns!' and went off like the wind up the hill towards the terrible battery that had made such deadly work among the Highlanders. It was the last we saw of our colonel, poor fellow! His body was found with both arms cut off. His pockets had been rifled. I once heard Major Clarke tell how he saw him wounded among the guns of the great battery, going at full speed, with the bridle-reins between his teeth, after he had lost his hands. Then we got among the guns, and we had our revenge. Such slaughtering! We sabred the gunners, lamed the horses, and cut their traces and harness. I can hear the Frenchmen yet crying 'Diable!' when I struck at them, and the long-drawn hiss through their teeth as my sword went home. Fifteen of their guns could not be fired again that day. The artillery drivers sat on their horses weeping aloud as we went among them; they were mere boys, we thought.[17]

There may be a debate as to who actually captured the eagle of the French 105th Ligne, but there is little doubt who plucked the bird from the French 45th. Here, the artist, Christopher Clark, paints Sergeant Charles Ewart in the act of cutting down an enemy lancer and two infantrymen, before carrying off the trophy.

After twenty-five years of sitting on the sidelines, listening to tales of stirring deeds in the Peninsula, the Greys and Inniskillings were not about to pass up the opportunity of proving their mettle now. Together with the 1st (Royals) they charged up the slope towards the French guns, which continued firing grape and cannister until the very last moment before they finally got in amongst the gunners. The slaughter was tremendous. The British dragoons had demolished the great infantry attack and had wreaked tremendous havoc amongst the French artillery. But even as they continued to slay the French gunners, the valley behind them was beginning to fill up with enemy cavalry, and in particular lancers. The way back to the Allied position was thus barred, and, with the horses blown and their riders exhausted, the Union

Lieutenant Colonel Richard Fitzgerald, 2nd Life Guards, one of the many British officers lost in the great British cavalry charge at Waterloo.

Brigade faced a terrible ordeal if they were to regain their own lines. There was nothing left but to run the gauntlet of enemy cavalry. It was a daunting prospect, as Sergeant Major Dickson later recalled:

> I shall never forget the sight. The cuirassiers, in their sparkling steel breastplates and helmets, mounted on strong black horses, with great blue rugs across the croups, were galloping towards me, tearing up the earth as they went, the trumpets blowing wild notes in the midst of the discharges of grape and cannister shot from the heights. Around me there was one continuous noise of clashing arms, shouting of men, neighing and moaning of horses. What were we to do?[18]

The men of the Union Brigade were left with little choice but to turn and fight their way out, and it was during this phase of the battle that the majority of their casualties occurred. As they tried to cross the valley, now strewn with the carnage of their own attack, the Union Brigade was taken in flank by enemy lancers, cavalry who showed no mercy whatsoever to either wounded or unwounded and who had but to lean over their horses in order to thrust their nine-feet long lances into the helpless bodies of their enemies. The brigade commander, Sir William Ponsonby, tried to escape, but his horse became stuck fast in a boggy ploughed field. Realising the game was up, Ponsonby took off his pocket watch and gave it to his aide-de-camp, Major Reignolds, telling him to save himself and give the watch to his wife. He had barely time to pass it over before the Polish lancers were upon him, driving their lances into him and killing him instantly. Thus, he was never to see the son that was born to his wife in February the following year. Reignolds was also speared, and so Ponsonby's watch disappeared either into the Waterloo mud or into the pockets of some enemy lancer.

The Scots Greys lost their commanding officer, James Hamilton, killed, along with seven other officers, including all three of its cornets. Eight other officers were wounded, whilst a further 220 men were either killed, wounded or taken at Waterloo, although we will never know how many of these casualties occurred during the great charge. The other British heavy cavalry regiments suffered similarly in trying to regain their own lines, although casualties might well have been higher had it not been for Vandeleur's light cavalry which now came to the assistance of their heavier comrades.

The problem lay in the fact that there had been no proper support. The Scots Greys should have been in the second line but had moved forward immediately prior to the charge in order to take shelter from the artillery barrage. Thus, all three regiments of the Union Brigade went forward leaving nobody in support. Away to the left of the brigade sat the light cavalry brigades of Vivian and Vandeleur. The two men watched with delight and then horror as the heavy cavalry first cut up the French infantry only to be severely attacked in turn by fresh French cavalry. The situation cried out for light cavalry support, but both Vivian and Vandeleur would not move without orders from Wellington. Both men knew the Duke's reputation for strict discipline. The entire army had registered its disgust, for example, when Norman Ramsay, of the Royal Horse Artillery, had been placed under arrest following the Battle of Vittoria after he had moved his battery against Wellington's orders. Neither man was willing to risk the same fate, not even when faced with the sight of hundreds of exhausted British dragoons trying to fight their way through the ranks of French cavalry. General Müffling, the Prussian liaison officer, was with them, and could not understand their reluctance to move, which he urged them to do. Both agreed with Müffling but shrugging their shoulders answered, 'Alas! We dare not! The Duke of Wellington is very strict in enforcing obedience to prescribed regulations on this point.'

At length, Vandeleur could stand it no more, and ordered his brigade to prepare to charge. Taking three squadrons each from the 11th, 12th and 16th Light Dragoons, Vandeleur led his men west, passing behind the Hanoverian brigades of Vinke and Best. He had to come this way because a deep sunken lane ran down towards La Haye and Papelotte, and prevented him from charging directly down into the valley from his original position. Furthermore, French infantry were attacking the latter farm and he had no desire to lose men even before he could extricate the heavy cavalry. Once at the Ohain road, Vandeleur's men charged down into the valley where the Union Brigade struggled against enemy lancers and cuirassiers. Charging with the 16th Light Dragoons was William Tomkinson:

> …we got forward as quickly as possible, charged, and repulsed a body of lancers in pursuit of a party of Scots Greys…The 12th on our left attacked and dispersed a considerable body of the enemy, and by being on our left, and not so much delayed with the lane, got in advance. We supported them, having formed immediately after our charge, and by forming line (with the 11th), presented a front which enabled the 12th to retire with safety, as likewise all men of the

2nd Brigade [the Union Brigade] that had retreated on this point. We had some difficulty in preventing the men of the 16th from attacking in small bodies, after the charge, those parties of the enemy which had pursued the 2nd Brigade. Had they done this, we should have got into the same scrape; at least, we could not have covered the retreat of the others, but must have retired to form ourselves.[19]

Vandeleur's men were supported in their charge by De Ghingy's Dutch light cavalry and together they managed to bring off the Union Brigade, but not before they too had sustained heavy casualties, including Frederick Ponsonby, commanding the 12th Light Dragoons. Ponsonby had served with great distinction in the Peninsula. He had charged with the 23rd Light Dragoons at Talavera, and had fought in a more than a dozen other actions. Now, at Waterloo, he was leading his men down into the muddy valley to come to the aid of the stricken Union Brigade. His regiment cut its way through a column of French infantry before falling upon the enemy lancers. He was fighting furiously in the midst of the enemy when he was set upon by enemy cavalry. His story remains one of the most vivid and gripping of all Waterloo stories:

> In the mêlée (thick of the fight) I was almost instantly disabled in both my arms, losing first my sword, and then my rein; and, followed by a few of my men who were presently cut down, no quarter being asked or given, I was carried along by my horse, till, receiving a blow from a sabre, I fell senseless on my face to the ground. Recovering, I raised myself a little to look around, being at that time in a condition to get up and run away, when a lancer passing by, cried out 'tu n'es pas mort, coquin!' and struck his lance through my back. My head dropped, the blood gushed into my mouth, a difficulty of breathing came on, and I thought all was over. Not long after, a skirmisher stopped to plunder me, threatening my life: I directed him to a small side pocket in which he found three dollars, all I had; but he continued to threaten, tearing open my waistcoat, and leaving me in a very uneasy posture.[20]

Frederick Ponsonby was to lie out on the battlefield throughout the rest of the day and through the night, surviving several scares, but lived to tell the tale. Others were not so lucky. In addition to Frederick's namesake, William Ponsonby, who had been killed, William Fuller, commanding officer of the King's Dragoon Guards, was killed, as was James Hamilton, commanding officer of the Scots Greys. Joseph Muter, commander of the Inniskillings, was wounded. Samuel Ferrior, who held a similar rank in the 1st Life Guards, was killed later in the day.

The British cavalry were given great support during this phase of the battle by Kempt's infantry brigade, who advanced down the slopes to the east of La Haye Sainte and kept up a withering fire on both the retreating French infantry and the French cavalry. At length, Vandeleur and the remnants of the Union Brigade returned to the Allied ridge, battered, bruised and covered with blood and mud. They were covered with glory too, for between them the Union and Household Brigades had brought Bonaparte's great infantry attack shuddering to a bloody halt. The cost was high, however. The two brigades suffered just over 1,000 casualties at Waterloo, the majority sustained during their charge. These losses left Wellington desperately short of heavy cavalry throughout the remainder of the battle. The Duke himself probably felt a mixture of delight and horror. He had seen over 15,000 French infantry bloodily repulsed by just 2,000 of his heavy cavalry, but their uncontrollable urge to attack the enemy's guns must have revived a few bad memories of similar episodes in the Peninsula. Uxbridge himself admitted to making a grave mistake in leading the charge, for once it had begun he was in no position to stop it. 'The *carrière* once begun, the leader is no better than any other man,' he later said. He was probably too hard on himself. Wellington's verdict on Uxbridge and his cavalry was as predictable as it was sarcastic. Riding over to him afterwards, he said simply, 'Well, Paget, I hope you are satisfied with your cavalry now.'[21]

The repulse of the French attack heralded a lull in the fighting in the centre. The fighting at Hougoumont continued, as did the French artillery barrage. Skirmishers duelled out in front whilst Wellington's men waited for Bonaparte's next throw of the dice. The Prussians, meanwhile, drew ever closer.

1 Lt. James Hope, *Letters from Portugal, Spain and France, during the memorable campaigns of 1811, 1812, & 1813, and from Belgium and France in the year 1815* (Edinburgh, 1819), p.248.
2 Harry Ross-Lewin, *With the 32nd in the Peninsula and other campaigns*, edited by John Wardell (London, 1914), p.270.
3 Lt.Col. Jonathan Leach, *Rough Sketches of the Life of an Old Soldier* (London, 1831), p.387.
4 Capt. John Kincaid, *Adventures in the Rifle Brigade* (London, 1830), pp.333–4.
5 N Ludlow Beamish, *History of the King's German Legion* (London, 1832), II. p.454.
6 Major Francis Duncan, *History of the Royal Regiment of Artillery* (London, 1879), II. 447.
7 Capt. RT Belcher, quoted in *Waterloo Letters*, edited by Maj.Gen. HT Siborne (London, 1891), p.355.
8 Hope, *Letters*, p.253.
9 Maj. R Winchester, quoted in *Waterloo Letters*, p.383.
10 Major S Waymouth, quoted in *Waterloo Letters*, p.44.
11 W Knollys, *Shaw the Life Guardsman* (London, 1885), pp.48–50.
12 Col. AK Clark-Kennedy, quoted in *Waterloo Letters*, p.72.
13 EB Low, *With Napoleon at Waterloo* (London, 1911), p.143.
14 Sgt. Charles Ewart to his brother, in *An Account of the Battle of Waterloo* (Edinburgh, 1815), pp.64–5.
15 Col. AK Clark-Kennedy, quoted in *Waterloo Letters*, pp.75–6.
16 Lt.Gen. The Earl of Uxbridge, quoted in *Waterloo Letters*, p.9.
17 Low, *With Napoleon*, pp.144–5.
18 Ibid. pp.145–6.
19 Lt.Col. William Tomkinson, *The Diary of a Cavalry Officer in the Peninsular War and Waterloo Campaign 1809–1815*, edited by James Tomkinson (London, 1894), p.301.
20 Sgt.Maj. Edward Cotton, *A Voice From Waterloo* (London, 1862), 6th edition, pp.264–5.
21 The Marquess of Anglesey, *One Leg; the Life and Letters of Henry William Paget, first Marquess of Anglesey* (London, 1961), p.135.

Chapter XI
A BOILING SURF
The French Cavalry Charges

I had the infantry for some time in squares, and we had the French cavalry walking about us as if they had been our own. I never saw British infantry behave so well.

Wellington to Beresford, 2 July 1815

The attack on Wellington's centre had considerably weakened his line. Not only had he lost the services of many hundreds of heavy cavalrymen, but his infantry, and in particular Pack and Kempt, had been likewise badly hit. He was also forced to detach a considerable number of men to escort as many as 3,000 French prisoners, taken during the French attack, back towards Brussels. This particular column caused no small panic in the capital, for as it moved slowly along the road from the battlefield, through the village of Waterloo and beyond, word spread that Wellington was beaten and that the French were advancing. Rumours were rife amongst the citizens, particularly the British residents, many of whom had already begun to pack and look towards Antwerp. It would be some while before the rumours were dispelled. These problems were of little consequence to Wellington, however, whose attention shifted constantly between his front and his left. Where would the next French attack come from? Were the Prussians any nearer?

It was past 3pm, and for a while there was a slight lull in the battle. The fight at Hougoumont continued, as did the French artillery barrage, but otherwise there was no renewed French infantry attack on Wellington's front. Therefore, Wellington took the opportunity to shore up his centre. With Picton dead, Kempt assumed command of the British 5th Division. The Hanoverian brigades of Vinke and Best were still relatively fresh and had not been unduly moved by the French infantry attack. Bylandt's battered brigade, meanwhile, was positioned behind the ridge whilst Sir John Lambert's British brigade, consisting of the 1/40th, 1/4th, 1/27th and 1/81st, was brought forward to take up a position on Wellington's left centre. The remains of

the two heavy cavalry brigades were left to lick their wounds close to the farm of Mont St Jean. Despite their great efforts during the early afternoon, they still had much fighting ahead of them. Wellington's attention then shifted to his right, where the fight around Hougoumont continued unabated. His earlier fears for his right flank were probably allayed, although he continued to keep at Hal and Tubize the 17,000 troops that he had placed there in case Bonaparte tried to move round his flank. Otherwise, he simply brought his westernmost brigades closer to the rear of Hougoumont.

In fact, Wellington could feel himself relatively satisfied with the way the day had gone so far. The weather had not been kind to the French, for it had delayed their attack. The delay, of course, was a crucial factor in the outcome of the battle, for as each minute passed, Blücher's Prussians marched ever closer to the battlefield. The Foot Guards, along with their Nassau and Hanoverian allies, continued to hold out at Hougoumont, whilst the first great infantry attack of the day, against Wellington's centre, had been bludgeoned to a halt by the British veteran infantry and driven back by the heavy cavalry. Only La Haye Sainte concerned him, for it lay tantalisingly close to the crossroads and would give the French a tremendous advantage if they could throw out the garrison and carry the place.

At Hougoumont, meanwhile, French infantry continued to probe away at the defences, swarming round the two gates and hammering away in vain at the walls. Saltoun's men continued to hold sway in the orchard, whilst any French troops brave enough to try the walls of the garden were easily dealt with. The Foot Guards were more than confident of holding on against the enemy infantry attacks, but a

The Duke of Wellington, obligatory telescope in hand, encourages a British infantry square during the afternoon of 18 June, in this painting by Hillingford.

whole new dimension was added when the French suddenly began to shell the place. The first few shells that came crashing into the château ignited the Great Barn, and soon afterwards the château itself. Despite the heavy downpour of the night before the flames spread rapidly and before long the buildings around the courtyard were ablaze. Matthew Clay found himself in one of the upper rooms of the château, along with several other men commanded by Lieutenant Gough of the Coldstream Guards. From their elevated position they were able to annoy the enemy skirmishers that continued to swarm around the place. The shells set the building alight and Clay and his comrades fought on with the smell of burning wood beginning to fill the air:

> Our officer placing himself at the entrance of the apartment would not permit any one to quit his post until our position became hopeless and too perilous to remain, fully expecting the floor to sink with us every moment, and in our escape several of us were more or less injured.[1]

The conditions inside Hougoumont quickly became intolerable. Alexander Woodford was one of those who found the heat and smoke difficult to bear. 'Several men were burnt,' he wrote, 'as neither Colonel Macdonnell nor myself could penetrate to the stables where the wounded had been carried.' One man who did make it was Corporal James Graham, of the Coldstream Guards. Earlier, Graham and his brother, Joseph Graham, had been amongst those who had hurled themselves at the north gate to close it after the French had burst in. Now, Joseph Graham lay wounded in the stables and in danger of being burned alive. James asked Macdonnell for permission to fall out for a minute in order to rescue his brother, which was duly granted. Both men survived. In the chapel there hung above the door a wooden statue of Christ on the Cross. It wasn't long before the flames came licking up the statue's feet. But, instead of taking hold and setting the statue fully alight, the flames fizzled out. The locals regarded the incident as some sort of miracle and even the defenders of Hougoumont were puzzled by the mystery.

The courtyard was to become like an inferno, with crashing timbers, burning embers, smoke and flames, and with the ever-present threat from the French outside, it is little wonder that the fight at Hougoumont has assumed epic proportions. It was, after all, the key to Wellington's right flank and needed to be held at all costs. The same importance was attached to the farm of La Haye Sainte. Inside, George Baring and his dwindling garrison had survived the first attack and had received valuable reinforcements in the shape of two companies of the 1st Light Battalion KGL, under Captains von Gilsa and Marschalck, and three companies of Nassauers. The two KGL companies took up defensive positions in the garden, along with some of Baring's men, whilst Graeme, Carey and Frank, and the Nassauers continued to defend the farm buildings themselves. The orchard, meanwhile, was abandoned. Baring knew it would only be a matter of time before the French came knocking on the gate once again. Sure enough, two French columns hove into sight, as Baring later recalled:

> About half an hour's respite was now given us by the enemy, and we employed the time in preparing ourselves against a new attack; this followed in the same force as before; namely, from two sides by two close columns, which, with the greatest rapidity, nearly surrounded us, and, despising danger, fought with a degree of courage which I had never before witnessed in Frenchmen. Favoured by their advancing in masses, every bullet of ours hit, and seldom were the effects limited to one assailant; this did not, however, prevent them from throwing themselves against the walls, and endeavouring to wrest the arms from the hands of my men, through the loop holes; many lives were sacrificed to the defence of the doors and gates; the most obstinate contest was carried on where the gate was wanting, and where the enemy seemed determined to enter. On this spot seventeen Frenchmen already lay dead, and their bodies served as a protection to those who pressed after them to the same spot.[2]

The Germans fought like tigers inside La Haye Sainte, shooting down their assailants and clubbing them with their muskets whenever they got too close to the opening in the west wall. How they must have regretted burning it for firewood the night before. Instead they had to make do with the bodies of the seventeen dead Frenchmen mentioned by Baring. At some point in the action the French set fire to the barn, which prompted swift action on the part of the defenders who used pots and camp kettles to bring water from the pond next to the south barn. The fire was brought under control and Baring's men were able to continue dealing with the French. They received good support from the 95th Rifles in the sandpit, their accurate Baker rifles shooting down scores of French troops who were attacking the eastern side of the farm. At length, the French, unable to break into the farm and coming under heavy fire both from British infantry and artillery, fell back. Like Hougoumont, the farm of La Haye Sainte would be the scene of a severe fight throughout the rest of the afternoon and early evening.

Throughout this latest French attack Wellington's men had been enduring an awesome artillery bombardment. Round shot and common shell came crashing into their lines once more. The common shells exploded, scattering deadly shards of sharp metal amongst the Allied soldiers, whilst the solid iron round shot simply ploughed into their bodies. The artillery bombardment, in fact, was for many the sternest test of the day. Enemy infantry fire was one thing; they could handle that, but artillery fire was another thing altogether, and the barrage at Waterloo was more intense than even the most experienced of Wellington's veterans could remember. Standing just to the west of the crossroads was Ensign Edmund Wheatley, of the 5th Line Regiment KGL. He walked up and down chatting and joking with younger officers who had not 'smelt powder':

> An ammunition cart blew up near us, [he later wrote] smashing men and horses. I took a calm survey of the field around and felt shocked at the sight of broken armour, lifeless bodies, murdered horses, shattered wheels, caps, helmets, swords, muskets, pistols, still and silent. Here and there a frightened horse would rush across the plain, trampling on the dying and the dead. Three or four poor wounded animals standing on three legs, the other dangling before them. We killed several of these unfortunate beasts and it would have been an equal charity to have performed the same operation on the wriggling, feverish, mortally lacerated soldiers as they rolled on the ground…We still stood in line. The carnage was frightful. The balls which missed us mowed down the Dutch behind us, and swept away many of the closely embattled cavalry behind them. I saw a cannon ball take away a Colonel of the Nassau Regiment so cleanly that the horse never moved from under him.[3]

Even the most harmless looking of shots were liable to prove fatal to anybody who was unlucky enough to get in their way, as Frederick Hope Pattison, of the 33rd, later pointed out:

During the battle, my attention was directed with much interest to what we termed 'spent cannon-balls,' leaping about the field and giving it much the appearance of a giant cricket match, so as almost to induce an earnest player to step forward to bat them. But woe betide the man who would be so presumptuous as to interfere with their course, for although they seemed harmless, they would instantly have cut him in two.[4]

As the shot and shell continued to rain in on Wellington's men, so casualties continued to mount. It was also somewhat galling to the British that they were unable to hit back. Their job was quite simple. They had to sit and take it until Blücher arrived with his Prussians. This was Wellington's plan and he had little choice but to stick to it, to soak up the intense French pressure and, hopefully, strike back when he was in a position to do so. This moment would arrive either when Blücher entered the battle or when the French had simply punched themselves out. The question was, would his men be able to hang on? If not, would Blücher arrive in time? Then, somewhere around 3pm, possibly earlier, while Wellington contemplated the possible outcome of the battle, a report reached him that small groups of darkly clad soldiers had been sighted away to the east. They were Prussians. Never one to betray his feelings, Wellington remained impassive, although deep down he must have realised immediately the significance of their arrival. Although these were just the vedettes of their advance guard, he knew that others must be following close behind them, and that it was only a matter of time before they began to make their presence felt on the battlefield. It also meant that he could begin to consider shifting troops from his left flank to his sorely tried right and centre.

Much has been made of the absence of many of Wellington's old Peninsular battalions, and it is entirely possible that during the Battle of Waterloo he must have longed for a few more of his faithful Peninsular veterans. But thus far his 'infamous army' showed no signs of breaking. The Guards held out at Hougoumont, whilst Baring and his dwindling band thwarted all attempts by the enemy to take La Haye Sainte. The great French infantry attack had likewise been repulsed, as had several enemy cavalry charges. But the French artillery barrage was slowly killing his army. Ironically, it was a move by the French, not Wellington, which brought relief to the stricken infantry behind the ridge. It was getting on towards 4pm when Wellington ordered his more exposed troops to withdraw behind the ridge a little in order to take shelter from the French artillery. Apparently, the French saw this 'retirement' as a sign of retreat; Wellington must be pulling back. Whatever the reason, the retirement was the cue for the French to begin a series of massed cavalry charges against Wellington's line, charges that finally brought some relief from the French artillery barrage.

Wellington himself was sitting upon Copenhagen, telescope in hand, and surrounded by his staff, when he noticed a great deal of movement in the enemy lines. A quick glance from him was enough to deduce that something was afoot, but not even he could believe what he was seeing. There, in the distance, arrayed between La Belle Alliance and the ground to the south of Hougoumont, thousands of French cavalry were drawn up, preparing to charge. Squadron after squadron lined up for what was to prove the last great cavalry attack of the Napoleonic era. In fact, it was just a prelude to a series of attacks that was to last for about two hours. Wellington scanned the enemy lines and saw line after line of cuirassiers, dragoons, hussars, lancers, carabiniers, horse grenadiers and chasseurs. It was a magnificent sight; but did Bonaparte really think he could do what no other French commander had yet achieved against unbroken British infantry, namely, to break them by cavalry attacks alone?

Only once before, at Albuera, had enemy cavalry managed to destroy British infantry, and even then it was due to the fact that the brigade in question, Colborne's, was not in square. In fact, a heavy downpour of rain and sleet blinded the British infantry on that occasion, rendering their muskets useless and shielding the enemy lancers from view until it was too late. The subsequent attack was devastating; of a brigade strength of 1,600 no fewer than 1,300 became casualties, but if they had been able to form square it is unlikely that the attack would have succeeded. Wellington's own cavalry had likewise generally failed to break French infantry squares. The only occasion when this had been achieved was on 23 July 1812 at Garcia Hernandez, when the heavy dragoons of the King's German Legion had a stroke of good fortune when a dying horse crashed into the side of the square, effectively creating a breach through which the other dragoons passed. By sending thousands of cavalry forward in the hope of breaking infantry squares, formed of steady troops, Bonaparte was gambling on very long odds indeed.

The task facing the British infantry, and indeed the other Allied units, was nevertheless daunting. The French cavalry force lining up in preparation for the charge was greater than anything Wellington's men had ever faced, and the coming test would be a very stern one indeed. However, there were several factors in Wellington's favour. His artillery remained in good shape, there being seven batteries arrayed along the top of the ridge. Many units of British infantry had suffered considerably from French artillery fire, but there were many more battalions still relatively fresh and in good strength. And then there was Wellington's own cavalry. Although the two heavy brigades had suffered during their great charge, there still remained the light cavalry. With the heavies temporarily out of action, the hussars and light dragoons took centre stage and they were to acquit themselves with great credit. Wellington was further helped by the French themselves, for they appeared to be lining up on a very narrow front with the intention of attacking the Allied line between the crossroads and Hougoumont. This represented a front of less than one thousand yards, which was far too narrow for the thousands of French cavalry to deploy effectively. They also attacked unsupported by either artillery or infantry. One of the golden rules of Napoleonic warfare was

that when cavalry attacked enemy infantry they were never to do it unsupported. Enemy infantry formed in squares presented a wonderful target to infantry and artillery, whose job it was to break them before allowing the cavalry to charge in and complete the job. It was this sort of combination that worked to such great effect at Salamanca, for example, when Le Marchant's heavy cavalry arrived on the scene at the very moment that Leith's 5th Division was breaking the French infantry squares with their musketry. The ensuing charge left eight French battalions completely destroyed. Would Wellington's men suffer the same fate or would they being able to withstand the great tide that was about to break over them? The Duke was about to find out.

The approach of the massed ranks of French cavalry was preceded by an increase in enemy artillery fire, the noise of which reached a crescendo before the guns were forced to stop firing, lest their shots strike their own men. The cessation of this barrage came as a welcome relief to Wellington's men who now found themselves facing yet another trial of strength and resolve. Howell Rees Gronow, of the 1st Foot Guards, was relieved when the artillery fire stopped, but later recalled vividly the scene which followed:

The 28th (North Gloucestershire) Regiment, still wearing their old Peninsular War stovepipe shakos, in square formation at Waterloo. The French cuirassiers can find no way through the square but ride round its sides hoping in vain for some sort of opening. One of the better Waterloo paintings by Wollen.

About 4pm the enemy's artillery in front of us ceased firing all of a sudden and we saw large masses of cavalry advance: not a man present who survived could have forgotten in after life the awful grandeur of that charge. You perceived at a distance what appeared to be an overwhelming, long moving line, which, ever advancing, glittered like a stormy wave of the sea when it catches the sunlight. On came the mounted host until they got near enough, whilst the very earth seemed to vibrate beneath their thundering tramp. One might suppose that nothing could have resisted the shock of this terrible moving mass. They were the famous Cuirassiers, almost all old soldiers, who had distinguished themselves on most of the battlefields of Europe. In an almost incredibly short period they were within twenty yards of us, shouting 'Vive l'Empereur!' The word of command, 'prepare to receive cavalry', had been given, every man in the front ranks knelt, and a wall bristling with steel, held together by steady hands, presented itself to the infuriated Cuirassiers.[5]

Cavalié Mercer had been waiting with his troop of horse artillery, out on Wellington's right flank, on the reverse slope behind Hougoumont. Suddenly, Sir Augustus Frazer came galloping up, his face, 'as black as a chimney sweep's', shouting, 'Left limber up, and as fast as you can', followed by, 'At a gallop, march!' The troop went flying off towards the main ridge, bounding over the ground towards the crest. Frazer explained that an enormous mass of French cavalry was preparing to charge and that he expected them to hit the ridge at any minute. Mercer later recalled the noticeable change of atmosphere when he entered the main arena:

> As he [Frazer] spoke, we were ascending the reverse slope of the main position. We breathed a new atmosphere – the air was suffocatingly hot, resembling that issuing from an oven. We were enveloped in thick smoke, and, *malgré* the incessant roar of cannon and musketry, could distinctly hear around us a mysterious humming noise, like that which one hears of a summer's evening proceeding from myriads of black beetles; and cannon shot, too, ploughed the ground in all directions, and so thick was the hail of balls and bullets that it seemed dangerous to extend the arm lest it should be torn off.[6]

The majority of Wellington's men would not have been privileged to see the awesome sight that was moving quickly towards them up the slopes of the ridge, for they were tucked away on the reverse slope where they had been enduring the French artillery barrage. Perhaps it was just as well. They certainly heard it, however, for the sound of thousands of horses' hooves thun-

Frustrated French cuirassiers struggling in front of the Allied squares on the afternoon of 18 June.

dering towards them was audible to everyone, whilst the shaking of the earth was felt everywhere on the battlefield. Having been given the order to receive cavalry, Wellington's men braced themselves in their squares, four ranks deep and bristling with Birmingham steel. The gunners on the ridge fired to the very last moment, with round shot and, as the range decreased, with cannister and grape, tearing huge lanes through the lines of French cavalry. Mercer again:

Our first gun had scarcely gained the interval between their squares [the Brunswickers], when I saw through the smoke the leading squadrons of the advancing column coming on at a brisk trot, and already not more than one hundred yards distant, if so much, for I don't think we could have seen so far. I immediately ordered the line to be formed for action – case shot! And the leading gun was unlimbered and commenced firing almost as soon as the word was given: for activity and intelligence our men were unrivalled. The very first round, I saw, brought down several men and horses. They continued, however, to advance…We were a little below the level of the ground on which they moved – having in front of us a bank of about a foot and a half or two feet high, along the top of which ran a narrow road – and this gave more effect to our case-shot, all of which almost must have taken effect, for the carnage was frightful. I suppose this state of things occupied but a few seconds, when I observed symptoms of hesitation, and in a twinkling, at the instant I thought it was all over with us, they turned to either flank and filed away rapidly to the rear. Retreat of the mass, however, was not so easy. Many facing about and trying to force their way through the body of the column, that part next to us became a complete mob, into which we kept a steady fire of case-shot from our six pieces. The effect is hardly conceivable, and to paint this scene of slaughter and confusion impossible. Every discharge was followed by the fall of numbers, whilst the survivors struggled with each other, and I actually saw them using the pommels of their swords to fight their way out of the mêlée. Some, rendered desperate at finding themselves thus pent up at the muzzles of our guns, as it were, and others carried away by their horses, maddened with wounds, dashed through our intervals – few thinking of using their swords, but pushing furiously onward, intent only on saving themselves. At last the rear of the column, wheeling about, opened a passage, and the whole swept away at a much more rapid pace than they had advanced.[7]

It appears that Mercer's men did not dash for cover beneath the squares of the infantry, but instead stood by their guns with their lighted portfires. Mercer's guns may well have brought scores of French cavalry crashing to the ground, but elsewhere they continued to pour forward. Wellington's infantry waited anxiously but impassive on the reverse slope, as the ground trembled beneath them, then, like a mighty tidal wave, thousands of French cavalry came sweeping over the crest. That imperturbable old campaigner, Thomas Morris, of the 73rd, had just woken up after an hour's sleep when the cavalry arrived:

Their appearance, as an enemy, was certainly enough to inspire a feeling of dread, – none of them under six feet; defended by steel helmets and breastplates, made pigeon-breasted to thrown off the balls. Their appearance was of such a formidable nature, that I thought we could not have the slightest chance with them. They came up rapidly, until within about ten or twelve paces of the square, when our rear ranks poured into them a well-directed fire, which put them into confusion, and they retired; the two front ranks, kneeling, then discharged their pieces at them. Some of the cuirassiers fell wounded, and several were killed; those of them that were dismounted by the death of their horses, immediately unclasped their armour to facilitate their escape.[8]

Cavalié Mercer, up on the ridge with his horse artillery, also watched in awe. He described the French charge as being like 'a heavy surf breaking on a coast beset with isolated rocks, against which the mountainous wave dashes with furious uproar, breaks, divides, and runs, hissing and boiling, far beyond the adjacent beach'.[9]

The outcome of the contest between the French cavalry and Wellington's infantry rested squarely upon the ability of the latter to remain steady and unflinching in the face of the cavalry's provocation. As long as they did so there was little chance of the French breaking the squares, for no matter how hard the French tried to make them, their horses simply would not charge home against four ranks of bayonets. Instead, the cavalrymen resorted to throwing their lances, firing their pistols and carbines, or simply hacking away with their swords whenever they closed. This, of course, was done only at extreme peril to the rider who risked being either shot or spitted upon the bayonets of the infantry. Gronow again:

When we received cavalry, the order was to fire low, so that on the first discharge of musketry the ground was strewed with the fallen horses and riders, which impeded the advance of those behind them and broke the shock of the charge. It was pitiable to witness the agony of the poor horses, which really seemed conscious of the dangers that surrounded them: we often saw a poor wounded animal raise its head, as if looking for its rider to afford him aid. There is nothing perhaps amongst the episodes of a great battle more striking than the debris of a cavalry charge, where men and horses are seen scattered and wounded on the ground in every variety of painful attitude. Many a time the heart sickened at the moaning tones of agony which came from man, and scarcely less intelligent horse, as they lay in fearful agony upon the field of battle.[10]

The French cavalry faced many problems during this phase of the battle. With each successive charge – and it is estimated that around sixteen charges were made in all – the ground, which was already boggy owing to the heavy overnight rain, grew even worse. The thunderous tramping of thousands of horses' hooves churned it up to such a degree that riding through it must have been extremely exhausting. Furthermore, each charge left an ever-increasing pile of dead and wounded men and horses, and it is said that in places the dead resembled a rampart. Another factor in the defeat of the French cavalry was Wellington's own cavalry. The heavies may well have been missing after their efforts earlier, but the light cavalry made several charges throughout the afternoon to deal with their French counterparts. Regiments would charge forward and meet them on the forward slopes, and in so doing broke up the charges before they could gain momentum. They met them on the crest of the ridge itself and did battle with them. They also waited for the French to run the gauntlet of Allied infantry fire between the squares before sweeping them away from the ridge, sending them off to the west beyond Hougoumont and back to their own lines. Finally, it should not be forgotten that all the French cavalry charges took place on a very narrow front of about 700 yards, from Hougoumont to La Haye Sainte. With such a narrow frontage at their disposal it is little wonder that the cavalry found it so difficult to pass through such a debris-strewn battlefield. The conditions within the squares were no less trying for the British infantry, as Howell Rees Gronow recalled:

During the battle our squares presented a shocking sight. Inside we were nearly suffocated by the smoke and smell from burnt cartridges. It was impossible to move a yard without treading upon a wounded comrade, or upon the bodies of the dead; and the loud groans of the wounded and dying were most appalling.

At four o'clock our square was a perfect hospital, being full of dead, dying and mutilated soldiers. The charges of cavalry were in appearance very formidable, but in reality a great relief, as the artillery could no longer fire upon us: the very earth shook under the enormous mass of men and horses. I shall never forget the strange noise our bullets made against the breastplates of Kellerman's and Milhaud's cuirassiers, six or seven thousand in number, who attacked us with great fury. I can only compare it, with a somewhat homely simile, to the noise of a violent hail-storm beating upon panes of glass.[11]

As each successive cavalry attack was repulsed, so the Allied infantry grew in confidence. Their squares had held firm against continuous attack, whilst at the same time they were spared the ordeal of having to face French artillery fire. Only when each tide of French cavalry had receded did the barrage, and the fire of French skirmishers, resume. This, in fact, caused greater damage than the cavalry attacks. In addition, the French cavalry grew more exhausted and desperate with each charge. Indeed, each charge involved an increasingly difficult ride up to the Allied ridge, a fight at the squares and a subsequent ride between them, and, for the survivors, a return trip to the safety of their own lines. In all, each charge involved a ride of around three miles. Thus, by the time the battle ended, any French cavalryman who had completed sixteen charges would have ridden something like forty-eight very exhausting miles. Undaunted, the French cavalry persisted in their attacks. Thomas Morris, of the 73rd, again:

The same body of the enemy, though baffled twice, seemed determined to force a passage through us; and on their next advance, they brought up some artillerymen, turned their cannon in our front upon us, and fired into us with grape-shot, which proved very destructive, making complete lanes through us; and then the horsemen came up to dash in at the openings. But before they reached, we had closed our files, throwing the dead outside, and taking the wounded inside the square; and they were again forced to retire. They did not, however, go further than the piece of cannon –

A square formed of Highlanders holds steady in the face of another determined attack by French cuirassiers and dragoons. As long as they remained steady there was little chance of the French breaking in.

waiting there to try the effect of some more grape-shot. We saw the match applied, and again it came thick as hail upon us. On looking round, I saw my left hand man falling backwards, the blood gushing from his left eye; my poor comrade on my right, also by the same discharge, got a ball through his right thigh, of which he died a few days afterwards.

Our situation, now, was truly awful; our men were falling by dozens every fire. About this time, also, a large shell fell just in front of us, and while the fuse was burning out, we were wondering how many of us it would destroy. When it burst, about seventeen men were either killed or wounded by it; the portion which came to my share, was a piece of rough cast-iron, about the size of a horse-bean, which took up its lodging in my left cheek; the blood ran copiously down inside my clothes, and made me rather uncomfortable. Our poor old captain was horribly frightened; and several times came close to me for a drop of something to keep his spirits up. Towards the close of the day, he was cut in two by a cannon shot.[12]

The sight of as many as 5,000 French cavalry – some estimates put the figure as high as 10,000 – swarming round the Allied infantry squares remains one of the most enduring images of the Battle of Waterloo. Time and time again the French charged but each time they were greeted with the same stoic resistance. 'The charge of the French cavalry,' wrote Howell Rees Gronow,

was gallantly executed, but our well-directed fire brought men and horses down, and ere long the utmost confusion arose in their ranks. The officers were exceedingly brave, and by their gestures and fearless bearing did all in their power to encourage the men to form again and renew the attack. The Duke sat unmoved, mounted on his favourite charger. I recollect his asking Colonel Stanhope what o'clock it was, upon which Stanhope took out his watch, and said it was twenty minutes past four. The Duke replied, 'The battle is mine; and if the Prussians arrive soon, there will be an end to the war.'[13]

Meanwhile, the French cavalry attacks continued, but at a much less frantic pace. Indeed, it was only with great effort that they managed to get up the slopes, through the debris of their earlier charges and on towards the Allied infantry. Mercer, whose men continued to blast away at the enemy, noted the slower pace.

On they came in their compact squadrons, one behind the other, so numerous that those of the rear were still below the brow when the head of the column was but some sixty or seventy yards from our guns. Their pace was a slow but steady trot. None of your furious galloping was this, but a deliberate advance, at a deliberate pace, as of men resolved to carry their point…On our part was equal deliberation. Every man stood ready at his post, the guns ready, loaded with a round-shot first and a case

Wellington and a few of his staff surveying the field of Waterloo in the late afternoon. The infantry bodyguard appears to be made up of Foot Guards. The artist has erroneously painted Wellington sitting on a white horse, whereas Copenhagen was, in fact, chestnut.

over it; the tubes were in the vents; the portfires glared and sputtered behind the wheels; and my word alone was wanting to hurl destruction on that goodly show of gallant men and noble horses...I thus allowed them to advance unmolested until the head of the column might have been about fifty or sixty yards from us, and then gave the word, 'Fire!' The effect was terrible. Nearly the whole leading rank fell at once; and the round-shot, penetrating the column carried confusion throughout its extent. The ground, already encumbered with victims of the first struggle, became now almost impassable...The discharge of every gun was followed by a fall of men and horses like that of grass before the mower's scythe.[14]

Those that passed through the guns again found themselves in the midst of Allied infantry squares, drawn up in checkerboard formation, each with its own zone of fire. The trick was to hold fire for as long as possible, for a volley delivered too soon, and by all four ranks, deprived the square of its firepower. Moreover, there was little need for too much firing as the French cavalry presented no real danger so long as the squares remained firm and steady. Nevertheless, the men continued firing, usually by ranks, and often at very close range as enemy cavalrymen came walking up in order to take a swipe or thrust with their swords, or a stab with their lances. Often, they got too close for their own good, as Thomas Morris described:

The next charge the cavalry made, they deliberately walked their horses up to the bayonet's point; and one of them, leaning over his horse, made a thrust at me with his sword. I could not avoid it, and involuntarily closed

my eyes. When I opened them again, my enemy was lying just in front of me, within reach, in the act of thrusting at me. He had been wounded by one of my rear rank men, and whether it was the anguish of the wound, or the chagrin of being defeated, I know not; but he endeavoured to terminate his existence with his own sword: but that being too long for his purpose, he took one of our bayonets, which was lying on the ground, and raising himself up with one hand, he placed the point of the bayonet under his cuirass, and fell on it.[15]

The French cavalry attacks continued until around 5.30pm, possibly later, when they petered out. Despite overrunning the British guns on numerous occasions, they had spiked not a single one of them, and on each occasion they retreated the British gunners were allowed to return to them and let loose shot after shot at the cavalrymen's backs. It is a mystery why not one of the guns was spiked, for it took just a single headless nail, driven into the touchhole, to render it ineffective. Each cavalryman carried a box of such nails, but none were used.

As the French cavalry tired, Wellington was able to feed in his own heavy cavalry. The British light dragoon regiments had been doing great service throughout the afternoon, but as yet the remnants of the two heavy brigades had not been used. However, as the French cavalry onslaught began to wane, Somerset's Household Brigade returned to the fray, making several effective charges. The Life Guards, in particular, were very active. Thomas Morris watched as they charged down the slope at a unit of cuirassiers, the Frenchmen opening their ranks, 'to allow them to ride in'.

It was a fair fight, [wrote Morris] and the French were fairly beaten and driven off. I noticed one of the Guards, who was attacked by two cuirassiers, at the same time; he bravely maintained the unequal conflict for a minute or two, when he disposed of one of them by a deadly thrust in the throat. His combat with the other one lasted about five minutes, when the guardsman struck his opponent a slashing back-handed stroke, and sent his helmet some distance, with the head inside it. The horse galloped away with the headless rider, sitting erect in the saddle, the blood spouting out of the arteries like so many fountains.[16]

The clash between the Life Guards and the French cuirassiers degenerated into a multitude of individual combats, one of which involved Samuel Godley, of the 2nd Life Guards. Godley was known as 'The Marquis of Granby' by his comrades on account of his bald head. He was no mean swordsman and during one fight lost his horse shot dead beneath him. He had barely got to his feet when he saw a cuirassier coming straight at him. Godley was quick enough to draw his sword, parry the blow of his adversary and then, after dealing him a deadly blow, rode off with the dead Frenchman's horse to the cheers of his comrades. The horse was later killed by cannon shot, and Godley himself badly wounded.

One of Godley's more famous comrades was the bare-knuckle champion, John Shaw, who had already killed his fair share of Frenchmen during the great cavalry charge earlier in the afternoon. The 25-year-old pugilist was in the thick of the mêlée, 'whirling his good blade swiftly around', striking all who came within reach of him. There are several accounts of Shaw's end, but it appears that after killing and wounding several of his adversaries his sword broke, after which he took off his helmet and began clattering the French with it before he was cut down and left for dead. Another account has him being shot down. Shaw was found at the end of the battle, bleeding to death on a dunghill. Recognising one of his comrades, Shaw said, 'Ah, me dear fellow, I'm done for.' He was found the next morning, 'lying dead, with his face leaning on his hand, as if he had breathed his last while in a state of insensibility…His death was occasioned rather by the loss of blood from a variety of wounds than the magnitude of one.'[17]

Wellington himself spent this phase of the battle riding between his infantry squares. Every now and then he had occasion to enter one for his own protection but appears never to have been personally threatened by the French. He must have been feeling very satisfied with matters at this point for the French had achieved nothing at all, save for the destruction of much of their own cavalry. In fact, the greater damage to Wellington's army had been inflicted by French infantry and artillery fire, which was about to recommence. In the meantime he could hear the reassuring boom of artillery fire away to the east as Blücher's men warmed to their task, the Prussians beginning to arrive in numbers on the battlefield.

It was close to 6pm and thus far Wellington's line continued to hold. Hougoumont was in flames but the 'Gentlemen's Sons' continued to keep the French out. But with the French cavalry attacks having come to nothing, attention turned once again to the farm of La Haye Sainte and to George Baring's small band of KGL infantry.

1 Matthew Clay, *A Narrative of the Battles of Quatre Bras and Waterloo, with the Defence of Hougoumont* (Bedford, n.d.), p.15.

2 N Ludlow Beamish, *History of the King's German Legion* (London, 1832), II, p.455.

3 Edmund Wheatley, *A Journal and Sketchbook kept during the Peninsular War and Waterloo Campaign*, edited by Christopher Hibbert (London, 1964), p.66.

4 Lt. Frederick Hope Pattison, *Personal Recollections of the Waterloo Campaign*, edited by Bob Elmer (London, 1997), p.37–8.

5 Capt. Howell Rees Gronow, *The Reminiscences of Captain Gronow*, edited by Nicolas Bentley (London, 1977), p.46.

6 Capt. Cavalié Mercer, *Journal of the Waterloo Campaign*, edited by Sir John Fortescue (London, 1927), p.169.

7 Ibid. pp.171–2.

8 Thomas Morris, *The Napoleonic Wars*, edited by John Selby (London, 1967), pp.77–8.

9 Capt. C Mercer, quoted in *Waterloo Letters*, edited by Maj.Gen. HT Siborne (London, 1891), p.216.

10 Gronow, *Reminiscences*, p.48.

11 Ibid. p.45.

12 Morris, *Napoleonic Wars*, pp.78–9.

13 Gronow, *Reminiscences*, p.46.

14 Mercer, *Journal*, pp.174–5.

15 Morris, *Napoleonic Wars*, p.79.

16 Ibid. p.79.

17 W Knollys, *Shaw the Life Guardsman* (London, 1885), pp.62–3.

Chapter XII
AN UNREMITTING SHOWER OF DEATH

Never did I see such a pounding match. Both were what the boxers call gluttons.

Wellington to Beresford, 2 July 1815

The repulse of the French cavalry charges brought on a renewal of their artillery barrage, and once again shell after shell came crashing into the Allied troops causing severe casualties. It also prompted the French to redouble their efforts to take La Haye Sainte. Thus far Baring and his men, who had been defending the farm heroically throughout the day, had thwarted all enemy attempts to break into the place, but by the early evening their ammunition had begun to run dangerously low.

They had watched in awe as the French cavalry had thundered up the crest beside them and had 'cheered with derision' when they were repulsed. But Baring now discovered that his men's constant firing had cost them much of their ammunition, and so an officer was sent scurrying out of the back of the farmhouse to request fresh supplies. Unfortunately, the ammunition set aside for Baring's men was stowed away in a cart which had been overturned on the Brussels road and so no ammunition was available. This was unknown to Baring at the time and he sent yet another officer to the rear but again nothing was sent forward. The only support sent to Baring came in the form of the skirmishers of the 5th Line Battalion KGL, under Captain von Wurmb, who was killed at the head of his men soon afterwards. Two hundred Nassauers were also added to the garrison but a third messenger again failed to bring back any fresh ammunition.

As the defenders firing began to wane, so French efforts to break in increased. One of their principal efforts was directed against the main entrance to the farm on its eastern side. The gate here was solidly built, but the French were able to climb up and fire over it into the courtyard. One of the defenders was Private Fredrick Landau, of the 2nd Light Battalion KGL, who stood at his post despite bleeding profusely from two head wounds. Baring tried to get him to go to the rear but he refused, largely on account of a large bag of gold which he had taken from the French. 'He would be a scoundrel that deserted you, so long as his head is on his shoulders!' Landau told Baring. Unfortunately, he lost his treasure later in the day when he was taken prisoner. Two other men, Dahrendorf and Lindhorst, of the same battalion, also distinguished themselves at La Haye Sainte. The former was one of the first to assist in putting out the fire that had taken hold of the barn. He remained in the building longer than anybody else until his leg was shattered by an enemy shot. Lindhorst, meanwhile, defended one of the many small breaches that had been made in the wall of the courtyard, and when his ammunition ran out he continued to fight on with his bayonet, a large stick and a brick.

The situation inside La Haye Sainte was now desperate, for a quick check of available ammunition revealed just three or four cartridges per man. The French continued to pour over the buildings, climbing up on to the roofs to shoot down at the defenders below who still struggled tenaciously to keep the enemy out. Baring's own account of the defence bears out the frustration he and his men felt at being denied much-needed ammunition, for without it there was no way he could maintain the post any longer:

> The enemy gave me no time for thought; they were already close by our weak walls, and now, irritated by the opposition which they had experienced, attacked with renewed fury. The contest commenced at the barn, which they again succeeded in setting on fire. It was extinguished, luckily, in the same manner as before. Every shot that was now fired, increased my

Men of the 2nd Light battalion KGL fight desperately to keep the French out of the farm of La Haye Sainte. Despite their heroic efforts the farm eventually fell, but only after fierce resistance which cost the garrison hundreds of casualties. Indeed, only forty-two men regained the safety of the Allied lines after the farm's capture.

uneasiness and anxiety. I sent again to the rear with the positive statement that I must and would leave the place if no ammunition was sent me. This was also without effect.

Our fire gradually diminished, and in the same proportion did our perplexity increase; already I heard many voices calling out for ammunition, adding, 'We will readily stand by you, but we must have the means of defending ourselves!' Even the officers, who, during the whole day, had shewn the greatest courage, represented to me the impossibility of retaining the post under such circumstances. The enemy, who too soon observed our wants, now boldly broke in one of the doors; however, as only a few could come in at a time, these were instantly bayonet-ed, and the rear hesitated to follow. They now mounted the roof and walls, from which my men were unfortunate marks; at the same time they pressed in through the open barn, which could no longer be defended. Inexpressibly painful as the decision was to me of giving up the place, my feeling of duty as a man overcame that of honour, and I gave the order to retire through the house into the garden.[1]

There were barely fifty men left to run for their lives when Baring gave the order to abandon the farm. Baring himself ran through a passage in the house, following others out into the garden behind. The remaining defenders followed but many were killed in the attempt. Indeed, there was a violent struggle in the passage, with muskets blasting off at close range and sabres being thrust by both friend and foe. Ensign Frank was one of those who tried to make good his escape through the passage. He was already suffering from one wound, but he managed to cut down one French soldier who was trying to shoot another KGL officer, Ensign George Graeme. No sooner had he done this than his arm was broken by a musket ball, fired at him from one end of the passage. In the confusion he managed to duck into a bedroom where he hid behind a bed, and here he lay undiscovered for the rest of the battle. The two men following him were not so lucky. They were caught by the French and shot without mercy. Like Frank, Graeme was one of the few lucky ones to survive to the farmhouse:

> We had all to pass through a narrow passage. We wanted to halt the men and make one more charge, but it was impossible; the fellows were firing down the passage. An Officer of our Company [Frank] called to me, 'Take care', but I was too busy stopping the men, and answered, 'Never mind, let the blackguard fire'. He was about five yards off, and levelling his piece at me, when this Officer stabbed him in the mouth and out through his neck; he fell immediately.
>
> But now they flocked in; this Officer got two shots, and ran into a room, where he lay behind a bed all the time they had possession of the house; sometimes the room was full of them, and some wounded soldiers of ours who lay there and cried out 'pardon' were shot, the monsters saying, 'Take that for the fine defence you have made'.
>
> An officer and four men came first in; the Officer got me by the collar, and said to his men, '*C'est ce coquin.*' Immediately the fellows had their bayonets down, and made a dead stick at me, which I parried with my sword, the Officer always running about and then coming to me again and shaking me by the collar; but they all looked so frightened and pale as ashes, I thought, 'You shan't keep me', and I bolted off through the lobby; they fired two shots after me, and cried out 'Coquin', but did not follow me.[2]

When Baring emerged from the house into the garden he looked around and still harboured hopes of defending it, but it was just a fleeting hope. With the French now swarming all over the farm and pouring into the garden, he skipped over the back hedge and ran the hundred yards or so back to the relative safety of the main Allied position. As he looked back he saw Captain Ernest Holtzermann being taken prisoner by the French, along with Lieutenant Tobin. He must have reflected with great pain upon the fact that of the 376 men with whom he had begun the defence of La Haye Sainte earlier in the day, and of the various reinforcements he had received, only forty-two were able to make good their escape.

Like Hougoumont, the defence of La Haye

The rear of La Haye Sainte, as it looks today. It was out of this exit that George Baring and the dazed survivors of the garrison escaped after the farm fell to the French during the early evening of 18 June.

Sainte was an epic action, but with less happy consequences. The lack of ammunition has long been a source of much discussion and debate, it appearing to be the main cause of Baring's failure to hold the farm. Many of the defenders were armed with Baker rifles and yet, even with the 95th Rifles nearby in the sandpit, it seems incredible that they were not able to supply the KGL men with some of their own rifle ammunition. James Shaw Kennedy, in his *Notes on the Battle of Waterloo*, was particularly critical of the way the business was handled, and thought spare ammunition should have been got into the place before the battle started. He spent the night of 18 June with Baring, and as they lay beneath the elm tree at the crossroads, the two men discussed the business at the farm.

This matter had certainly been grossly mismanaged. The arrangement for the brigades getting their spare ammunition was, that each brigade should communicate with the guard over the ammunition, and order forward what was wanted. How the brigade failed to do this has not been explained, as so many superior officers fell in the action. Baring could not account for it, which I know from our having slept together on the ground close to the Wellington Tree on the night after the action, when he mentioned his having sent more than once for a supply of ammunition and his having received no answer. The unexplained want of ammunition by Baring's battalion is placed in an extraordinary view when it is considered that the battle of Waterloo lasted eight hours and a half, and that all three brigades of the division got the ammunition they required, with the exception of this one battalion. The simple fact of Baring's application for spare ammunition having been made by him late in the day, when, owing to the enemy's position, there could be no certainty of its being got into the place, proves an extraordinary oversight. The spare ammunition should have been sent for early in the morning. What were 60 rounds per man for the defence of such a post?[3]

Whatever the reason, the fact remained that La Haye Sainte was now in French hands. It was about 6.30pm and the battle was entering its critical stage. Blücher's Prussians were beginning to make an impact on the battle away to the east, driving on towards the village of Plancenoit, which lay behind Bonaparte's right flank. Wellington, meanwhile, was still holding firm despite the dreadful pounding his men were taking from enemy artillery, but with the fall of the farm he could expect things to get worse.

No sooner had La Haye Sainte fallen than the French started to bring up guns in order to blast away at Wellington's centre. Without the garrison of the farm to hinder and harry them the French gunners were relatively free to go about their deadly business. That being said, there were still plenty of green-jacketed riflemen across the Brussels road who took out the odd gunner with their accurate Baker rifles. But despite this irritating rifle fire the French artillery got on with their job of trying to punch a hole through the Allied centre, a business that was carried on at an extremely short range. Indeed, one might almost say it was point blank range, for the distance from the French guns to the British and KGL troops at the crossroads was no more than two or three hundred yards. In some places the French brought their guns to within a mere 100 yards of the Allied position before they began blasting away with cannister and grape shot.

French infantry, too, were brought forward for what was certain to be yet another attack on the centre. Christian Ompteda watched the developments in his front whilst sitting upon the recently acquired horse of his adjutant, Lieutenant Schuck, who had been killed. His brigade was paying a heavy price for having the honour of standing at the crossroads, having suffered severe casualties during the day. Next to Ompteda was Lieutenant Colonel Linsingen, commanding the 5th Line Battalion KGL, and as the two men watched the French troops deploying down in front of them, General von Alten's adjutant, Lord Somerset, rode up with orders to attack them. This order was received with some astonishment by Ompteda, who pointed out a body of cuirassiers lurking in a fold in the ground, waiting to pounce on any unwary enemy infantry. Somerset rode off but returned a short while afterwards with von Alten and the Prince of Orange, upon which von Alten repeated the order. Ompteda again remonstrated, adding that if he were to go forward he should at least be supported by cavalry. Turning to the cavalry in front, the Prince of Orange explained that these were Dutch cavalry. We can well imagine the incredulity with which this statement was received by Ompteda, who diplomatically pointed out that they were, in fact, cuirassiers. But the prince would not be swayed. The proud young man could not be seen to have changed his mind in the presence of others and insisted that Ompteda carry out the order. 'I must still repeat my order to attack,' he said, 'in line with the bayonet, and I will listen to no fur-

Christian Ompteda commanded the 2nd KGL Brigade at Waterloo. He lost his life as the result of a gross error by the Prince of Orange, who ordered him to attack La Haye Sainte, even when French cavalry were seen waiting nearby.

Wellington, accompanied by a member of his ever-dwindling staff, encourages a British square at Waterloo.

ther arguments.' Ompteda simply sighed and said in a loud voice, 'Well, I will,' and, realising his time had come, turned to Linsingen and asked him to look after his two teenage nephews, Charles and Louis, who were with him. Then, drawing his sword, he put spurs to horse and slowly led the 5th Line Battalion KGL down the slopes towards La Haye Sainte and to its destruction. With Ompteda was Edmund Wheatley, one of the few English officers with the King's German Legion:

> Colonel Ompteda ordered us instantly into line to charge, with a strong injunction to 'walk' forward, until he gave the word. When within sixty yards he cried 'Charge', we ran forward huzzaing. The trumpet sounded and no one but a soldier can describe the thrill one instantly feels in such an awful moment. At the bugle sound the French stood until we reached them. I ran by Colonel Ompteda who cried out, 'That's right, Wheatley!'
>
> I found myself in contact with a French officer but ere we could decide, he fell by an unknown hand. I then ran at a drummer, but he leaped over a ditch through a hedge in which he stuck fast. I heard a cry of, 'The Cavalry! The Cavalry!' But so eager was I that I did not mind it at the moment, and when on the eve of dragging the Frenchman back (his iron-bound hat having saved him from a cut) I recollect no more.[4]

Wheatley was, in fact, one of the lucky ones, or at least he was for the moment, for no sooner had Ompteda led his two hundred men forward than the cuirassiers drew their swords and sprang from their cover to deliver the charge that he had so tragically predicted. Advancing in line, the 5th Line presented a wonderfully tempting invitation to the French cavalry, who in an instant charged and completely rode down the line, cutting and hacking in all directions until only six officers and eighteen stunned men were able to return to their own lines. Linsingen himself had his horse shot under him, and as he lay pinned beneath it, he raised his head to see the French cavalry sweep in and destroy his comrades. Fortunately, he managed to free himself and, taking hold of Ompteda's two nephews, who struggled to follow their uncle, he spirited them back to the safety of the sunken lane, at the crossroads. One of the survivors of the charge was Captain Berger, who followed Ompteda as he rode alone into the French mass:

> I hastened to follow him as quickly as the miry state of the ground permitted. I kept my eyes on him and on the enemy. I saw that the French had their muskets pointed at the colonel, but did not fire. The officers struck the men's barrels up with their swords. They seemed astonished at the extraordinary calm approach of the solitary horseman, whose white plume showed

him to be an officer of high rank. He soon reached the enemy's line of infantry before the garden hedge. He jumped in, and I clearly saw how his sword-strokes smote the shakos off. The nearest French officer looked on with admiration without attempting to check the attack. When I looked round for my company I found I was alone. Turning my eyes again to the enemy, I saw Colonel Ompteda, in the midmost throng of the enemy's infantry and cavalry, sink from his horse and vanish.

So died he – a man of noble soul, distinguished in mind and character, fitted to render his Fatherland further high services – a hero's death.[5]

The French officers had initially refused to fire upon Ompteda as he took them on single-handed, but they could not simply stand and allow him to continue cutting away at their men. Somebody had to stop him and it was left to a private soldier to put an end to his brave demonstration with a single shot. Ompteda was found dead later that night by his aide-de-camp, von Brandis, lying hard by the garden hedge. His uniform had been rifled by the French but his body had not been stripped. 'The singed appearance of the bullet-hole in the collar of his coat showed that the fatal ball had been fired into his neck close to him in the last desperate struggle amid the masses of the foe.'[6]

Edmund Wheatley recovered his senses and found himself lying in a ditch with Ompteda close by him, on his back, 'his head stretched back with his mouth open, and a hole in his throat'. Wheatley was then taken prisoner and bundled unceremoniously away by a group of rough French infantry. Meanwhile, up on the ridge, both von Alten and the Prince of Orange were left to reflect upon their disastrous decision that had sent Ompteda and his men to their deaths. Orange may well have been treated over-harshly by historians for his part in the mishap to the 69th at Quatre Bras, and to the Lünebergers at Waterloo, but the blame for this tragedy lies fairly and squarely at his royal feet.

The fall of La Haye Sainte ushered in the most critical phase of the Battle of Waterloo. In some places, French guns were now as close as one hundred yards from Wellington's line, whilst those just south of the crossroads were a mere two to three hundred yards away. The British troops at the crossroads themselves, Lambert's brigade, suffered appalling casualties, with the 27th Inniskillings suffering in particular. The regiment lost 105 officers and men killed and no fewer than 373 wounded, by far and away the heaviest losses sustained by any British regiment at Waterloo. John Betty, Andrew Gardner and William Talbot, in addition to the quartermaster and the two assistant-surgeons, were the only officers of the 27th to come through unscathed. As John Kincaid, of the 95th, famously remarked afterwards, 'The twenty-seventh regiment were lying literally dead, in square, a few yards behind us,' adding, 'I had never yet heard of a battle in which every body was killed; but this seemed likely to be an exception, as all were going by turns.'[7]

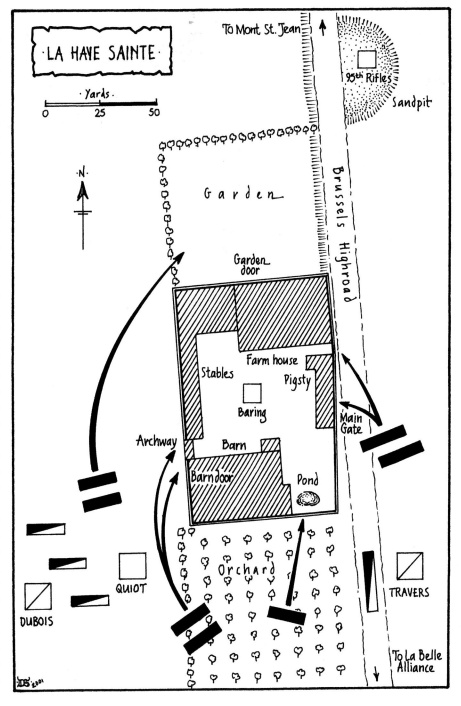

Away to the west, Maitland's Foot Guards had also been taking heavy punishment, this time from a strong force of French voltigeurs who had crept up the slopes to open fire on them as they stood in square. Therefore, Wellington had them advance down the slope to drive them off, as Henry Davis later recalled:

> After the attacks of the enemy's cavalry had been repelled, a strong force of enemy infantry was pushed forward, who kept up a galling fire on the part of the line where the battalion to which I belonged was posted. In order to drive them back the Battalion, not waiting to deploy into line (which in consequence of large masses of the enemy's cavalry still hovering about would have been unsafe), opened from the centre of the rear face of the square, that face and the two flank faces bringing their right and left shoulders forward until in line with the front face, thus forming an irregular line of four deep. They then advanced, drove back the French infantry, and in the midst of the murderous fire of the enemy's artillery, re-forming square with as much coolness as on parade, returned to their former position.[8]

The 52nd and 71st advanced also, and thus the French infantry were thrown back, for the time being at least. But there was little respite from the enemy's artillery barrage which continued its unremitting shower of death. Despite the barrage, many British soldiers, exhausted with fatigue brought on as a result of the last few days' marching, lay down and fell asleep. Some of them were destined never to wake, being struck by enemy shells. An anonymous private of the 71st Highlanders was one of those who managed to sleep during the artillery barrage:

> We were so overcome by the fatigue of the two days' march that, scarce had we lain down, until many of us fell asleep. I slept sound for some time while the cannonballs, plunging in amongst us, killed a great many. I was suddenly awakened. A ball struck the ground a little below me, turning me heel-over-head, broke my musket in pieces and killed a lad at my side. I was stunned and confused and knew not whether I was wounded or not. I felt a numbness in my side for some time.[9]

In addition to French artillery fire, Wellington's men suffered from the fire of the many French voltigeurs who advanced to the Allied ridge from where they kept up a continuous and destructive fire. But at least Wellington's men were able to reply to this harassing fire by sending forward their own light troops to engage them. Otherwise, they had little option but to stand there and take whatever the French threw at them. Cavalié Mercer had been in action with his troop of horse artillery whilst the voltigeurs crept forward once more and appeared to make a target of him as he rode up and down in front of his men:

> This quieted my men; but the tall blue gentlemen, seeing me thus dare them, immediately made a target of me, and commenced a very deliberate practice, to show us what very bad shots they were and verify the old artillery proverb, 'The nearer the target, the safer you are.' One fellow certainly made me flinch, but it was a miss; so I shook my finger at him, and called him *coquin*, etc. The rogue grinned as he reloaded and took aim. I certainly felt rather foolish at that moment, but was ashamed, after such bravado, to let him see it, and therefore continued my promenade. As if to prolong my torment, he was a terrible time about it. To me it seemed an age. Whenever I turned, the muzzle of his infernal carbine still followed me. At length bang it went, and whiz came the ball close to the back of my neck, and at the same instant down dropped the leading driver of one of my guns (Miller), into whose forehead the cursed missile had penetrated.[10]

This sort of show certainly encouraged the men, although it is doubtful whether the unfortunate driver appreciated Mercer's gesture. Sergeant William Lawrence, of the 40th Foot, had served in South America, in the Peninsular War, and in North America. Lawrence's battalion formed part of Sir John Lambert's brigade, the other battalions being the 1/4th, 1/27th and 1/81st, all four being veterans of the Peninsular War. The brigade had watched from their position just in front of the farm of Mont St Jean until just after the repulse of the French infantry attack by Picton's men, when they were brought forward into a position in Wellington's second line to the east of the Brussels road. The second line it may have been, but it was no less dangerous a position, with many enemy shells bouncing and skimming through the front line troops into the ranks of those behind. The 1/40th had barely taken up their new station when they suffered their first casualties. Lawrence himself was used to the smell of battle but even he felt apprehensive when he was called to protect the Colours during the afternoon on 18 June:

> This, although I was used to warfare as much as any, was a job I did not at all like; but still I

went as boldly to work as I could. There had been before me that day fourteen sergeants already killed and wounded while in charge of those colours, with officers in proportion, and the staff and colours were almost cut to pieces...I had not been there more than a quarter of an hour when a cannon-shot came and took the captain's head clean off. This was again close to me, for my left side was touching the poor captain's right, and I was spattered all over with his blood.[11]

The gradual appearance of the Prussians on the eastern fringe of the battlefield enabled Wellington to move some of his brigades west to bolster the hard-pressed right and centre. Accordingly, the two light cavalry brigades of Vivian and Vandeleur, which had been largely inactive, save for the latter brigade's intervention during the charge of the Union Brigade, were moved to the west of the crossroads. The arrival of these two brigades 'was to give confidence to the troops almost worn out with the protracted and murderous combat', wrote Vivian afterwards. Even the remnants of the two heavy brigades were brought forward to stiffen the line. Meanwhile, the garrison inside the

blazing inferno of Hougoumont continued to hold out confidently whilst the Nassauers maintained the left flank at Papelotte and La Haye.

How Wellington himself escaped injury throughout the long and bloody day is a mystery, for members of his staff were falling at his side all day long. The Prince of Orange fell, badly wounded by a musket ball, whilst William De Lancey, Acting Quartermaster General, was mortally wounded by a cannon shot that struck him in the back and plucked him from his horse. Fitzroy Somerset was wounded, as was Alexander Gordon, mortally, whilst Charles Fox Canning, who had been one of Wellington's aides in the Peninsula was yet another who met his end at Waterloo. Little wonder that Wellington was moved to remark after the battle that the 'finger of Providence' had been upon him throughout the day to ensure he did not meet a hero's end in the way that England's other great hero, Nelson, had done, ten years earlier at Trafalgar. Wellington's great friend, the Spanish general, Miguel Alava, had been at Trafalgar too, where he had fought on the side of the French against Nelson. He had been at Wellington's side in the Peninsula and here he was again at Waterloo, witnessing a

'Guns to the Front!' A troop of Royal Horse Artillery brings its guns into action at Waterloo, in this painting by Wollen.

British officers and men cheer Wellington as he rides between the Allied squares at Waterloo. Bearskins were certainly not worn during by the British during the battle, despite the artist having included them here.

level of destruction that he had never seen in Spain. Alava, in fact, was one of the few members of Wellington's staff to come through the battle unscathed.

Meanwhile the slaughter continued. Up on the Allied ridge the French barrage was so fierce that even the Foot Guards were hard pushed to stand there and take it. Colour Sergeant Charles Wood, of the 3/1st Foot Guards, had seen service in Holland, Sicily, Spain and southern France. He was also a devout Christian and during the time his battalion had been quartered at

Hovis, near Enghien, he had preached three times each Sunday and once on Wednesdays. Needless to say, Wood also considered the 'finger of Providence' to have been upon him at Waterloo, particularly with the battle being fought on a Sunday. 'It was the Sabbath-day,' he later wrote to a friend, 'and while you were praying too, and praising the King of Glory in his Church, I was doing the same in the field of blood; I was truly in the spirit of a Christian and a soldier on the Lord's day.'[12] His faith was truly tested during the early evening at Waterloo when the French artillery began to take its toll of his battalion:

> Their cannon…raked us with grape, cannister, and horse-nails; and our line was so shattered that I feared they could not stand; in fact, I was for a moment really afraid they would give way; and if we had given way it would have gone hard with the whole line, as our third battalion and the rifle battalion of the KGL were the manoeuvre of the day. Our Officers exerted themselves to the very uttermost, as also the Sergeants; Major-General Maitland, Colonel Lord Saltoun, Colonel Reeve, and Brigade-Major Gunthorp, were in the front face of the square, in the hottest part of the contest; our loss at this time was tremendous. It was at this juncture that I picked up Ensign Purdo's coat, which was covered with blood, lying on a dead horse. The Ensign belonged to our battalion; he was killed and stripped by the plunderers during some of our manoeuvres. I stepped about twenty-five paces before the line and waved the coat, cheering the men, and telling them that while our Officers bled we should not reckon our lives dear. I thought that if anything would stimulate the men, this would be effective.[13]

Wood's dramatic gesture certainly steadied the men, as did a brave deed by Captain Goodwin Colquitt, of the same regiment. At one point during the French barrage a shell came spluttering into his battalion's square, the fuse fizzing away on top. The consequences for the tightly packed formation would have been dire had it not been for Colquitt's swift and extremely brave action, for he picked up the shell and threw it back as far as he could, the shell exploding well away from the square. Colquitt's brother had died of wounds received at the taking of Seville in August 1812, and so he had good reason to stay alive. The enemy shells continued to wreack havoc, however, forcing the sergeants of the Foot Guards to use their pikes in order to keep the men in check, as Charles Wood described in his letter:

> The sergeants placed their pikes (lengthways) against the men's backs in line (for they were getting eight or ten deep) and bore them up by their shoulders by main strength. Some of the men kept firm in the line, but others fell back to get out ammunition, and others were begging ammunition in the rear as all their own was spent, which, with our continuous loss, quite unsteadied the line; so the pikes were intended to prevent any from falling back for ammunition, as we wanted the men to use the bayonet, for now depended the honour of Britain, and the safety of Europe.[14]

Suddenly the firing ceased, but only momentarily, and as the smoke cleared and the cacophony died down, Wellington's men peered through the gloom and saw dark masses gathering away to the south. The ringing in their ears must have been tremendous but it did not stop them hearing the loud cheers that rang out as a lone horseman, riding a white horse, led the enemy columns forward from La Belle Alliance where they had mustered. Wellington knew he had beaten off everything that Bonaparte had thrown at him, and now, with the Prussians arriving in ever-growing numbers, the decisive moment of the Battle of Waterloo had finally arrived; Bonaparte's Imperial Guard was coming.

1 N Ludlow Beamish, *History of the King's German Legion* (London, 1832), II. p.459.

2 Maj. GD Graeme, quoted in *Waterloo Letters*, edited by Maj.Gen. HT Siborne (London, 1891), pp.408–9.

3 Gen. Sir James Shaw Kennedy, *Notes on the Battle of Waterloo* (London, 1865), pp.122–3.

4 Edmund Wheatley, *A Journal and Sketchbook kept during the Peninsular War and Waterloo Campaign*, edited by Christopher Hibbert (London, 1964), p.70.

5 Christian Ompteda, *A Hanoverian English Officer a Hundred Years Ago*, translated by John Hill (London, 1892), pp.312–3.

6 Ibid. p.313.

7 Capt. John Kincaid, *Adventures in the Rifle Brigade* (London, 1830), p.342.

8 Lt. Col. H. Davis, quoted in *Waterloo Letters*, pp.256–7.

9 Anon, *A Soldier of the 71st*, edited by Christopher Hibbert (London, 1975), p.107.

10 Captain Cavalié Mercer, *Journal of the Waterloo Campaign*, edited by Sir John Fortescue (London, 1927), pp.173–4.

11 Sgt. William Lawrence, *Autobiography of Sergeant William Lawrence, a hero of the Peninsular and Waterloo Campaigns*, edited by GN Bankes (London, 1886), p.210.

12 Col. Sgt. Charles Wood, *Some Particulars of the Battle of Waterloo, being an extract of a letter from C/Sergeant C.W. Third Battalion First Regiment of Foot Guards* (Halifax, 1816), p.4.

13 Ibid. p.6.

14 Ibid. p.7.

Chapter XIII
THE GLINT
OF VICTORY

A peel of ten thousand thunders burst at once on their devoted heads,
the storm swept them down, as a whirlwind which rushes over the ripe corn.

Digby Mackworth, describing the effect of the Foot Guards' fire
on Bonaparte's Imperial Guard

Wellington's men had heard stories about Bonaparte's illustrious Imperial Guard but they had yet to meet them on the field of battle. The Guard had remained firmly at Bonaparte's side throughout his campaigns in central Europe, and as he paid only a fleeting visit to the Peninsula, during the winter of 1808–9, so the Guard did likewise. Thus, the Battle of Waterloo was to provide the stage for the great showdown between Wellington's infantry and Bonaparte's Guard. Wellington himself knew all about them, about their reputation and how Bonaparte had invariably employed the Imperial Guard only to tip the scales in his favour at the most crucial moments on the battlefield. It was clear to him that Blücher's Prussians, battling their way into the shattered village of Plancenoit, were taking a heavy toll of the French defenders, leaving Bonaparte with little option but to play his final card. It is highly probable that Wellington, ever the cool, calculating and very professional soldier, had nothing on his mind on that hot, choking summer's evening, other than how he was to deal with this latest French attack. But it is entirely possible that, even at this most crucial moment of the battle, he relished the prospect of finally facing the Imperial Guard.

Of course, reputations were all very well, but actually living up to them on the battlefield was another thing altogether, and Wellington's men were not about to let the French enhance their reputation at their expense. The mounted officers up on the Allied ridge watched, impassive and with great interest, as the large enemy columns began to take shape away in the distance. In fact, it soon became clear that these columns were five large squares, the Imperial Guard obviously not wanting to taste the bitter dish that was served up by the British heavy

cavalry earlier in the day. Starting from La Belle Alliance, the five squares left the Brussels road soon after, marching to their left and taking the same route that had been used by the French cavalry only a couple of hours earlier. Bonaparte himself led the advance, riding out in front with his generals until he halted about 600 yards from Wellington's line. His Guard continued past him, cheering his name and wishing him long life. All along Wellington's line, British officers watched with a mixture of awe, anxiety and excitement. Maitland's Foot Guards, meanwhile, adopted an air of disinterest. Sir John Colborne, commanding the 52nd, had seen most things in the Peninsula having served throughout the war with great distinction. However, he had never seen Bonaparte. But, as he peered through his telescope he clearly saw the unmistakable figure, in his grey greatcoat, by now on foot, and walking with his hands behind his back. It was the only time Colborne saw Bonaparte in his life. The red-jacketed infantry on the reverse slope could see none of this, of course, but they could hear the French bands playing the same old tunes as they came on. The British had made them dance to their own tune in the Peninsula, however, and they were determined to do the same here.

Supporting the Imperial Guard as it picked its way steadily over the debris of the French cavalry attacks were other French units, marching parallel with the Brussels road towards La Haye Sainte. With the farmhouse in French hands they were free from flanking fire, and the newly installed garrison cheered as the pace of this latest attack increased. French cavalry and artillery also moved forward in support, advancing behind the five squares. The advance of the Imperial Guard was hampered by the bad state of the ground that had been severely churned up by thousands of French cavalry. In addition to this, hundreds of men and horses lay scattered about the field, causing the infantry to step out every now and then to avoid a corpse or a wounded soldier. In the midst of the squares Imperial eagles could be seen glinting in the evening sunlight as they were carried into battle for what was to prove the last time. It was all massively impressive to the watching French who believed, with good reason, that the hour had come. The Guard was going into action. Victory was at hand.

Waiting in silence behind the ridge were a few thousand British redcoats who begged to differ, along with several battalions of Hanoverians and Brunswickers. As soon as the French came within range, Wellington's artillery opened up, first with round shot and common shell, and then, as the range shortened, with cannister and grape. The French struggled to maintain order across the bad ground as their ranks were decimated by British, KGL and Dutch-Belgian artillery fire. 'Every one felt how much depended on this terrible moment,' wrote Digby Mackworth, Lord Hill's aide-de-camp, 'a black mass of the Grenadiers of the Imperial Guard with music playing and the great Napoleon at their head came rolling onward from the Farm of the "Belle Alliance"; with rapid pace.'[1]

It was clear from the direction of the French attack that Halkett's and Maitland's brigades would bear the brunt of it, whilst the remains of Kielmansegge's brigade would have to tackle the French troops on the right of the Imperial Guard. In addition, Wellington could call upon Baron Chassé's Dutch-Belgian division, which he had brought across from the west prior to the attack. Chassé was a veteran of the Peninsular War but had fought on the side of the French. Indeed, only two years before Waterloo, Chassé had held the village of La Hermandad at Vittoria against repeated British attacks. His loyalties appear never to have been in doubt, however, and he was there on the ridge, waiting patiently to bring his men into action.

Although the British artillery did great execution amongst the oncoming French, they did not escape lightly, for the French artillery that came forward in support of their infantry did a great deal of damage themselves. Indeed, had it

The 1st Foot Guards are seen here repulsing the Imperial Guard during the latter's final attempt for victory at Waterloo. Having brought the French to a halt, the Guards are advancing to drive the French back at bayonet point.

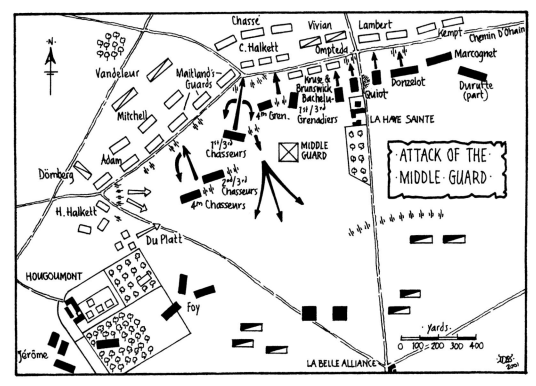

not been for the fire of a Dutch battery under Captain Krahmer de Bichin, Mercer's battery would have been annihilated by a nearby French battery. Fortunately, the 'beastly drunken Belgians', as Mercer described them, saw them off with a few well directed shots.

At last, the Imperial Guard began to ascend the Allied ridge. Apart from some British skirmishers and batteries of artillery, there was no sign of Wellington's army. There is little doubt that the French were well aware of Wellington's reverse slope tactic, or that there were more than a few bearskinned warriors who knew exactly what to expect when they reached the crest of the ridge. They knew full well the power of British musketry and knew also that when it was delivered by the red-jacketed infantry it was likely to be very unpleasant. The sun was sinking slowly by this time and the shadows that were cast up by the tall, bearskinned French on to the smoke which drifted about the ridge were said to have given the French the impression of being giants. Finally, they reached the crest, cheering and shouting 'Vive l'Empereur!' but no sooner had they reached Wellington's line than a solitary voice was heard above the din. It was Wellington himself. 'Stand up Guards!' he shouted, and with the order 'Make Ready! Fire!', hundreds of British infantry sprang up in front of the French and unleashed a devastating fire into their packed ranks. The French had been expecting a hot reception, but the sudden appearance of King George's finest soldiers appears to have

rooted them to the spot. Not for the first time in his life Wellington was in the thick of the action, and he could not resist taking personal command of the Foot Guards. Watching the great clash of arms was Digby Mackworth:

> The French moved on with arms sloped 'au pas de charge'. They began to ascend the hill [and] in a few seconds they were within a hundred paces of us, and as yet not a shot had been fired. The awful moment was now at hand – a peal of ten thousand thunders burst at once on their devoted heads, the storm swept them down, as a whirlwind which rushes over the ripe corn. They paused, their advance ceased, they commenced firing from the heads of their columns, and attempted to extend their front, but death had already caused too much confusion among them. They crowded instinctively behind each other, to avoid a fire which was intolerably dreadful.[2]

Ensign Howell Rees Gronow was in the thick of it himself. He had watched from the reverse slope as the Imperial Guard grew ever nearer:

> We saw the bearskin caps rising higher and higher, as they ascended the ridge of ground which separated us and advanced nearer and nearer to our lines. It was at this moment that the Duke of Wellington gave his famous order for our bayonet charge, as he rode along the line: these are the precise words he made use of – 'Guards, get up and charge!' We were instantly on our legs, and after so many hours of inaction and irritation at maintaining a purely

defensive attitude – all the time suffering the loss of comrades and friends – the spirit which animated officers and men may easily be imagined. After firing a volley as soon as the enemy were within shot, we rushed on with fixed bayonets and that hearty 'hurrah' peculiar to British soldiers.[3]

Not far from Gronow was Harry Weyland Powell, who later recalled the effect of the Foot Guards' musketry on the French squares:

They [the French] continued to advance till within fifty or sixty paces of our front, when the brigade were ordered to stand up. Whether it was from the sudden and unexpected appearance of a corps so near them, which must have seemed as starting out of the ground, or the tremendously heavy fire we threw into them, La Garde, who had never before failed in an attack suddenly stopped. Those who from a distance and more on the flank could see the affair, tell us that the effect of our fire seemed to force the head of the column bodily back. In less than a minute 300 were down. They now wavered, and several of the rear divisions began to draw out as if to deploy, whilst some of the men in their rear beginning to fire over the heads of those in front was so evident a proof of their confusion, that Lord Saltoun (who had joined the Brigade, having had the whole of his Light Infantry Battalion dispersed at Hougoumont) holloaed out, 'Now's the time, my boys.' Immediately the brigade sprang forward. La Garde turned and gave us little opportunity of trying the steel.[4]

Ensign Swinburne, of the 3/1st Foot Guards, had been out in front, skirmishing with his men, when the Imperial Guard advanced. He rejoined the rest of his battalion and soon after received the command to rise and fire. 'This the French received and I think they were not more than 15 yards from us. They were so close that most of our men fired from the charging position (I mean without bringing the musket to the shoulder).'[5]

The French were shocked and stunned by the appearance of the long, red line of British infantry, which now poured volley after volley into their ranks. It was a scene that would have been familiar to many a Peninsular veteran, the same scenario having been played out on many a dusty Spanish battlefield. With the French brought to a halt, the men gave three loud cheers before charging their bayonets and driving forward into the thick, grey smoke. When they emerged they found the grenadiers and chasseurs of the Imperial Guard in utter disarray, the officers struggling to maintain order and the front ranks trying desperately to reload and fire. In fact, the French managed to get off at least one withering volley before they were overwhelmed by Maitland's Foot Guards, who went crashing into the French with their bayonets. At least one Guardsman, Hughes, use the butt of his musket to flatten the French, as Gronow recalled:

'The Battle of Waterloo, the height of the battle, and the rout of the French.' This painting by Pierre Hellemans depicts the closing stages of the battle, with the French army beginning to disintegrate.

Numerous anomalies are to be found in this picture, although it does capture the atmosphere of the evening at Waterloo rather well. Wellington raises his hat in the air as the signal for his embattled but victorious army to advance.

It appeared that our men, deliberately and with calculation, singled out their victims, for as they came upon the Imperial Guard our line broke, and the fighting became irregular. The impetuosity of our men seemed almost to paralyse their enemies: I witnessed several of the Imperial Guard who were run through the body apparently without any resistance on their parts. I observed a big Welshman of the name of Hughes, who was six feet seven inches in height, run through with his bayonet and knock down with the butt-end of his firelock, I should think a dozen at least of his opponents.[6]

The fate of these Frenchmen was decided when Sir John Colborne ordered his battalion, the 52nd, to wheel round to their left in order to fire upon the French left flank. The regiment had achieved great things in the Peninsula where, as part of the famous Light Division, it had fought in countless actions, although nothing had been as significant as the move which Colborne now ordered. Frederick Adam, commanding the brigade, asked Colborne what he intended doing, at which the latter replied, 'To make that column feel our fire.' No sooner had the words left his lips than the 52nd hurried to their feet and, wheeling round to their left, brought themselves parallel with the left flank of the French infantry. The French were already reeling from the destructive fire of Maitland's Foot Guards, and when the 52nd opened up with a rolling fire, the game was up.

Assailed from front and flank, the Imperial Guard began streaming away to the rear, first those at the back of their formation and then those in front. The 71st Regiment came forward too, to add their weight to the British attack. 'Go on, go on!' cried Wellington as he watched Colborne, 'They won't stand!' And so the 52nd continued pushing forward, driving the French back whilst the Foot Guards poured forward likewise from the crest.

Farther east, the other French squares were attacking and here they met with some success, at least initially. Two squares of the Imperial Guard hit Wellington's line either side of the place where the road to Braine l'Alleud meets the track which runs from Hougoumont. This was Colin Halkett's sector. The Imperial Guard drove up the slope to the crest where they were met by the 2/30th and 2/73rd, both in a four-deep line. Ensign Edward Macready was with the 30th and watched the Imperial Guard as it came on:

> As they rose step by step before us, and crossed the ridge, their red epaulettes and cross-belts put on over their blue great-coats, gave them a gigantic appearance, which was increased by their hairy high caps and long red feathers, which waved with the nod of their heads as they kept time to a drum in the centre of their column. 'Now for a clawing,' I muttered, and I confess, when I saw the imposing advance of these men, and thought of the character they had gained, I looked for nothing but a bayonet in the body, and I half breathed a confident sort of wish that it might not touch my vitals.[7]

On Macready's right were the 33rd and 2/69th. The British met the French attack with a withering fire but did not stop it. Instead, the French slowly began to drive back the redcoats, whilst behind them some Brunswickers and Nassauers were only stopped from running away by Vivian's cavalry. The French artillery had done a fine job in softening up the British line prior to the attack, much of the damage being done by two guns which Macready claimed were sited on the crest itself. These fired grape into the square of the 30th and 73rd – the two regiments had formed a single square – causing severe casualties. Thus, when the Imperial Guard arrived they found the British reeling from the fire of the French artillery. 'That there was a great giving way near this point about this period is certain,' wrote Macready, as the British began to fall back in the face of this latest determined attack:

> Officers were jammed together and carried along by the pressure from without, many of the latter, some cursing, others literally crying with rage and shame, were seizing the soldiers and calling on them to halt, while these admirable fellows, good-humouredly laughing at their excitement, were struggling get out of the mêlée, or exclaiming, 'By God, I'll stop, Sir, but I'm off my legs.'[8]

According to Thomas Morris, of the 73rd, Halkett's brigade was cut to pieces. Colin Halkett himself was shot through the cheeks whilst trying to rally his men and had to be led from the field. It was a desperate position for everybody up on the ridge but not a man deserted his post. With Halkett removed to the rear, command of the brigade passed into the hands of Colonel William Elphinstone, of the 33rd, who rode up and down the line brandishing his

sword in the air, shouting, 'Come on, my brave fellows! Let us die like Britons, sword in hand, or conquer.' His stirring battle cry brought a cheer from the battered remnants of the brigade, but still the enemy fire continued. Fortunately, Detmer's brigade from Chassé's division was thrown into the action and opened fire on the French at close range. Krahmer's battery of artillery, that had earlier saved Mercer, was also brought forward, opening up on the Imperial Guard with grape and cannister. This allowed the hard-pressed British infantry to turn about and return to the crest, and, slowly but steadily, the French began to give way. Volley after volley was poured into the French, both from Halkett's men in front and Detmer's men on their flank. The French troops at the rear of their formation, sensing the attack had come to a halt and with musketry and grape flying all around them, turned and began streaming away to the south. Those at the front, hemmed in by those behind, could do nothing but stand and fight, the majority of the front ranks being cut down. Then, suddenly, the fire slackened and then stopped altogether. 'The fire of the enemy,' wrote Hope Pattison,

> which had been decimating our ranks…suddenly relaxed and almost in an instant ceased entirely, so that when the smoke had disappeared, not a man [of the French] was to be seen except those who were retreating in great disorder and consternation.[9]

It was true. When Hope Pattison and his comrades emerged from the smoke, they gazed out across the battlefield to see the Imperial Guard in full retreat. Away to their right Maitland's Foot Guards strode manfully forward, bayoneting and shooting all who stood in their way, while farther to the right Colborne's veteran infantry drove on, keeping up a galling fire on the French in order to hasten their retreat. The attack by the Imperial Guard, Bonaparte's final throw of the dice, had failed.

The defeat of the Imperial Guard was the death knell for the French Army at Waterloo. It seemed inconceivable to them that this last attack had been thrown back by an army such as that which now stood defiantly atop the ridge of Mont St Jean. 'The Guard is defeated!' rang out along the length of the French line, precipitating a sudden collapse in both morale and discipline. The French units attacking on the right of the Imperial Guard close to the crossroads were driven back also, leaving Wellington's men victorious on all parts of their line. Already the Prussians were tearing into Bonaparte's rear, and with the Imperial Guard and their supporting troops streaming back in defeat away from the Allied ridge, the French Army suddenly began to disintegrate. 'The Prussians are here!' cried many, whilst others shouted angrily, 'We are betrayed!'

It was about 8pm when the Imperial Guard was hurled back from Wellington's ridge. Their defeat sent shockwaves reverberating throughout the rest of the French Army, but although thousands of them began running from the battlefield soon afterwards, there remained many units that maintained their discipline, many of which hovered at the foot of the ridge. Having seen the Imperial Guard defeated, Wellington, 'with the glint of victory in his eye', was not about to let the French off the hook and knew the time was right for his army to advance and finish what Maitland and Halkett had started. And so, raising himself in his saddle for all to see, he took off his cocked hat and waved it high above his head. Everybody who saw it knew what it meant, and in an instant a great cheer went up, growing louder and louder as it was picked up by everybody who remained standing on the ridge. It was the signal to advance. The battle was won.

1 Digby Mackworth, MSS Journal.
2 Ibid.
3 Capt. Howell Rees Gronow, *The Reminiscences of Captain Gronow*, edited by Nicolas Bentley (London, 1977), p.48.
4 Capt. HW Powell, quoted in *Waterloo Letters*, edited by Maj.Gen. HT Siborne (London, 1891), p.255.
5 Ensign Thomas Swinburne, British Library Add.MSS. 34708.
6 Gronow, *Reminiscences*, p.48.
7 Anthony Brett-James, *The Hundred Days* (London, 1964), p.155.
8 Ibid. p.331.
9 Lt. Frederick Hope Pattison, *Personal Recollections of the Waterloo Campaign*, edited by Bob Elmer (London, 1997), p.43.

Chapter XIV
THE GRAND FINALE

No cheering, my lads, but forward, and complete your victory!
Wellington to his men, at the moment of victory

The sight of Wellington, raising himself in his saddle and waving his hat above his head to signal the general advance, remains one of the most enduring images of the Battle of Waterloo. What a moment it must have been. There had been other poignant moments in his career, such as the time when he bade farewell to Portugal for the last time before embarking on his decisive 1813 campaign. 'Farewell Portugal,' he said, turning in his saddle, 'for I shall never see you again.' And when he rejoined his army at Sorauren, in July 1813, the cheers that rolled out along the length of the British line must have touched even his heart, the men not usually being given to open displays of adoration. Here, at Waterloo, he had seen his friends cut down around him, whilst his men had been subjected to the greatest of punishments. But they had come through this tough examination and had emerged victorious, and the huge roar that greeted Wellington's gesture was as much an explosion of relief as it was of triumph. John Kincaid, still on his feet near the crossroads, recalled the moment in his memoirs:

> Presently a cheer, which we knew to be British, commenced far to the right, and made every one prick up his ears; – it was Lord Wellington's long wished-for orders to advance; it gradually approached, growing louder as it grew near; – we took it up by instinct, charged through the hedge down upon the old knoll, sending our adversaries flying at the point of the bayonet. Lord Wellington galloped up to us at the instant, and our men began to cheer him; but he called out, 'No cheering, my lads, but forward, and complete your victory!'[1]

With the French in retreat, Wellington took the opportunity to send his cavalry down in pursuit

of them. This job, of course, fell to the light cavalry, the heavies having suffered earlier in the day. With the cavalry having charged, the rest of Wellington's men came tumbling down the southern slopes of the ridge to ensure that the enemy were not given the chance to reform, not that that ever looked likely, what with the Imperial Guard having been defeated and with the Prussians on the battlefield in full force. When they emerged from the smoke and gloom that hung about over the ridge, Wellington's men discovered it to be a very fine summer's evening, with the sun shining as it began to dip low beneath the horizon. The stifling heat and the smell of burnt cartridges gave way to fresher air, and all of a sudden the whole atmosphere changed. No longer were they being subjected to intense enemy fire, but they were enjoying their great moment, they were pushing the French back, driving them towards their own staging positions. One officer enquired as to the direction of the advance. 'Why, straight ahead to be sure,' replied Wellington, pointing ahead of him.

It was not all plain sailing, however, for several French units refused to be intimidated by the great Allied advance and instead remained in tight formation. As the light began to fade, these units caused Wellington's men much trouble. The speed of the Allied advance resulted in some British regiments finding themselves with French troops behind them, and these, opening fire, caused heavy casualties even at this late stage of the battle. Orange flashes lit up the gloom as the two sides exchanged volleys, whilst here and there men were shot down in error by their own sides. George Farmer, of the 11th Light Dragoons, left a vivid account of the confused fighting that followed the Allied advance:

'The Duke gives the magic word. "The whole line will advance!" ' is the caption for this spirited painting by Wollen. The debris of the French cavalry attacks lies scattered around on the ground as Wellington and his men begin their final advance.

There was a heart-stirring cheer begun, I know not where, but very soon audible over the whole of our front; and we, too, were ordered to leap into the saddle and move forward! On we went at a gallop, dashing past the weary yet gallant footmen, and, shouting as we went, drove fiercely and without check up to the very muzzles of a hostile battery. A furious discharge of grape met us, and thinned our ranks. Before it, man and horse went down; but the survivors, never pulling bridle or pausing to look back, scattered the gunners to

the winds, and the cannon were our own. Just at this moment, Sergeant Emmet of the 11th, whom I covered, received a shot in the groin, which made him reel in the saddle, from which he would have fallen, had I not caught him; while at the same time a ball struck me on the knee, the bone of which was saved by the interposition of my unrolled cloak...There was a momentary check, during which the men demanded one of another, what regiment this was. I do not know how the discovery of their own absolute intermingling might have operated, had not an officer called aloud, 'Never mind your regiments, men, but follow me.' In an instant I sprang to his side, and, seeing a mass of infantry close upon us, who, by the blaze of musketry, we at once recognised to be French, he shouted, 'Charge!' and nobly led the way. We rushed on; the enemy fired, and eight of our number fell, among whom was our gallant leader. A musket-ball had pierced his heart: he sprang out of his saddle, and fell dead to the ground. Another check was the consequence, and almost instinctively we recoiled: neither, indeed, was the movement inopportune, for the impetuosity of a mere handful had carried them into the middle of a retreating column, and their destruction, had they lingered there, must have been inevitable.[2]

Sir Hussey Vivian had led the 10th and 18th Hussars down the slopes against the French infantry with 'a good hearty damn', but found squadrons of enemy cavalry still lurking in the darkness. He ordered the 18th to halt in support of the 10th, whilst he himself led the latter in a charge against some French cavalry. Having scattered them he rode back to the 18th but was attacked en route by a cuirassier. Vivian had lost the use of his right arm at the Croix d'Orade, in April 1814, and so was at a distinct disadvantage.

I was fortunate enough to give him [the cuirassier] a thrust in the neck with my left hand (for my right was in a sling, and I was just capable of holding the reins with it only), and at that moment I was joined by my little German orderly, who cut the fellow from his horse.[3]

As he continued his ride, he saw a dragoon of the King's German Legion struggling to free himself from beneath his wounded horse. As he lay there a French lancer came up and blew his brains out. When he reached the 18th Hussars, Vivian called on them to join him in an attack on some French infantry. 'Yes, General, to hell if you will lead us,' came the reply. The attack was beaten off, but the 18th reformed, being joined by the 1st Hussars KGL and a weak squadron of the 10th Hussars under Major Howard. Another charge was delivered against an enemy infantry square but once again it was unsuccessful. In fact, the charge cost Howard his life, as Captain Taylor later recalled:

Major Howard said that having been ordered to attack he thought it a ticklish thing not to do it, and gave the order accordingly and did it with effect, though the enemy stood well, the officers being wounded close to the bayonets, and Major Howard falling so that a man in the front ranks struck him with the butt end of his musket.[4]

Colonel James Sleigh, of the 11th Light Dragoons further highlights the confusion:

Another painting depicting the moment of victory. Hat in hand, Wellington gives the signal for the general advance. When asked in which direction, Wellington is reputed to have said, 'why, straight ahead to be sure.'

After enduring everything the French could throw at them, Wellington's men are ordered to advance and complete their victory. The British troops here cheer and wave their shakos in the air as they begin their advance through the smoke and down into the valley which lay littered with the debris of earlier French attacks.

We took the last battery and received their last fire, which was given when the brigade, then under my command, was so close that I saw the artillerymen fire their guns; fortunately the ground was undulating, and we only lost by the fire Lieutenant Philips of the 11th [Light] Dragoons, and Hay of the 16th [Light] Dragoons. It was after this, when continuing our advance, that the 1st Hussars came up in the rear of our brigade, and from its being nearly dark were all but in collision with the 11th and 16th, which regiments, knowing there was a brigade

of French cavalry on our right, went threes about, and were in the act of charging, when they recognised the 1st Hussars by knowing their cheer; it was very dark, and the men knew of the French brigade being behind them.[5]

With the light cavalry brigades of Vivian and Vandeleur actively engaged against the retreating French Army, the commanding officer of the Allied cavalry, Lord Uxbridge, could reckon his cavalry to have turned in a good performance at Waterloo. His heavy cavalry may well have

The 71st Highland Light Infantry turn a captured French gun upon its previous owners during the closing stages of the Battle of Waterloo. The regiment was careful to chalk its number upon the barrel to stake their ownership.

suffered severely earlier in the afternoon, but at least he had had the satisfaction of seeing them destroy the great French infantry attack to the east of the Brussels road. The light cavalry had done well also, making several effective charges throughout the day, particularly during the French cavalry attacks. Now, with the French in full retreat, Uxbridge rode beside Wellington, down the slope to the west of La Haye Sainte. Suddenly, a shot came whizzing over the neck of Wellington's horse, striking Uxbridge in the knee. 'By God, sir, I've lost my leg!' exclaimed Uxbridge as he looked down at his shattered knee. Given the history between the two great men, it is hardly surprising that Wellington, turning slowly to him, replied simply, 'By God, sir, so you have!' before turning his attention once more to the thousands of British soldiers who continued to race onwards towards La Belle Alliance and the former French position. Uxbridge, meanwhile, was carried from the field by his aide, Seymour, and six Hanoverians.

The advance continued. Sergeant David Robertson and his comrades in the 92nd had set off 'at full speed', not bothering to load their muskets. Instead they simply bayoneted any Frenchmen who got in their way. 'The French at length ran off,' he wrote, 'throwing away knapsacks, firelocks, and everything that was cumbersome, or that could impede their flight.' As they approached La Belle Alliance, they saw a

French column still standing and offering resistance. 'We rushed upon it like a legion of demons…we speedily put an end to their resistance.'[6] Thomas Morris's battalion, the 2/73rd, came down off the ridge in a four-deep line. Major Kelly had ordered the regiment's bullet-ridden Colours to be taken from the staff and given to Sergeant Weston, who rolled them round his body for safekeeping. The 73rd then advanced a short distance before halting. They then returned to a position just fifty yards from where they had been fighting during the day.

Meanwhile Adam's brigade, being well in advance of the other British infantry brigades, continued to lead the way. The brigade advanced with the 52nd on the left and the 71st on the right, with the two companies of the 3/95th supporting them. As they passed La Haye Sainte the officers on the far left of the line ran over to it to see what was going on inside, but the French had abandoned the place. The brigade then overran some enemy guns and the 71st began frantically chalking their regimental number upon them, as if to lay ownership to them. Two companies of the 52nd also fired into a squadron of the 23rd Light Dragoons by mistake. Soon enough, the brigade reached the original French positions from where all but a few squares of the Imperial Guard had fled. One of these continued fighting despite being called upon to surrender. 'Merde' was their famous

Captain Joseph Thackwell is wounded leading the 15th Hussars in a charge against French grenadiers of the Imperial Guard on the evening of Waterloo. After successive shots had disabled both of his arms, Thackwell took the reins of his horse between his teeth.

Yet another painting showing Wellington at the moment of victory at Waterloo. A dead Frenchman lies biting the dust, as British infantry charge bayonets and advance.

reply, leaving the British with little option but to continue pouring their fire into them. While these gallant soldiers were dying for their beloved Emperor, Bonaparte himself was making good his escape by way of Genappe, at first fleeing in his carriage and then, when this became jammed in the narrow streets of the town, by horse.

Shortly after Adam's brigade had reached the initial French position, other British and Allied units began to join them. The shattered remnants of Lambert's brigade arrived, having first thrown some of their number into La Haye Sainte, which had been abandoned. Pack's brigade arrived also, the wild Highlanders of the 92nd accidentally setting off a few ammunition wagons that had been abandoned by the enemy, whilst Kempt's men, having marched down the slopes, arrived too. By now it was almost dark, and in the dim light British troops came under fire from the Prussians who were emerging from the road leading to Plancenoit. British light cavalry, in particular, came in for some punishment, exchanging sabre cuts with their allies before the mistake was realised.

Not all of the British troops were able to join in the general advance. Cavalié Mercer had seen his beloved battery of horse artillery shattered by French artillery fire during the enemy's final attack. While the advance was taking place Mercer was surveying the scene around him. On his right was McDonald's troop, commanded by Lieutenant Sandilands, which had suffered also:

We were congratulating ourselves on the happy results of the day, when an aide-de-camp rode up, crying, 'Forward, sir! – forward! It is of the utmost importance that this movement should be supported by artillery!' at the same time waving his hat much in the manner of a huntsman laying on his dogs. I smiled at his energy, and, pointing to the remains of my poor troop, quietly asked, 'How, sir?' A glance was sufficient to show him the impossibility and away he went.

Our situation was indeed terrible; of 200 fine horses with which we had entered the battle, upwards of 140 lay dead, dying or severely wounded. Of the men, scarcely two-thirds of those necessary for four guns remained, and these so completely exhausted as to be totally incapable of further exertion. Lieutenant Breton had three horses killed under him; Lieutenant Hinks was wounded in the breast by a spent ball; Lieutenant Leathes on the hip by a splinter; and although untouched myself, my horse had no less than eight wounds, one of which – a graze on the fetlock joint – lamed him for ever. Our guns and carriages were, as before mentioned, altogether in a confused heap, intermingled with dead and wounded horses, which it had not been possible to disengage from them. My poor men, such at least as were untouched, fairly worn out, their clothes, faces, etc., blackened by the smoke and spattered over with mud and blood, had seated themselves on the trails of the carriages, or had thrown themselves on the wet and polluted soil, too fatigued to think of anything but gaining a little rest. Such was our situation when called upon to advance![7]

At around 9pm Wellington arrived at La Belle Alliance, followed shortly afterwards, by happy coincidence, by Blücher himself. The two commanders shook hands warmly but neither could speak each other's language. 'Mein lieber Kamerad!' cried Blücher, to which Wellington replied in French, 'Quelle affaire!' Given the confusion that followed the French rout, it is not surprising that the decision was taken to conduct the pursuit with Prussian troops only, in order to avoid more instances of 'friendly fire'. In any case, Wellington's men were thoroughly exhausted after the efforts during the day and were in no state to effect a pursuit. At the same time a band struck up 'God save the King'. It was a momentous occasion, carried out in almost total darkness, but one that vindicated the two men's strategy. The campaign had opened inauspiciously, with a total breakdown in communications between the two armies, but through the endeavours of the two men and of their armies they had come together on the day to crush Bonaparte and his army once and for all.

1 Capt. John Kincaid, *Adventures in the Rifle Brigade* (London, 1830), p.343.
2 George Farmer, *The Light Dragoon*, edited by GR Gleig (London, 1850), pp.157–8.
3 Vivian, quoted in *Waterloo Letters*, edited by Maj.Gen. HT Siborne (London, 1891), p.164.
4 Lt.Col. TW Taylor, quoted in *Waterloo Letters* , p.176.
5 Lt.Gen. JW Sleigh, quoted in *Waterloo Letters*, p.108.
6 Sgt. David Robertson, *The Journal of Sergeant D. Robertson, late 92nd Foot, comprising the different campaigns between the years 1797 and 1818* (Perth, 1842), p.159.
7 Capt. Cavalié Mercer, *Journal of the Waterloo Campaign*, edited by Sir John Fortescue (London, 1927), pp.180–1.

Chapter XV
19 June:
The Crowning Carnage

*Well, thank God, I don't what it is like to lose a battle; but certainly nothing can be
more painful than to gain one with the loss of so many of one's friends.*

Wellington to Dr Hume, 19 June 1815

After leaving Blücher Wellington turned Copenhagen round and together they began the long ride back across the battlefield and on to headquarters in the village of Waterloo. It was just as well that it was dark, as it spared him the full horror of the battlefield at night, although the human disaster that surrounded him was still visible to a degree, the moon having cast its own pale light over the scene. With the battle having been fought over such a small area, and with the numbers of dead and wounded being so high, the battlefield presented a truly horrific sight. Wellington had seen large numbers of dead and wounded soldiers in the Peninsula, but these had been spread over large areas. Badajoz was the worst sight, the

majority of the 3,500 casualties being crammed into a small space, barely three hundred yards long, at the foot of the breaches. But nothing compared with this. It is doubtful whether the ringing in his ears, caused by the tremendous din throughout the day, spared him the groans and moans of thousands of wounded soldiers, still lying out on the battlefield.

The bodies of scores of British heavy cavalrymen lay thick on the ground on either side of the main road, just south of La Haye Sainte, marking the high tide of their great charge earlier in the day. As he passed the farm itself Wellington would have noticed piles of dead and wounded Frenchmen who had been struck down in their efforts to take the place. At the

Wellington and Blücher exchange handshakes close to the aptly-named La Belle Alliance in the late evening of 18 June 1815. Having already fought a battle at Wavre the same day, the Prussians marched to Waterloo where they engaged the French in a fierce action at the village of Plancenoit, behind the French right. They then engaged in a vicious pursuit of the beaten French army, leaving Wellington's men on the field of Waterloo.

Another version of the meeting between Wellington and Blücher. A band nearby struck up, 'God Save the King,' as the two men congratulated each other.

back of the farmhouse lay Christian Ompteda, an old comrade from the Peninsula, who had died as a result of a whim on the part of the young Prince of Orange, who had been wounded himself. Nearer the crossroads, where the bodies of the 27th Inniskillings lay dead in square formation, lay another old comrade of Wellington's, Sir Thomas Picton. The fiery Welshman had never really been one of Wellington's 'inner circle', and, indeed, Wellington considered him rather rough. 'Picton's are very bad,' was Wellington's verdict on Picton's dinner parties when asked by a young officer new to the Peninsula. However, he was the sort of man Wellington needed when there was fighting to be done, and as he trotted past the crossroads he almost certainly mourned the death of his old Peninsula comrade.

The road north to the village of Waterloo was strewn with the debris of battle, but at length Wellington reached his headquarters. It lay opposite the church of Saint Joseph's, inside which scores of British soldiers lay wounded or dying. After he had dismounted he gave Copenhagen a pat on the hind quarters, at which the horse kicked out violently and came close to injuring or even killing his master. According to his cook, James Thornton, Wellington arrived back at his quarters at midnight having already arranged for a hot dinner to be served when he returned. Indeed, Thornton had been awoken at 4am on

18 June at Wellington's house in Brussels in order to pack some provisions in a basket. Wine, tea and sugar were packed up and sent off. Soon afterwards, Thornton himself found a horse and, accompanied by Wellington's butler, set off for Waterloo. He was standing in the entrance passage to the house when Wellington arrived and, turning to some officers in the passage, asked how they were. Then, upon seeing Thornton, he said, 'let us have dinner directly'.[1]

The dinner was served in a bedroom upstairs. In Wellington's own bed lay his close friend and aide-de-camp, Alexander Gordon, whose leg had been amputated on the battlefield earlier on. The operation, performed by Dr Hume, was not enough to prevent Gordon from fast slipping away and, indeed, by morning he had joined the ever-growing list of fatalities. With the dinner laid by Thornton, Wellington sat down. In front of him were places for all of his staff but only Miguel Alava, his old Spanish friend, joined him. The grime of battle was still on his face as Wellington began his belated meal. Presently, the door opened and in came Müffling who exchanged a few words with the diners before leaving. Every now and then an orderly would came in, causing Wellington to glance up, hoping that, by chance, one of his friends would enter. But none did. They had either been killed or wounded, or were still busy at the scene of the day's victory. And so it left

A British officer calls upon the Old Guard to surrender at Waterloo. The request was met with the famous reply, 'Merde!', by Colonel Cambronne, who was wounded and taken prisoner shortly after. Having refused to surrender, the Guard took to its heels along with the rest of the French army, with the Prussians in hot pursuit.

just Wellington and Alava to dine alone, the two men drinking a toast to the memory of the Peninsular War.

When dinner was done, Wellington retired to bed and quickly fell asleep. He had not long been asleep when he was woken up by Dr Hume, who told him that Gordon had just died. The doctor then went on to read the long list of casualties that he had so far received: Canning, Gordon, Picton, Chambers, Eeles, Reignolds, Stothert, L'Estrange, Smyth, Marschalk, Crofton, Currie and Curzon, all killed, and this was only the staff. The list of wounded was, naturally, even longer, and included several of Wellington's most senior officers: the Prince of Orange, Fitzroy Somerset, Uxbridge, Cooke, Kempt, Pack, Grant, Adam, Colin Halkett, Barnes and Elley. Sir William De Lancey was also amongst the latter, but he too would die of his horrific wound. Wellington was informed of the death of Sir William Ponsonby later on. There were scores of regimental officers, good men who had shared in Wellington's triumphs in the Peninsula, who had been struck down also.

During six years of war in the Peninsula Wellington had only been known to shed tears publicly on two occasions; once at Burgos, in October 1812, following the burial of his friend, Edward Cocks, and, six months earlier, at Badajoz, on the morning after the storming of the fortress. On that occasion, Wellington had looked down into the smouldering breaches to see the shattered remains of the 4th and Light Divisions who had made over forty unsuccessful attacks. The huge pile of British and Portuguese corpses moved him to tears for the first time in the war. Now, at Waterloo, with Dr Hume having read out the long list of casualties, the tears began to flow once again. Little wonder he was moved to whisper, 'Well, thank God, I don't know what it is like to lose a battle; but certainly nothing can be more painful than to gain one with the loss of so many of one's friends.'

Unable to sleep, Wellington slid out of his bed and dressed himself. He had gone to bed without having washed, and the grime of battle still clung to his face. The tracks of his tears were still visible upon his cheeks when he sat down at his desk, picked up his pen and began to write to Earl Bathurst:

My Lord, Buonaparte [sic] having collected the 1st, 2nd, 3rd, 4th and 6th corps of the French army and the Imperial Guards, and nearly all the cavalry on the Sambre, and between that river and the Meuse, between the 10th and 14th of the month, advanced on the 15th, and attacked the Prussian posts at Thuin and Lobez, on the Sambre, at day light in the morning.[2]

In his famous *Waterloo Despatch*, published in *The Times*, on Thursday 22 June, Wellington described the three days' fighting in his usual clear and precise way, singling out several officers for praise. He did not forget to add his own thanks to Marshal Blücher, saying, 'I should not do justice to my feelings or to Marshal Blücher and the Prussian army, if I did not attribute the successful result of this arduous day, to the cordial and timely assistance I received from them.' He was also moved to praise his own army, writing, 'It gives me the greatest satisfaction to assure your Lordship, that the army never, upon any occasion, conducted itself better.'

Wellington did not finish the despatch, but early on the Monday morning, 19 June, no doubt still exhausted, he took himself off to Brussels where he completed it. He then gave it to Major Henry Percy who took it, along with the two captured French eagles, back to London. Other letters were written also, one of which was to his brother, William:

> It was the most desperate business I was ever in. I never took so much trouble about any battle, and never was so near being beat. Our loss is immense particularly in that best of all instruments, British infantry. I never saw the infantry behave so well.[3]

At 8.30am he penned another letter, this time to Lady Frances Webster, informing her of his victory. 'My loss is immense,' he wrote, 'The finger of Providence was upon me, and I escaped unhurt.'[4]

Meanwhile back on the battlefield, Wellington's men had been enduring what was, for some, an unforgettable night. For many others it was their last. The British Army was in no condition to move after their exertions during a day when they had fought the French to a standstill before delivering the knock-out blow. The cost had been tremendous. No fewer than 1,781 British and KGL officers and men were killed at Waterloo, and 5,734 wounded. A further 810 were listed as missing, many of whom were almost certainly killed. The total British casualty figure of

With the battle over, there remained the huge task of gathering in the thousands of wounded who lay scattered far and wide across the battlefield. In some instances, wounded soldiers lay out on the battlefield for days before they were brought in. The treatment being given to this wounded Highlander is an extremely sanitised and romantic version. The reality was, sadly, much worse.

8,325 is just 700 short of the entire force with which Wellington landed in Portugal back in the summer of 1808. French losses were put as high as an incredible 30,000, not including around 6,000 prisoners. 250 French guns were taken also during the battle and in the immediate pursuit. Altogether, it is estimated that over 40,000 men lay dead, wounded and dying around the battlefield.

Wellington's men camped for the night on the battlefield. It was an eerie and unpleasant night, with thousands of groaning wounded men, and neighing horses, all around them, for whom there was little that could be done until daylight. The majority of the wounded needed water desperately, and many simply faded away through the lack of it. Meanwhile the dazed and exhausted survivors tried to get some sleep on a battlefield covered with bleeding humanity. Cavalié Mercer, 'devoured by a burning thirst', pulled down the painted cover of one of his limbers and fashioned a tent from it. He tried to sleep but in his excitement found he could only doze. Mercer's experiences on the battlefield that night were beautifully and vividly brought to life in one of the most descriptive passages in his journal:

The field of Waterloo the morning after the battle. The horrendous spectacle which followed the battle was made worse by the relatively compact nature of the battlefield. Hundreds of wounded soldiers died at the hands of peasants who wandered over the field at night, finishing off war's deadly work with a quick thrust of the knife to both wounded Allied and French soldiers alike.

From one of these dozes I awoke about midnight, chilled and cramped to death from the awkward doubled-up position imposed upon me by my short and narrow bed. So up I got to look around and contemplate a battlefield by the pale moonlight. The night was serene and pretty clear; a few light clouds occasionally passing across the moon's disc, and throwing objects into transient obscurity, added considerably to the solemnity of the scene. Oh, it was a thrilling sensation thus to stand in the silent hour of the night and contemplate the field – all day long the theatre of noise and strife, now so calm and still – the actors prostrate on the bloody soil, their pale wan faces upturned to the moon's cold beams, which caps and breastplates, and a thousand other things, reflected back in brilliant pencils of light from as many different points! Here and there some poor wretch, sitting up amidst the countless dead, busied himself in endeavours to stanch the flowing stream with which his life was fast ebbing away. Many whom I saw so employed that night were, when morning dawned, lying stiff and tranquil as those who had departed earlier. From time to time a figure would half raise itself from the ground, and then, with a despairing groan, fall back again. Others, slowly and painfully rising, stronger, or having less deadly hurt, would stagger away with uncertain steps

across the field in search of succour. Many of these I followed with my gaze until lost in the obscurity of distance; but many, alas! After staggering a few paces, would sink again on the ground, probably to rise no more…Save these I have mentioned, no living being moved on the moonlit field; and as I cast my eyes at the lustrous lamp of heaven, I thought on the thousand dear connections far, far away, on whose peaceful dwelling it now looked down, their inmates sleeping in tranquil security, ignorant of the fatal blow which had now forever severed them from those they loved, whose bodies encumbered the ground around me.[5]

Thomas Morris, of the 73rd, spent the last few moments of twilight passing amongst his wounded comrades, trying to bind their wounds and placing them in more comfortable positions. However, he was unable to give them any water for there was none to be found anywhere.

The cries and shrieks of the poor creatures [he later wrote] would have been dreadful in the night, if we could have heard them; but the continued discharges of the artillery during the battle, had so affected the drums of the ears, that we could scarcely hear anything for two or three days afterwards, but the roar of cannon.

We lay on the ground that night. I fell asleep, but woke again about midnight, almost mad, for want of water, and I made up my mind to go in search of some. By the light of the moon, I picked my way among the bodies of my sleeping, as well as of my dead comrades; but, the horrors of the scene created such a terror in my mind, that I could not muster courage to go by myself, and was turning back to get my brother along with me, when on passing where a horse was lying dead, on its side, and a man sitting upright with his back against the horse's belly, I thought I heard the man call to me, and the hope that I could render him some assistance, overcame my terror. I went towards him, and placing my left hand on his shoulder, intended to lift him up with my right; my hand, however, passed through his body, and I then saw that both he and his horse had been killed by a cannon ball.[6]

Morris went back to wake his brother, and the two men went to search the canteens of their sleeping comrades, looking for water. The two wily Cockneys finally found one slung around the neck of a man named Smith, and duly exchanged it with their own empty one. In the morning, Morris heard Smith 'blustering and swearing' about the theft of his canteen, and

threatening to run the culprit through. Morris wisely kept silent.

The perils on the battlefield at night were not confined to natural causes. No sooner had the battle ended and darkness descended, than scores of local peasants came scurrying out from their homes and hovels to begin scouring the battlefield for treasures. There was gold lace a plenty, expensive swords, pistols, quality boots and clothing and other valuable trinkets, such as gilt badges and shako plates. All had their own worth. Then, of course, there were purses, often full of coins. Indeed, although many dead and wounded soldiers had been relieved of their purses while they were lying helpless, many more still retained theirs. By looting the dead and wounded of a few coins here and there the peasants quickly began to amass a considerable sum. Often, helpless soldiers, hanging on for dear life, would be put out of their misery by a quick knife thrust from one of the scavenging rogues, amongst whom the women were often the worst. Many a British and French soldier, having fought bravely throughout the day, had his fight for life terminated in this most callous way.

Meanwhile many of the survivors continued to search for food and drink. George Farmer and some of his comrades of the 11th Light Dragoons came across one of the many grass huts which the French had thrown up earlier that morning. Inside they found raw meat of every description; pork, beef, and mutton, scattered about the floor. But such was the revolting condition of it – some pieces still had plenty of hair on them – that few of the men could eat it, and indeed the Light Dragoons rode off quietly across a battlefield, the likes of which neither they nor Farmer had ever seen before:

I never shall forget, so long as memory remains by me, the adventures of that extraordinary night. In the first place, the ground, whithersoever we went, was literally strewed with the wreck of the mighty battle. Arms of every kind, – cuirasses, muskets, cannon, tumbrels, and drums, which seemed innumerable, cumbered the very face of the earth. Intermingled with these were the carcasses of the slain, not lying about in groups of four or six, but so wedged together, that we found it, in many instances, impossible to avoid trampling them where they lay under our horses' hoofs. Then, again, the knapsacks, either cast loose, or still adhering to their owners, were countless. I confess that we opened many of these latter, hoping to find in them money, or articles of value, but not one – which I, at least, examined – contained more than the coarse shirts and shoes that had belonged to the dead owners, with here and there a little package of tobacco, and a bag of salt. And what was worst of all, when we dismounted to institute this search, our spurs for ever caught in the garments of the slain, and more than once we tripped up, and fell over them.[7]

Sergeant William Lawrence, of the 40th, ended the day camped on the ground formerly occupied by the French, having pursued them about a mile at the end of the battle. When the 'hungry and tired tribe of men', as Lawrence described his battalion, encamped, their first priority was to light a fire and cook some food, but what wood they had was wet through. Some of the men went looking for fuel as Lawrence described:

One of our company, named Rouse, who went out in search of sticks, came across one of the enemy's powder-wagons that we had taken in the battle amongst the rest of the many other things, and immediately commenced cutting the cover up for fuel; but his hook coming in contact with a nail of some other piece of iron and striking fire, as a natural consequence the remains of the powder in the wagon exploded and lifted the poor fellow to a considerable height in the air. The most remarkable thing was that he was still alive when he came down and able to speak, though everything had been blown from him except one of his shoes.[8]

Apparently, Rouse survived the explosion but died in a Brussels hospital a few days later, 'raving mad'. Lawrence's men eventually lit a fire and had the good fortune to find a sack, abandoned by some French gunners, which contained a large ham and two fowls. And so, while thousands of men endured a traumatic night around them, Lawrence and his comrades, enjoyed their meal 'as much as men ever did'.

A red glow in the sky to the west of the battlefield marked the blazing château of Hougoumont. The Foot Guards had held on here throughout the day against repeated French attacks. 'You see, Macdonnell held Hougoumont,' a delighted Wellington said to Müffling, who had earlier doubted whether the Guards would be able to keep the French out. The 'Gentlemen's Sons' emerged from their bastion to find hundreds of Frenchmen outside and in the surrounding woods. Inside the château, a dazed Matthew Clay wandered round, looking over the scene of this most famous fight.

The fire unobstructed continued its ravages, and having been unnoticed by us in the eagerness of the conflict, destroyed many of the buildings, where (in the early part of the action) many of the helpless wounded of both armies had been placed for security. On proceeding into a kind of kitchen, the wounded [were] being arranged all around as far as possible from harm's way. On again going into the yard it being evening, and perceiving a clear glowing fire rising from the ruins of a stable or some other outhouse, I took the opportunity of cooking the remaining portion of pork which I had stored away in my haversack as before stated, and after having placed it upon the fire and quietly awaiting its being cooked, discovered that the glow of fire arose from the half consumed body of some party who had fallen in the contest; my meat, which was unsavoury in the morning, became much more so by its re-dressing. Having now found a little veal (in a cooking pot hanging over a small fire) smothered with dust and fragments of broken ruins, but sufficiently cooked, I most gladly partook of it.[9]

Shortly afterwards Clay was ordered to fall in, along with another man, in order to look for fuel, after which they made their way up the slope at the rear of Hougoumont where they deposited their loads, 'in time to answer our names at the evening roll call'.

And so the night wore on. Wellington's men did not know it but the vast majority of them had fought their last battle. Waterloo was to prove the last great battle of the Napoleonic Wars and, apart from a few minor skirmishes on the road to Paris, there would be no more fighting for them. 'The three days' fight is over,' wrote William Wheeler, in anticipation of further action, and one wonders just how many British soldiers realised that the Great War with France was all but over. Probably not many, not that they really cared at such moments. What they did know, however, was that they had just taken part in one of the greatest battles in history, in which they had finally come face to face with the Corsican ogre and had emerged victorious.

Gradually, the first streaks of light began to appear on the horizon in the direction of Papelotte. In contrast to the previous morning, Monday 19 June dawned fine but chilly. The dawn came as a welcome relief to the men still camped on the battlefield, and at last they were able to wander in search of fuel, food and water, to discover who lived and who did not, and to begin gathering the wounded for transportation

The Duke of Wellington begins his famous Waterloo Despatch. *He could not sleep in his own bed for it was occupied by the dying Alexander Gordon, his aide and close friend. The* Despatch *was completed in Brussels on Monday 19 June.*

to the many hospitals that had been established in the area, in Waterloo and in Brussels. The gradual light of day revealed the full extent of the horror of the battlefield. The previous night had ended with Wellington's men still engaged until darkness set in, but now, with the new day and with no enemy present, they were able to look out over a sea of dead, dying and wounded soldiers. Horses, caps, muskets, breastplates, knapsacks, helmets, swords, wagons, carts – an enormous amount of battlefield debris, enough to fill all the museums of the world, lay scattered thick on the ground in all directions. When Sergeant David Robertson, of the 92nd, woke on the morning after the battle he went out to view the battlefield:

> The scene which then met my eyes was horrible in the extreme. The number of dead was far greater than I had ever seen on any former battlefield. The bodies were not scattered over the ground but were lying in heaps – men and horses mixed promiscuously together. It might truly have been called the 'crowning carnage', for death had indeed been here, and had left visible evidences of his grim presence in the misery and devastation that surrounded us. I turned away with disgust from this heart-melting spectacle, and had scarcely arrived at my headquarters when every person that could be spared was sent out to carry the wounded to the road side, or any other convenient place where the wagons could be brought to convey them to hospital.[10]

John Kincaid had fought his way from Lisbon to Toulouse, surviving scores of actions, but even he had never seen such a battlefield before.

> The field of battle, next morning [he wrote] presented a frightful scene of carnage; it seemed as if the world had tumbled to pieces, and three-fourths of everything destroyed in the wreck. The ground running parallel to the front of where we stood was so thickly strewed with fallen men and horses, that it was difficult to step clear of the bodies; many of the former still alive, and imploring assistance, which it was not in our power to bestow.
>
> The usual salutation on meeting an acquaintance of another regiment after an action was to ask who had been hit? But on

The ruins of Hougoumont, painted after the battle. Scores of wounded Guardsmen perished in the flames that engulfed the Great Barn after they had been taken there for 'safety'. On the right of the painting stands the chapel, the last remaining part of the original château.

this occasion it was 'Who's alive?' Meeting one, next morning, a very little fellow, I asked what had happened to them yesterday? 'I'll be hanged,' says he, 'if I know anything at all about the matter, for I was all day trodden in the mud and galloped over by every scoundrel who had a horse; and, in short, that I only owe my existence to my insignificance.'[11]

William Tomkinson, of the 16th Light Dragoons, rode over the battlefield on the morning of the 19th, and thought the battlefield between La Haye Sainte and Hougoumont looked more like a breach carried by storm, rather than a regular battlefield. There were so many wounded that he feared many would remain where they lay for a second night. As he continued his ride he came across three men of the 32nd lying together, having been wounded by grapeshot.

> They begged a little water from me with such earnestness that I got off and gave them a taste of some brandy I had in a flask. The first two I gave it to were wounded in the leg, and on my putting it to the mouth of the third, who was wounded in the body, one of the others requested me to give him his share, for his comrade was wounded in the belly, and the brandy would only do him harm. I was aware it was not good for any, yet having been out all night,

and probably having had nothing on the 18th, I thought a taste could not injure them. They begged me to send their doctor, and were afraid they would remain out a second night. A man of one of the Highland regiments was employing himself in carrying water to the wounded on both sides, and had been doing so from daylight. Many were looking after plunder, and excellent French watches were sold at a low rate.[12]

Harry Ross-Lewin, of the 32nd, was out on the battlefield looking for a new horse, having given up his own to one of the field officers of his own regiment who had had his horse shot under him on the 18th. He quickly found a horse which had belonged to an officer of the Imperial Guard, upon which he took himself off across the battlefield.

> The mangled bodies of men and horses, broken gun-carriages, caps, helmets, cuirasses, arms, drums, harnesses, accoutrements, pieces of battered uniforms, knapsacks, letters, and cards, that were strewed abundantly in all directions, and the crops levelled by the trampling of infantry and cavalry in the strife, plainly marked the extent of the field, and gave undeniable evidence of the fury of the conflict that had raged there on the preceding day.[13]

As the morning wore on numerous burial parties busied themselves in interring the dead. Naturally, regiments preferred to bury their own dead, but in many cases it was impossible to distinguish friend from foe and both were alike cast into the same grave. Ross-Lewin again:

> A sergeant of the 12th light dragoons, who was with a burying party where our left had been stationed, had found, just as I came up to him, the bodies of two young cornets of his regiment, in search of which he had been for some time. I remarked to the sergeant that his regiment must have suffered dreadfully, judging from the number of bodies which I saw lying around me in the light cavalry uniform; but he said that the dead at that spot were not all British, although the uniforms did appear to be very nearly the same. To be satisfied of this, I alighted, and had to examine the buttons before I could distinguish with any certainty between the dead of our dragoons and those of the French that lay mixed with them.[14]

Many of the dead had been stripped almost completely naked, however, and it was totally impossible to tell which nationality they were, not that it mattered too much. To the majority of the phlegmatic British one corpse was much like the next. Down at Hougoumont, the fire in the château was still smouldering when Howell Rees Gronow returned to view the scene of the fight there:

> I came first upon the orchard and there discovered heaps of dead men, in various uniforms: those of the Guards in their usual red jackets, the German Legion [sic] in green, and the French dressed in blue, mingled together. The dead and the wounded positively covered the whole area of the orchard; not less than two thousand men had fallen there. The apple trees presented a singular appearance; shattered branches were seen hanging about their mother-trunks in such profusion that one might almost suppose the stiff-growing and stunted tree had been converted into the willow: every tree was riddled and smashed in a manner which told that the showers of shot had been incessant…we had not advanced for many minutes before we met several of our gallant companions in arms who had been wounded. They were lying in waggons of the country and had been abandoned by the drivers. Some of these poor fellows belonged to our regiment and on passing close to one of the waggons, a man cried out, 'For God's sake, Mr Gronow, give us some water or we shall go mad.' I did not hesitate for a moment, but jumped into the cart and gave the poor fellow all the water my flask contained. The other wounded soldiers then entreated me to fill it with some muddy water which they had descried in a neighbouring ditch half filled by the rain of the preceding day. As I thought a flask would be of little use among so many, I took off my shako, and having first stopped up with my belcher handkerchief a hole which a musket ball had made in the top of it, filled it with water several times for these poor fellows, who were all too severely wounded to have got it for themselves and who drank it off with tears of delight.[15]

As heartless as it may appear, there were men in Wellington's army whose main concern after the battle was not the wounded but the immense amount of discarded equipment that lay strewn across the battlefield and that had to be accounted for. It was a logistical nightmare for Wellington's staff, for in the Peninsula orders had been issued for the collection of arms and equipment after each action. Indeed, units from all regiments would collect from the dead and wounded their arms and accoutrements and report the numbers collected to the Quartermaster General. Here, at Waterloo, there were simply thousands of discarded muskets and sets of accoutrements, and in some cases barely enough men to gather them. Whether or not this practice was continued at Waterloo is not clear. After all, losses had been very great, and every man would be needed soon to follow the French into France.

The work of gathering the wounded continued throughout 19 June, but by evening it was clear that the task would not be completed. Indeed, many of the wounded lay out on the battlefield for days afterwards, after the army had gone, leaving them in the care of surgeons and as many men as could be spared. Wellington gave orders that one officer, one NCO and three privates for every one hundred men wounded were to remain in Brussels for both the preservation of order and the care of the wounded. In addition to British and Allied wounded, many French soldiers were also taken to Waterloo, the surrounding villages and to Brussels, where they received care and attention from British surgeons. For the majority of the enemy, however, there was little prospect of surviving the long days on the battlefield. Their own army had fled on the night of 18 June, and with nobody but sympathetic British surgeons and the odd local, many simply perished before they could be gathered up and attended to.

Night descended once again on the field of Waterloo, but whilst thousands of wounded were left to spend a second night on the battlefield, the majority of the British Army were already marching away towards Nivelles. Matthew Clay and his comrades of the 3rd Foot Guards marched off on the afternoon of 19 June before halting for the night in a small field in sight of Nivelles, near to which was a small stream,

> …in which we cleansed ourselves from our uncomfortable state, caused by excessive perspiration, marching through the clouds of dust, bespattered with dirt, laying on the wet ground by night, biting off the ends of cartridges, and being for many hours warmly engaged amongst spreading burning fragments of destruction in the château of Hougoumont. Now came the time for the distribution of rations, camp kettles all in requisition, and a general cooking along the hedgerows, the issue of rations and liquor, and the buzz of congratulations taking place with men of different companies with their townsmen and old acquaintances, sitting or reclining on the ground, each listening to the narrative of his comrade, having been separated from each other during the contest. Had any of our enquiring friends in England been present in this said field in which was our bivouac, they would have listened with the deepest interest to the tales that were told on the night of the 19th of June 1815.[16]

There were, doubtless, hundreds of different stories being told and retold by Wellington's men on the night of 19 June. The fires were then trimmed, blankets produced and the victorious army settled down for the night. The following morning the army would finally move away, for already Wellington had issued orders for the advance south and the invasion of France.

1 James Thornton, *Your Obedient Servant* (London, 1985), p.102.

2 Wellington to Earl Bathurst, 19 June 1815. *The Despatches of Field Marshal the Duke of Wellington* (London, 1832).

3 Elizabeth Longford, *The Years of the Sword* (London, 1969).

4 Wellington to Lady Frances Webster, 19 June 1815, *Supplementary Despatches and Memorandum* (London, 1857).

5 Capt. Cavalié Mercer, *Journal of the Waterloo Campaign*, edited by Sir John Fortescue (London, 1927), pp.182–3.

6 Thomas Morris, *The Napoleonic Wars*, edited by John Selby (London, 1967), p.82.

7 George Farmer, *The Light Dragoon*, edited by GR Gleig (London, 1850), pp.159–60.

8 Sgt. William Lawrence, *Autobiography of Sergeant William Lawrence, a hero of the Peninsular and Waterloo Campaigns*, edited by GN Bankes (London, 1886), p.213.

9 Matthew Clay, *A Narrative of the Battles of Quatre Bras and Waterloo, with the Defence of Hougoumont* (Bedford, n.d.), pp.16–17.

10 Sgt. David Robertson, *The Journal of Sergeant D. Robertson, late 92nd Foot, comprising the different campaigns between the years 1797 and 1818* (Perth, 1842), pp.160–1.

11 Capt. John Kincaid, *Adventures in the Rifle Brigade* (London, 1830), pp.347–8.

12 Lt.Col. William Tomkinson, *The Diary of a Cavalry Officer in the Peninsular War and Waterloo Campaign 1809–1815*, edited by James Tomkinson (London, 1894), p.317.

13 Harry Ross-Lewin, *With the 32nd in the Peninsula and other campaigns*, edited by John Wardell (London, 1914), pp.282–3.

14 Ibid. pp.284–5.

15 Capt. Howell Rees Gronow, *The Reminiscences of Captain Gronow*, edited by Nicolas Bentley (London, 1977), pp.52–3.

16 Clay, *A Narrative*, pp.19–20.

Chapter XVI

THE ADVANCE TO PARIS

One can tolerate being shot at by those fine grenadiers of the Russian and Prussian Guards…
But how could one be a good soldier under that little sugar-loaf with a peak, with the inelegantly
cut red jacket, those grey trousers clinging to knock knees?

A Parisian onlooker at a review, horrified by the appearance of Wellington's infantry

Although the Battle of Waterloo was over the war itself was not, and so, early on the morning of 20 June Wellington's army began the advance south from their bivouacs around Nivelles. The march took them to Mons and Binche, with the cavalry occupying the villages between Mons and Roeulx. Before Wellington left his headquarters at Nivelles, he issued a General Order to his army, reminding them of their duties once they had crossed the French border. He reminded them also that, 'nothing should be taken either by officers or soldiers, for which payment be not made'. It was Wellington's polite way of saying there was to be no plundering. The commissaries, he declared, would see to the needs of his men, 'in the usual way'.

Wellington, ever the diplomatic soldier, was well aware of the dangers of invading an enemy country, and he did not simply mean the dangers from a hostile army. He issued his order with memories of Spain in mind, where guerrillas had operated against the occupying French armies to great effect. He simply could not afford to allow similar opposition to his own army to occur in France, even though it looked as if the coming campaign would be a relatively short one. When he had last invaded France, in October 1813, following the crossing of the Bidassoa, he found his Spanish allies were hell bent on retribution following years of often brutal French occupation. Not wishing to see the French turn on his own men, he ordered over 30,000 Spanish troops to return to Spain, thus considerably weakening his army, but it paid dividends when the people of southern France realised Wellington's army would not plunder them, which is what they had expected. Thus, an easy relationship developed between invader and invaded.

While Blücher's Prussians carried on a vigorous pursuit of the beaten French, Wellington's army made good their advance in easy stages. On 21 June, on the second anniversary of the Battle of Vittoria, Wellington crossed the French border and established his headquarters at Malplaquet, the scene of the Duke of Marlborough's bloodiest victory on 11 September 1709. How strange it is that Wellington's campaign linked two centuries of British battles; Malplaquet, Waterloo and Mons – for, ninety-nine years after Wellington's men marched across the field of Malplaquet, the Old Contemptibles would do the same during that momentous summer of 1914.

Before reaching Paris, Wellington and Blücher would have to pass the triple line of fortresses which they believed might yet present a problem. In the event, they proved no barrier at all. Three fortresses stood in Wellington's path: Valenciennes, Cambrai and Peronne. The first of these was blockaded on the night of 21 June, as was Le Quesnoy, another Vauban-type fortress. Prospects for a swift end to the campaign were good, as Wellington's intelligence indicated that the French were in 'a wretched state', with large numbers deserting to return to their homes.

On 23 June one of the two British brigades, Johnstone's, from Sir Charles Colville's 4th Division, along with Major Unett's battery of 9-pounders and Grant's cavalry brigade, marched to Cambrai to summon the place to surrender. Wellington's orders stated that if the governor refused to surrender, Colville was to open fire with his artillery upon the citadel only, the town apparently being loyal to the King.

The Duke's written summons the Governor would not receive, [wrote Colville] and he gave himself as usual some foolish airs, upon which

The bridge over the Dyle at Genappe in 1815. The small bridge caused tremendous traffic jams in the town during the flight of the French Army after the battle of Waterloo. Indeed, it caused Bonaparte to abandon his carriage and continue his escape on horseback.

I treated the citadel to six and twenty howitzer shells and about a dozen round shot, and moved the troops off with but the casualty of two men wounded.[1]

Wellington himself came over to Cambrai the following day, bringing with him the other brigade of infantry, Sir Neil Campbell's, along with two more batteries of artillery under Lieutenant Colonel Webber Smith and Major Brome. A brief inspection by Wellington convinced him that the place was particularly strong and well manned, and would require a regular siege. Nevertheless, he left Colville to make preparations for an assault if he thought he could achieve it. Plans were duly made for an assault to take place on the evening of the 24th. Colville divided his infantry into three columns; the first, consisting of the light companies of Johnstone's brigade, under Campbell, was to escalade the walls at the angle formed by the Valenciennes gateway and the curtain of the place. The second column, under Sir William Douglas of the 91st, and led by Lieutenant Gilbert of the Royal Engineers, was to escalade a large ravelin close to the Amiens road. The third column, consisting of Colonel Mitchell's brigade, was to force the outer gate of the Courve Port in the hornwork, and once across both ditches, which were to be crossed by way of the rails of the drawbridge, would attempt to force the main Paris Gate. The assault was timed for 6pm and would be covered by the three batteries of artillery.

I had made all my arrangements [wrote Colville] and the attack was to have commenced at six in the evening, when about a quarter of an hour before that time, two French officers came out to meet me, one from Douai, the general camp in the Department du Nord, with proposals to the Duke of Wellington for an armistice on account of the abdication of Napoleon: the other was immediately addressed to myself, but including the additional act of the Provisional Government in favour of Napoleon 2nd. It was now my turn to ride the high horse, so sent him back word I knew no such person as Napoleon 2nd, and that if in an hour he did not surrender both the town and citadel for the King of France, I must do my best to force him. The escalade of the north of the town by three small columns accordingly took place at 8 o'clock, while the fire of my eighteen pieces of artillery kept down theirs in the citadel excepting three flank guns that couldn't be got at, and two small ones in the town ramparts, which annoyed the troops as they debouched from the cover they had been placed in.[2]

Campbell's light companies scampered forward under cover of the British guns and quickly set about throwing up their ladders against the walls of the town. The men were quickly up and over the ramparts without too much opposition and, dropping down inside the place, they set about opening the Valenciennes Gate. Once this had been done they lowered the drawbridge.

Mitchell's men, meanwhile, poured forward to attack the Paris Gate but found it too strong. Fortunately, the ditch near the gate had not been cleared of reeds and mud and thus the escarp was not as high as it should have been. This allowed the British troops to place their ladders and scale the walls which were still about forty feet high, and presented quite an obstacle. Opposition was again light, and with the British guns blazing away above their heads, the men succeeded in their attack. William Wheeler, of the 51st, was one of the stormers at Cambrai:

> We had collected what ladders and ropes we could find in the farm houses, then we began splicing to enable us to scale the walls if necessary. A flag of truce was sent to the Town but they were fired at, which caused them to return, and a ball had passed through the trumpeter's cap. We were now ready for storming and were only waiting the order to advance. In a short time our field pieces opened when a shell, I believe the first thrown from the howitzer, set a large building on fire. We now pushed on to the works, near the gate, got into the trenches, fixed our ladders and were soon in possession of the top of the wall. The opposition was trifling, the regular soldiers fled to the citadel, and the shop-keepers to their shops.[3]

Wheeler then added with some sarcasm that the townspeople who now welcomed the British with cheers had only a few minutes earlier been firing on them from the ramparts. They had 'forgot to wash the powder off their lips caused by biting off the cartridges when they were firing on us from the wall'.

The town was carried in less than half an hour, with the loss of eight dead and twenty-nine wounded. This still left the citadel in French hands, but Colville had shut this up and it surrendered the following day. The greatest difficulty Colville faced was in preventing his men from plundering the place. They assumed, naturally, that they had a right to do so, as this was very much the convention of the day, but Colville had to bear in mind Wellington's order, issued four days earlier. Nevertheless, the British troops did not go away empty handed, as William Wheeler wrote:

> We had picked up some money in the town, or more properly speaking we had made the people hand it over to us to save us the trouble of taking it from them, so we were enabled to provide ourselves with what made us comfortable.[4]

The capture of Cambrai at least allowed a few of Johnstone's brigade to taste action, as the brigade had been absent from the field of Waterloo on 18 June. It was a very small consolation, but at least they had not been completely idle during the campaign. Some of Wheeler's comrades, meanwhile, were killed after the town was taken when they were engaged in a bit of plundering. A sergeant, a corporal and four men, having got completely drunk, found what they thought was a barrel of brandy. In fact, it was a barrel of gunpowder. In his attempt to make a 'bung hole', the corporal fired into it with his musket while the others waited eagerly with their mess tins to catch the brandy. The barrel blew up, of course, and Wheeler's 'brandy merchants' were all mutilated and scorched.

The following day, 25 June, King Louis XVIII – 'His pottle belly Majesty' as Wheeler called him – entered Cambrai, cheered by his 'loyal' subjects. A distinctly cynical Wheeler added that the papers no doubt described Louis as being welcomed by their beloved subjects, how he 'wept over the sufferings of his beloved people', and how he entered the town without a single soldier. 'But the papers will not inform you,' he wrote, 'that the 4th Division and a brigade of Hanoverian Hussars were in readiness within half a mile of this faithful city, and if the loyal citizens had insulted their king, how it was very probable we should have bayoneted every Frenchman in the place.'[5]

Despite the success at Cambrai, Wellington was evidently not satisfied with the overall situation regarding his army. Even as 'Old Bungy Louis' was entering Cambrai, Wellington was writing a stinging letter to the Prime Minister, complaining of shortages in his army and the state of his troops, the Dutch in particular. In a letter, bearing echoes of his notorious 'infamous army' outburst, he wrote:

> We have not one quarter of the ammunition which we ought to have, on account of the deficiency of our drivers and carriages; and I really believe that, with the exception of my old Spanish infantry, I have got not only the worst troops, but the worst equipped army, with the worst staff that ever was brought together.[6]

It is difficult to account for this latest outburst, particularly as his army had delivered to him the crowning glory of his illustrious military career. Perhaps it was just one of those days.

On 26 June Wellington's army arrived in front of Vermand, a few miles beyond which lay

The bridge as it looks today.

Peronne, situated on the Somme river, and the last of the fortresses between Wellington and Paris. Like Cambrai, Peronne was a strong place, its walls constructed in accordance with the principles laid down by the great engineer, Vauban. With the garrison intent on making a fight of it, Wellington detached Sir John Byng, now commanding the 1st Corps, with Maitland's brigade of Guards with orders to take the place. They were to be supported by a brigade from Chassé's Dutch-Belgian division. Four Dutch 9-pounders were also attached to the force.

Without waiting for the Dutch-Belgians to arrive, Maitland's Foot Guards began the eleven-mile march from their position close to Vermand on the morning of 26 June. Whilst not being in the same category as Badajoz or Ciudad Rodrigo, two of the great fortresses in Spain, Peronne was still a difficult place to attack, with its entire eastern and southern sides being covered by the wide Somme. Attacking forces were, therefore, presented with only the western and northern sides of the town. The western wall was a strong one, with bastions at its northern and southern ends, and with a further bastion midway between the northern end and the citadel which jutted out from the wall about halfway along its length. The wall was in turn protected by a series of ravelins. The northern wall, of narrow length, was likewise protected on either flank by a bastion, and had the added protection of an extensive hornwork which itself had an exterior ravelin.

Not long after the Guards had reached Peronne, Wellington himself arrived and, after summoning the town to surrender, he proceeded to make a brief reconnaissance of the place. It was fairly obvious to him that the key to the town was the hornwork to the south of the main walls. He also wished to take the place as quickly as possible and had no desire to embark upon a lengthy siege, and so arrangements were made for an attempt at storming the hornwork without delay.

The task was given to the 3/1st Foot Guards, their attack being preceded by the light companies of the brigade, under Lord Saltoun. Men from the 2/1st Foot Guards would follow, carrying bundles of fascines. The 3/1st Foot Guards were divided into two columns; the first, which would attack the left face of the right bastion of the hornwork, and the second, to attack the ravelin of the hornwork, before passing through its gate which was to be blown open by engineers attached to the column. All being well, the cap-

ture of the hornwork would prompt the governor of the town to surrender.

Having formed his men, Saltoun rushed forward into the ditch of the ravelin, where they came under fire from the French troops inside. Saltoun himself had a lucky escape when he was struck by a grapeshot whilst in the act of mounting a ladder. By a stroke of good fortune the shot struck his purse, which was full of coins, thus lessening the blow. He was not disabled and he pressed on with his men. The ravelin was carried whilst the gate to the hornwork was duly blown up by the engineers, leaving the Guards to charge through the smoke and into the body of the place. The hornwork was thus carried without too much trouble, and with the loss of just one man killed and eight wounded. Saltoun, with a wound 'to his purse', didn't bother to return himself wounded.

With the hornwork carried, the four Dutch-Belgian guns were brought forward, opening fire upon the bastion at the north-west flank of the main walls of the town. According to some accounts, the guns were sited inside the newly won hornwork, whilst the *History of the Grenadier Guards* states that they were sited to the west of the town. It is of little real consequence, however, for only a few shots were actually fired. Byng sent forward his acting quartermaster-general, Lieutenant Colonel the Hon. James Stanhope, with a flag of truce, and the garrison surrendered the town soon afterwards. The French soldiers, mainly National Guardsmen, were then allowed to return to their homes.

The storming of the hornwork at Peronne by Saltoun and the 1st Foot Guards was accomplished beneath the watching eyes of Wellington himself. His military career had stretched back to Flanders, and to India, with victories at such places as Assaye, Argaum and Gawilghur. It continued through Portugal and Spain, where he gained further laurels at battles such as Talavera, Salamanca, Badajoz, Vittoria, and the Nivelle, and had culminated at Waterloo, which had been his crowning glory. But it was here, at this relatively insignificant French town, that the years of the sword finally came to an end for the Duke of Wellington, for never again would he lead his men through the fire and smoke of battle.

There were still many miles to cover before Wellington finally reached Paris, but, to all intents and purposes, the fighting was over for him and his army. With the fall of Peronne they had a clear run to Paris. The Prussians, meanwhile, involved themselves in a series of sharp fights with French troops as they too advanced towards Paris. However, the avenging Prussians had more than just the advance on their agenda. After having suffered the ravages of war and occupation at the hands of successive French armies Blücher's men were intent on inflicting as much pain and damage on the French people as they possibly could. James Gibney, of the 15th Hussars, was one who saw the trail of destruction left by the Prussians.

> These gentlemen literally ransacked many houses, and we coming after them as we did, were uncommonly bad off. They were like a swarm of locusts, making all barren around them. Indeed, for miles round they seem to have wantonly destroyed all they could lay their hands on. If revenge for the French occupation of Berlin a short time previously was their object, they certainly obtained it.[7]

It wasn't just the Prussians who misbehaved. The Dutch troops, who had been ordered to support the Guards at Peronne, arrived at 9pm, well after the place had surrendered. A few Belgian cavalrymen arrived also, and after cutting the ropes of the drawbridge, broke into the town. Colonel Stanhope, who had arranged the truce and capitulation, was forced to defend himself after they refused to leave the town. In fact, the French governor had to draw his own sword to help him.

With Paris only a few days away, Wellington became more aware of the need for a peaceful resolution to the campaign. While the Prussians would probably have relished the prospect of sacking Paris, Wellington knew that an attack on the French capital would prove to be extremely costly to both sides. 'It appears to me,' he wrote to Blücher on 2 July,

> that, with the force which you and I have under our command at present, the attack of Paris is a matter of great risk. I am convinced it cannot be made on this side with any hope of success. The army under my command must then cross the Seine twice, and get into the Bois de Boulogne before the attack can be made; and even then if we should succeed the loss would be very severe. We must incur a severe loss, if it is necessary, in any case. But in this case it is not necessary.[8]

By this, Wellington was referring to negotiations he had been having with the French commissioners with a view to the city capitulating peacefully, thus avoiding the need for an attack.

Furthermore, in a few days the Bavarian, Austrian and Russian armies would arrive, which, as Wellington said, would guarantee a successful assault, 'with a comparatively trifling loss'. However, he still favoured a diplomatic rather than a military solution:

> It is true we shall not have the vain triumph of entering Paris at the head of our victorious troops, [he continued] but, as I have already explained to your Highness, I doubt our having

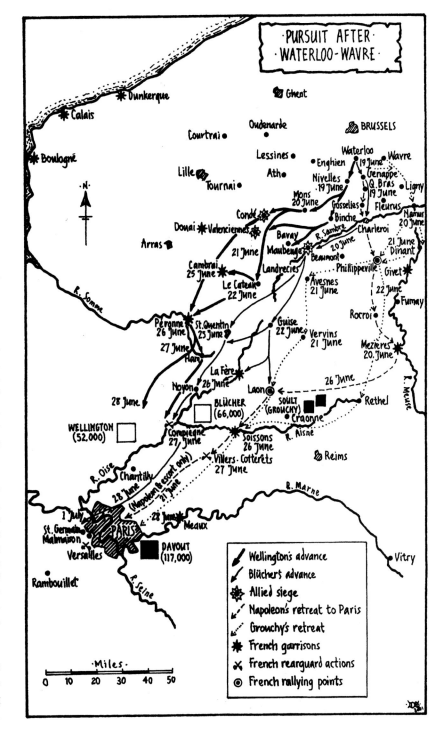

the means at present of succeeding in an attack upon Paris; and, if we are to wait till the arrival of Marshal Prince Wrede to make the attack, I think we shall find the Sovereigns disposed, as they were last year, to spare the capital of their ally, and either not to enter the town at all, or enter it under an armistice, such as it is in your power and mine to sign this day.[9]

The armistice to which Wellington referred contained four main points. First, that the Allied armies remained in their present positions on the outskirts of Paris. Second, that the French Army retreated from Paris across the Loire river. Third, that Paris be given over to the National Guard until King Louis ordered otherwise. Finally, a time was to be fixed for notice to break off the armistice. 'By adopting this measure,' wrote Wellington, 'we provide for the quiet restoration of His Majesty to his throne; which is that result of the war which the Sovereigns of all of us have always considered the most beneficial for us all, and the most likely to lead permanently to peace in Europe'.

Despite Wellington's hopes for a quick end to the campaign, the fighting continued. Early on the morning of 3 July the French attacked the Prussians at Issy, supported by twenty guns.

The Prussians, in fact, had already reached Versailles, skirmishing daily with the French, but this latest attack proved to be the final clash between the two old enemies. The French were driven back and later on the same day an armistice, the Convention of Paris, was concluded between the French and the Allies. The following day the French withdrew from Paris and marched to the banks of the Loire, leaving the British and Prussian troops to take possession of the suburbs of St Denis, St Ouen, Clichy and Neuilly. The following day they took Montmarte and on 6 July the Prussians entered Paris, the British remaining outside the city.

Wellington harboured genuine fears that the occupation of Paris by the avenging Prussians would provoke the citizens into a rising that would retard all of the progress which had been made to secure a peaceful occupation of Paris and a lasting peace. 'You may depend upon it,' he wrote to Lord Castlereagh, 'that if one shot is fired in Paris, the whole country will rise in arms against us.'[10] As it turned out, the only real attempt at Prussian retribution came, ironically, from Blücher who tried to blow up the Pont de Jena, named after Bonaparte's victory over the Prussians in October 1806. The plan was

Hougoumount a year after the battle.

actually foiled by Wellington himself. 'The destruction of the bridge of Jena,' he told Blücher, 'is highly disagreeable to the King and to the people, and may occasion disturbance in the city.'[11]

On 7 July 1815, three weeks after the Battle of Waterloo, the Allies entered Paris, and the following day King Louis XVIII returned to his capital. The British Army took up residence in the Bois de Boulogne, where camps were established. These camps were soon receiving scores of visits from many a curious Parisian tourist, anxious to discover just who these men were who had helped bring about the downfall of their Emperor for the second successive year. As for Bonaparte, he had abdicated for the second time on 22 June. On the very day that the French King returned to Paris, the former Emperor was at Rochefort, taking ship for America. His ship, *La Saale*, had barely set sail before Captain Maitland in HMS *Bellerophon* sailed into view, barring the way. After a brief exchange between the two men Bonaparte surrendered and was duly taken back to England. The great bogeyman was not allowed to set foot on English soil, however, but was kept on board ship until the British government decided what to do with him. At length the decision was taken to send Bonaparte to the distant mid-Atlantic island of St Helena, where he died in 1821.

Back in Paris, Wellington's men began making themselves at home in the Bois de Boulogne, which was to be their camp for the next three years. Reinforcements were despatched to France to make good the losses in the old battalions whilst new regiments were sent out to join the occupying force. Other regiments, like the famous 43rd Light Infantry, also joined. This regiment, which had formed part of the Light Division in the Peninsula, had returned from service in America but had not arrived in time to take part in the Battle of Waterloo. In fact, the regiment landed at Ostend on the very day the battle was fought. But now the regiment arrived to join their British comrades in occupation of their old enemy's capital city.

No sooner had the various Allied powers taken possession of Paris than the victory parades began in earnest. Indeed, reviews were a common sight for Parisians who would look on, usually with disinterest, while the endless columns of Russian, Austrian, Prussian and British troops filed past. On Saturday 24 July some 13,000 Prussian Guards were to hold a review in the presence of the Allied sovereigns, with Wellington's army, 65,000 strong, holding their own two days later. The Prussian Guards

duly held their review and it is said that even some of the British troops admitted that they had never seen such a fine body of men. The Duke, apparently hearing one such comment, turned to the admiring spectators, and said simply, 'Ah, but I will show you on Monday some men that can lick these fellows.'[12]

The parades were carried on with all the pomp and circumstance that the victorious armies could muster. The Austrian, Prussian and Russian armies were always well turned out. 'Uncommonly well dressed in new clothes, smartly made, setting the men off to the greatest advantage,' was how Cavalié Mercer described them. This was in stark contrast to the appearance of Wellington's British troops, however, who were their usual phlegmatic selves, turning out in their characteristically nonchalant style, and unconcerned at their shabby appearance. As late as 25 July they paraded before Emperor Alexander, the King of Prussia and the Austrian Emperor, still wearing the same uniforms they had worn at Waterloo on 18 June. Cavalié Mercer watched the parade with a wince of pain, occasioned by the appearance of his fellow countrymen:

> Our infantry – indeed, our whole – appeared at the review in the same clothes in which they had marched, slept, and fought for months. The colour had faded to a dusky brick-hue; their coats, originally not very smartly made, had acquired by constant wearing that loose easy set so characteristic of old clothes, comfortable to the wearer, but not calculated to add grace to his appearance. *Pour surcrot de laideur*, their cap is perhaps the meanest, ugliest thing ever invented. From all these causes it arose that our infantry appeared to the utmost disadvantage – dirty, shabby, mean, and very small.[13]

It transpired that the Allied sovereigns were none too impressed by the appearance and size of the British infantry, particularly when compared to their own, very shiny troops. Their views were communicated to an amused Wellington who remarked, 'Ay, they are small; but your Majesties will find none who fight so well.' Wellington had never cared too much about the appearance of his men. Indeed, one of his old Peninsular officers famously remarked that, 'Provided we brought our men into the field well appointed, and with sixty rounds of ammunition each he never looked to see whether their trousers were black, blue, or grey; and as to ourselves, we might be rigged out in all the colours of the rainbow it we fancied it.'[14]

The surviving part of the walls of Peronne. It was here that the last action of the British Army took place on its advance to Paris.

A nineteenth-century photograph of La Belle Alliance. It was close to this inn that Wellington met Blücher at the end of the battle.

The shabby appearance of the British infantry came as a mighty blow to the citizens of Paris who found it hard to come to terms with the fact that their Emperor and his army had been defeated by such a poorly turned out band. It simply added insult to injury. One onlooker recorded his pain in his diary:

> Oh! It was really like being beaten twice over, *bis mori*, to have been beaten by an army as badly turned out as the English army was. One can tolerate being shot at by those fine grenadiers of the Russian and Prussian Guards, who look so masculine and military; to receive sabre cuts from those old hussars from Brandenburg and Silesia, typical of light cavalry. But how could one be a good soldier under that little sugar-loaf with a peak, with the inelegantly cut red jacket, those grey trousers clinging to knock knees?[15]

However, he did notice one difference between the British troops and the other Allied soldiers that endeared the former to him:

> I did notice one thing to England's credit; on the 50,000 breasts that I watched go past, I saw no ribbons, none of that jewellery which bedecks the armies of the rest of Europe. Only at rare intervals did I see a medal hanging from a violet ribbon on some officer's breast. Love of country, the glory of old Albion – that is what has to suffice for British troops to make them fight with such admirable courage.[16]

The citizens of Paris would have to wait another year before they would see any British troops wearing medals, for the Waterloo Medal was not awarded until 1816, and was the first campaign medal to be awarded to the British Army. The veterans of the Peninsular War would have to wait until 1848 before they received any campaign medal. What an utter disgrace this was, that the men who had fought so gallantly for six years for their King, country and regiment, should have to wait so long. It would probably not have bothered them too much, however, had not the Waterloo Medal been awarded in 1816. Indeed, it was not uncommon to see British troops, who had not served in the Peninsula but had fought at Waterloo, brawling on the Champs Elysées with resentful Peninsular veterans.

The parades were at first a regular occurrence in Paris, but in time they became less frequent, and so Wellington's men settled down to long periods of inactivity in their camp in the Bois de Boulogne. Drilling and sightseeing occupied most of their time, which was done under the curious gaze of the population, although even their curiosity waned after a few months. 'All mistrust and dislike of each other are at an end,' noted Cavalié Mercer, and such was the easy pace of life in post-Bonaparte Paris that Wellington was able to order the return to England of several British battalions before the end of 1815. On 23 November 1818 the last British regiment to leave Paris marched for England. That regiment was, appropriately, the 52nd, that had served throughout the Peninsular War and had delivered the decisive blow against the Imperial Guard at Waterloo.

For Johnny Kincaid, of the 95th, Waterloo was 'the last, greatest, and most uncomfortable heap of glory that I ever had a hand in'. There were, no doubt, many veterans in Wellington's army who thought the same thing. There were no more battles for them to fight, nor indeed for Wellington. Their march together had taken them from the rugged slopes of Roliça, to the far more gentle slopes of Waterloo, and although the majority of his Peninsular regiments were not present at the scene of Wellington's final triumph, the 'Johnny Newcomes' did a fine job, standing alongside those veterans who were. The old Peninsular army would have been proud of them.

Wellington's own part in the Battle of Waterloo continues to cause heated debate, his alleged duplicity towards the Prussians being the latest in a series of criticisms levelled against him. Indeed, Wellington's critics, beginning with Bonaparte himself, have tried in vain to find fault with his generalship during the campaign. Amongst other things, they criticise his choice of position, his refusal to believe that the French would not attack by way of Mons, his scattering of the Anglo-Dutch Army prior to hostilities, and his lacklustre performance in concentrating on 16 June. One would almost believe that Wellington actually lost the battle. Books on the Waterloo campaign invariably contain a chapter on Wellington's mistakes, and it is undeniable that he made some. However, the fact remains that when he came face to face with Bonaparte on 18 June 1815, he emerged triumphant. And when he read Bonaparte's own criticism of his performance during the campaign, he replied in the best possible way, with a response that ought to serve as a riposte to all his critics. 'Damn them,' he said, 'I beat them, and if I were surprised, if I did place myself in so foolish a position, they were the greater fools for not knowing how to take advantage of my faults.'[17]

It is, therefore, quite appropriate that we should leave the last word to Wellington who, when asked by Thomas Creevey whether the French had fought better than usual at Waterloo, replied, 'No, they have always fought the same since I first saw them at Vimeiro.' And he added, 'By God! I don't think it would have been done if I had not been there.'

1 John Colville, *Portrait of a General; A Chronicle of the Napoleonic Wars* (London, 1980), p.205.
2 Ibid. p.206.
3 William Wheeler, *The Letters of Private Wheeler 1809–1828*, edited by Capt. BH Liddell Hart (London, 1951), p.175.
4 Ibid. p.176.
5 Ibid. pp.176–7.
6 Wellington to Bathurst, 25 June 1815, *The Despatches of Field Marshal the Duke of Wellington* (London, 1832).
7 Dr Thomas Gibney, *Eighty Years Ago, or the Recollections of an old Army Doctor*, edited by his son, RD Gibney (London, 1896), pp.223–4.
8 Wellington to Blücher, 2 July 1815. *Despatches.*
9 Wellington to Blücher, 2 July 1815. *Despatches.*
10 Wellington to Castlereagh, 14 July 1815, *Despatches.*
11 Wellington to Blücher, 12 July 1815, *Despatches.*
12 Lt.Gen. Sir FW Hamilton, *The Origin and History of the First or Grenadier Guards* (London, 1874), III, p.60.
13 Capt. Cavalié Mercer, *Journal of the Waterloo Campaign*, edited by Sir John Fortescue (London, 1927), p.299.
14 Lt. William Grattan, *Adventures with the Connaught Rangers 1809–14*, edited by Charles Oman (London, 1902), p.50.
15 Anthony Brett-James, *The Hundred Days* (London, 1964), p.214.
16 Ibid. pp.214–15.
17 SGP Ward, *Wellington* (London, 1969), p.95.

WELLINGTON'S ARMY DURING THE WATERLOO CAMPAIGN
(British and KGL units in bold)

Commander-in-Chief: Field Marshal the Duke of Wellington
Quartermaster General: Colonel William De Lancey

First Corps: The Prince of Orange. 25,400 infantry, 56 guns

1st British Division. Lt.Gen. Sir George Cooke. 4,061 infantry, 12 guns
1st British Brigade. Maj.Gen. Sir Peregrine Maitland.
2/1st Foot Guards, 3/1st Foot Guards.
2nd British Brigade. Maj.Gen. Sir John Byng.
2/Coldstream Guards, 2/3rd Foot Guards.
Artillery: **Sandham's** British and **Kuhlmann's** KGL Field batteries.

3rd British Division. Lt.Gen. Sir Charles Alten. 6,970 infantry, 12 guns.
5th British Brigade. Maj.Gen. Sir Colin Halkett.
2/30th, 33rd, 2/69th, 2/73rd.
2nd KGL Brigade. Colonel Christian Ompteda.
1st and 2nd Light Battalions KGL.
5th and 8th Line Battalions KGL.
1st Hanoverian Brigade. Maj.Gen. Count Kielmansegge
Bremen, Verden, York, Lüneberg, Grubenhagen Battalions, Jaeger Corps.
Artillery: **Lloyd's** British and **Cleeves's** KGL Field Batteries.

2nd Dutch-Belgian Division. Lt.Gen. Baron de Perponcher. 7,700 infantry, 16 guns
1st Brigade. Maj.Gen. Count de Bylandt.
7th Line, 27th Jaegers, 5th, 7th and 8th Militia.
2nd Brigade. Prince Bernhard of Saxe-Weimar.
2nd Nassau (3 batts.) Reg. Of Orange-Nassau.
Artillery: Byleveld's Horse and Stievenaar's Field Batteries.

3rd Dutch-Belgian Division. Lt.Gen. Baron de Chassé. 6,669 infantry, 16 guns
1st Brigade. Maj.Gen. Detmers.
2nd Line, 35th Jaegers, 4th, 6th and 19th Militia.
2nd Brigade. Maj.Gen. D'Aubreme.
3rd, 12th and 13th Line, 36th Jaegers, 3rd and 10th Militia.
Artillery: Krahmer's Horse and Lux's Field Batteries.

Second Corps. Lt.Gen. Lord Hill. 24,033 infantry, 40 guns

2nd British Division. Lt.Gen. Sir Henry Clinton. 6,833 infantry 12 guns.
3rd British Brigade. Maj.Gen. Adam.
1/52nd, 1/71st, 2/95th (6 coys), 3/95th (2 coys).
1st KGL Brigade. Col. G. Du Plat.
1st, 2nd, 3rd and 4th Line Battalions.
3rd Hanoverian Brigade. Col. Hew Halkett.
Bremervorde, Osnabruck, Quakenbruck and Saltzgitter Landwehr Battalions.
Artillery: **Bolton's** British Field and **Sympher's** KGL Horse Artillery.

4th British Division. Lt.Gen. Sir Charles Colville. 7,212 infantry 12 guns.
4th British Brigade. Col. Mitchell.
3/14th, 1/23rd, 51st.
6th British Brigade. Maj.Gen. Johnstone.
2/35th, 1/54th, 2/59th, 1/91st.
6th Hanoverian Brigade. Maj.Gen Sir James Lyon.
Lauenberg and Calenberg Battalions, Nienburg, Hoya and Bentheim Landwehr Battalions.
Artillery: **Brome's** British and Rettberg's Hanoverian Field Batteries.

1st Dutch-Belgian Division. Lt.Gen. Stedman. 6,389 infantry, 8 guns.
1st Brigade. Maj.Gen. Hauw.
4th and 6th Line, 16th Jaegers, 9th, 14th and 15th Militia.
2nd Brigade. Maj.Gen. Eerens.
1st Line, 18th Jaegers, 1st, 2nd and 18th Militia.
Artillery: Wynard's Battery.

Lt.Gen. Anthing's Dutch-Belgian Indian Brigade.
5 infantry battalions, 1 Field Battery.

Reserve. 20,563 infantry, 912 cavalry, 52 guns

5th British Division. Lt.Gen. Sir Thomas Picton.
   7,158 infantry, 12 guns
8th British Brigade. Maj.Gen. Sir James Kempt.
1/28th, 1/32nd, 1/79th, 1/95th.
9th British Brigade. Maj.Gen. Sir Denis Pack.
3/1st, 1/42nd, 2/44th, 1/92nd.
5th Hanoverian Brigade. Col. Von Vincke.
Hameln, Gifhorn, Hildesheim and Peine
   Landwehr battalions
Artillery: **Rogers's** British and Braun's
   Hanoverian Field batteries.

6th British Division. Lt.Gen. Sir Lowry Cole.
   (Absent at Waterloo, getting married)
10th British Brigade. Maj.Gen. Sir John Lambert.
1/4th, 1/27th, 1/40th, 2/81st.
4th Hanoverian Brigade. Col. Best.
Verden, Luneburg, Osterode, and Munden
   Landwehr battalions.
Artillery: **Unett's** and **Sinclair's** British Field
   Batteries.

Brunswick Corps. Duke of Brunswick. 5,376
   infantry, 912 cavalry, 16 guns.
8 Batts. Infantry, one regiment of Hussars, a
   squadron of lancers, 2 batteries of artillery.

Nassau Contingent. General Kruse. 2,880 infantry.
3 Batts. 1st Regiment.

Unattached artillery: **Bean's** and **Ross's** British
   Horse Artillery Batteries.

Cavalry. Lt.Gen. The Earl of Uxbridge. 10,155
   troopers, 36 guns.

1st British Brigade. Maj.Gen. Lord Edward
   Somerset.
**1st Life Guards, 2nd Life Guards, Royal Horse
   Guards.**
2nd British Brigade. Maj.Gen. Sir William Ponsonby.
**1st (Royal) Dragoons, 2nd Dragoons (Scots
   Greys), 6th (Inniskilling) Dragoons.**
3rd British Brigade. Maj.Gen. Sir William Dornberg.
**1st and 2nd Light Dragoons KGL, 23rd Light
   Dragoons.**

4th British Brigade. Maj.Gen. Sir John Vandeleur.
11th, 12th and 16th Light Dragoons.
5th British Brigade. Maj.Gen. Sir Colquhoun Grant.
2nd Hussars KGL, 7th and 15th Hussars.
6th British Brigade. Maj.Gen. Sir Hussey Vivian.
1st Hussars KGL, 10th and 18th Hussars.
7th British Brigade. Col. Sir F. Arentschildt.
3rd Hussars KGL, 13th Light Dragoons.
1st Hanoverian Brigade. Col. Estorff.
Cumberland Hussars, Prince Regent's Hussars,
   Bremen and Verden Hussars.
Artillery: **Bull's (howitzers), Gardiner's, Mercer's, Ramsay's, Webber-Smith's and
   Whinyates** British Horse Artillery Batteries.

Dutch-Belgian Cavalry. 3,405 troopers, 8 guns.
1st Brigade. Maj.Gen. Tripp.
1st and 3rd Dutch Carabiniers, Belgian Carabiniers.
2nd Brigade. Maj.Gen. De Ghigny.
4th Dutch Light Dragoons, 8th Belgian Hussars.
3rd Brigade. Maj.Gen. Van Merlen.
5th Belgian Lt Dragoons, 6th Dutch Hussars.
Artillery: Petter's and Gey's half batteries of
   horse artillery.

Total Strength by Nationalities

Nation	*infantry*	*cavalry*	*guns*
British	20,310	5,911	90
KGL	3,285	2,560	18
Hanoverians	13,793	1,682	12
Brunswick	5,376	922	16
Nassau	7,308		
Dutch-Belgian	18,838	3,405	56
Total	**68,910**	**14,480**	**192**

BIBLIOGRAPHY

An Account of the Battle of Waterloo (Edinburgh, 1815).

Anglesey, the Marquess of. *One Leg; the Life and Letters of Henry William Paget, first Marquess of Anglesey* (London, 1961).

Anon. *A Soldier of the 71st*. Edited by Christopher Hibbert (London, 1975).

Anton, J. *Retrospect of a Military Life* (Edinburgh, 1841).

Batty, Capt. Robert. *An Historical Sketch of the Campaign of 1815* (London, 1820).

Beamish, N. Ludlow. *History of the King's German Legion*. (London, 1832).

Booth, J. (A Near Observer), *The Battle of Waterloo* (London, 1815).

Bowles, Captain George. *A Series of Letters to the First Earl of Malmesbury, his family and friends, from 1745 to 1820*. Edited by his grandson, the Earl of Malmesbury (London, 1870).

Brett-James, Anthony. *The Hundred Days* (London, 1964).

The Capel Letters, 1814-1817. Edited by the Marquess of Anglesey (London, 1955).

Chandler, David. *Waterloo: The Hundred Days* (London, 1981).

Chesney, Col. Charles. *Waterloo Lectures: A Study of the Campaign of 1815* (London, 1907).

Clark-Kennedy, AE *Attack the Colour! The Royal Dragoons in the Peninsula and at Waterloo* (London, 1975).

Clay, Matthew. *A Narrative of the Battles of Quatre Bras and Waterloo, with the Defence of Hougoumont* (Bedford, n.d.).

Colville, John. *Portrait of a General; A Chronicle of the Napoleonic Wars* (London, 1980).

Cotton, Sgt. Maj. Edward. *A Voice From Waterloo* (London, 1862), 6th edition.

The Despatches of Field Marshal the Duke of Wellington, Edited by John Gurwood (London, 1832).

Douglas, Sergeant John. *Douglas's Tale of the Peninsula and Waterloo*. Edited by Stanley Monick (London, 1997).

Duncan, Major Francis. *History of the Royal Regiment of Artillery* (London, 1879).

Ellesmere, Francis. *Personal Reminiscences of the Duke of Wellington* (London, 1904).

Farmer, George. *The Light Dragoon*. Edited by GR Gleig (London, 1850).

Fletcher, Ian. *Gentlemen's Sons: The Foot Guards in the Peninsula and at Waterloo* (Speldhurst, 1992).

Fletcher, Ian. *Wellington's Regiments* (Staplehurst, 1995).

Fortescue, Sir John. *History of the British Army* (London, 1920).

Frazer, Col. Augustus. *Letters of Augustus Frazer, KCB, commanding the Royal Horse Artillery in the Army under the Duke of Wellington, written during the Peninsular and Waterloo campaigns*. Edited by Edward Sabine (London, 1859).

Gardyne, Lt.Col. C. *The Life of a Regiment* (Edinburgh, 1929).

Gibney, Dr Thomas. *Eighty Years Ago, or the Recollections of an old Army Doctor*. Edited by his son, RD Gibney (London, 1896).

Grattan, Lt. William. *Adventures with the Connaught Rangers 1809-14*. Edited by Charles Oman (London, 1902).

Gronow, Captain Howell Rees. *The Reminiscences of Captain Gronow*. Edited by Nicolas Bentley (London, 1977).

Hamilton, Lt.Gen. Sir FW *The Origin and History of the First or Grenadier Guards* (London, 1874).

Hamilton-Williams, David. *Waterloo: New Perspectives* (London, 1993).

Haswell, Jock. *The First Respectable Spy: The Life and Times of Colquhoun Grant, Wellington's Head of Intelligence* (London, 1969).

Hay, Captain William. *Reminiscences 1808-1815 under Wellington*. Edited by Mrs SCI Wood (London, 1901).

Haythornthwaite, Philip J. *Waterloo Men: The Experience of Battle 16-18 June 1815* (Marlborough, 1999).

Hope, Lt. James. *Letters from Portugal, Spain and France, during the memorable campaigns of 1811, 1812, & 1813, and from Belgium and France in the year 1815* (Edinburgh, 1819).

Howarth, David. *A Near Run Thing* (London, 1968).

James, Surgeon Haddy. *Surgeon James' Journal 1815*. Edited by Jane Vansittart (London, 1964).

Kennedy, Gen. Sir James Shaw. *Notes on the Battle of Waterloo* (London, 1865).

Kincaid, Captain John. *Adventures in the Rifle Brigade* (London, 1830).

Knight, Corporal. *British Battalion at Oporto* (London, n.d.).

Knollys, W. *Shaw the Life Guardsman* (London, 1885).

Lawrence, Sgt. William. *Autobiography of Sergeant William Lawrence, a hero of the Peninsular and Waterloo Campaigns*. Edited by GN Bankes (London, 1886).

Leach, Lt.Col. Jonathan. *Rough Sketches of the Life of an Old Soldier* (London, 1831).

Longford, Elizabeth. *The Years of the Sword* (London, 1969).

Low, EB. *With Napoleon at Waterloo* (London, 1911).

Mackinnon, Col. Daniel. *Origin and History of the Coldstream Guards* (London, 1837).

Mackinnon, Col. Daniel. MSS, RHQ Coldstream Guards.

Mackworth, Digby MSS Journal, 1809–1815.

Maxwell, Sir Herbert. *The Life of Wellington; the Restoration of Martial Britain* (London, 1899).

Mercer, Captain Cavalié. *Journal of the Waterloo Campaign*. Edited by Sir John Fortescue (London, 1927).

Morris, Thomas. *The Napoleonic Wars*. Edited by John Selby (London, 1967).

Müffling, Karl von. *Passages from my Life* (London, 1853).

Ompteda, Christian. *A Hanoverian English Officer a Hundred Years Ago*. Translated by John Hill (London, 1892).

Pattison, Lt. Frederick Hope. *Personal Recollections of the Waterloo Campaign*. Edited by Bob Elmer (London, 1997).

Picton, Sir Thomas. *Memoirs of Lieutenant General Sir Thomas Picton*. Edited by HB Robinson (London, 1835).

Robertson, Sergeant David. *The Journal of Sergeant D. Robertson, late 92nd Foot, comprising the different campaigns between the years 1797 and 1818* (Perth, 1842).

Robinson, Maj. Gen. CW *Wellington's Campaigns 1808–1815*. (London, 1906).

Ropes, John Cadman. *The Campaign of Waterloo* (New York, 1893).

Ross-Lewin, Harry. *With the 32nd in the Peninsula and other campaigns*. Edited by John Wardell (London, 1914).

Short, Ensign Charles. MSS, NAM (GS 202).

Siborne, Maj.Gen. HT (Ed.). *The Waterloo Letters* (London, 1891).

Siborne, Captain William. *The Waterloo Campaign* (London, 1990).

Simmons, Major George. *A British Rifleman. The Journals and Correspondence of Major George Simmons, Rifle Brigade, During the Peninsular War and the Campaign of Waterloo*. Edited by Willoughby Verner (London, 1899).

Stanhope, Philip Henry, Earl. *Notes of Conversations with the Duke of Wellington* (London, 1888).

Swinburne, Ensign Thomas. British Library Add. MSS. 34708.

Supplementary Despatches and Memorandum of Field Marshal the Duke of Wellington. Edited by his Son, the 2nd Duke (London, 1857).

Thornton, James. *Your Obedient Servant* (London, 1985).

Tomkinson, Lieut.Col. *The Diary of a Cavalry Officer in the Peninsular War and Waterloo Campaign 1809-1810*, Edited by James Tomkinson (London, 1894).

Uffindell, Andrew, and Coram, Michael. *On the Fields of Glory: The Battlefields of the Waterloo Campaign* (London, 1996).

Ward, SGP *Wellington* (London, 1969).

Weller, Jac. *Wellington at Waterloo* (London, 1967).

Wheatley, Edmund. *A Journal and Sketchbook kept during the Peninsular War and Waterloo Campaign*. Edited by Christopher Hibbert (London, 1964).

Wheeler, William. *The Letters of Private Wheeler 1809-1828*. Edited by Capt. BH Liddell Hart (London, 1951).

Wood, Colour Sergeant Charles. *Some Particulars of the Battle of Waterloo, being an extract of a letter from C/Sergeant C.W. Third Battalion First Regiment of Foot Guards* (Halifax, 1816).

INDEX

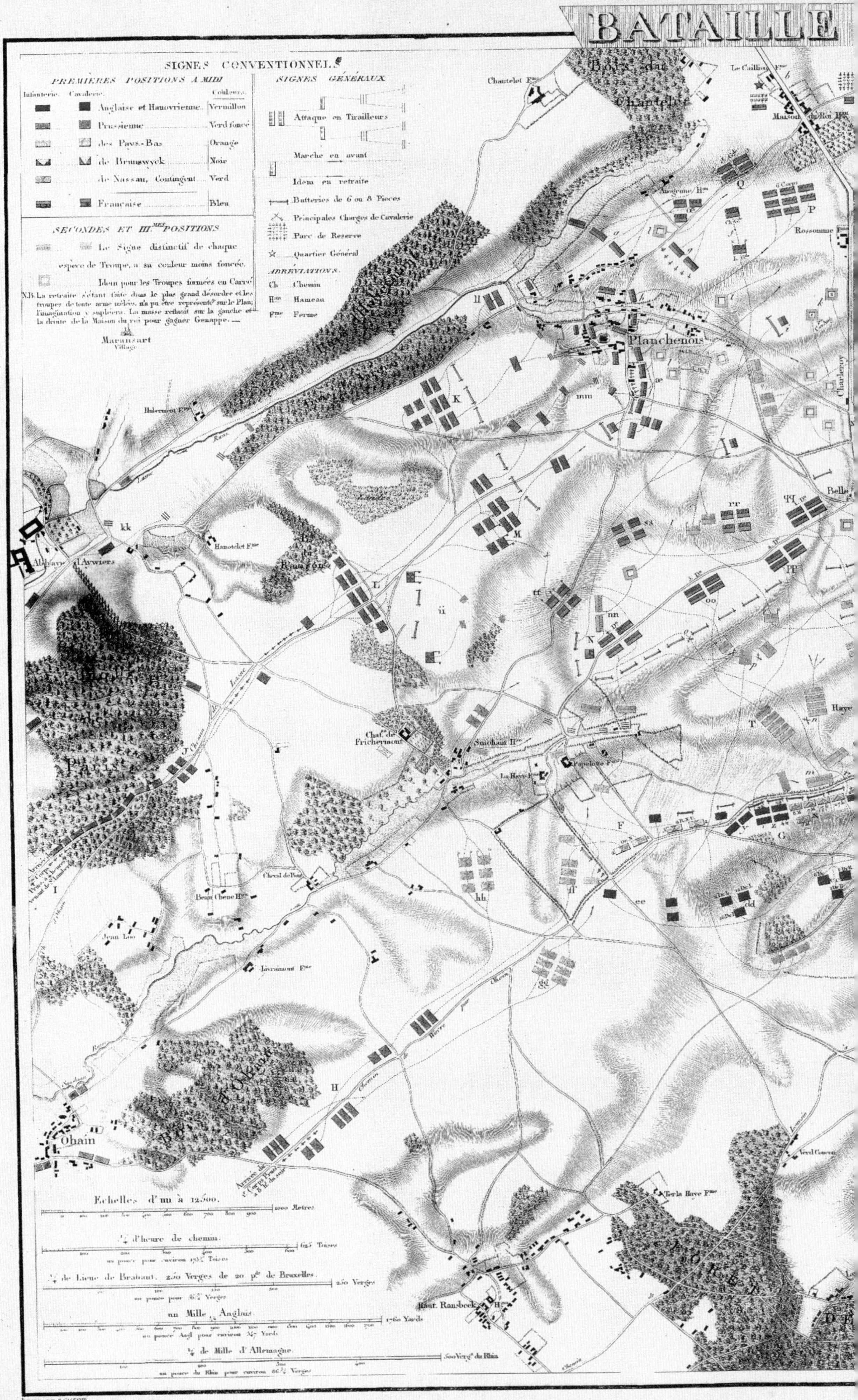

BATAILLE

Maransart
Village

Habermont Fme

Abbaye d'Aywiers

Hanotelet Fme

Beau Force

Chat. de Frichermont

Smohain Hau

La Haye Fme

Planchenois

Chantelet Fme

Le Caillou Fme

Maison du Roi Hau

Rossomme

Bella

Haye

Beau Chene Hau

Cheval de Bois

Jean Louis

Lavraimont Fme

Obain

Haut Ransbeck Hau

Verd Coucou

Ter la Haye Fme

Dessiné par E. Carton.
Druk: Topografische Dienst, Emmen